Theatre, activism, subjectivity

Manchester University Press

Series editors
MARIA M. DELGADO
MAGGIE B. GALE
PETER LICHTENFELS

Advisory board
Michael Billington, Sandra Hebron, Mark Ravenhill, Janelle Reinelt, Peter Sellars, Joanne Tompkins

This series will offer a space for those people who practise theatre to have a dialogue with those who think and write about it.

The series has a flexible format that refocuses the analysis and documentation of performance. It provides, presents, and represents material which is written by those who make or create performance history, and offers access to theatre documents, different methodologies, and approaches to the art of making theatre.

The books in the series are aimed at students, scholars, practitioners, and theatre-visiting readers. They encourage reassessments of periods, companies, and figures in twentieth-century and twenty-first-century theatre history, and provoke and take up discussions of cultural strategies and legacies that recognise the heterogeneity of performance studies.

To buy or to find out more about the books currently available in this series, please go to: https://manchesteruniversitypress.co.uk/series/theatre-theory-practice-performance

Theatre, activism, subjectivity

Searching for the Left in a fragmented world

Edited by
Bishnupriya Dutt and Silvija Jestrovic

MANCHESTER UNIVERSITY PRESS

Copyright © Manchester University Press 2024

While copyright in the volume as a whole is vested in Manchester University Press, copyright in individual chapters belongs to their respective authors, and no chapter may be reproduced wholly or in part without the express permission in writing of both author and publisher.

Published by Manchester University Press
Oxford Road, Manchester, M13 9PL

www.manchesteruniversitypress.co.uk

British Library Cataloguing-in-Publication Data
A catalogue record for this book is available from the British Library

ISBN 978 1 5261 7856 5 hardback
ISBN 978 1 5261 9550 0 paperback

First published 2024
Paperback published 2026

The publisher has no responsibility for the persistence or accuracy of URLs for any external or third-party internet websites referred to in this book, and does not guarantee that any content on such websites is, or will remain, accurate or appropriate.

EU authorised representative for GPSR:
Easy Access System Europe – Mustamäe tee 50,
10621 Tallinn, Estonia
gpsr.requests@easproject.com

Typeset by Newgen Publishing UK

Contents

List of illustrations	page vii
List of contributors	ix
Foreword – Partha Chatterjee	xv
Acknowledgements	xxi
Introduction: Searching for the Left in a fragmented world – Silvija Jestrovic and Bishnupriya Dutt	1

Part I: Activism

1 Performing the Constitution as an insurgent document – Nivedita Menon	23
2 Revolution: like, share, subscribe – Dragan Todorovic	38
3 The 'hunger artists': Hunger protests, prisons, and insurgent citizenship – Anupama Roy and Ujjwal Kumar Singh	56
4 Of quiet resistance: *Shy Radicals*, divergent world-making, and the poetics of statecraft – Anika Marschall	73

Part II: Theatre

5 Acting politically: Making performance in the eye of history – Adrian Kear	93
6 Theatre of the streets: Of working-class strikes, protests, and democratisation of life – Bishnupriya Dutt	112
7 *The Cheviot* and its legacies: Dramaturgies of the Left in Scottish theatre – Trish Reid	129
8 Between the Right and the Left: Staging political, emotional, and social polarisations on the Canadian stage – Yana Meerzon	145
9 The indiscreet charm of Left nostalgia: Reeking redolence in the contemporary – Ameet Parameswaran	163

10 Staging revolution: Utpal Dutt's *Kallol* (1965) and the question of 'spectacular' aesthetics in Calcutta's Leftist theatre practice – Trina Nileena Banerjee   180
11 Love in the time of revolution: Exploring the political theatre of Utpal Dutt – Mallarika Sinha Roy   199

Part III: Subjectivity

12 Revolutionary intimacies: Friendship, love, and theatre – Silvija Jestrovic   219
13 The fraught act of speaking for/about the communist women – Urmimala Sarkar Munsi   236
14 One always fails to speak of the things one loves: Memories of border crossings – Shirin M. Rai   257
15 Why I am still a socialist – Janelle Reinelt   275

Index   288

List of illustrations

6.1 *Chakkajam*, 21 November 1988, at the Artists Rally in support of the seven-day industrial strike (photo by Safdar Hashmi) *page* 116

8.1 *The Assembly* by Alex Ivanovici, Annabel Soutar, and Brett Watson, directed by Chris Abraham, a Porte Parole Production. Actors featured in the photo (left to right): Amélie Grenier, Christina Tannous, Alex Ivanovici, Brett Watson, Pascale Bussières, and Nora Guerch (photo credit: Maxim Côté) 150

8.2 *The Assembly* by Alex Ivanovici, Annabel Soutar, and Brett Watson, directed by Chris Abraham, a Porte Parole Production. Actors featured in the photo (left to right): Sean Colby, Tanja Jacobs, Jimmy Blais, and Ngozi Paul (photo credit: Maxim Côté) 151

8.3 *The Assembly* by Alex Ivanovici, Annabel Soutar, and Brett Watson, directed by Chris Abraham, a Porte Parole Production. Actors featured in the photo (left to right): Ngozi Paul and Jimmy Blais (photo credit: Maxim Côté) 156

9.1 Rafeeq and Kunjami interacting, with *mathi* being fried on stage (courtesy of Jino Jospeh) 170

9.2 Members of the cultural organisation listening as Rafeeq is on the bicycle in one of his ruminations about *mathi* and life (courtesy of Jino Joseph) 171

9.3 Celebration or the 'retake' of life towards the end of the performance (courtesy of Jino Joseph) 176

10.1 Still from Utpal Dutt's *Angar* (1959) (photograph by Sambhu Banerjee) 185

10.2 Still from Utpal Dutt's *Kallol* (1965) (photograph by Sambhu Banerjee; courtesy of the Utpal Dutt Foundation) 190

13.1 Covers of *Chalar Pathey* and *Ek Shathey*, two women's periodicals published by the women's organisations belonging to the Communist Party of India (CPI) and the Communist Party of India (Marxist) (CPI(M)) (© author)   237
14.1 NFIW – the women's wing of the Communist Party of India (CPI) (© author)   265
14.2 Satya M. Rai with the Cuban Ambassador, Eloy Valdez, 1970s (© author)   269

List of contributors

Trina Nileena Banerjee is an Assistant Professor in Cultural Studies at the Centre for Studies in Social Sciences, Calcutta. Her essays have been published in several edited volumes and national/international journals. She writes in both Bengali and English. She has also been a theatre and film actress, as well as a journalist and fiction writer. Her book *Performing Silence: Women in the Group Theatre Movement in Bengal* was published by Oxford University Press (India) in 2021.

Partha Chatterjee is a political theorist, political anthropologist, and historian. He is Professor Emeritus of Anthropology, Columbia University, New York, and Honorary Professor, Centre for Studies in Social Sciences, Calcutta, where he was the director from 1997 to 2007. He is the author of more than thirty books and edited volumes in English and Bengali. He was a founding member of the Subaltern Studies Collective. His books include *The Black Hole of Empire* (Permanent Black, 2012), *Lineages of Political Society* (Permanent Black, 2011), *Politics of the Governed* (Permanent Black, 2004), *A Princely Impostor? The Strange and Universal History of the Kumar of Bhawal* (Princeton University Press, 2002), *The Nation and Its Fragments* (Oxford University Press, 1993), and *Nationalist Thought and the Colonial World* (Oxford University Press, 1986). Chatterjee delivered the Ruth Benedict lectures in April 2018, which was published in an expanded version as *I Am the People: Reflections on Popular Sovereignty Today* (Columbia University Press, 2019). His most recent book is an edition of a found manuscript titled *The Truths and Lies of Nationalism as Narrated by Charvak* (State University of New York, 2021). He is also a playwright whose play *Chokher Bali (Sand in My Eye)* was staged at Barnard College in 2016.

Bishnupriya Dutt is Professor of Theatre and Performance Studies in the School of Arts and Aesthetics, Jawaharlal Nehru University, Delhi.

Her recent publications include *Maya Rao and Indian Feminist Theatre* (Cambridge University Press, 2022); 'Post-Colonial Imaginations: Afro-Asian Dialogues in the Past and Present' (in Miriam Haughton *et al.* (eds), *Theatre, Performance and Commemoration*, Methuen, 2023); and 'Performing Gestures at Protest and Other Sites' (in Shirin Rai *et al.* (eds), *The Oxford Handbook of Politics and Performance*, Oxford University Press, 2021). She is currently the President of the International Federation for Theatre Research, a Distinguished Fellow at Temporal Communities, Free University, Berlin (2023), and visiting Leverhulme Professor at the Royal Central School of Speech and Drama, UK. Bishnupriya has been involved in active theatre in Calcutta since the 1960s with the Little Theatre Group and later with People's Little Theatre, where she performs and directs.

Silvija Jestrovic is Professor of Theatre and Performance at the University of Warwick. She has been awarded the Leverhulme Major Research Fellowship for her project 'Whose Freedom? Dramaturgies of Freedom and the Aesthetic of Solidarity'. Her books include *Theatre of Estrangement* (University of Toronto Press, 2006), *Performance, Space, Utopia: Cities of War, Cities of Exile* (Palgrave Macmillan, 2012), and *The Author Dies Hard* (Palgrave Macmillan, 2020). She co-edited *The Oxford Handbook of Politics and Performance* (Oxford University Press, 2021) with Shirin Rai, Milija Gluhovic, and Mike Saward, and with Ameet Paramewaram she co-edited the special issue of *Studies in Theatre and Performance* Performing 'Worksites of the Left' (2019). Silvija is Senior Editor of the journal *Theatre Research International*.

Adrian Kear is Professor of Theatre and Performance at Wimbledon College of Arts, the University of the Arts London. His research investigates the relationships between performance and politics in public life and creative practice. Adrian's books include: *Theatre and Event: Staging the European Century* (Palgrave Macmillan, 2013); *Thinking through Theatre and Performance* (with Maaike Bleeker, Joe Kelleer, and Heike Roms – Bloomsbury, 2019); *International Politics and Performance: Critical Aesthetics and Creative Practice* (with Jenny Edkins – Routledge, 2013); *Psychoanalysis and Performance* (with Patrick Campbell – Routledge, 2001); and *Mourning Diana: Nation, Culture and the Performance of Grief* (with Deborah Lynn Steinberg – Routledge, 1999).

Anika Marschall works as an Assistant Professor at Utrecht University. In her research she investigates vexed relations between theatre, migration, and human rights, questions of racialisation, performance, and institutional critique. She was the author of *Performing Human*

Rights: Artistic Interventions into European Asylum (Routledge, 2023), and her latest co-authored book *Intersectional Theatre Practice* will be published in 2025 by Cambridge University Press.

Yana Meerzon teaches in the Department of Theatre, University of Ottawa, and served as President of the Canadian Association for Theatre Research in June 2020 and 2022. Yana's research interests are theatre of exile and migration, and cultural and interdisciplinary studies. She is the editor of nine collections and author of four books, with the latest one, *Performing Nationalism in Russia*, being published by Cambridge Element in 2024. Her current research project is titled 'Between Migration and Neo-Nationalism(s): Performing the European Nation – Playing a Foreigner'. She is the co-editor (with S. E. Wilmer) of *The Palgrave Handbook of Theatre and Migration* (Palgrave Macmillan, 2023) and the Palgrave book series *Theatre and Migration*.

Nivedita Menon, Professor at the Centre for Comparative Politics and Political Theory, Jawaharlal Nehru University, Delhi, is the author of *Secularism as Misdirection: Critical Thought from the Global South* (Permanent Black and Duke University Press, 2023/2024) and *Seeing like a Feminist* (Penguin, Zubaan, 2012). As well as research papers in Indian and international journals, her previous books include *Recovering Subversion: Feminist Politics beyond the Law* (Permanent Black, 2004) and (co-written with Aditya Nigam) *Power and Contestation: India after 1989* (Zed Books, 2007, second edition Orient Blackswan, 2014). She has also edited two volumes, *Gender and Politics in India* (Oxford University Press, 1999) and *Sexualities* (Zed Books, 2007), and co-edited *Critical Studies in Politics: Exploring Sites, Selves, Power* (Orient Blackswan, 2013).

Ameet Parameswaran is an Assistant Professor of Theatre and Performance Studies in the School of Arts and Aesthetics, Jawaharlal Nehru University, Delhi. His monograph is titled *Performance and the Political: Power and Pleasure in Contemporary Kerala* (Orient Blackswan, 2017), and he has recently co-edited with Silvija Jestrovic the special issue 'Worksites of the Left' in the journal *Studies in Theatre and Performance* (2019).

Shirin M. Rai is a Distinguished Research Professor in the Department of Politics and International Studies, SOAS, University of London. She is a Fellow of the British Academy. Before joining SOAS, she was Professor of International Political Economy at the University of Warwick, where she was the Founder Director of the Warwick Interdisciplinary Research Centre for International Development (WICID). Rai's research interests lie in performance and politics, gender and politics, and feminist international political economy. Her latest book, *Depletion: The Costs of Care and the Struggles to Reverse It*, will be published in 2024 by Oxford University Press. She is also a lead co-editor (with Milija Gluhovic, Silvija Jestrovic, and Michael Saward) of the *Oxford Handbook of Politics and Performance* (Oxford University Press, 2022).

Trish Reid is Professor of Theatre and Performance and Head of the School of Arts and Communication Design, University of Reading. She is a Principal Fellow of the Higher Education Academy and the author of *Theatre & Scotland* (Palgrave Macmillan, 2013) and *The Theatre of Anthony Neilson* (Bloomsbury, 2017). With Professor Liz Tomlin (Glasgow), she is co-editor of the new Cambridge University Press series *Elements in Theatre, Performance and the Political*. She is also co-editing the *Routledge Companion to Twentieth-Century British Theatre* (2023).

Janelle Reinelt is Emeritus Professor of Theatre and Performance at the University of Warwick. She was President of the International Federation for Theatre Research (2004–2007). She has published widely on politics and performance, receiving the 'Distinguished Scholar Award' for lifetime achievement from the American Society for Theatre Research (2010) and an honorary doctorate from the University of Helsinki in 2014. Books include *The Grammar of Politics and Performance*, with Shirin Rai (Routledge, 2015), and *Gendered Citizenship: Manifestations and Performance*, with Bishnupriya Dutt and Shrinkhla Sahai (Palgrave Macmillan, 2017). More recently, she published 'Resisting Rancière', in *Rancière and Performance*, edited by Fryer and Conroy (Rowman & Littlefield, 2021).

Anupama Roy is a Professor in the Centre for Political Studies at Jawaharlal Nehru University, Delhi, who works on citizenship, political anthropology of political institutions, political ideas, and gender studies. She is the co-author of the book *Election Commission of India: Institutionalising Democratic Uncertainties* (Oxford University Press, 2019) and author of *Citizenship Regimes, Law and Belonging: CAA and the NRC* (Oxford University Press, 2022), *Citizenship in India* (Oxford India Short Introduction Series – Oxford University Press, 2016), *Mapping Citizenship in India* (Oxford University Press, 2010, reprinted 2015), and *Gendered Citizenship: Historical and Conceptual Explorations* (Orient Longman, 2005, paperback 2013). She co-edited *Dimensions of Constitutional Democracy* (Springer, 2019) and *Poverty, Gender and Migration in South Asia* (Sage, 2008).

Urmimala Sarkar Munsi is a Professor in the School of Arts and Aesthetics, Jawaharlal Nehru University, Delhi. Her current work is on changing landscapes of dance in India, sex-trafficking and the designing of survival processes for survivors of trafficking, and politics of performance. Urmimala is currently the President of World Dance Alliance Asia Pacific. She is the co-guest editor with Aishika Chakraborty of 'The Dancing Body: Labour, Livelihood and Leisure' in the journal *South Asian History and Culture* (2023). Her most recent books are *Uday Shankar and His Transcultural Experimentations: Dancing Modernity* (Palgrave Macmillan, 2022) and *Mapping Critical Dance Studies in India* (Springer, 2024).

Ujjwal Kumar Singh is a Senior Professor in the Department of Political Science at Delhi University. He obtained his master's degree from Delhi University and his PhD from the School of Oriental and African Studies (SOAS), University of London. He is the author of *Political Prisoners in India* (Oxford University Press, 1998, paperback 2001) and *The State, Democracy and Anti-Terror Laws in India* (Sage, 2007). He has co-edited *Towards Legal Literacy: An Introduction to Law in India* (Oxford University Press, 2008, paperback 2015) and was the editor of *Human Rights and Peace: Ideas, Laws, Institution and Movements* (Sage, 2009). His co-authored book *The Election Commission of India: Institutionalising Democratic Uncertainties* was published by Oxford University Press in 2019.

Mallarika Sinha Roy is an Assistant Professor in the Centre for Women's Studies at Jawaharlal Nehru University, Delhi. She received her D.Phil (PhD) from the University of Oxford in 2008. Her research monograph is titled *Gender and Radical Politics in India: Magic Moments of Naxalbari (1967–1975)* (Routledge, 2011). Her research interests include social movement studies, ethnography and oral history, gender and political violence, gender and theatre, and the history and politics of South Asia. Her recent publications are essays in peer-reviewed journals such as *Theatre Research International*, *South Asian History and Culture*, *Feminist Review*, the *Indian Journal of Gender Studies*, *Contemporary South Asia*, *Feminism & Psychology*, and the *Journal of South Asian Development*. Her co-edited book *Displacement and Citizenship: Histories and Memories of Exclusion* (with Papori Bora, Vijaya Rao, and Shambhavi Prakash) has been recently published by Tulika (2019). She has been Co-PI in international collaborative academic projects with the University of Warwick, the University of Liverpool, and the University of Cambridge, funded by the British Academy and the Arts and Humanities Research Council, UK. She has also been a bilingual contributor to a range of cultural press in India.

Dragan Todorovic is Head of the Warwick Writing Programme, University of Warwick. His novel *Diary of Interrupted Days* (Random House Canada, 2009) was shortlisted for the Commonwealth Writers' Prize, the Amazon

First Novel Award, and other awards. His memoir *The Book of Revenge* (Random House Canada, 2006) won The Nereus Writers' Trust Non-Fiction Prize and was shortlisted for British Columbia's National Award for Canadian Non-Fiction. His collection of interactive poetry *Five Walks on Isabella Street* (Astound, 2008) was the winner of the Astound International Competition. Several of his stories have been anthologised. Dragan has written and directed twenty-four radio plays and two TV documentaries, and hosted over 150 live TV interviews (on the Culture Channel and 3K, Serbia). He is the author of the biographies of Tom Waits and Bruce Springsteen. He has translated Charles Bukowski, Tom Waits, Rod McKuen, Erica Jong, Billy Collins, Louise Glück, Adolfo Bioy Casares, and others. His articles in Canadian magazines have been shortlisted for the National Magazine Award, and he has been part of the prestigious Creative Non-Fiction programme at Banff Centre for the Arts. His aural essay *In My Language I Am Smart* was performed at Deep Wireless Festival and on CBC Radio One, and published on a CD in 2012. His sound works were recently featured on Earlid, a space dedicated to sound art. His new collection of poetry, *When Is Train Passing through Here? (Kad prolazi voz?)* was published in 2022 by Koraci in Serbia.

Foreword

The predominant mood of the chapters brought together in this volume is, the editors admit, one of melancholy and nostalgia. But that is not, they claim, the same as surrender and the acceptance of defeat. These chapters also constitute an act of recovery. There is much that is still left of the Left. Throwing aside the pervasive sentiments of hopelessness and dejection, this volume sounds a clarion call for a renewal of the battle against an exploitative, fraudulent, and morally decrepit capitalist order.

I fully endorse that call because it is both compelling and timely. There have been numerous outbursts around the world of popular frustration and anger against the depredations wrought by continued capitalist accumulation through methods that dispossess, pauperise, and humiliate ordinary people. The glaring income inequalities that keep widening in virtually every country, irrespective of whether the economy is growing or stagnant or in recession, bring out in stark relief the inherently unjust distribution of wealth and wellbeing under contemporary capitalism. There can be no question about the legitimacy and urgency not only of mounting an opposition to the rule of capital but also – let us not forget – of finding alternative ways of organising the material and moral life of society.

That task is not easy. The enormity of the challenges is apparent in the careful analyses the contributors to this volume have made in their accounts of several recent attempts around the world at retrieving the partisan practices of the Left. Let me mention a few of them. Many recent protests around the world, from the Arab Spring to the Occupy movements, have tried to overcome the well-known rigidities of the old methods of mass mobilisation through front organisations of Leftist parties by turning to the new digital communications media in order to bring together people from diverse locations. But these media are vulnerable to manipulation; the Right can sow confusion and even steal the agenda of the Left. To take another example, protests in Indian cities against a discriminatory citizenship law were marked by spontaneous performances of the Indian constitution as a document that promises liberty, equality, and justice for all. Yet such performances showed little transformative potential. How does one reconcile the entanglement of some of the brilliant work of socialist dramaturgy with recent revivals of nationalism in places like Scotland or Catalonia or Greece? Is nationalism no longer an enemy of the Left in the heart of capitalist Europe? Or have new fault lines opened up between core and periphery within Europe, redefining the bonds of solidarity between its oppressed peoples? And what do the new retrievals of Leftist theatre practices have to say about that old problem of the relation between party discipline and the ethical individual, both female and male? Have we discovered new principles to harmonise our personal and collective obligations?

These are difficult questions that complicate the task of recovering those lessons from the heritage of the Left that may have been swept away by the surge of capitalist time. Let me point to one such basic concept of the Leftist tradition that is almost completely missing in the contributions to this volume. That is the concept of class. There are, of course, good reasons for this absence. The robust history of Leftist cultural production in Europe until the middle of the twentieth century was built around a clearly identifiable social entity called the industrial working class, which constituted a substantial majority of working people in every country. Even with the more or less universal spread of school education, there were distinct differences between working-class and middle-class cultures. These differences began to blur from the 1960s and had largely vanished by the 1980s. Among the factors that brought about this change were the decline of manufacturing and extractive industries and the dominance of the financial sector, much greater access for students from working-class families to university education, the proliferation of service occupations, the demand for technically proficient workers in the new automated industries, etc. The result was a major transformation of the occupational structure of European societies. Alongside were changes in the cultural sphere marked by the entry of television into every home and the capture of mass entertainment and sports by corporate owners and advertisers. What resulted was the spread of a standardised middle-class lifestyle across the overwhelming majority of the population, with subtle gradations by income brackets that were believed to be open to upward mobility from one generation to the next. The working class in the old sense disappeared.

It would be overly simplistic to claim that this provides a causal account of why Leftist cultural practices declined in the West by the turn of the twenty-first century. But it does provide the background to at least two major political developments of our time. The first is the replacement, in the heartland of the capitalist West, of class by something called 'the people'. Not since the American and French Revolutions or the nationalist upsurges in the nineteenth century has the term 'people' evoked so much political passion in the West as it has in recent years. The antagonists are no longer labour versus capital, the working class versus the capitalists, but the people versus a tiny band of super-wealthy tycoons – the enemies of the people. The new opposition was expressed in slogans such as 'we the ninety-nine percent versus they the one percent'. This, to follow Ernesto Laclau's analysis, is the classic form of populist reasoning. Has Leftist politics transformed itself into populism?

That, of course, is not true, because populism can be both Right wing and Left wing, and is, in most cases, a mix of both. Some commentators – Chantal Mouffe being one of the most prominent among them – have argued for a distinct Left populism as a viable political path that could recuperate the heritage of the Left for the present moment. Some of the contributors to this volume appear to endorse this view. The difficulty with the Left populist position is that it assumes that since class has entirely disappeared from the social formation, the diverse mass of the people, if suitably energised by the rhetorical power of populist solidarity, could force the motley collection called the elite to make concessions that would lessen the hardship of ordinary people and improve their lives. Why, if successful, the people could even make a bid to transform the social order. The trouble with this claim is that whereas all the other classes have indeed fragmented, the owners of capital in every capitalist society today continue to retain their class organisations as well as class consciousness, as was shown in their decisive interventions during the financial crisis of 2008–2009 as well as the COVID pandemic. Where will Left populism find the political resources to challenge the dominance of an organised capitalist class?

The second major development of our time that is connected to changes in the Western capitalist world in the second half of the twentieth century took place in Asia and Africa following the dissolution of the European colonial empires. The trajectory of class in the politics of the Left in the ex-colonial countries is quite different from what happened in the West. The size of the capitalist manufacturing sector there, and thus of the industrial working class, in relation to the total economy or the total population was very small. Besides, the sector was typically dominated by colonial capital, which meant that working-class movements, even when led by Communist or Socialist Parties, became allied with the wider anti-colonial nationalist movement. The search for a broad platform of mass mobilisation led Leftist parties to look for alliances of the working class with the politically advanced middle class and the far more numerous peasantry. Even though the script of socialist revolution acquired from Europe prompted these parties to declare a theoretical adherence to working-class leadership, in actual fact Leftist movements in Asia and Africa were mostly built on the support base of peasants and were led by the middle-class intelligentsia.

This had important consequences for both the politics as well as the cultural productions of the Left in the non-Western world. The progressive section of the middle class acquired its social and political orientation through colonial education and exposure to international currents of ideas. They constructed, in their own countries, the forms of a modernist aesthetic in literature, art, music, and theatre that challenged, even as they drew upon, traditionally popular forms of performance. The aesthetic criteria that would endow a work with the quality of progressive modernity were often in sharp contrast with those valued by popular audiences. This led to difficulties, and prolonged debates, in Left circles. Works that were considered to be of great aesthetic merit would fail to impress large audiences, while those that did gain popularity might be accused of having pandered to retrograde tastes. The task of reaching the masses was often difficult to reconcile with that of educating them in Leftist values.

Given these characteristics of the class structure of many non-Western postcolonial countries, the slide of anti-colonial nationalist parties towards populism came much earlier than the latter's recent advent in the West. In India, for instance, Indira Gandhi employed characteristically Leftist populist rhetoric to consolidate her authoritarian dominance in the 1970s. In the southern Indian state of Tamil Nadu, the two regional parties that have held power in that state for over fifty years have set up an unbroken tradition of competitive populist politics. Other regional parties in other states have followed suit. In many such instances, political and cultural organisations claiming a distinct Left identity have adopted similar populist slogans, even if only on tactical grounds. On the other hand, the Hindu nationalist Bharatiya Janata Party, which, under Narendra Modi, has ruled India since 2014, has deftly combined its ideological thrust of consolidating the Hindu majority against increasingly marginalised and threatened minorities with populist benefit programmes for the poor. Thus, the well-known phenomenon of populist tactics being combined with both Left-wing and Right-wing ideological agendas has been on clear display in India.

These difficulties, many of which have indeed been explored in detail in this volume, raise a crucial question that must be answered by those interested in reviving Leftist politics in the domain of cultural production. What is the social force that can act as the agent in this exercise of recovery? It is becoming clearer by the day that without such an identifiable social category – whether or not it can be called a class is not of vital importance – which possesses an organised form and can articulate its own interest as the universal interest of society as a whole, appeals – no matter how passionate – to an inchoate mass called the people will never transcend the domain of tactics and will remain perennially open to manipulation and disruption by ruling groups. If the task of the Left is not just to be relevant but to assume a transformative role, then that is a question to which an answer must be found.

I am not, of course, suggesting that it is up to theatre workers to find that answer. But I do think that there is something in the social location of theatre in the contemporary world that gives it a vantage point that the other arenas of cultural production lack. Theatre is the one sphere of public entertainment today that is largely outside the grasp of corporate investors and advertisers (with the exception of Broadway in New York and the West End of London). Of course, state funding is often important, and sometimes crucial, for significant theatrical productions. That entails its own problems of political interference, partisanship, and corruption. But then Left cultural activists often argue that a Leftist government comes to power through a political process in which theatre workers are also participants, and, consequently, patronage of theatre is part of the political agenda of such a government. In any case the vast bulk of theatre activity in most of the world today is carried out by small groups operating with tiny budgets supplemented by sheer hard work, enthusiasm, and commitment to a cause. That generates, I believe, a rare set of favourable conditions for creativity and bold innovation.

Those are qualities that are of the essence in finding an answer to the question of identifying the appropriate agent of transformation of our contemporary world. If one looks back a few decades, one will find that the ideological dominance of global finance capital and neoliberalism was built largely on the efforts of technical experts located in universities, research laboratories, and think tanks, journalists working in a variety of print and visual media, and creative artists in cinema, television, and advertising. These were the people of the intelligentsia who provided the ideas, facts, and narratives for politicians to transform public opinion in favour of globalised neoliberal policies. A similar effort is needed on the part of a new generation of the intelligentsia to shift the tide towards the revival of Leftism. Creative artists in the theatre, by virtue of their relative independence from the clutches of big finance, can, I believe, contribute significantly to this effort.

In particular there are two areas – one in contemporary Western society and the other in the postcolonial world – where the narrative and affective powers of theatre could, I think, generate vivid and constructive accounts of new lines of social differentiation. In Western Europe and North America the least attractive jobs in the economy are performed by immigrants who are victims of racist discrimination and xenophobic hatred. The old litany of multiculturalism is too jaded to facilitate the inclusion of these people into a reconstructed social formation. That is where theatre could make a significant contribution. On the other hand, in many Asian and African countries, globalised capital accumulation has caused the collapse of traditional occupations, leading, on the one hand, to the growth of massive new settlements of informal labour, and, on the other, to desperate efforts by hundreds of thousands to flee to richer countries where, if they manage to get in, they end up as exploited and hated immigrants. There is a great need for a different narrative that can both identify the new fault lines and imagine a more prosperous social order that offers harmony and hope. Historically, that was the mission of the Left.

Partha Chatterjee

Acknowledgements

Our book, *Theatre, activism, subjectivity: Searching for the Left in a fragmented world*, is the culmination of the British Academy funded Partnership and Mobility project 'Cultures of the Left: Manifestations and Performances'. The project encompassed many interdisciplinary dialogues, colloquia, and publications, and a high-profile international conference – we are very grateful to the British Academy for this funding that enabled us to connect scholars and artists from India, the UK, the US, Canada, Serbia, Germany, France, and others. During the project, we became an international community of scholars, artists, and activists exploring the legacies and current potentialities of the Left – that in this global climate of fragmentation and uncertainty, the rise of the Right seems more pertinent than ever. This book came into being through many different voices – some featured within its covers, others contributing to its shaping in various, yet invaluable modes.

For Bishnupriya, growing up in the politically charged post-colonial India, with democratic and agonistic processes at work and urging for social citizenship and egalitarianism, cultures of the Left made sense of the times. Her cultural conditioning and legacy, she owes to the two very brave theatre activists, her parents, who risked their lives to be pioneers of political theatre in post-independent India.

Silvija, who grew up in socialist Yugoslavia, has never overcome the feeling of loss and sorrow over a certain kind of collectivity, solidarity, care for commons, and multicultural social set-up that have been violently destroyed. She is deeply grateful to everyone who has been in the project and who contributed to this collection for awakening the hope that a world where capitalism indeed has an alternative could be reimagined.

Special thanks go to the inimitable Janelle Reinelt for her intellectual generosity, guidance, and friendship – she has remained our most wonderful motivator and mentor. We are also most grateful to Elaine Aston for her camaraderie, support, and wisdom. Our collaborators and fellow travelers from Warwick, JNU, SOAS, and the Centre for Social Science in Kolkata, respectively, made this journey inspiring and unforgettable: Miljia Gluhović, Ameet Parameswaran, Urmimala Sarkar Munsi, Shirin Rai, Anupama Roy, Trina Nilina Bannerjee, Mallarika Sinha Roy, and the indomitable Partha Chatterjee and Samik Bandopadhyay as our mentors and advisors, were the backbone of the project and publication. Many senior and early career scholars joined us on the way: Nivedita Menon, Chantel Mouffe, Dragan Todorovic, Ujjwal Singh, Anika Marschall, Yana Meerzon, Adrian Kear, Trish Reid, Anuradha Kapur, Igor Štiks, Jelena Vasiljević, Andy Lavender, Snežana Golubović Nicholas Rideout, Amanda Stuart-Fisher, Liz Tomlin, Vicky Angelaki, Komita Dhanda, and many of our students and colleagues. To Tony Fisher we owe special thanks for being constantly in dialogue with us as he worked on politics and performance, opening many new insights and critical perspectives. All our collaborators and colleagues showed a very high level of commitment and enthusiasm in keeping our optimism up, while hoping academic writing and research will affect ground level politics and build resistances.

We would ardently like to thank our two institutions: JNU, the radical University which continues to fight for academic freedom and progressive free thinking against all odds and to keep our faith in collectivities, collaboration, and struggles, through a very rare comradeship; and the University of Warwick for generous and collegial support. We especially thank our colleagues Tim White, Nicholas Whybrow, Nadine Holdsworth, Yvette Hutchison, and anna six, as well as the Humanities Research Council, the Warwick Institute of Advanced Studies, and the Connecting Culture GRP for additional financial support. Special gratitude goes to our dear, late college and friend, Jim Davis – who always championed international connections and dialogues and whose legacy continues to inspire us.

Both of us owe a lot to our colleagues in the International Federation for Theatre Research, and its vibrant discussion forums, particularly the Feminist Research Working Group and Political Theatre Working Group.

A very special thanks to our series editors: Maria Delgado, Vice President of IFTR and dear friend and colleague, for her enthusiasm and dedication to academic diversity and political cultures; and Maggie Gale and Peter Lichtenfels for supporting this book with kindness and generosity. Heartfelt thanks to the editorial and production team at Manchester University Press and Newgen Publishing, including Paul Clark, Matthew Frost, Kate Hawkins, Pete Gentry, and Helen Flitton for her great help and eye for detail. Our gratitude also goes to Aastha Gandhi, who came to our rescue during the indexing process; and Semanti Basu, whose editorial help in the pre-manuscript submission process was much appreciated. We thank Ana Isabella Todorovic @AnArt for granting us her original artwork featured on the cover.

To our families, Ahvana and Ana, we hope they will inherit a more egalitarian and just world and if things get worse, as are the indications at the moment, we hope our work and writings will continue to inspire them to keep the struggle and resistances alive. The book is dedicated to them and to many of our students who think in such terms to stand against poverty and class – to poor and stigmatised groups fighting for a just and egalitarian world.

Introduction: Searching for the Left in a fragmented world

Silvija Jestrovic and Bishnupriya Dutt

Questions of the Left

In her documentary novel *The Years*, the Nobel laureate Annie Ernaux remembers the collective political hopes on the Left following the end of the Cold War era and the fall of the Iron Curtain: 'We waited, indeed hoped, for some fusion between Communism and Democracy, the market economy and Lenin's planning. We longed for an October Revolution with the happy ending' (Ernaux 2017: 118). Instead, former socialist/communist countries went through a period of ruthless privatisation (not only of companies and factories but also of mountains, rivers, and forests, leaving a trail of destitution behind) under the euphemism of 'transition' to the free market. Subsequently, cuts to health and social care, education, and the cultural sector became trends not only exclusive to countries emerging from the ruins of communism but also among the richest of the rich (the UK after fifteen years of Conservative rule being a case in point). Even though Ernaux's hope and disillusionment are located in the Western European experience, the suburbs of Paris to be precise, a similar melancholy motivated us at first. Indeed, the initial question was asked in the spirit of melancholy but also retrieval, while our histories and memories of the Left were coming from various directions – the Global South (India), Eastern Europe, and the West (Europe and North America). It started as a legacy project looking at remnants of the past and how they manifest in the present: what is left of Left institutions, practices, critical discourses, and its other cultural manifestations at the present juncture? And what is worth salvaging?

What's Left of the Left (Cronin et al. 2011) was the seed out of which this volume grew. It first emerged from shared global histories, memories, and experiences of the political and cultural Left (albeit from very different geographical and socio-political locations) and from the consciousness that this legacy needed to be revisited, rethought, and retrieved. As variations of this question began to increasingly (re-)emerge in politics, history, and philosophy, and through artistic and documentary works,[1] we realised that our shared yet different cultural and political experiences of the Left and the interdisciplinary potential of theatre and performance studies, within which we predominately (although not exclusively) work, could offer a unique insight and contribution. The British Academy Partnership and Mobility grant that we received (from 2016 to 2019) enabled us to embark on a cross-cultural journey in search of the Left. While the physical journey mainly stretched from the UK to India and back, on our intellectual journey we travelled to many more places – past and present, rural and urban, from street to stage, to the theatre and the home. More voices from different cultural, linguistic, geographical, and disciplinary backgrounds came on board (some are featured here and others contributed elsewhere and in different forms).[2]

Quickly, our initial search for the Left became less tentative by responding to the urgency of the ever-shifting political realities of our time. We started asking after the grand ideological narratives of communism have crumbled,[3] how can a Leftist ethos to address contemporary inequalities of class, caste, gender, and race against the backdrop of the rising Right and mounting environmental crisis be recuperated? From the moment we first asked 'What's left of the Left?' to the time that the first drafts of the chapters in this collection were completed, Narendra Modi had solidified his power in India, Donald Trump had won and then lost the US presidency, and while fuelled by the Right-wing populist rhetoric of xenophobia, the Brexit vote was cast in the UK. In Brazil Bolsonaro, like Trump, won and then lost the elections as the Amazon was burning. The victory of the far-Right party Brothers of Italy was yet another warning sign for Europe that the Right was on the rise. When the global pandemic struck, it put an additional twist on these constellations, starkly exposing local and global inequalities of class, caste, race, and gender. 'The pandemic is a portal' wrote Arundhati Roy in her eponymous article calling upon us to re-examine, this time in the context of the pandemic, the deadly workings of capitalism (Roy 2020). During the process of completing this collection, the general context(s) from which we have worked has felt like a constantly shifting ground. Paradoxically, retrieving the remains of the Left from the past and in the present became infused with a growing sense of urgency to respond to the rising Right of our time, to the crisis of the global Left, but also to the increasing sense of crisis of capitalism itself. In our times of political confusion – when Leftist agendas and struggles often collapse or become appropriated by the Right – the necessity of recovering the Leftist ethos of solidarity, social justice, and care for the commons seems more urgent than ever. How does one grapple with the complexities of the Left, its theatres and theatricalities, its modes of activism, its subjects and subjectivities?

We live in a fragmented world, in an overflow of information and stimuli reinforced through ever-growing technology that in one minute opens democratic spaces of dialogue (even through dissensus), only to turn into a cacophony that makes listening impossible and any debate meaningless in the next. Forms of political activism and political art are often watered down and marginalised in the global political arena where 'perception management' (Roy 2020: 622) and 'manufacturing of consent' (Herman and Chomsky 2019) have replaced ideological positions and often work more effectively in swaying publics than political programmes and policies. How to be political and to act politically as an individual within a very fragmented collective, where single-issue agendas often pull apart groups that would normally be allied, is a vexing question. However, our fragmented world is different from the sense of the fragmentation emerging from the traumas of the First World War, and still different from the divided world of the Cold War era that, notwithstanding, also included the Non-Aligned Movement that endeavoured to carve a third way beyond the then dominant East–West binary. This fragmentation stems from two contradictory aspects: 1) the capitalist spectacle – with its all-penetrating tentacles – that in various scripts keeps reinscribing that 'there is no alternative'; and 2) the growing (even if still somewhat formless) hunch that this capitalist orthodoxy is starting to crumble. In her chapter 'Capitalism: A Ghost Story' Arundhati Roy points to this contradiction when she writes about the powerful symbiosis of neoliberal economics and politics:

> Gradually, one imagination – a brittle superficial pretence of tolerance and multiculturalism (that morphs into racism, rabid nationalism, ethnic chauvinism or warmongering Islamophobia at a moment's notice) under the roof of the single overarching, very unplural economic ideology – began to dominate the discourse. It did so to such an extent that it ceased to be perceived as an ideology at all. It became the default position, the natural way to be. (2019: 643)

Nonetheless, Roy also notes that this discourse has started to shift, singling out the Occupy movement as an event that (re)introduced an alternative vocabulary and vision of the world (even if its immediate effects were less than hoped for). Indeed, small- and larger-scale events of Leftist political resistance worldwide and the Left as an actual and actualised democratic political option (for example, the Left governance in Kerala, Podemos in Spain, and Syriza in Greece remain impactful even when teetering between success and decline, and there are also Lula's recent return to power in Brazil and Gabriel Boric's electoral victory in Chile)[4] further indicate that a radical alternative imagining of the world is taking place even if in a fragmented manner when two steps forward always come with one step back. They do contribute, however, to the growing sense that in Engels and Marx's words, 'Capitalism has conjured up such gigantic means of production and exchange, that it is like the sorcerer who is no longer able to control the powers of netherworld whom he has called up by his spells' ([1884] 1998: 17).

On the one hand, we see the confusion of values, a collapsing of the Left and the Right, for example, when demands for workers' rights become coupled with anti-migrant sentiments, where the quest for freedom and against the neoliberal state becomes backed with conspiracy theories, and when the Right appropriates the rhetoric and strategies of the Left. On the other hand, there is an urgent call to recuperate the idea of care for the commons (the direct meaning of the word communism), rethink the economy of growth in favour of sustainability, and re-examine individualism to forge new collective imagination rooted in solidarity. As these processes unfold, the binaries of Left and Right might eventually become obsolete, but the antagonistic ethics of these opposite sides of the political and ideological spectrum should never become conflated and interchangeable.

Through the lens of performance and politics, this collection zooms in on the context-specific dimensions, analogies, and micro-histories of the Left to better understand the larger picture. It proposes a search for the Left not from totalising Leftist ideological positions and partisan politics but from ethical dimensions through smaller-scale Left-leaning struggles, not from the political to the aesthetic but from the potentiality of art to offer new political imagination and critique, not from the individual subordinated to the collective but from the dialectics of subjectivity and collectivity. This is not an attempt at a sweeping global overview of Leftist cultures either but a collection that brings together culture-specific and comparative perspectives. This book searches for fragments of and on the Left, past and present, through which to rethink and patch a fragmented world.

Such an approach might appear counterintuitive as both the idea of communism and the Subject[5] within it are constituted through big political events that have the capacity to change the course of history. Left aesthetics are often viewed as being in service of political ideas rather than their dialectical manifestation, while for the Left activism to sustain itself, the individual's submergement within the collective (more specifically, if we are to follow Jodi Dean, within party discipline[6]) is seen as inevitable. Here, however, we examine the bigger picture from below – from smaller-scale, context-specific junctures in time and place. The assumption here is not that the big picture is mechanically reflected in miniature but rather that on the micro-plane, things often manifest and unfold at different frequencies and even follow different laws. In other words, what is effective politically and viable ethically on a large scale might prove challenging, even unsustainable, on a smaller scale. It is there, on the micro-plane, that the Left emerges not only as a political idea and action (in big strokes) but as a practice of everyday life.

The Left is framed here as a large umbrella term for a range of progressive cultural and political practices, as well as a way of living/being in the world. The focus on plural cultural Lefts draws attention to different histories of Leftist political and cultural practices and to the dialectics between official and unofficial Lefts – between the totalising ideological framework and its smaller-scale manifestations. The conceptual focus is on the dialectics of the macro- and the micro-plane of the Leftist histories, legacies, and current forms of resistance as they occur through different dramaturgies of activism but also through theatre and everyday life. Drawing from both past and present, using the interdisciplinary hermeneutics of theatre, politics, and performance, we refine our overarching questions of the Left: how to do activism, make theatre, and be in the world through the Leftist paradigms and ethos? What are the political, cultural, personal, and collective dramaturgies through which to recuperate the Leftist care for commons for our time?

Playing the field

In the early days of the project we anchored on the *Idea of Communism* (Badiou 2010) – an edited volume of chapters by leading Marxist scholars, compiled through a seminar that retained a dialogical mode for exploring in earnest the conceptual and critical approaches to addressing the dynamics of culture and politics with the intent of recovering the progressive values of Left philosophical discourses. The collection covered a multitude of issues: citing relevant critical discourses on subjects, subjectivities, and presence (Badiou, Balso, Rancière), history and critical reflexivity of Left historical transgressions, cultural freedom, and culture revolutions (Russo, Buck-Morss), rights and will (Douzinas), and the very foundational principles inherent in communism – community, collective, and solidarities (Eagleton, Hallard, Hardt, Negri, Nancy). The publication and our discussions gestured towards rethinking theatre and performance practices in terms of a paradigm shift without discarding the essence of what we can term Left cultural politics. It seemed more urgent than ever to reconsider taxonomic distinctions of the term 'Left cultural politics' to apply to multiple practices in a terrain where various modes of struggle occur to build resistance against hegemonic cultural processes.

In 2019, midway through the project, we organised a conference in Venice called 'Cultures of the Left in the Age of Right Wing Populism'. As the title suggests, it was to make sense of the Right-wing populism sweeping across the world, depoliticising cultural practices and decimating what the Left has always prioritised: the people, the notion of the popular (not merely empirical data), empathetic encounters, or collective struggles, and people's movements. Chantal Mouffe, the keynote speaker at our conference, and her then latest publication – *For a Left Populism* (2018) – became a critical point of debate in relation to formulations of hegemony, such as Partha Chatterjee's, which regards populism as apparently consistent with democratic rationality in terms of a peculiar differential demand based on equivalence but also a 'crisis of hegemony' emanating from the 'tactical contraction of the integral state during the phase of neo-liberal governmentality' (Chatterjee 2020: xiv). In the Indian context – one of the focus areas of this book and the location from which Chatterjee writes – in the face of growing authoritarianism, an undermining of the liberal state, and a decline of political parties with coherent ideologies and trade union – has led to a dangerous nexus between the state and Right-wing conservative forces, mobilising and dividing people on lines of caste and religion, while personality cults are pivots on which consensus is mobilised. For Chatterjee, the pessimism of the times is countered by citing Antonio Gramsci and asking 'What social forces will lead counterhegemonic projects of transformations?' (Gramsci, quoted in Chatterjee 2020: xvii). This prompts us, through the research, interaction, and now the publication, to ask how activism, theatre, and resistances can be a catalyst and at the same time be symptomatic of this scenario.

Rustom Bharucha's work *Terrorism and Performance* (2014) traces the complexities further to show how hegemonic discourses are constructed, such as around terrorism, which he says is distinct from actual incidents of terror or the figure of the terrorist and manages perceptions, degenerating into Islamophobia and divisive communal politics and reinstating binaries of violence and victimhood. Bharucha, too, seeks out examples from India and all over the world, where responsible artistes, theatre-makers, and performance activist-artists create works that challenge, halt, disrupt, and interrupt the power structures which construct and disseminate these hegemonic discourses – precisely a kind of 'disjunction' and 'anachronism' that challenges the hegemonic common sense and 'assumes that only the language of performance can legitimately address the terror of our times' (Bharucha 2014: 24).

The intimidating tendencies of totalitarian hegemonic populism and counter-hegemonic performance practices, and eloquent references to Marxist ideas and critical literature, led us to regard our work as an intervention into the scholarship in the domain of theatre and performance studies. Since the first decade of the twenty-first century, a rising tide of new scholarship has claimed that political theatre is redundant, politics and theatre should be uncoupled at best, and that theatre studies should instead look inward to examine the apparatus of performance/theatre itself (Lehmann 2006; Read 2008; Kelher 2009; Ridout 2013). [7] The common stance that informs this strand of theatre and performance studies scholarship is that it is becoming increasingly difficult to create effective, meaningful theatre works to counter mass cultural practices. Although theatre's internal apparatus and mechanisms are key to understanding progressive performance practices and have always been so, they are supplemental or dialectical to the practice itself, as Nicholas Ridout tells us in *Passionate Amateurs: Theatre, Communism and Love* (2013). However, as Ridout further argues, they cannot replace theatre's role in the public domain as an important institution of civil society and shared experience to build theatrical communities and be part of a collective struggle, particularly at a time when it is much needed. *Passionate Amateurs* on the one hand regards the internal mechanism, such as economics, social constitution, amateur status, aesthetics, and experimental works, as imperative, while on the other hand it acknowledges the importance of building theatrical communities and emanance between actors and spectators, and underlies the tension between aesthetic experiments and capitalist cultural economics shaped by time, investment, and profit motifs closely related to labour (Ridout 2013).

However, the influential vein urging for a fragmented approach to theatre practices (Lehmann 2006; Read 2008; Kelher 2009) continues to argue that looking at political theatre in today's context could be regarded as naïve, obsolete, or even complicit with the neoliberal culture of consumption and spectacularisation of cultures. Janelle Reinelt reads such tendencies, particularly Read's claims that 'to politicise performance requires us to do away with the ideas of political theatre if not political theatre itself' (in Reinelt 2015: 242), as detrimental and his attempts at reconceptualising certain key terms that characterise political theatre as imminently dangerous. Rai and Reinelt's *Grammar of Politics and Performance* (2015) warns against the consequences of such an approach that would denigrate the critical components that characterise political practices – 'interests, representations, identities, and re-distributions' (Rai and Reinelt 2015: 6). They offer a counter realm of aesthetic analysis, which urges for a return to engaging with the partisan thematic of the practice itself and focusing on the material and social-political structures of power, governance, and activism to explore the possibilities of (political, social, or cultural) transformations.

Reinelt's influential keynote at the International Federation for Theatre Research (IFTR) conference in 2014 (Reinelt 2015) urged the academic community to reconsider their approaches to cultural politics. With Raymond Williams's classic lines – 'What I came to say' – and through Williams's various concepts, she formulated a critical perspective around the current debates, offering new methodological approaches to political theatre in the times of wide-scale depoliticisation. To recover the concept of culture as productive, processual, and egalitarian, Reinelt asks the vital question 'what is left to recuperate, renegotiate, rethink and re-perform' from the Leftist projects. She offers various strategies: performances that unravel the materiality of cultural processes, and practices that undermine hierarchies between elite and popular culture and build on the utopian projection of a common culture (Reinelt 2015: 236).

Given that many of us never dared to depart from our basic investment in cultural politics and, historically, the genre in which we worked or researched, Reinelt's reference to Williams's concept of residual and emergent cultures as antagonistic or counter to the dominant hegemonic cultures allowed us in many ways to revert to histories of political theatre and struggles and find relevance in actual practices of the contemporary times. Not only was there a spurt of new production of landmark political theatre from the past but also residues of social movements, such as feminist practices that started reappearing in new emergent protest and performance strategies. It allowed us to understand who we are and what our works signify at this critical juncture. Partha Chatterjee's keynote at the IFTR conference in 2015 (later published in *Theatre Research International* in 2016) similarly indicates such a need for theatre practices (read political theatre) which directly address issues and establish long-term lines of communication in fostering or facilitating changes within democratic practices. A departure from what was implied in his work on populism or political society, Chatterjee reinvents a critical role for the political theatre, particularly for those with strong Left leanings, as does Tony Fisher (2023). One of Fisher's examples is directly related to the Leftist street theatre group Janam. He writes that 'by articulating itself in relation to "issues" the activist theatre constitutes itself as a site for mobilisation of the popular democratic force otherwise known as the "people"' (Fisher 2023: 153). Taking off from Fisher and Chatterjee – a Left commitment at the centre – the chapters here, however, explore a diverse range of trajectories that are expressions of political theatre in today's context or what is historically relevant. Progressive Left theatre has never remained modular or monolithic but reflects how politics and performances vary and contribute to specific contexts but also intersect.

Liz Tomlin, in her book *Political Dramaturgies and Theatre Spectatorship* (2019), and Vicki Angelaki, in *Social and Political Theatre in 21st Century Britain: Staging Crisis* (2017), indicate new works and repertoires in the context of British theatre where collective spectatorship is the priority, connecting text and new modes of theatrical practices into the area of spectatorship. Moreover, they both highlight the tensions between the logic of autonomy vis-à-vis the collective. Like Reinelt, Tomlin includes a strong critique of Rancière's influential philosophical discourse on the distribution of the sensible and the limitations of dissensus, which is individualistic, momentary, and does not have the political efficacy that Williams advocates in reimagining the idea of the spectator citizen and the processes that build political communities.

Since we did our research and wrote the chapters, Tony Fisher's *Aesthetic Exception* (2023) has elaborated on the debate and mapped a genealogy rather than a history (which Fisher sees as the problem of the history of political theatre, theoretical debate, and practices). *Aesthetic Exception* also urges us not to fall into the binaries of, as he explains, aesthetics and propaganda or autonomy (read aesthetics experiments) and efficacy. Unlike Reinelt and Tomlin, Fisher is critical of ideological theatre and hegemonic didacticism but is heavily invested in a critical theatre of conjuncture, which associates with the politics of the times, exposing its own locations within the conjuncture and in terms of its reinventing aesthetics, employs a displacement effect, jeopardises cultural aesthetics, and disturbs theatre's mode of complicity and habituation. In terms of the critical theatre of conjuncture, the political is inherent in the aesthetics. Fisher insists that the political and social situation necessitates its existence, and reverting back to Gramsci, via Hall, he writes that theatre must be grasped through the specifications of its conjunctural determinants – tactics and agitations (as opposed to strategy or propaganda) that 'constitutes the exemplary sites for hegemonic struggles, ... the immediate terrain on which political action inescapably happens' (Fisher 2023: 171).

A number of our collaborators and contributors to the volume, meanwhile, expanded their research and published critical works in the interdisciplinary field. *The Oxford Handbook of Politics and Performance* (2021) is one such comprehensive edited volume, which initiated a prolonged conversation between scholars in both politics and performance across different geographical areas. It highlighted politics and performance as co-constituent disciplines that foreground ways in which theatre is political and politics is performative. This vein of combining politics with performative manifestations and performances is reflected in two very significant publications: Anupama Roy's *Citizenship Regimes, Law and Belonging: The CAA and the NRC* (2022) and Nivedita Menon's *Secularism as Misdirection: Conversations from the Global South* (2023).

What the state of the field in politics and performance indicates and the book gestures towards is that the academic discourse in the field has since understood the need for progressive cultural projects within definite practices adhering to Leftist and Marxist imaginations based on cultural materialism. This also brings back the argument that to look at the political theatre genre, among many others, as merely an aesthetic practice needs reassessment, a critical historiography, and a disciplinary symbiosis of politics and performance. However, Anandita Bajpai's edited book *Cordial Cold War: Cultural Actors in India and the German Democratic Republic* (2021), Ania Loomba's *Revolutionary Desire: Women, Communism and Feminism in India* (2019), and Kavita Panjabi's *Unclaimed Harvest: An Oral History of the Tebhaga Women's Movement* (2017) explore local forms of Left cultural practices, not simply as the mechanical emanation of Left ideology into practice but rather they map how in every iteration, new practices and the plurality of the Leftist ideas are constructed, negotiating both local and international issues. These are some of the works our collection builds on while taking the debate more strongly into the context of theatre and performance studies and the intersection between politics and performance.

Drawing from the epistemologies of theatre and performance scholarship on the one hand and political, social, and cultural analysis on the other, this collection relies on interdisciplinary voices and vocabularies to understand the dynamics between theory and practice – the unfolding of radical politics and aesthetics, and the relationship between the individual and the collective. Combining history and historiography with contemporary performance, political and cultural analysis is vital to our aim of addressing the legacies of the Left and the ways in which they have shaped (or could be retrieved to shape) contemporary forms of Leftist theatre, activism, and lifestyle. Moreover, this comparative approach to the past and the present allows for analogies to emerge that point not only to distinct dramaturgies of the Left but also to the performativity of Leftist legacies and their echoes in today's practices.

Activism, theatre, subjectivity: concepts and contents

The interwoven themes of theatre, activism, and subjectivity shape both the content and the key conceptual frameworks of this collection, comprising *worksites of the Left*, *scales*, and *biography*. First, in intertwining the lens of theatre and performance with radical political thought and action, various modes of performance – from activist/political to theatrical/political to personal/political – are understood here as *worksites of the Left* within which to recuperate the Leftist ethos and praxis.[8] The term 'worksite' itself is immediately linked to the verb 'to do/delat' (as in Chernishevsky/Lenin's famous question: '*Chto delat?*' (What is to be done?)).[9] It is the site where 'doing', 'work', or 'labour' of some kind or another takes place. In the vocabulary of theatre dramaturgy, doing is action. It implies conflict or agon. Various doings/actions take place when a worksite is shaped into being: legal and juridical, political, social, artistic, discursive, and embodied. In Brechtian terms, however, the key question is not so much 'What is this action, what is the doing?' but rather 'How is this action, how is this doing performed?' '*Kak delat?*' rather than '*Chto delat?*'

Second, the worksite concept enables a better understanding of the importance of micro-histories and micro-practices of the Left within larger historical moments and manifestations. How can theatre and performance, different modes of political dissent (large scale and small), and everyday practices of living politically tackle the burning question 'What is to be done?' How can micro-practices of the Left, for example notions such as micro-communism or minimal communism, serve as worksites and modelling of what might become possible on a larger scale? How do micro-practices formulate and embody a dialectical critique of the politics and ideology that underpin them?

Third, biography and autobiography are proposed as a conceptual and methodological approach to access the subjective and the personal viewed both in their everydayness and within larger historical narratives. Biography and autobiography are the genres within which we recognise the potential to explore the workings of the micro- and macro-scales in a range of modes as material to further conceptualise notions such as micro-communism and as a means of political self-reflection.

The collection is structured into three parts – Activism, Theatre, Subjectivity – that are identified as *worksites of the Left*. These worksites enter into dialogue with one another from their various, and at times overlapping, locations: from the street to cyberspace, from prison to theatre, and from the public stage to home. The activism worksite foregrounds scales, especially in terms of the collective (from larger-scale mass events to individual, smaller-scale interventions), while the subjectivity worksite especially favours the biographical material and autobiographical voice with various degrees of intimacy and distance. The section on theatre is placed physically in the middle, whereby theatre is viewed as a site of intersection of both activism and subjectivity – of living/being on the Left and of acting politically. This tripartite structure reflects the conceptual journey of the book: from the collective to the individual – from political action to political subjectivity (and back) – as we explore dramaturgies, theatricalities, and the performativities of these categories.

Political activism is perhaps the most obvious area where politics becomes performative, and performance turns political. It is the sphere of political spectacle, yet it is often marked by strong performative acts of collective defiance. It is where, as in Patti Smith's song *People Have the Power*, we can see and feel revolutionary thought in action. The focus on activism highlights the collective and individual interventions that inform our thinking about the Left publics where theatricality and performativity emerge as devices or as by-phenomena. Nivedita Menon's opening chapter 'Performing the Constitution as an insurgent document' starts from the intersection of politics and performance to navigate dissensus and its manifestations in public spaces. The chapter highlights the performativity of the Indian constitution while questioning its capacity for radical politics. She relates tribal and lesbian, gay, bisexual, and transgender (LGBT) issues to Leftist politics and practices of activism as she zooms in on the tribal *Pathalgadi* movement and the ways in which they perform 'insurgent constitutionalism'.

While street and open public space are the main stage on which the insurgent constitution performs in Menon's chapter, Dragan Todorovic takes us to the aporias of hyperspace and its relationship to actual, physical sites of political activism in his chapter 'Revolution: Like, share, subscribe'. He problematises ways in which dissensus and consensus are managed through these different sites and how between the hyperspaces and embodied resistance in situ, Left agendas often become defused and co-opted by the Right. Activism is seen here as a worksite with the strongest mobilising potential (both on the street and in the hyperspace), yet in our hyper-mediatised world, it is also vulnerable to manipulation and prone to confusion. Drawing from a range of protest activities from the Occupy movement to the '1 in 5 Million' protest in Serbia, Todorovic examines the protest strategies and the question of leadership as he calls for more resilient Leftist practices of utilising both the hyperspace and the street.

Anupama Roy and Ujjwal Kumar Singh's chapter 'Hunger artists' adds prison to the list of worksites of Leftist activist practices. The adjective 'insurgent' is also the keyword of Roy and Singh's chapter as they trace Gandhian activism, suffragists, Irish Republicans, and 'revolutionary terrorists' through their examination of archival sources, memoirs, prison writings, interviews, documentaries, and films. Hunger fasts are explored here as examples of radical political practices and protest strategies of the Left. Even though they take place in confinement, they bring visibility and traction to the cause. Like Menon's 'insurgent constitution', Roy and Singh's 'insurgent citizenship' foregrounds radical protest practices at the intersection of the individual and the collective and in relation to the state and the power apparatus.

Conversely, Anika Marschall's chapter 'Of quiet resistance' looks at the 'shy radicalism' of the artist and activist Hamja Ahsan and takes the activist discourse from the collective to the individual while exploring the radical political potential of neurodiverse subjectivity as a form of Leftist activism. Drawing from identity politics, including questions of race, gender, disability, and religion and from his neurodiverse perspective, Marschall argues that Ahsan's 'shy radicalism' devises a new vocabulary of dissent, which she names 'the quiet resistance'. Ahsan's aesthetics and politics of 'shy radicalism' emerge here as a new form of small-scale Leftist activism. Yet like Todorovic's critique of and search for new forms of Leftist activism in the cacophony of both the street and the hyperspace, Menon's theatricality and performativity of the constitution and its capacity to protect tribal and LGBT rights, and the silence and noise of hunger fasts as forms of Left protests in prisons that Roy and Singh explore, Marschall too, in a way, seeks to identify new forms of 'insurgent citizenship' that are germane to the cultures of the Left. She finds them in the dramaturgies of 'quiet resistance'. In these four chapters that address different forms of radical Left-leaning activism, forms of insurgent citizenship emerge (at times overtly, at other times discreetly) on different scales – from macro to micro, from loud to quiet, from collective to individual and back.

The theatre worksite highlights theatrical performance and the stage (whether it be the proscenium arch or the street) as a site that, in its heterotopic nature, can show the operation of various scales revealing the politics of the personal and the collective. The section opens with Bishupriya Dutt's chapter 'Theatre of the streets: Of working class strikes, protests, and democratisation of life' that explores the intersection of the street and the theatre as a site of radical dissensus through a feminist historiographic perspective. It focuses on the work of the female theatre directors Moloyashree Hashmi and Anamika Haksar as they forge unique Leftist dramaturgies of street theatre that highlight issues of labour, workers' rights, and the aesthetics of workers' theatre. Moreover, Dutt asserts a postcolonial lens – juxtaposing proscenium arch theatre, as a legacy of Indian colonial aesthetics, to various postcolonial experimentations with space.

Drawing on Mouffe's notion of Left populism, Yana Meerzon further engages with the dramaturgies of the Left in her chapter 'Between the Right and the Left: Staging political, emotional, and social polarisations on the Canadian Stage', examining the form of documentary theatre and assembly to address political dissensus. The form of political assembly is brought down to the scale of a theatrical stage whereby Meerzon addresses the political responsibility of the audience situated between the irreconcilable discourses of the Left and the Right.

Ameet Parameswaran's 'The indiscreet charm of Left nostalgia' is set in the context of the postcolonial nationalism of Kerala (currently the only remaining Leftist state in India). He focuses on zooesis, globality, and Leftist nostalgia while analysing the depiction of class, caste, and poverty on stage. He engages with the questions of scale and theatre-within-the-theatre as specific dramaturgical devices that enable these investigations.

All the chapters in this section variously explore what Trish Reid, in her chapter on socially engaged theatre in the Scottish context, *The Cheviot and its legacies*', calls 'dramaturgies of the Left'. Reid shows how Leftist politics has been channelled within the work of John McGrath, exploring the paradoxical relationship of the socialist engagement and Left-leaning dramaturgies on the one hand and nationalism on the other.

Trina Banerjee and Adrian Kear grapple, in different ways, with the relationship between aesthetics and politics. Banerjee's approach is historiographic as she looks at the large-scale designs in Utpal Dutt's Leftist theatre and its departure from minimalism. In her chapter 'Staging revolution' she demonstrates how aesthetic choices ranging from minimalism to spectacle become, within the cultural public sphere of the Left, ideological battles. Using Brecht's notion of *gestus* as one of the key elements of conceptual framing, Adrian Kear's 'Acting politically: Making performance in the eye of history' asks 'how does history see us when we ourselves are historical beings living in and through the storm of history?', and what does it mean to act politically in theatre? Drawing from a range of scholarships that consider the notion of gesture and *gestus* as the 'reopening of historical perspective and performative possibility', he turns to the performances of Anna Deavere Smith and the issues of race and racism to explore the potentiality of aesthetics and politics in taking a political stand on the stage.

Mallarika Sinha Roy's essay 'Love in the time of revolution' on Utpal Dutt's 'passionate politics' continues to grapple with aesthetics and politics, showing how affective registers establish stronger feminist aspects in the Leftist political theatre. Exploring the ethical framing of Dutt's imagination of love, Roy points to the link between historical accountability of theatrical forms and the transgressive possibilities of notions of love and romance on the revolutionary stage with audiences of different communities, religions, and castes. Both Kear and Roy, invoking Brecht, unpack methodologies of theatre-making, as well as of being a theatre-maker on the Left.

The term 'subjectivity' in the eponymous worksite of this collection connotes both an individual and a political subject who has, through acting politically, undergone the process of subjectification (Badiou 2010). To realise this kind of subjectivity, one needs to live the life of activist doing/making, that is, to adopt the stanza of acting politically as a lifestyle. The term 'subject' here implies both individual agency and subjection to the collective and to the greater good – the dialectics of which the chapters in this section probe and negotiate. This multifaceted notion of subjectivity foregrounds both the relationship between the individual and the collective as well as the asymmetries between the Left of big events and ideas on the one hand and the Left of everyday life and micro-communist practices on the other. Biographical and autobiographical narratives and testimonies offer a special insight into these dynamics between political theory and lived experiences and a new critical understanding of the quotidian performativity of the

Left. Connecting to Mallarika Sinha Roy's chapter that offers biographical glimpses into Utpal Dutt's life to understand the role of revolutionary love in theatrical aesthetics and politics of his work (in the theatre worksite) and to Marschall's consideration of Hamja Ahsan's unique subjectivity and biographical dimensions to foreground the subversive political potential of 'shy radicalism' (in the activist worksite), the chapters in this section range from historical biographies to autobiographical reflections to explore ways of performing subjectivity politically.

Identifying the notion of political friendship as a form of micro-communism, Silvija Jestrovic turns to the biography of Eleanor Marx to look for dialectical intersections of personal and political in 'Revolutionary intimacies' of theatre, friendship, and love. Urmimala Sarkar Munsi's chapter 'The fraught act of speaking for/about the communist women' points to the importance of feminist readings of biographical narratives and testimonies as she traces the female voices of the Indian Left. Indirectly linking Dutt's highlighting of feminist historiographies in the context of Leftist street theatre dramaturgies (in the theatre worksite), Sarkar Munsi demonstrates not only how women's experiences of being communist differ but also how their biographical narratives become interventionist political texts that challenge both the patriarchy within the movement and the dogmatic dimensions of the Communist Party itself.

In 'One always fails to speak of the things one loves: Memories of border crossings', Shirin Rai continues to explore political contradictions inherent in the dialectics between individual agency and party doctrine in the context of the Indian Left and through the life and work of her parents. In her chapter the intersection of the political and the personal of her parent's biographies and her own autobiographical voice becomes a hermeneutical device of probing into revolutionary dreams and disillusionments as well as a means of digging deeper into one's own political subjectivity.

In Janelle Reinelt's closing chapter 'Why I am still a socialist', the autobiographical voice and insight also figures as an epistemological device of political self-knowledge through which to examine the relationship between the personal and the political in the context of the American Left and socialist artist practices on stage. These chapters variously show the tensions in the processes whereby the individual becomes and acts as a political subject while also pointing to somewhat underexplored intersections of patrilineages and matrilineages of the Left (which in this collection also subvert the from-father-to-son pattern in favour of the trajectory from mothers and fathers to daughters).

While the geographical focus of the book is broad, the aim was not to be all-encompassing but rather place a limited number of geopolitical and cultural contexts in dialogue. Some of the chapters have been newly commissioned for this proposed collection, and others have developed through a continuous cross-cultural dialogue with one another. The international and collaborative dimensions of this book have enabled us to think about the cultures of the Left in this fragmented world through a cross-cultural lens and to understand the context-specific practices and struggles that underpin its broad theoretical framework. We hope that by limiting the geographical scope of the collection, we might be able to zoom in more closely on the given contexts and eventually inspire further research focusing on other geographies. Moreover, looking at distinct Left cultures further allows a certain degree of decolonising of our *worksites of the Left* and a dialogical, cross-cultural approach to theatre's politics and aesthetics, activist practices, and Leftist subjectivities. The geographical strands are interwoven through both analogies and contrasts as we find evidence of cross-fertilisation and as we discover divergent paths in the dramaturgies of the Left.

Through these performative, cross-cultural junctions of Leftist histories and current practices, the contours of the new Leftist political subject(s) begin to emerge through fragments of bodies, voices, vocabularies, and gestures, in different spaces and geographies. This subjectivity acts politically from the intersection of the personal and the collective, from the crossover of politics and poetics where the dialectics of small-scale communism shape the dramaturgies of the Left. This is a journey of an always-evolving political subject within the larger solidaristic collective process of 'performing' (and eventually realising) the idea 'that the world [even our very fragmented world] could be otherwise' (Buck-Morss 2013), while never fully subjecting to its dogmas, not even to one's own political ideals.

Notes

1 The three volumes of *The Idea of Communism* have been published from 2010 to 2016; also Tariq Ali's *The Idea of Communism (What Was Communism)* (2009), Enzo Traverso's *Left-Wing Melancholia: Marxism, History and Memory* (2016), Wendy Brown's 'Resisting Left Melancholy' (1999), Jodi Dean's *The Communist Horizon* (2012), and so on. In theatre and film Lola Arias's *Atlas of Communism* (2016), Milia Turajlic's documentaries, *Cinema Komunisto* (2011), and the *Labudovic Reels* (2022) are some of the recent examples.

2 Other forms and formats of contribution include the special issue of *Studies in Theatre and Performance*, 'Performing Worksites of the Left' (2019), through talks and workshops (at the University of Warwick, at Jawaharlal Nehru University, at the IFTOK Festival in Karela, at the conference Cultures of the Left in the Age of Right Wing Populism in Venice, and also in the Cultures of the Left report that emerged at the onset of the pandemic), and through

performances lectures and artistic works (for example *The Last Pioneer* by Snezana Golubovic and a performance lecture by Liz Tomlin).

3 There are the exceptions of China, who maintains the communist label while allowing privatisation of industrial and technological production, creating a class of the super-rich yet keeping the iron fist approach when it comes to political dissent and minority rights, and Cuba, where the potential of communist governance has been dwarfed by the longest-standing trade embargo imposed by the US (partially lightened under Obama's administration, and most recently by Biden's, following Trump's full reinstatement of the sanctions) and its authoritarian regime.
4 For more on Left-wing activism in different places of the world see Ibrahim and Roberts (2019).
5 See Alain Badiou (2010).
6 Dean (2019).
7 Both Tomlin (2019) and Reinelt (2015) attribute Jacques Rancière's (1995, 2009) influential works to the logic of autonomy of theatre position (Tomlin 2021: 5).
8 See also Jestrovic and Parameswaran (2019).
9 Nikolay Chernyshevsky was the first to ask in his book *What Is to Be Done?*, first published in 1863 (English edition from Cornell University Press 1989). Lenin's *Chto delat?* pamphlet was written in 1902. See also Althusser (2020).

Bibliography

Ali, Tariq. 2009. *The Idea of Communism (What Was Communism)*. Calcutta: Seagull.
Althusser, Louis. 2020. *What Is to Be Done?* Cambridge: Polity.
Angelaki, Vicky. 2017. *Social and Political Theatre in 21st Century Britain: Staging Crisis*. London: Methuen Drama Engage.
Badiou, Alan. 2010. 'The Idea of Communism.' In *The Idea of Communism*, edited by C. Douzinas and S. Žižek, pp. 1–15. London: Verso.
Badiou, Alan. 2012. *In Praise of Love*, translated by P. Bush. London: Serpent's Tail.
Badiou, Alan. 2015. *In Praise of Theatre*, translated by A. Bielski. Cambridge: Polity.
Bharucha, Rustom. 2014. *Terror and Performance*. London: Routledge.
Brown, Wendy. 1999. 'Resisting Left Melancholy.' *Boundary* 26(3): 17–19.
Buck-Morss, Susan. 2013. 'A Commonist Ethics.' The Committee on Globalization and Social Change. https://globalization.gc.cuny.edu/2011/11/susan-buck-morss-a-commonist-ethics. Accessed on 14 April 2023.
Chatterjee, Partha. 2016. 'Theatre and the Publics of Democracy: Between Melodrama and Rational Realism.' *Theatre Research International* 41(3): 202–217. doi:10.1017/S0307883316000419.
Chatterjee, Partha. 2020. *I Am the People*. Delhi: Permanent Black.
Chernyshevsky, Nikolay. 1989. *What Is to Be Done?*, translated by M. R. Katz. Ithaca: Cornell University Press.
Cronin, James E., George W. Ross, and James Shoch. 2011. *What's Left of the Left: Democrats and Social Democrats in Challenging Times*. Durham, NC: Duke University Press.
Dean, Jodi. 2012. *The Communist Horizon*. London: Verso.

Dean, Jodi. 2019. *Comrade*. London: Verso.
Douzinas, Costas, and Slavoj Žižek. 2010. *The Idea of Communism 1*. London: Verso.
Engels, Frederick, and Karl Marx. [1884] 1998. *Manifesto of the Communist Party*, translated by S. Moore. Torfaen: Merlin.
Ernaux, Annie. 2017. *The Years*, translated by A. L. Strayer. London: Fitzcarraldo.
Fisher, Tony. 2023. *The Aesthetic Exception: Essays on Art, Theatre and Politics*. Manchester: Manchester University Press.
Herman, Edward S., and Noam Chomsky. 2002. *Manufacturing Consent: The Political Economy of the Mass Media*. New York: Patheon Books.
Horvat, Srećko. 2016. *The Radicality of Love*. Cambridge: Polity.
Ibrahim, Joseph, and John Roberts (eds.). 2019. *Contemporary Left Wing Activism*, Volumes 1 and 2. London: Routledge.
Jestrovic, Silvija, and Ameet Parameswaran. 2019. 'Performing Worksites of the Left'. *Studies in Theatre and Performance* 39(3): 217–223.
Kelleher, Joe. 2009. *Theatre & Politics*. Basingstoke: Palgrave Macmillan.
Lehmann, Hans-Thies. 2006. *Postdramatic Theatre*, translated by K. Jürs-Munby. Oxford and New York: Routledge.
Lenin, Vladimir I. 1902. *Chto delat?* www.marxists.org/archive/lenin/works/1901/witbd/index.htm. Accessed on 25 April 2023.
Menon, Nivedita. 2023. *Secularism as Misdirection: Critical Thought from the Global South (Theory in Form)*. Delhi: Permanent Black.
Mouffe, Chantal. 2018. *For a Left Populism*. Brooklyn, NY: Verso.
Rai, Shirin M., and Janelle Reinelt. 2015. *The Grammar of Politics and Performance*. London: Routledge.
Rai, Shirin M., Milija Gluhovic, Jestrovic Silvija, and Michael Saward (eds.). 2021. *The Oxford Handbook of Politics and Performance*. Oxford: Oxford University Press.
Ranciere, Jacques. 1995. *On the Shores of Politics*, translated by L. Heron. London and New York: Verso.
Ranciere, Jacques. 2009. *The Emancipated Spectator*, translated by G. Elliott. London and New York: Verso.
Read, Alan. 2008. *Theatre, Intimacy, Engagement: The Last Human Venue*. Basingstoke: Palgrave Macmillan.
Reinelt, Janelle. 2015. '"What I Came to Say": Raymond Williams, the Sociology of Culture and the Politics of (Performance) Scholarship.' *Theatre Research International* 40(3): 235–249. doi:10.1017/S0307883315000334.
Ridout, Nicholas. 2013. *Passionate Amateurs: Theatre, Communism and Love*. Ann Arbor, MI: University of Michigan Press.
Roy, Anupama. 2022. *Citizenship Regimes, Law and Belonging*. Delhi: Oxford University Press.
Roy, Arundhati. 2019. 'Capitalism: The Ghost Story.' In *My Seditious Heart*, pp. 622–655. London: Penguin.
Roy, Arundhati. 2020. 'The Pandemic Is a Portal.' *Financial Times*, 3 April. www.ft.com/content/10d8f5e8-74eb-11ea-95fe-fcd274e920ca. Accessed on 8 April 2023.
Sanjukta, Sunderasan. 2020. *Partisan Aesthetics: Modern Art and India's Long Decolonization*. Stanford, CA: Stanford University Press.
Taek-Gwang Lee, Alex, and Slavoj Žižek. 2016. *The Idea of Communism 3*. London: Verso.

Traverso, Enzo. 2016. *Left-Wing Melancholia: Marxism, History and Memory*. New York: Columbia University Press.
Tomlin, Liz. 2019. *Political Dramaturgies and Theatre Spectatorship: Provocations for Change*. London: Methuen Drama Engage.
Žižek, Slavoj. 2013. *The Idea of Communism 2*. London: Verso.

Part I

Activism

1

Performing the Constitution as an insurgent document

Nivedita Menon

In April 2019, on the eve of the general elections that would bring the Hindu supremacist Bharatiya Janata Party (BJP) into power for a second term, the performance artist Maya Rao staged an event at a women's march. Ceremoniously, she stripped herself of her sari and then slowly reclothed herself with cloth inscribed with the values of the Preamble to the Constitution – 'Equality, Liberty, Fraternity'. This performance invokes the well-known scene from the *Mahabharata* of the stripping of Draupadi in the royal court by the Kaurava Duhshasana and her being saved from public nudity by the god Krishna, who miraculously lengthens her strip of cloth indefinitely until Duhshasana is exhausted and gives up the attempt. Here Rao drew on the wellspring of Hindu culture to subvert it, to indicate instead that the protection of the powerless will today emanate from the Constitution.

By the end of the first term of the BJP, the Hindutva project of establishing Hindu *rashtra* (Hindu nation) was well in place. Minorities and Dalits,[1] as well as dissident voices even from within the Hindu community, were terrorised and often killed.[2] Legal and mob-implemented diktats on whom to love, what to eat, targeted lynchings, and assassinations had already all become the norm. A parallel project of this government is accelerated predatory capitalism, in which the state acts as an agent for crony capitalists. Through all of this there was a growing sense that asserting the values of the Constitution was a powerful tool of resistance.

Jignesh Mevani, a charismatic young Dalit leader and now a member of the Gujarat state legislature, said to a journalist before the 2019 elections that he would go to the prime minister and place before him a copy of the Constitution and a copy of the *Manusmriti*, the ancient text that sets out the hierarchical caste system, and ask him to choose (Mevani 2018). Mevani was referring to the police complaints against himself and other activists and their potential arrests for attending a massive assembly of Dalits. This dramatic counter-position of the Constitution to the caste order has a long history going back to B. R. Ambedkar, and highlights the insurgent possibilities in the Constitution.[3]

Similarly, the passing of the Constitutional Amendment Act (CAA) in December 2019, excluding Muslims of neighbouring countries from seeking refugee status in India, which the BJP Home Minister indicated was the first step towards disenfranchising Muslim citizens of India (although later he denied this), evoked massive countrywide protests, led by Muslims but including all sections of society. These protests, beginning at the end of 2019, and continuing with vigour until COVID restrictions began to be implemented with severity in March 2020, were remarkable for their performances of the Preamble to the Constitution that guaranteed equal rights to all citizens. The twenty-four-hour sit-ins occupied public spaces for months in different parts of the country, and these sites became festivals celebrating the Constitution through music, dance, spoken-word performances, speeches, wall art, and periodic recitations of the Preamble. In addition, public readings of the Preamble were organised at multiple sites in the country, where hundreds of people would show up just to read aloud the Preamble in different local languages as well as in English. Women overwhelmingly led these protests. The most well-known of these protest sites is Shaheen Bagh, a Muslim neighbourhood in Delhi, which has acquired iconic and legendary status (Mustafa 2020; Us Salam and Ausaf 2020; Khalid 2021).

Chandrashekhar Azad, founder of Bhim Army (Ambedkar's first name), a mass social movement for the dignity of Dalits, has been arrested more than once. At his meetings, attended by thousands of Dalit youths, he routinely holds up a Hindi copy of the Constitution (*Hindustan Times* 2020). His face is on an iconic poster that is widely publicised by the Bhim Army, in which he sports a proud moustache and stylish dark glasses, a direct performative challenge to the vicious caste system in which Dalit men have been physically attacked for daring to grow moustaches, ride a horse to their weddings as upper castes do, or dress well.

These are just a few instances of the way the Constitution has been owned, reiterated, and cited as the source of political legitimacy by different kinds of movements challenging injustice in the twenty-first century. This chapter will study two such movements that have performed the Constitution with the goal of radical social transformation: the tribal *Pathalgadi* ritual and the queer movement's legal challenge to Section 377 of the Indian Penal Code.

Politics and performance

What does it mean to perform? As with the question 'What is art?', the answer tends to fluctuate between 'everything is performance' and 'only very specific acts are performance'. Assuming the dense field of discussion on this question in philosophy, political theory, and performance studies (systematically outlined in Rai *et al.* 2021: 1–27), I will draw out the particular sense in which I use the concept of 'performing' in this chapter. My own understanding at one level draws on Judith Butler's conceptualising of performativity as the 'reiterative and citational practice by which discourse produces the effects it names' (1993: 2). In this sense every aspect of life implies performance, not 'mere' performance as opposed to something real or natural but performance as constitutive of our subjectivities. Yet as with 'What is art?', we do need to have a narrower understanding of performance too, when it is a structured, conscious enactment. In this sense I would differentiate performance from performativity. Performance refers to deliberate enactments of a phenomenon, emotion, or story for the public domain, while performativity constitutes our very subjectivity. Similarly, an understanding that 'the political' refers to every site in which power relations operate (home, kitchen, classroom) has to be accompanied by a recognition of specific dynamics and actions that can be defined as more narrowly political (movements, elections, public protests), in which there is a conscious presentation of subjectivities in the public domain *as political* and as aiming to bring about some transformation.

Here, while I see the value of understanding performance broadly, as some performance theorists such as Diana Taylor do, for whom performance indicates a dense field of multiple dimensions ranging from performativity to staged enactments (Taylor 2003), I feel the need to narrow the concepts of politics and performance if we are to indicate the specificity of particular phenomena. So, it is a deliberate choice here to narrow the conceptual field in this instance while retaining the potential to expand both terms in other contexts.

In addition I suggest the need to distinguish between artistic performances that may be political, by which I mean performances in spaces delineated for the purpose of performance, whether on a stage, the street, or in a warehouse, and performances whose very existence is tied to a political movement or campaign and have no other purpose beyond the political aim. This distinction is crucial because in a democracy, artistic performance, however political, must be protected infinitely and at every level, while political performance could expect to face state repression of varying degrees. When the border between these two kinds of performance is blurred by the state and artistic performances are censored, growing authoritarianism may be recognised.

So, while accepting that 'politics is performative, performance is political, and both of these matter to understanding our worlds' (Rai et al. 2021: 4), in this chapter my attempt is to narrow down the terms 'political' and 'performance' so that they capture something specific. I will use both politics and performance in their narrower senses – consciously political performances produced as such in the public domain with an implied, accompanying recognition of embodiment, including verbal utterances. I attempt to demonstrate, through two case studies, that the Indian Constitution is being performed as a potentially radically transformative document, even an insurgent one.

Can a constitution be insurgent?

Insurgency implies revolting against established authority, not necessarily with arms. To be an insurgent is to resist an established order. How, then, can a constitution be insurgent? After all, does a constitution not establish an order? Yes, generally, a constitution is a set of principles that legitimises a new order. However, it would be a mistake to read the Indian Constitution as expressing a singular will and a singular order.

By using the term 'insurgent' alongside 'constitution', I am reformulating an argument I made earlier in which I referred to a dilemma that arises at the interface of radical political practice with the logic of constitutionalism (Menon 2004). By 'constitutionalism' I refer to a specific method adopted by modern democracies of safeguarding the autonomy of the individual self. It is now generally recognised, however, that this objective is achieved by a process of enforcing universal norms that marginalise, render obsolete, and delegitimise contesting worldviews and value systems. This particular method of organising democracies has a specific history and arose in a particular geopolitical location, that is, in Europe in the seventeenth century. By historicising this method, we remind ourselves, to use Upendra Baxi's words, that 'much of the business of "modern" constitutionalism was transacted during the early halcyon days of colonialism/imperialism. That historical timespace marks a combined and uneven development of the world in the processes of early modernity ... [C]onstitutionalism inherits the propensity for violent social exclusion from the "modern"' (2000: 1184–1185). The drive of constitutionality, I argue then, is towards the erasure of any kind of normative ethic that differs from its own unitary central ethic. The dilemma that faces radical politics is what I termed the 'paradox of constitutionalism' – that is, the tension in which the need to assert various and differing moral visions comes up against the universalising drive of constitutionality and the language of universal rights.

Constitutions are usually seen as legal documents that embody a certain new dispensation or structure of power and which become our reference points in the context of the resolution of disputes among different sections of people. Thus, Marxists, for instance, might talk of bourgeois or socialist constitutions – and there certainly is an element of truth in the characterisation of many modern constitutions as bourgeois, in that they protect property rights and civil rights, not economic democracy. However, that does not exhaust the full meaning of what constitutions are, for what we see in contemporary India is that the Constitution no longer lives the singular life that liberal constitutionalism laid out for it but has become, for many sections of the population, a call to radical transformation as well. The Constitution has broken out of the confines of the liberal imagination that attempts to keep it in the safe custody of constitutional experts.

There are two reasons for this, I suggest. First, the Indian Constitution is not merely a liberal document in any sense. It reflects a variety of political opinions from Left to Right, emerging from a mass anti-imperialist struggle, and, therefore, it tries to balance the individual and the community, equality, and special provisions for historically disadvantaged groups, the drive towards industrialisation and the rights of the peasantry. This mid-twentieth-century moment was very different in time and space from that which produced the constitutions of the West, which in a sense marked a closure of and an end to political ferment. The Indian Constitution, on the contrary, is seen by all participants as the *beginning* of a journey towards what the Preamble promised (Menon 2008).

The second reason why the Constitution is emerging as the banner of revolt for some struggles is the nature of Indian democracy, which has rarely remained confined to participation in elections. Of course, there are many movements that would definitely not accept the Indian Constitution as a basis of legitimation, but here I am talking only about the many movements that do express their anger towards governments by reasserting the vision of the Constitution. The explosion of mass movements across the country over the past decades, and especially over the term of the ongoing regime of the BJP since 2014, is an indication that continuous democratic participation in decision-making has come to be taken for granted by the people. There is, thus, a growing divide between the people and the ruling elites, including all political parties.

In other words the Indian Constitution is not a document that has managed to establish one unitary order. If it was meant to legitimise the Brahminical,[4] patriarchal class society that India is, it certainly failed, for it ended up reflecting the heterogeneity of impulses of the anti-imperialist moment. It ended up, therefore, being a porous document with one foot in the future. While I do not suggest that the Constitution exhausts all possibilities for radical politics, it certainly seems to offer some kinds of movements and the resources to think in radically transformative terms.

Performances in time and space

We come now to two contemporary movements through which we see the Constitution acquiring new life – the *Pathalgadi* movement in the tribal belt across Jharkhand, Chhattisgarh, and Odisha in central India, and the campaign against Section 377 of the Indian Penal Code that criminalised same-sex desire – to reveal a politics of performing what I term 'insurgent constitutionalism'. I suggest that while both are mass movements that actively and consciously perform the Constitution, *Pathalgadi* performs the Constitution in *spatial* terms and *outside formal structures and institutions*, and the latter performs the Constitution in *temporal* terms and *within the formal institution of the law*.

Here I understand any extra-linguistic performance as spatial (occupying the dimension of space) and purely linguistic speech as temporal (occupying only the dimension of time). A spatial performance also necessarily involves the dimension of time, but a temporal performance need not occupy a space. This aspect of language is finely drawn out by Oliver Sacks in his discussion of sign language, in the claim that sign is unique in its 'linguistic use of space' (Sacks 2012: 69). Drawing on William C. Stokoe (1979), Sacks alerts us to the way in which sign is a 'language in four dimensions'. Stokoe says that while speech has only one dimension (its extension in time), writing has two dimensions (space outside the body and time), models have three dimensions in space, but only sign employs the fourth dimension – 'the three spatial dimensions available to a signer's body as well as the dimension of time' (Sacks 2012: 71). Taking off from here, I suggest that purely linguistic performances (involving interpretation of words) occupy the dimension of time alone, while performances of the body or outside the body occupy both time and space. It is in this sense that I see *Pathalgadi* as a spatial performance of the Constitution and the movement against Section 377 as a temporal performance.

Pathalgadi

Sweeping across the tribal belt of the states of Jharkhand, Chhattisgarh, and Odisha since early 2018 is a political movement in which the tribal people have reworked a tradition of putting up stone slabs across their lands. Traditionally, *Pathalgadi* is a generic name for this ritual performed by many tribes of this region for several purposes – during the last rites of a person who has died, to perpetuate the existence of ancestors, to demarcate a village boundary, to show the existence of generations in the claims to land. Thus, there are many kinds of *Pathalgadi*, which have different names;

for example, the burial ritual is called *sasandiri*, and the stones that make a public declaration of customary rights are called *hukumdiri*.

The contemporary political performance of this tradition, which is called *Pathalgadi*, involves the erecting of giant, green, painted, stone slabs with lettering on them asserting tribal sovereignty over their lands, prohibiting the entry of government officials and other 'outsiders'. Some of them list the names of those martyred in the cause of tribal autonomy. The *Pathalgadi* revolution is capturing the imagination of village after village, and wherever these stand, the movement declares, marks the limit of authority of the Indian government. The erecting of such slabs is a ceremonial process involving the whole village (Louis 2021: 39–41).

The current movement draws on a practice initiated after the Panchayat (Extension to Scheduled Area) Act (PESA) that was passed in 1996, which explicitly gave tribal people rights over their lands. This legislation was the outcome of a long struggle and negotiations with the government. Two eminent former bureaucrats who have worked with the tribal people for decades and acted as conduits to the government in getting PESA passed, B. D. Sharma and Bandi Oraon, suggested using the *Pathalgadi* tradition to put up stone slabs inscribed with rules and provisions of the PESA in villages to raise awareness about this legislation. It is during this time that the word '*Pathalgadi*' gained popularity, eventually replacing a more commonly used traditional word for burial death rituals, '*sasandiri*'. Now the word '*Pathalgadi*' is used for burial rituals as well (Kiro 2018). So there is an interesting way in which contemporary political practice has seeped through and renamed the traditional one. Inscribed on the majority of the stone slabs are these words taken from PESA 1996: 'every village shall have a gram sabha [village council] … and every gram sabha shall be competent to safeguard and preserve the traditions and customs of the people, their cultural identity, community resources, and the customary mode of dispute resolution'.

Customary modes of dispute resolution refer to the traditional institutions of tribal communities that exercise social, moral, religious, economic, and political authority over them, most of which preserved their own distinct cultural identities through their unwritten codes of conduct and traditional mechanisms to enforce these codes. The customary laws of the tribes and jurisdiction of the traditional council were marginalised by the introduction of statutory Panchayati Raj Institutions (PRI, that is, state-mandated village councils) all over the country including tribal areas in 1992 (Rao n.d.). The PES Amendment of 1996 is seen as having restored these rights to tribal communities, but the PRI continue to hold sway, and the assertion of PESA is part of what the *Pathalgadi* movement is about. It is true that customary tribal councils are often patriarchal and entrench the rights of local, traditional elites, but on the other hand, PRI often act as agents of the Indian state in the dispossession of tribal communities. Moreover, central legislation has consistently eroded the community rights of tribals to their lands, so the struggle is at many levels (Chandran 2020).

Many of the stones directly invoke the Constitution, in which collective ownership of tribal lands is protected by the Fifth Schedule and other specific articles. British colonial rule began the process of dispossessing tribal people of their land, forests, and water (*jal*, *jangal*, and *jameen*) in the interests of capitalist expansion, and the independent Indian state continued this process. Tribal people make up less than 10 per cent of India's 1.3 billion population but account for 40 per cent of people who were uprooted from 1951 to 1990 due to dams, mines, industrial development, and wildlife parks (Chandran 2020). The history of the militant struggle of the tribal people against this dispossession also started in the nineteenth century and continues today.

These regions have been in ferment for decades, but the immediate trigger for the current militant phase of the *Pathalgadi* movement can be traced to 2016 when amendments were proposed by the BJP government of Jharkhand to two key legislations that protect tribal rights to their land. The legislation was passed but aroused such widespread opposition that it had to be withdrawn. Subsequently, the same effect was achieved by the BJP government at the centre by the passing of amendments to another legislation in 2017, that is, the Land Acquisition Act 2013. The amendments enable the acquisition of tribal land for 'development', reduce the scope for social impact assessment, and also reduce the powers of the *gram sabha* to merely giving 'advice'. This legislation received the assent of the governor in 2018. What is more, the copy of the Amendment Bill, which finally got the assent of the President, has been kept out of public circulation by the government, and what can be viewed is only the Draft Bill.

All of this has aroused deep anger in the region, exacerbated by the kinds of methods state agencies use to discredit the movement. For instance, there were reports in the media at the time the amendments to the Land Acquisition Act were passed of the gang rape of five non-governmental organisation (NGO) women workers, allegedly by *Pathalgadi* activists. These women were performing a street play against human trafficking in a *Pathalgadi* village. It was claimed in the media that *Pathalgadi* activists were responsible because of their antipathy to *dikus*, or outsiders, entering a *Pathalgadi* village (Sarkar 2018). The police accused *Pathalgadi* activists of this rape. One of them, a relative of one of the rape survivors, was jailed. Church personnel were also implicated by the police in the crime.

It is common in India for NGOs working on different issues to use different kinds of performances, such as songs and street plays, to draw attention to the issues they work on. (These are both performances as well as political gestures in the narrow sense that I am using these terms.) The performance team, in this case, was engaged by an NGO of Christian nuns, '*Asha Kiran*', to perform a street play on human trafficking and the out-migration of tribal girls. *Asha Kiran*, with its awareness programme, has long tried to conscientise the poor and marginalised on their human and fundamental rights. It also campaigned for promoting *gram sabha* functioning at the grassroots, so it was not in fact against *Pathalgadi* but rather in support of the movement. Many rights activists, therefore, saw the entire episode (including the rapes) as staged by the state as a warning to the Church authorities to stop supporting *Pathalgadi* (Report on Gang Rape 2018).[5]

The survivors of the incident were kept under 'police protection' for twenty days, and so during all this time the only version of the event in public was the one circulated by police sources. When the women who survived the rape were finally released from 'police protection', the only one of them ready to speak to the media was very clear that the rapists were outsiders, not *Pathalgadi* activists. She also identified one of the rapists who surrendered to the police, from photographs in the media, as part of a 'pro-police Maoist splinter group'.[6] These are the all-too-familiar dirty tricks the state agencies play against people's movements (Iqbal 2018).

All of this has aroused enormous anger across the area. However, the expression of this anger is through the performative assertion of the supremacy of the Indian Constitution, while the government in power has, in letter and spirit, eroded its provisions.

Inhabitants of the village of Ghagra told a journalist:

> We wanted to do the Pathalgadi programme peacefully, without confrontation or fighting with anyone. We wanted to erect a stone on the basis of our Adivasi[7] parampara (custom). Our aim is simply to inform people, to educate them about Adivasi customs. Why does the state have a problem with that? Pathalgadi is our culture … We want to tell them that this is how our law is. The law for Adivasis is completely different from that for others. And everything should work according to law. (Iqbal 2018)

Several leaders of the *Pathalgadi* movement – including former senior bureaucrats – have been arrested under charges of sedition. The movement faces the full might of state repression. However, a second rung of leadership has emerged, and the movement appears to be gaining strength, discussing the setting up of an Adivasi Educational Board, an Adivasi bank, and other such institutions through public meetings held under trees (Sundar 2018; Tewary 2018). In 2021, after a lull due to COVID, there has been a resurgence of the movement (Saran 2021).

It is telling that the performative act of erecting traditional tombstones to invoke the Constitution and legal provisions as a mode of declaring tribal sovereignty over their lands is declared by the government as sedition, which is conduct or speech inciting people to rebel against the authority of a state. It appears that the current government places its own authority over the authority of the Constitution. However, both the *Pathalgadi* movement and the state response to it suggest that the Indian Constitution has the potential to challenge centralisation, authoritarianism, and dispossession of indigenous peoples for the benefit of capitalist land acquisitions.

The *Pathalgadi* movement, in short, does not just assert constitutional rights; it performatively inscribes the Constitution across the lands over which it declares sovereignty. The document establishing the modern republic of India is thus reanimated through a traditional ritual, reinvesting this performance with so much power that the older name for the burial ritual, *sasandiri*, is replaced by the new name, *Pathalgadi*, indicating the presence of a political performance within the tribal ritual.

The queer movement and Section 377

The decriminalising of same-sex desire in India came out of a decades-old movement as well as legal interventions that produced the Constitution and constitutional values as the highest authority. This required legal challenges to a colonial-era provision, Section 377 of the Indian Penal Code, which criminalised sexual acts 'against the order of nature', understood to refer to bestiality and homosexuality. This invocation and assertion of the Constitution was a performance at several levels involving petitions in court, articles in the media, and public demonstrations at Queer Pride. Here I will consider only the legal interventions and the responses by the courts.

The public visibility of the queer movement in India allied to feminism can be traced to the 1990s. The politics of this movement has always tried to locate sexuality and sexual identity within other identity-producing networks of class, caste, and community identity, both acknowledging them as well as demanding inclusion within them. There are, of course, Hindu supremacist strands within queer politics, as well as those individuals who want no other social transformation beyond decriminalising same-sex desire. However, the movement as a whole, like feminist politics in India, tends towards the Left and is generally mistrustful of the state. The decision by the NGO Naz Foundation to file a Public Interest Litigation in 2001, challenging the constitutional validity of Section 377, therefore, was not universally welcomed by the movement, partly because it did not come out of widespread discussions within the movement and partly because many members felt that the work of social transformation should precede entry into legal processes. Nevertheless, in the seventeen years that followed, many other petitioners joined in, including, among others, a coalition called Voices Against 377, parents of gay children, psychiatrists, and a group of teachers of whom I am one.

The Naz petition, as well as Voices Against 377, highlighted constitutional values in making the argument that Section 377 violated fundamental rights guaranteed by the Constitution. Similarly, the teachers' petition argued against Section 377 on the basis of implicit constitutional values. As teachers, we made the argument that Section 377 vitiates for everybody (and not just for gay people) the general atmosphere of free expression, learning, enquiry, and dignity that an academic environment should ensure. That we oppose Section 377 because of its existence on the statute books legitimises an atmosphere that runs counter to the spirit of openness and acceptance of difference that should mark modern academic spaces. The existence of Section 377, we argue, is not only an affront to those who are non-heterosexual, but it is an affront to each and every person in the academy who believes that every teacher and student has dignity that should be respected and that learning is a continuous and lifelong process, in which fixed ways of thinking are continuously challenged and reshaped by the winds of change.[8]

The first landmark in this long journey was the judgement by the Delhi High Court in 2009 that 'read down' Section 377 to exclude sex between consenting adults. The judgement anchored its decision in the petitions that invoked the Constitution. The judgement declared Section 377 as violative of the rights to equality and to life and personal liberty guaranteed by Fundamental Rights assured by the Constitution, asserting that the underlying tenet of the Constitution is 'inclusiveness'.

Justices A. P. Shah and S. Muralidhar declared:

> In our view, Indian Constitutional law does not permit the statutory criminal law to be held captive by the popular misconceptions of who the LGBTs are. It cannot be forgotten that discrimination is antithesis of equality and that it is the recognition of equality which will foster the dignity of every individual.[9]

The Supreme Court overturned this judgement in 2013, holding that amending or repealing Section 377 should be a matter left to the Parliament, not the judiciary. Curative petitions were submitted by the Naz Foundation and others, and the Supreme Court decided that they would be reviewed by a five-member Constitutional Bench. Five eminent individuals of the LGBTQ community filed a fresh writ petition before this Bench. Finally, in 2018, this Constitutional Bench held that same-sex relations came under 'individual choice and autonomy', which is rooted in the constitutional structure. Section 377 was, thus, struck down for consenting adults.[10]

In the course of the long process of legal intervention, one of the key arguments that were made by the petitioners against Section 377 and reiterated in the Delhi High Court judgement of 2009 that read down the section was that popular morality cannot prevail over constitutional morality, an idea derived from B. R. Ambedkar, one of the key architects of the Constitution:

> Thus, popular morality or public disapproval of certain acts is not a valid justification for restriction of the fundamental rights under Article 21. Popular morality, as distinct from a constitutional morality derived from constitutional values, is based on shifting and subjecting notions of right and wrong. If there is any type of 'morality' that can pass the test of compelling state interest, it must be 'constitutional' morality and not public morality.[11]

I see this invocation of the Constitution by different sections of democratic movements that challenge a colonial-era provision that criminalised same-sex activity as a performance in time unfolding through linguistic speech, in which constitutional morality gets produced as a supreme value by the petitioners.[12]

As an aside, we may note that after the first Supreme Court judgement, which upheld Section 377, a lawyer, Danish Sheikh, who was involved with the campaign, produced what I would call a political-artistic performance in space: he wrote a play, *Contempt*, based on individual testimonials and actual transcripts of the courtroom deliberations. This play has been performed several times (Phukan 2018) and is now published, along with another play, in a volume titled *Love and Reparation: A Theatrical Response to the Section 377 Litigation in India* (Sheikh 2021).

The Indian Constitution turns out not to be a simple seal of legitimacy on ruling dispensations of caste, class, and gender. It is a document that emerged from the acute conflicts and contestations in the anti-colonial struggle *outside* and from the contentious debates *inside* the constituent assembly. Its vision, therefore, was never singular. Rather, it became something of a manifesto of a future state of affairs, where the ethos of egalitarianism would be decisive. The invocation of the Constitution in the twenty-first century, then, is not necessarily simply a demand for legal changes but can indicate, rather, alternative visions of democracy in practice that go beyond obeying a government elected every five years.

Notes

1 The political term of self-reference by the former Untouchable castes, officially referred to as Scheduled Castes by the Constitution.
2 Hindutva is the name given to the modern politics of Hindu supremacist nationalism, as opposed to the wide range of heterogeneous practices and beliefs brought under the umbrella term Hinduism. Hindutva is the modern political ideology behind the Hindu *rashtra*.

The Constitution as an insurgent document 35

3 Dr B. R. Ambedkar was the Chairman of the Drafting Committee of the Indian Constitution. He was a powerful voice from the 'Untouchable' caste of Mahars, and he saw the Constitution as a means to establish equal citizenship, as the final authority to supercede the traditional caste order that marked Hinduism.
4 Brahmins are the highest caste in the Hindu caste order, and 'Brahminical' refers to a socio-economic order in which the caste hierarchy is protected and maintained.
5 Jharkhand has a tribal Christian population of 14.4 per cent while the Hindu tribals account for 39.7 per cent. Hindu nationalist forces have long been claiming 'forced conversions' among tribals of the entire region by Christian organisations that work with the tribal people on everyday issues. Hindu nationalist forces also periodically run 'reconversion' drives of Christian tribals, implying their 'return' to the Hindu fold, although in fact Adivasis have their own pre-Hindu religion, so they are in effect being converted to Hinduism.
6 These areas are also the heartland of armed Maoist activity against the Indian state, and the state response has included the setting up of counter-insurgency groups among local Adivasis, some of them by the local police under the guise of splinter groups from within the Maoist organisation but in fact acting for the Indian state and local police.
7 Adivasi is the general word used for the indigenous tribal and ethnic groups of the Indian nation state, referred to in the Indian Constitution as Scheduled Tribes. This term is also applied to such groups in other parts of the Indian subcontinent. Adivasi is not the name of a tribe, of which there are many, with different names and histories, but a general name for indigenous peoples.
8 The sixteen teachers and academics are from universities and research institutes in Delhi, Mumbai, and Chandigarh, and in order of their names on the petition, they are: Nivedita Menon, Aditya Nigam, Ranjani Mazumdar, Kamal Mitra Chenoy, Anuradha M. Chenoy, Ankita Pandey, Partha Pratim Shil, K. P. Jayasankar, Satish Deshpande, Janaki Srinivasan, Shilpa Phadke, Shoba Venkatesh Ghosh, Mary. E John, Anjali Monteiro, Shohini Ghosh, and Janaki Abraham.
9 Naz Foundation vs Government of NCT of Delhi and Others 2009.
10 The three key judgements are: Naz Foundation vs Government of NCT of Delhi and Others 2009; Suresh Kumar Koushal and Another vs Naz Foundation and Others 2013; and Navtej Singh Johar vs Union of India Ministry of Law and Others 2018. For a brief outline of the history of legal interventions on Section 377, see the Supreme Court Observer: www.scobserver.in/court-case/section-377-case.
11 Naz Foundation vs Union of India 2–7-2009 WP(C) No.7455/2001 at Para. 79.
12 I am not going into the different kinds of queer critiques made regarding the campaign and the judgement – for instance, of the recourse to law (rather than bringing about radical social transformation) or of the reliance on the right to privacy (rather than challenging the liberal notion of privacy that protects compulsory heterosexuality). This chapter is meant to highlight only the way in which a mainstream legal document, the Constitution, has been performed by radical movements that challenge the very class and gender basis of the Indian state, in such a way as to render the Constitution insurgent.

Bibliography

Baxi, Upendra. 2000. 'Constitutionalism as a Site of State Formative Practices.' *Cardozo Law Review* 21(4): 1183–1210.

Butler, Judith. 1993. *Bodies That Matter*. New York and London: Routledge.

Chandran, Rina. 2020. 'Reform of Customary Laws Urged to Protect India's Indigenous Land.' *Reuters*, 4 February. www.reuters.com/article/us-india-landrights-lawmaking-trfn-idUSKBN1ZY0MK. Accessed on 6 February 2020.

Ezrahi, Yaron. 2012. *Imagined Democracies: Necessary Political Fictions*. New York: Cambridge University Press.

Hindustan Times. 2020. 'Constitution in Hand, Bhim Army Chief Azad Returns to Jama Masjid in Delhi.' 27 August. www.hindustantimes.com/india-news/constitution-in-hand-bhim-army-chief-chandrashekhar-azad-returns-to-jama-masjid/story-HnxbbUUs3Gj5fHCDG6wMDN.html. Accessed on 28 August 2020.

Iqbal, Javed. 2018. 'Jharkhand Gang Rape Survivor's Account Upends Narrative of Pathalgadi Role.' *The Wire*, 26 July. https://thewire.in/rights/jharkhand-Pathalgadi-movement-gang-rape-police-firing. Accessed on 27 July 2018.

Khalid, Umar. 2021. 'Ita Mehrotra's Book Portrays the Shaheen Bagh Protest for the Multitude of Things It Was.' *The Caravan*, 13 September.

Kiro, Santosh K. 2018. 'The State's Violent Response to Tribal Discontent Is Fuelling the Pathalgadi Movement.' *The Wire*, 29 June. https://thewire.in/rights/jharkhand-Pathalgadi-movement-abduction-violence. Accessed on 30 June 2018.

Louis, Prakash. 2021. *Fr. Stan Swamy: A Maoist or a Martyr?* Delhi Media House and Kottayam: Sahitya Pravarthaka Cooperative Society.

Menon, Nivedita. 2004. *Recovering Subversion: Feminist Politics beyond the Law*. Delhi: Permanent Black and University of Illinois Press.

Menon, Nivedita. 2008. 'Citizenship and the Passive Revolution: Interpreting the First Amendment.' In *Politics and Ethics of the Indian Constitution*, edited by R. Bhargava, pp. 189–210. Delhi: Oxford University Press.

Mevani, Jignesh. 2018. 'Will Ask PM to Choose between Manusmriti and Constitution.' *The Quint*, 11 January. www.thequint.com/news/india/mevani-will-ask-pm-to-choose-between-manusmriti-and-constitution. Accessed on 20 January 2018.

Mignolo, Walter. 2011. *The Darker Side of Western Modernity: Global Futures, Decolonial Options*. Durham, NC: Duke University Press.

Mustafa, Seema (ed.). 2020. *Shaheen Bagh and the Idea of India*. Delhi: Speaking Tiger Books.

Rai, Shirin, Milija Gluhovic, Silvija Jestrovic, and Michael Saward. 2021. 'Introduction: Politics and/as Performance, Performance and/as Politics.' In *The Oxford Handbook of Politics and Performance*, edited by S. Rai, M. Gluhovic, S. Jestrovic, and M. Saward, pp. 1–27. Oxford: Oxford University Press.

Rao, N. Sambasiva. n.d. 'Interface of Tribal Self-Governance Institutions and Statutory Panchayats: A Study in the Scheduled Areas of Andhra Pradesh.' National Institute of Rural Development and Panchayati Raj. http://nirdpr.org.in/nird_docs/srsc/srsc230217–19.pdf. Accessed on 20 April 2022.

Report on Gang Rape. 2018. *Report on the Gang Rape of Street Play Members in Jharkhand*. The Free Library. www.thefreelibrary.com/Report+On+The+Gang+Rape+Of+Street+Play+Members+In+Jharkhand-a0545000513. Accessed on 5 May 2018.

Sacks, Oliver. 2012. *Seeing Voices*. London: Picador.
Saran, Bedanti. 2021. 'Pathalgadi Movement Gets More Refined, Demands Implementation of Rules.' *Hindustan Times*, 19 March. www.hindustantimes.com/cities/ranchi-news/Pathalgadi-movement-gets-more-refined-demands-implementation-of-rules-101616172925508.html. Accessed on 20 March 2021.
Sarkar, Debashish. 2018. 'Pathalgadi Masterminds Arrested in Kochang Gangrape of 5 Tribal Girls.' *Hindustan Times*, 22 July. www.hindustantimes.com/india-news/Pathalgadi-masterminds-arrested-in-kochang-gangrape-of-5-tribal-girls/story-iTwScm2DOeytFNkZgrXQdJ.html. Accessed on 23 July 2018.
Sheikh, Danish. 2021. *Love and Reparation: A Theatrical Response to the Section 377 Litigation in India*. Kolkata: Seagull.
Sundar, Nandini. 2018. 'Pathalgadi Is Nothing but Constitutional Messianism so Why Is the BJP Afraid of It?' *The Wire*, 16 May. https://thewire.in/rights/Pathalgadi-is-nothing-but-constitutional-messianism-so-why-is-the-bjp-afraid-of-it. Accessed on 17 May 2018.
Taylor, Diana. 2003. *The Archive and the Repertoire: Performing Cultural Memory in the Americas*. Durham, NC: Duke University Press.
Tewary, Amarnath. 2018. 'The Pathalgadi Rebellion.' *The Hindu*, 14 April. www.thehindu.com/news/national/other-states/the-Pathalgadi-rebellion/article23530998.ece. Accessed on 15 April 2018.
Us Salam, Zia, and Uzma Ausaf. 2020. *Shaheen Bagh: From a Protest to a Movement*. New Delhi: Bloomsbury India.

2

Revolution: like, share, subscribe

Dragan Todorovic

While desperate struggles that involve all the traditional elements of protest (skirmishes with security forces, mass arrests, victims of the state-inflicted violence) still take place on the ground, the internet has emerged as a new site of political debate, persuasion, and confrontation. What used to be about actual people on the actual ground, barricades, oppression, tear gas, and truncheons, now is mostly about avatars, pictures of witty placards, and online pressure. How does activism from online platforms correspond to actions on the ground? Does it aid or hinder new scenarios of resistance? Are the results better? To grapple with these questions, I will draw from a range of political movements from a broadly Left-leaning political spectrum and from different socio-political and geographical contexts that have at least one commonality – they are all initiated and organised online. Manifesting in a modified scenario of traditional protest struggles, the intermittent protest emerges here as a prominent mode of activist-organising.

Production of the needs

News distribution has been in constant flux for the past century. The change has often been initiated by technological advancement, but each new step in delivery has changed the reception and the way we consume news, and every such change has shifted the positioning of the news as a factor in democratic changes. The whole history of the news media in the past century can be viewed through the fight to keep the role of the news editor unchallenged and irreplaceable as the mediator between the stream of events and the interest of the public and, often, the authorities. From traditional newspapers of the nineteenth and twentieth centuries to the absolute rule of the radio and even the early days of television, the situation was, at its core, unchanged: the editor as the keeper of knowledge and the consumer on the opposite end receiving that knowledge – one-way traffic, with direct influence on the population.

The arrival of the commercially available internet in the early 1990s introduced a new paradigm of distribution: news consumers are finally completely free to choose their sources, and these are not necessarily big and tested content providers. This opened the way for alternative sources, which do not require much money to operate. Furthermore, not only are consumers able to personalise their content, but they are also able to publish. What they choose to publish is not controlled by anyone, and if they are not engaging in illegal activities, small publishers can choose to fight for a good cause, or they can claim the Earth is flat. Facebook was introduced in 2004 and Twitter in 2006. Their arrival has confirmed this trend and irrevocably changed the information structure. An increasing number of people are getting their news from social media.[1]

This is a situation theoretically ideal for the Left, at least when it comes to demographics. Why the Left? By far, the biggest users of the internet are young people – for study purposes, for gaming, for social networking, for jobseeking, for media streaming – and they traditionally vote Left. YouGov research published on the eve of the UK General Election in 2019, for example, showed that the age of the voters directly correlated to their political preferences: 51 per cent of those in the age group of 18–29 intended to vote for Labour, and only 20 per cent for Conservative. In the 60–69 age group the votes were mirrored: 56 per cent for the Conservatives, and only 17 per cent for Labour (FitzPatrick 2019). The age groups in between fit in precisely within this trend: the older the voters, the more likely they are to vote on the Right.[2] To add to this, all search parameters that are considered signifiers of the Left political interest (from Marxist thinkers to general socialist issues, to literature, arts, and so on) are on the rise and are generally winning over the conservative search terms, suggests Google Trends (de Pony Sum 2018). However, when contemplating the search interest numbers, it is worth noting that this also might mean that the conservative voters are migrating towards the means of information that do not necessarily fall under search engine statistics – YouTube and social networks are such areas (on social networks, only those posts explicitly marked as Public will be indexed by Google). Indeed, what is the Right doing on the internet?

With the internet, effectively, the chain of causality is immediate. Reporting on something can bring immediate corrective action, the implementation of which is then reported in real time, closing the circle. Through this process, social media becomes not only a critical source but also an organiser. Thus, it acquires characteristics of a *political party light*, capable of fast organisation of large numbers of people regardless of where they stand on the political spectrum.

It is worth noting here how social media functions *both* as a source of information and a campaigning platform, and most often this is synchronous, where information morphs into a political call to action, and the campaign is fuelled by the distributed information. This is not a traditional situation where a political candidate is knocking at your door to ask what *you* think should be their priorities and explaining how their party would solve it – this is a situation where a political centre controls the information you receive, preparing it so it is calculated to pique your interest: it does not only respond to political needs of the constituency (online and offline) but also shapes them.

This process is then repeated easily, daily, with minimal costs involved, turning into a system of political grooming. True problems are often ignored in this process, and slogans are bleached until all they contain is some form of a call to action and all specific promises have been removed. For example, Donald Trump's 'Make America Great Again!' in 2016 had previously been used by Ronald Reagan in 1980 ('Let's Make America Great Again'). It is rather telling to note that Hillary Clinton used the same slogan for her radio campaign in 2008, and the Democratic candidate John Kerry's presidential campaign in 2004 offered a slightly different 'Let America Be America Again'. The seed of this can be traced to 'America First' – the 1920 campaign theme of Warren G. Harding, the Republican candidate who was tapping into isolationist and anti-immigrant sentiment after the First World War.

Such recyclable slogans are not part of political programmes, so the campaign strategists are given wide freedoms in choosing them. They are battle cries, not promises, and, as with any battle cry, what counts is the noise, not the content. Political slogans are miniature scripts that facilitate *performing engagement* on social networks, which can be observed as social stages, constructed and operating within the architecture and mechanism of the panopticon. One can observe all, but one is, in return, observed by all. The performative effect here is of utmost importance. Political gestures seek large stages, and social networks are the largest stages we have today.

Hyperspace has no centre

I use the term 'hyperspace' because it is the umbrella wide enough to cover not only social media but also a modern form of communication systems, from WhatsApp to Viber, Signal, Telegram, Messenger, and so on, as well as the ground space of the internet and the somewhat undefined Dark Web, not to mention email, podcasts, and blogs. The term is wide enough to include the multitude of the developments and directions in the information distribution of today and its performativity. Traditionally defined as Euclidean space with more than three dimensions, hyperspace is a term in transition – a non-linear space based on the internet that contains a network of interlinked text, media, and communication. The performativity of this space is also such that it spills over into the physical world, onto the ground.

Movements stemming from hyperspace are based on horizontal democracy, where all voices have the same importance, leaders are not recognised, and decisions are only loosely binding. On the opposite side stands the political establishment, based on the pyramidal organisation. Pyramidal structures expect that the process of negotiation should be based on high representatives deliberating on the list of topics. With hyperspace movements, this is impossible since these organisations have neither representatives nor, arguably, clearly defined and firmly set goals. Indeed, they do not seem to be able to negotiate, opting instead to state their claims and wait for them to be fulfilled. Between vertical structures of the state and horizontal democracy of the hyperspace movements, translation is needed, but it is impossible as it would have to be not the usual transposition of meaning but a completely new system of thinking. This untranslatability is at the core of the paradox of the hyperspace movements.

Hyperspace is not linear. It is based on a network in which the nodes connected are all on the same plane, and hierarchy is absent. The whole purpose of hyperspace, the reason why it has been created, is to allow the free flow of knowledge. Movement is possible in all directions at once. There is no 'right direction' in hyperspace, and maps become obsolete. Search engines have been established as a solution for this problem, but any search today will yield millions of directions, of which at least several tens will be generally useful. No maps. As Frederic Jameson argues, 'Postmodern hyperspace has finally succeeded in transcending the capacities of the individual human body to locate itself, to organize its immediate surroundings perceptually, and cognitively to map its position in a mappable external world' (1992: 44). Without maps, hyperspace does not have a moral centre, perceived or real. When social movements conceived online land on the street, they state their claims, produce some terrific placards that reach considerable success on Instagram, and then go home to get some rest before Monday morning. The establishment, in most cases, chooses to safely tolerate such movements. When it does not, it moves the fight to where the focus is – to the hyperspace.

The following example is illustrative: the Serbian Progressive Party (Srpska napredna stranka – SNS) has been the ruling party since 2012. It has consolidated its power and its influence on the media, and there are very few independent media outlets remaining. Its leader, Aleksandar Vučić, the President of Serbia, has been a member of the far-Right groups and parties in the past but has reinvented himself as a moderate keeper of the stability in the Balkans – the main reason why the world community so readily looks the other way when his party uses state resources for its own political gains. Vučić flatly denies any influence of the media, but occasionally leaked reports reveal the level of attention this party of the Right spectrum gives to online informational wars.

A report from the December 2018 meeting of the Central Board of the Serbian Progressive Party stated that the Party had 3,456 employees working on social networks as 'bots', and they had left over ten million comments on 201,717 posts on Twitter, Facebook, and Instagram. In the twenty-four hours leading to the meeting, the report says, the Party bots have posted 43,000 comments to 1,147 social network posts. These numbers tell us clearly how it works: each voice of dissent is drowned in about fifty angry comments on average (*OzonPress* 2018). Political fight transferred into hyperspace becomes a bodiless fight. Hence, the demarcation line between a bot and an activist also can become dangerously porous.

Attaching an avatar[3] to personal space on a social network is an act of accepting membership, declaring it, and inviting one's peers to join – all in one. However, this ease of use means the ease of disuse at the same time. Facebook, for example, gives the option to apply a specific protest avatar for a certain period, after which one's profile picture will automatically resort to the default version. One can choose the length of time during which to be affiliated with the cause.

Weekend mutinies

Social media can work well in staging protests, as shown multiple times and in several countries across the globe. It is a fast and efficient medium for the almost instantaneous organisation of street protests. Is social media, however, capable of organising a sustained movement? What happens when social media becomes the central organising point?

On 23 November 2018 the leader of the Serbian Left Movement, Borko Stefanović, was attacked during a public event in the town of Kruševac, and he and two members of his team ended up in hospital. While the images showing them with bloodied heads were scarce in the state-controlled media, the social media filled in the gaps, and the news about the attack spread throughout the country and its significant diaspora. Calls to action came from several sides (opposition parties and non-governmental organisations (NGOs)), but citizen groups were faster than the ever-quarrelling opposition parties, and a week later several thousand citizens walked in protest from the public square in the centre of Belgrade to the National Assembly, refusing to accept any one party as the organiser of the event. This was a genuine grassroots movement.

Asked for a comment, the Serbian president Aleksandar Vučić said, 'Even if there were five million people on the streets, I would change nothing. Let them win the elections' (in Veselinović 2019).[4] Vučić effectively christened the protests, as the protesters, in response, adopted the slogan '#1of5 million' and continued to hold protest walks every Saturday. The protests spread, first through other major Serbian cities and then through smaller towns, where the calendar was different, but it was always a specific day every week. In spring 2019 the intermittent protests were taking place in over thirty Serbian cities, mostly on Saturdays. Over 1,400 university professors signed the petition in support of the protests, students got involved, and a number of artists, authors, and other public personalities encouraging protesters kept growing daily.

A few months later the portal Balkan Insight wrote:

> The disparate opposition to Vučić has yet to consolidate around a single leader or decide on a strategy for fast-approaching parliamentary elections in mid-2020. From tens of thousands at their height in February, the weekly protests in Belgrade now gather barely a few hundred. They once boasted simultaneous rallies across the country, taking aim at what critics say is Vučić's authoritarian tilt since the Progressives came to power in 2012. (Zivanovic 2019)

A year after they had started, towards the end of 2019, #1of5 million petered out. In some cities (Kragujevac), the final attempts at gathering ended in such small numbers that the participants went together for a drink in a café. Much criticism back and forth ensued on social media, but the protests never returned.

What had happened? As the protests went on, for the first few months the curve of engagement moved up. Support was widening, reporting on social media became almost professional when some of the leading press photographers started reporting from the gatherings, and the weather steadily improved as the spring slid towards summer. However, the authorities chose to avoid most instances of repression, limiting the police presence to small numbers, there mostly to keep an eye on traffic, and concentrating their anti-protest efforts on the media war, one-sided as the majority of the media in Serbia are in the hands of the regime or its allies.

Was there anything specific in the local culture that led to such development? Should this be observed as a localised process? Comparison with similar intermittent protests held in Morocco,[5] for example, shows that this was not the case. Something else is at play here: the avoidance of repression by the authorities. In his analysis of the Moroccan events, Ben Ahmed Hougua writes:

> The protests tend to be more prevalent during both high and low levels of repression, while they are less prevalent when coercion is moderate. These variations resonate with the backlash hypothesis developed by Francisco (1995,

1996) to explain the escalation of mobilisations after harsh repression. The hypothesis suggests that if repression demobilises the number of activists in the short term, it engenders contentious actions in the long term, especially when the practice of police coercion is applied indiscriminately to community members (Mason and Krane 1989). Rising stakes complicate protests, but they also mobilise masses in the long run (backlash hypothesis). (Hougua 2020: 29)

In Serbia neither political concessions nor any repression emerged, and this lowered the stakes. The protesters protested, the authorities ignored, and the police regulated traffic: it looked as if the protests had become a regular part of normal life, and routine kills everything. While coercive regimes invariably tend to resist mass mobilisation efforts, if such efforts succeed – and it is hard to prevent them considering the speed of online communication and the massive scale of participation – they can avoid serious consequences if they control their response. Furthermore, by refusing to accept leadership from any opposition party, not even the Serbian Left, despite the fact that the attack on its leader was the impetus for the protest, the groups of citizens recruited through social networks practically opted to make #1of5million a leaderless protest, and that – in combination with intermittency – led to the protests remaining wide open for all sorts of uninvited satellites and their interventions. What started as a grassroots protest against political violence in Serbia soon swelled into general eco protests (the Don't Drown Belgrade movement joined the protests without claiming it was participating as an organised group but nevertheless displaying its slogans), then widened further towards other political aims, ending up infested by Right-wing groups (Obraz, and other far-Right movements), which used the presence of the crowd to demand Kosovo to be reinstated as part of Serbia[6] by any means necessary. The combination of the regime ignoring the protests with the moral dilemmas imposed by the differing goals of the participants led to diminishing numbers and, ultimately, to the protests petering out.

This is something that often happens with leaderless protests. Most protests organised through social media are leaderless because there seems to be no reason for anyone to be recognised as the leader, but also because this improves the security of the protests, as the traditional policing technique of stopping the crowd by arresting the leaders cannot work.

Dahlum points at the paradoxical lack of flexibility where one would expect the opposite:

> Organized movements are better able to withstand government overreactions. Leaderless movements appear to be less effective at manoeuvring around government repression, maintaining nonviolent discipline, and negotiating or bargaining with the government. As a result, even when the government offers concessions, horizontal or leaderless movements tend to intensify. ... When governments accommodate leaderless movements, it simply emboldens those

movements to ask for more. ... Leaderless movements – which don't organize the relationships among a movement's different groups – risk allowing centralized groups with tighter discipline to outmanoeuvre the more inclusive majority. (Dahlum et al. 2019: 3)

Leaderless protests carry some serious problems within. Demands keep growing, making negotiations difficult. The effective ending of the protests can only be hoped for as the decisions stemming from negotiations are not universally accepted, but perhaps the biggest danger lies in the opportunity for unwelcome groups and individuals to infiltrate the crowd, and this can lead, among other things, to conflict, drastically raising stakes, and, ultimately, to the breach of safety. Leaderless protests make it harder to resolve the conflict and achieve anything beyond short-term concessions. There is no long-term strategy or plan because these require leadership.

Intermittent protests

The speed and ease offered by social media in organising protests have introduced the concept of intermittent protests. Although this phenomenon was known before the creation of social media, in the pre-internet past intermittency was mostly caused by repression. Now, it has become a tool for increasing the numbers on the streets, allowing those generally interested in the cause but not directly affected to join the protests outside of their working hours. The internet is already making participation a low-barrier exercise – with intermittent protests, the barrier is even lower.

An internet search for the term 'weekend activism' reveals a wide diapason of offers with a multitude of organisations, from Extinction Rebellion (UK) to March & Rally (USA), to Nordic Resistance Movement (Sweden), to Fridays for Future (Canada), to Jewish Activism Summer School (Germany), to All Hands On (UK), to Viva! (Vegan activists) (UK), to Insulate Britain (UK), to Alternative Pride (UK). What sounds like a derogatory description has gained a position on the programme of potential political actions – on the global level. We are practically facing a menu of protests offered in our spare time.

This ease of recreational engagement is, again, most obvious on social networks, which can be seen as shopping malls of slacktivism engagement. Signalling consonance with an idea/cause is often confused with participating. Applying public statements on social networks is a sign of networked individualism but little else. Can a click of the computer mouse translate into a political fight? Evgeny Morozov writes:

> 'Slacktivism' is the ideal type of activism for a lazy generation: why bother with sit-ins and the risk of arrest, police brutality, or torture if one can be as

loud campaigning in the virtual space? Given the media's fixation on all things digital – from blogging to social networking to Twitter – every click of your mouse is almost guaranteed to receive immediate media attention if it's geared towards noble causes. That media attention doesn't always translate into campaign effectiveness is only of secondary importance. (Morozov 2009)

Moreover, when creating a post on Facebook several options regarding how that post can be used are offered, one of which is 'support non-profit'. The options available are anywhere from the usual health-related and animal welfare charities to organisations with a more or less obvious political background, such as Wounded Warrior Project, Help for Heroes, Healing Venezuela, the Armed Forces Charity, and so on. Here engagement does not require a conscious decision. It is an automatic action, a reflex movement of a finger.

The theory of '*connective* action' (Bennet and Segerberg 2012: 743) proposes a substitute for the traditional notion of *collective* action. Where in the forms of collective action collective identity is required, connective action is based on flexible and temporary connections among individuals facilitated by digital communication and results in a personalised engagement with protest activity. Perhaps the key word in this concept is flexibility: flexibility of the connections, but also the flexibility of the obligations. Connective action contains no concept of membership or obligation, not even loyalty. 'Thousands Take to the Streets in Europe for a Fourth Consecutive Weekend of Anti-Racism Protests' was the title of *Euronews* on 20 June 2021 (Tidey and Dell'Anna 2021). The article is an amalgamated report from protests held on that Saturday in different parts of Europe. The report states: 'Other protests took place in the French capital, including a demonstration near the US Embassy by the Black African Defense League, and a march linked to recent violence involving Chechens in the French city of Dijon.' Another part of the same article says: 'These weekend's crowds in the UK capital were reportedly smaller and more socially distanced than those seen in the first two weeks after George Floyd's death.'

A similar report, published in March in the *Guardian*, says:

> Climate protesters from as many as 60 countries have gathered in person and online for Fridays for Future, a movement created by the Swedish activist Greta Thunberg. Campaigners raised local issues alongside the globally co-ordinated campaign #cleanupStandardChartered, which calls on the London-headquartered Standard Chartered to divest from coal in emerging markets. (Vinter 2021)

Nonetheless, the performative elements of the protest have turned it into a community event in which a plethora of issues was mentioned without any specific demands.

The images from some of the events show that the atmosphere of tension had evaporated, allowing the event to take carnivalesque overtones. When this happens, protesters compete in innovation, turning *protest* into an *exuberant celebration of protest*.

The original cause becomes a distant reason, occasionally present on the placards. Instead of the political goals (does anyone among the participants hope that such protests will bring change, or has here the *travelling being more important than arriving* notion also taken root?), aesthetic goals take over, and they translate into the attractiveness of performance, which might have a political dimension, but that is now of tertiary importance. The order is: 1) picturesque/social post ready; 2) innovative/smart/self-promoting; 3) political goal. The intermittent character of protests allows for variable themes to be set, depending on the developments in the previous weeks, and allows for such themes to be different from place to place while all events remain under the umbrella of the same movement.

Irregularity, both in terms of the frequency of gathering and in terms of the thematic goals of the events, gives a chance to both the protesters and the system to recharge. This is not a simple energy replenishment: both sides – more importantly – learn, and during the breaks in activity can systematise that knowledge. Maps are drawn on all sides; phones are charged, but so are tasers. In general, the new means of communication level the chances of the protesters to outrun and outsmart the police, so it is the authorities who profit from the breaks in demonstrations. The state prefers attrition when the stakes have not been raised, as the third principle of thermodynamics applies here, too: entropy will set in as the temperature falls. This is, for example, what happened in the Hong Kong protests of 2019, attempted as a remedy to the failed 'Umbrella' protests[7] of five years before:

> The state employed the strategy of attrition effectively in handling the movement. After the use of force by the police in the first week of protests, the police and the government refrained from further repressive actions. Rather, the state allowed the inconveniences and nuisances caused by the occupation to accumulate, which facilitated the pro-government forces' counter-mobilisation efforts. (Lee *et al.* 2019: 5)

Can intermittent protests ever be successful? Although examples of this are exceptionally rare, and I had to do a very wide search for a good example of this, it seems that certain conditions must be fulfilled. One such example is DACO. DACO is an acronym for the Delta Avenue Citizens Organization. The organisation had been formed in 1965 in a US Midwestern city of about 66,000 citizens[8] as a response to the proposed building of a large bridge to connect to the area where the concerned citizens lived – around Delta Avenue (Lindgren 1987). The sole purpose of DACO was to defeat this project, as they feared that a bridge into their area would mean highly increased traffic that would ultimately destroy the neighbourhood.

When citizens identified a threat to their neighbourhood, they decided to act, mobilised others, and began researching the political decisions surrounding this issue so they could fight it, an activity that stretched over the next twenty-plus years. The group was based on solidarity and loosely structured, but at the first meeting a chair was elected, and over the years sixteen people had been elected to that position – there always was a leader. The group chose to be concentrated exclusively on the fight against the proposed bridge. The goal had never been changed, never broadened, and DACO never established any ties with the larger social movement networks. The latter would normally mean suicide for an interest group, but not in this case – it might have helped the organisation to survive and ultimately win. One more detail: DACO made it publicly known that the organisation would immediately disband if the goal was achieved. Public action of the group was rare and can be classified as clearly intermittent, yet the organisation was successful. Their success factors include steady focus on the issue, a clear leadership structure, unchanging demands, and keeping the pressure consistent but never violent. Still, there is an obvious caveat – this was an unapologetically single-issue movement. Hence, it was of little consequence whether its members agreed on anything else or if they stood on different sides of the political spectrum. But what happens if more than a bridge is at stake and if the issue concerns more than a neighbourhood community? This is the question of activist movements and scales and to what extent small-scale activist success could be translated on strategies applied to larger-scale issues and larger numbers of participants.

Schrödinger's city

Is the traditional continuing performance of a huge crowd in the centre of a capital still much more effective than intermittent and online protests? We need to ask several prior questions before attempting to give the answer to this question.

Why do protesters walk? Pilgrimage is a journey towards the place of moral and/or spiritual gravity. Protest walks are political pilgrimages, but on the road to recalibrating their centre of gravity, protesters also perform other important socio-political functions. According to de Certeau, they transform streets into spaces through their walks.[9] They reclaim the public space which regimes tend to empty out. As for the authorities, the beauty of the deserted square is the beauty of a well-controlled society. Finally, the political pilgrims are exiles from the public sphere turning agonistic space into agora by performing return. This is a public act but also a very private act: the internal is externalised.

How does a public space get emptied of citizens, alienated, and removed from the available reality? Rules and regulations – some of which generally affect public order, while others can be specific to a limited agora – tend to grow until any attempt to gather en masse must be approved by the authorities. Michel Foucault demonstrated in his book *Discipline and Punish* how the system moved away from punishing through inflicting pain on the body towards creating an omnipresent control – 'eyes that must see without being seen' (Foucault 1995: 171). Central to this concept is the architecture of surveillance. Foucault positioned the military camp as the ideal of such architecture, as this structure allowed for clear geometry of always visible paths and total control at any given moment. To this take on surveillance, founded in the eighteenth century with Bentham's panopticon and Haussmann's restructuring of Paris, modern governments have added camera surveillance and – recently – facial recognition software. The process is finished: it is impossible to exit the habitat without being noticed and recorded. Thus, modern regimes do not necessarily strive for the beauty of deserted squares anymore because they are using cameras to achieve a less obvious panopticon. The architecture of isolation has given place to the architecture of total control. The agora is preferred full.

Paradoxically, to perform a protest walk means to perform, at the same time, leaving and return, exile and repatriation: leaving the state of misbalanced society and returning to the desired equilibrium, reclaiming the sweetness of exile and retesting the pain of repatriation. (A walk is always towards the perceived moral centre. In oppressive regimes, destinations are often public buildings where the power is concentrated: Parliament, TV, some of the ministries.) This process of simultaneous negation/affirmation is creating a map, a map that shows the areas of friction, the buildings of power, and the streets of protest. Protesters write themselves into the reality of space, which is a social construct.

Quantum physics operates with the concept of quantum superposition. Simplified, this means that two distinct states of a system can exist at the same time. Applied to the reality we occupy, the quantum superposition means that the city simultaneously exists and does not exist – much like the secretive cat from Erwin Schrödinger's thought experiment. It needs to be stopped in one state by the act of measuring. The city is very much a Schrödinger's cat: until touched by feet, it is not confirmed; its map is only imaginary, a geometry of ideatic spaces drawn by the idealistic planners. 'Space is practised place. Thus, the street geometrically defined by urban planning is transformed into a space by walkers' (de Certeau 1984: 17). Protest walks perform not only recognition of space but are also the measuring that confirms the possibility of a city. Once the city is reconfirmed by protest walks, political healing can have its chance. If the protest walks have been peaceful and the stakes have not been raised, the chances of success of such forms of political protest are significant.

Power, unclaimed

What is missing in online and intermittent protests?[10] Foucault claims that 'Power must be analysed as something which circulates ... And not only do individuals circulate between its threads; they are always in a position of simultaneously undergoing and exercising this power' (Foucault 1980: 98). *Power* and *resisting power* are entangled; one carries the seed of the other (the yin and yang sign is a good visual representation of this dichotomy). Paddison *et al.*, however, warn that there is a significant problem with the balance – power feeds on the status quo; it can wait while *resisting power* often draws its strength from speed:

> Resisting power can involve very small, subtle and some might say trivial moments, ... but it can also involve more developed moments when discontent translates into a form of social organisation. ... In order for these resistances to occur, power has to be exercised and realised, both by the leaders (in a form that can become dominating in its own right) but also in a more 'grassroots' fashion by everyday people finding that they have the power to do and to change things. (Paddison *et al.* 2000: 3)

In the cases of *weekend activism*, we see the protesters who are not ready to test their own power. Whatever is achieved during the day of protest in terms of media attention will be wiped away during the rest of the week by the regime-inclined media and by the never-ending avalanche of events.

Here, too, we can apply the concept of quantum superposition. *Resisting power* is another case for Schrödinger's experiment: until touched by concrete actions, be it by walks or some other form of *concrete* activity, it is not confirmed. Revolutionary changes throughout history have been brought by long, persistent marches of millions. Weekend and online activism have powers that are only imaginary, a march of avatars through the escapist space in which the Establishment doesn't have immediate interest.

In his seminal book *Social Movements 1768–2004*, Charles Tilly introduced three elements he considered basic for all social movements: a sustained effort (campaigns instead of single, one-time acts like petitions, open letters, etc.), varied political performances (public meetings, vigils, rallies, solemn processions, demonstrations, petition drives, PR statements, etc.), and what he calls WUNC (an acronym for worthiness, unity, numbers, and commitment). WUNC simply means that the more people commit to the cause, show up for protests, and display their unity, the greater the chances are for the political establishment to take heed and at least think about how the issue will affect the next elections.

Intermittent protests fall on the first hurdle: they do not really make for a campaign; instead, they should be observed as a series of single events. As their membership varies from weekend to weekend, it is difficult to establish WUNC, too (commitment and numbers are hard to prove, but unity is also an issue). *Keyboard warriors* have even less chance according to Tilly: commitment is very low when the protest remains online only; the number of 'likes' is not the same as the headcount on the street. Performing political protest on the main streets is physical and nearly impossible to ignore. Performing the same protest online relies on the hope that the people who have the power to make changes in society are looking your way. If you are disenfranchised – and chances are this is precisely the reason you are protesting – they seldom are.

Victory?

The idea mentioned in the Extinction Rebellion proclamation, about mobilising 3.5 per cent of the population to achieve system change, comes from the article published by the Weatherhead Center for International Affairs, affiliated with Harvard University, in which professor Erica Chenoweth talks about her research into non-violent resistance, which – surprisingly – shows that non-violent civil resistance is far more successful in creating broad-based change than violent campaigns are (Nicholasen 2019). However, four vital conditions have to be met: 1) a significant and diverse *sustained* (emphasis mine) participation; 2) the movement has to initiate a shift in loyalty among security forces and other elites; 3) the campaign needs more than just protests; there needs to be a lot of variation in the methods they use; 4) when campaigns are repressed – which is inevitable for those calling for major changes – they must not descend into chaos or resort to violence. (This somewhat differs from Tilly's WUNC, but points 1 and 3 are identical.)

Chenoweth's research shows that the numbers needed for victorious protests are seemingly small: only 3.5 per cent of the population needs to support them. However, in the UK that means 2,380,000 people out on the streets. Two of the largest mass protests in the 2000s – 15 February 2003: the 'Million' march against the Iraq war; and 19 October 2019: the 'Million' march against Brexit – both reached around a million participants.

In the US the magic number is 11.5 million. In Russia it is over 5 million. Fifty-three million for China. Indian protesters need 47 million supporters on the move. The government of Brazil would feel pressured to make changes only if 7.5 million people should rise against it. The numbers start telling a different story when seen in absolute quantities and not as a percentage, but there is an interesting suggestion here: the more populous the country, the more difficult it is to initiate changes by protests. The inertia of the system and the pyramidal structure of power serve as protective layers that are difficult to peel off.

Another detail that is hidden here is the fact that the success of the protest movements has been measured against democratisation as the goal. However, democracy is not a universal cure, nor can it be a measure of political success. Myanmar, Libya, Tunisia, and Serbia are some of the recent examples where democracy had triumphed only for the country to face a plethora of serious problems and continuing political strife, now often worse than it had been before the protests.

The trend of online activism has gained momentum in the 2000s for several reasons, among which the wish to engage elites should not be underestimated (see number 2 above on Chenoweth's list). How else can a social movement in its early stages engage public names than through appealing to them online? The immediate question: why do we expect that political elites should turn to issues that have been the object of protest in the first place? We presume that the media coverage of protests should inform the elites of the problems in society, 'out on the street' – but such a direct line does not exist, as is amply proven in the research reported in the article 'The Media as a Dual Mediator of the Political Agenda-Setting Effect of Protest' (Vliengenthart et al. 2016). Rather, there is a circular road: a protest is an event and media reports about the event, and if such reports are many and repeated, the public starts to investigate the issue behind the protest, which in turn might lead to the questions being asked in the assembly. It is impossible to see how an online campaign can achieve this, as the core is missing – an online campaign is not an event, as defined by Deleuze: 'Every event is revolutionary due to an integration of signs, acts and structures through the whole event. Events are distinguished by the intensity of this revolution, rather than the types of freedom or chance' (cited in Williams 2013: xi).

What is, then, to be done? If it is true that the internet inherently leans to the Left, what can the Left do with such a chance? The receipt which does not guarantee the success of political protest (nothing can) but increases its chances seems to be:

- Do use social networks, but only for organisation and promotion.
- Counting on the avatars as the end means is counterproductive.
- Make sure that the protests are transferred into the reality of the main streets as soon as possible. (They can be intermittent, but not in regular intervals, and at least some of them have to happen on working days.)
- Work on increasing your WUNC. Aim to draw the attention and win the support of the elites.
- When under pressure, increase the WUNC.
- Do not resort to violence, as that will raise the stakes and endanger the whole movement.

And, whatever you do, do not count on pretty pictures. 'Revolution will not be televised' (Scott-Heron 1971). The revolution will not come from Silicon Valley. The revolution will not be tweeted. The revolution will not be posted on users' walls.

The revolution will not be liked.

Notes

1. The Pew Research Centre Report from 2019 shows that 71 per cent of American adults use Facebook (FB), of which 52 per cent get their news on FB; 74 per cent use YouTube, of which 28 per cent watch it for the news; and 23 per cent use Twitter, out of which 17 per cent get their news there.
2. It might be interesting to add that the General Election of 2019 resulted in the Conservative Party receiving a landslide majority of eighty seats. The Conservatives made a net gain of forty-eight seats and won 43.6 per cent of the popular vote – the highest percentage for any party since 1979. This might be a hint at how inclined young voters are to go out and vote.
3. 'Avatar' is a concept of representation, which in traditional Buddhism means an incarnation, embodiment, or manifestation of a person or idea. Today the commonly used meaning of avatar is that it is an icon or a figure representing a particular person in an online space.
4. It might be of interest to note that one of Vučić's advisers is Tony Blair, who, in a situation more serious for his rule, safely ignored a million people on the streets of London on 15 February 2003, protesting the British involvement in Bush's war against Iraq.
5. A series of demonstrations across Morocco between 20 February 2011 and the autumn of 2012, part of the Arab Spring protests. Demands revolved around political reforms, aiming at limiting King Mohammed's powers.
6. Kosovo is a partially recognised state in southeast Europe. Serbia has historically considered Kosovo as part of its territory, as defined in its Constitution. After an armed uprising, and the bombing of Serbia by NATO in 1999, Kosovo unilaterally declared its independence from Serbia in 2008, gaining recognition by fewer than half of the member states of the United Nations. It remains a disputed territory.
7. The Umbrella movement was a political movement that emerged during the 2014 Hong Kong protests. It was named after the use of umbrellas in defence from the Hong Kong police's use of pepper spray to disperse the crowd. The seventy-nine-day occupation of the city demanding more transparent elections was an internet-organised, leaderless movement, adhering to the principle of non-violent civil disobedience.
8. The article reporting on this NGO hides the name of the city on purpose – there is a significant military presence in the area.
9. 'Space is practised place. Thus, the street geometrically defined by urban planning is transformed into a space by walkers' (de Certeau 1984: 117).

10 By intermittent protests here, I mean the protests that are scheduled over weekends and holidays, attempting to gather larger numbers. This does not include movements utilising guerrilla tactics – performing sudden actions in irregular intervals. The key difference is predictability through regularity of the intervals of protest.

Bibliography

Beckett, Charlie. 2011. 'Ritual, Spectacle, Protest, and the Media.' LSE Polis Blog, 19 October. https://blogs.lse.ac.uk/polis/2011/10/19/ritual-spectacle-protest-and-the-media/. Accessed on 30 December 2022.

Bennett, Lance W., and Alexandra Segerberg. 2012. 'The Logic of Connective Action, Information.' *Communication and Society* 15(5): 739–768.

Chenoweth, Erica, Sirianne Dahlum, Sooyeon Kang Dahlum, et al. 2019. 'This May Be the Largest Wave of Nonviolent Mass Movements in World History: What Comes Next?' *The Washington Post*, 16 November. www.washingtonpost.com/politics/2019/11/16/this-may-be-largest-wave-nonviolent-mass-movements-world-history-what-comes-next. Accessed on 13 September 2021.

Dapiran, Anthony. 2019. '"Be Water!": Seven Tactics That Are Winning Hong Kong's Democracy Revolution.' *New Statesman*, 1 August. www.newstatesman.com/politics/2019/08/be-water-seven-tactics-that-are-winning-hong-kongs-democracy-revolution-2. Accessed on 21 March 2023.

De Certeau, Michel. 1984. *The Practice of Everyday Life*, translated by S. Rendall. Berkeley, CA: University of California Press.

Democracy Now. 2011. 'Interview with Cornel West.' 24 October. www.democracynow.org/2011/10/24/dr_cornel_west_we_are_in (at 53:20). Accessed on 22 December 2022.

De Pony Sum. 2018. 'Internet Searches Increasingly Favour the Left over the Right Wing of Politics.' Medium (blog), 4 October. https://medium.com/@sumdepony/internet-searches-increasingly-favour-the-left-over-the-right-wing-of-politics-8122f92fcd9f. Accessed on 18 March 2023.

FitzPatrick, Sam. 2019. 'General Election: Who Will Win the Youth Vote?' YouGov, 22 November. https://yougov.co.uk/topics/politics/articles-reports/2019/11/22/general-election-who-will-win-youth-vote. Accessed on 21 March 2023.

Foucault, Michel. 1980. *Power/Knowledge*. New York: Pantheon Books.

Foucault, Michel. 1995. *Discipline and Punish*, second edition, translated by A. Sheridan. New York: Vintage Books.

Francisco, Ronald A. 1995. 'The Relationship between Coercion and Protest: An Empirical Evaluation in Three Coercive States.' *Journal of Conflict Resolution* 39: 263–282.

Francisco, Ronald A. 1996. 'Coercion and Protest: An Empirical Test in Two Democratic States.' *American Journal of Political Science* 40(4): 1179–1204.

Hougua, Ben Ahmed. 2020. 'Intermittent Breaks of Public Order in the Moroccan Political Context: An ARDL Approach to the Dynamics of Protest Mobilisations, 1997–2018.' *Contemporary Arab Affairs* 13(2): 27–53.

Jameson, Frederic. 1992. *Postmodernism: Or, the Cultural Logic of Late Capitalism*. London: Verso.

Lee, Francis L. F., Samson Yuen, Gary Tang *et al.* 2019. 'JCL, Hong Kong's Summer of Uprising.' *China Review* 19(4): 1–32.

Lindgren, H. E. 1987. 'The Informal-Intermittent Organization: A Vehicle for Successful Citizen Protest.' *The Journal of Applied Behavioural Science* 23(3): 397–412.

Mason, D., and D. A. Krane. 1989. 'The Political Economy of Death Squads: Toward a Theory of the Impact of State-Sanctioned Terror.' *International Studies Quarterly* 33: 175–198.

Morozov, Evgeny. 2009. 'The Brave New World of Slacktivism.' *Foreign Policy*, 19 May. https://foreignpolicy.com/2009/05/19/the-brave-new-world-of-slacktivism. Accessed on 1 May 2021.

Nicholasen, Michelle. 2019. 'The Lasting Power of Nonviolent Resistance – Part 1.' Epicentre (blog), 24 January. https://epicenter.wcfia.harvard.edu/blog/lasting-power-nonviolent-resistance. Accessed on 5 April 2023.

OzonPress. 2018. 'Naprednjačka strogoća: Ko ne plati članarinu do ponedeljka nek se spremi za smenu.' 2 December. www.ozonpress.net/politika/naprednjacka-strogoca-ko-ne-plati-clanarinu-do-ponedeljka-nek-se-spremi-za-smenu. Accessed on 14 April 2019.

Paddison, Ronan, Chris Philo, Paul Routledge *et al.* (eds). 2000. *Entanglements of Power: Geographies of Domination/Resistance*. New York: Routledge.

Satoshi, Yamamoto. 2019. '"Be water": Hong Kong Protesters Learn from Bruce Lee.' 13 November. www3.nhk.or.jp/nhkworld/en/news/backstories/745. Accessed on 12 September 2021.

Scott–Heron, Gil. 1971. *The Revolution Will Not Be Televised*. Track B on Pieces of a Man. Ace Records.

Tidey, Alice, and Alessio Dell'Anna. 2021. 'Thousands Take to the Streets in Europe for Fourth Consecutive Weekend of Anti-racism Protests. *Euronews*, 20 June. www.euronews.com/2020/06/20/anti-racism-protests-take-place-across-france-and-the-uk. Accessed on 5 September 2021.

Tilley, Charles. 2004. *Social Movements 1768–2004*. Abingdon: Routledge.

Veselinović, Stefan. 2019. '"1 od 5 miliona": Dva meseca na ulicama Beograda i Srbije, šta dalje.' BBC News na srpskom, 1 February. www.bbc.com/serbian/lat/srbija-47092431. Accessed on 5 April 2023.

Vinter, Robin. 2021. 'Climate Protesters Gather in Person and Online for Fridays for Future.' *Guardian*, 19 March.

Vliegenthart, Rens, Stefaan Walgrave, Ruud Wouters *et al.* 2016. 'The Media as a Dual Mediator of the Political Agenda-Setting Effect of Protest: A Longitudinal Study in Six Western European Countries.' *Social Forces* 95(2): 837–859.

Williams, James. 2013. *Gilles Deleuze's Difference and Repetition: A Critical Introduction and Guide*, second edition. Edinburgh: Edinburgh University Press.

Zivanovic, Maja. 2019. 'Serbian Opposition at Sea on Anti-Government Protest Anniversary.' *Balkan Insight*, 6 December. https://balkaninsight.com/2019/12/06/serbian-opposition-at-sea-on-anti-government-protest-anniversary/. Accessed on 10 September 2021.

3

The 'hunger artists': Hunger protests, prisons, and insurgent citizenship

Anupama Roy and Ujjwal Kumar Singh

State practices of citizenship involve performative acts of naming, which produce citizens of a particular kind, framed by and subject to the laws of the state. Through such practices, citizenship gets construed as a carefully guarded space fraught with questions of belonging. James Holston describes this space as an *assemblage* of 'entrenched and insurgent forms' which exist 'in tense and often dangerous' relationships with each other (2008: 33). The tension in the space of assemblage emerges with the insurgent 'irrupting' in and unsettling of the site inhabited by the entrenched. This chapter focuses on hunger fasts in *prisons* as sites that are configured differently from the street/square/maidan in terms of the spatial framing of state power and the performative power of 'irruption'.

For Erving Goffman (1961), the prison is a 'closed world' – a 'total institution' – in which 'inmates' live a sequestered and regimented life. The 'encompassing or total character' of prisons is manifest in the 'barriers' to 'social intercourse with the outside' – through *fortified spaces* enabling physical entrapment (1961: 4) and a *regulatory regime* where 'a small staff' places all aspects of life of a 'large group of inmates' into tightly arranged 'enforced activities' under a 'single authority' to fulfil 'the official aims of the institution' (1961: 6–7). The official aims of prisons are understood variously – as punitive, correctional, and reformative. Prisons have, however, also been seen as sites of concentration/accumulation of state power, made effective through what Michel Foucault calls the 'carceral network', which consists of 'institutions, techniques and disciplines of detention taken together' (Guha 1977: 14). Yet prisoners, as David Arnold argues in his study of colonial prisons in India, are not 'docile bodies' (Arnold 1994: 150) under constant surveillance in cells under the panopticon gaze: 'so many cages, so many small theatres, in which each actor is alone, perfectly individualised and constantly visible' (Foucault 1985: 200). Prisons have witnessed innumerable 'revolts' against the disciplinary 'gaze'. This chapter focuses on hunger protests as one form of 'revolt against the gaze' to trace the performative aspects of insurgent citizenship in contexts where the *public* is assumed to be absent.

Recalling Franz Kafka's 1922 creation – *A Hunger Artist* – this chapter sees the performance of 'hunger' producing various publics. Unlike the progressive marginalisation of the hunger artist in Kafka's story, hunger protests inside prisons make 'powerlessness' *complex* (Sassen, 2011), producing an effect *on* power to make prisons permeable institutions. The self-starving body transforms into an insurgent body 'daring to execute a radical and self-harming performance' as a dissident act, which brings out the 'grotesqueness' of state power (Kraidy 2016: 5–6). This chapter focuses on *colonial* prisons as institutions embodying dominative power and as sites of insurgent citizenship, where hunger as a protest form interlaces narratives of protest across different time spaces. The chapter concerns itself with two hunger protests – the *anshan* of Hindustan Socialist Revolutionary Association (HSRA) prisoners in India in 1929, and the hunger strike by Irish Republican prisoners in Britain in 1981. In the late 1920s and 1930s the HSRA represented an influential strand in the anti-colonial movement in India which sought to make nationalism and socialism part of the Left-radical movement. The Irish Republicans, through different phases of their resistance against Britain, waged a powerful struggle for the creation of a unified Ireland founded on the principles of socialism and republicanism. These protests serve as pegs to string a narrative of resistance spun around the 'spectacle' of 'death' that accumulated around the starving bodies of prisoners and the power of speech that the bodies assumed in death. Ironically, even as self-starving prisoners interrupted the spectator regime of the corporeal state, they also led to the entrenchment of a medico-legal carceral regime embodying the custodial state. The dissident bodies of prisoners became sites for the standardisation of force-feeding as a life-saving measure for those in the custodial care of the state.

Courting hunger/courting death

In Kafka's story the spectacle of fasting was staged as a commercial performance for the public. Fasting was performed live by the hunger artist for forty days, after which public interest was likely to wane, but also, as Kevin Grant points out, as the replication of Christ's forty-day fast in the desert (Grant 2019: 6). Public excitement for the show was sustained by generating both curiosity and suspicion among the spectators. The emaciated body of the artist was inscribed with a set of meanings in which the codes of seeing were framed by the public's apprehensions of its own mortality.

Writing about a 'hunger striker' who died of anorexia nervosa a year after her release from Armagh, a prison where women Irish Republicans were incarcerated, Maud Ellmann contemplates the impossibility of *knowing* exactly why the hunger striker of Armagh destroyed herself and what *self*-starvation meant to *her*. Ellmann writes:

> even if she died of *sheer despair*, her hunger was a form of speech; and speech is necessarily a dialogue whose meanings do not end with the intentions of the speaker but depend upon the understanding of the interlocutor. Her body was enmeshed in social codes that preceded and outlasted its brief consciousness. In particular, it was entangled in the rival ideologies of nation, gender, and religion, and racked by all their passionate intensities. It was in the form of hunger that these forces battled for expression, ravaging the very flesh on which they were inscribed. (1993: 3)

Unlike the 'dialogue' that accumulates around starvation as a 'self-lacerating' (Elmann 1993: 2) *form of protest*, the starving body of the hunger artist in Kafka's story produced for public consumption was construed as incapable of 'speech'. Towards the end of the story, however, amid the indifference of the people who trooped past the hunger artist's cage, placed now in the circus compound competing for attention with the robust antics of circus animals and artists, the hunger artist's voice is heard for the first time. The voice is prompted by the curiosity of the overseer, who discovers that, completely unnoticed and forgotten, the hunger artist was *still fasting*:

> 'Forgive me, everybody,' whispered the hunger artist. ... 'I always wanted you to admire my fasting.' ... 'But you shouldn't admire it,' said the hunger artist. ... 'Because I have to fast, I can't help it,' ... 'because I couldn't find the food I liked. If I had found it, believe me, I should have made no fuss and stuffed myself like you or anyone else.' These were his last words, but in his dimming eyes remained the firm though no longer proud persuasion that he was still continuing to fast. (Kafka 1922)

At the conclusion of the story, the artist's craft of hunger regresses into a *personal pathology*. Indeed, the public had been deceived. The artist starved himself because there was no food that he liked. The gluttonous public and the abstemious artist constitute a binary along which the wasted body of the hunger artist is reinscribed to produce a script of moral outrage. Yet the disruptive narrative of hunger spun by the dying artist could well be construed as a moment of 'turning back' and 'turning on' (Anderson 2010: 9). Patrick Anderson writes that 'practices of self-starvation reflect an eminent moment of agential presence even as they conceptually and symptomatically eventuate the death of the subject'. The manner in which self-starvation performs subjectivation begins from the basics of the practice itself: 'a structured and sustained refusal to rehearse and perform normative eating, resulting in emaciation (among other physical effects) and, in the end, death' (Anderson 2010: 9). Yet hunger as a form of *protest* in prisons, in 'caged' spaces sequestered from the public, had to be anchored in an idiom of 'courage' – invoking the higher morality of hunger as a mode of politics – to steer clear from any semblance of 'personal pathology'. This was affirmed as follows by the Catholic Church, which refused to condemn Terence MacSwiney's fast to death in 1920 as suicide:

> No hunger striker aims at death. Quite the contrary, *he desires to live*. He aims at escaping from unjust detention, and to do this is willing to risk death, of which he has no desire, not even as a means. *His object is to bring the pressure of public opinion to gear upon an unjust aggressor* to secure his release and advance a cause for which he might face certain death in the field. (O'Neill, cited in Swinney 1993: 428; emphasis added)

A rational justification for courting death was crucial for preventing the fast from becoming a manifestation of personal despair or pathology. It was also important for forming a community within the prison *and* among the public *at large*. As we shall see later, while questioning the ethics of force-feeding, dissident voices in the medical community anchored their ethical dilemma on the volitional and purposive nature of the act of self-starvation. The HSRA prisoners in India and the Irish Republican prisoners in Britain asserted that they were political prisoners and not criminals. Their claims to political prisoner-hood drew from the premise that they were imprisoned for having presented themselves as political adversaries to the ruling regime and possessed an inalienable right to be treated with dignity inside the prison. Hunger became 'political' when the striker transformed the suffering body into a 'statement', giving speech to 'the wordless testimony of the famished flesh', holding thereby 'the body to ransom' (Ellmann 1993: 17). In order to be able to 'make mortality into a bargaining chip', it was imperative that the hunger strikers *'declare the reason for their abstinence'* (Ellmann 1993: 17). Without this 'self-narration', argues Lucy Fiske, the political act can too easily be subsumed by individual pathologising explanations (2016: 120). By giving a *reason* for courting hunger, the famished body became both a *metaphor for speech* – producing a community of affect, in which 'hunger' was made intelligible in a shared code of meanings around ideas of freedom and equality – and an *embodiment of political courage* – as a dissident body interrupting the power of the state by refusing to participate in its rituals of ruling. Holloway Sparks describes courage as 'a commitment' that is persistent even in the 'face of risk, uncertainty, or fear' (1997: 76). As a 'virtue' ascribed to soldiers, courage 'has often been constructed as a quintessentially masculine trait, tied intimately to conceptions of manhood and to the performance of violence' (1997: 76). Sparks, however, looks at Rosa Parks's *refusal* to vacate her seat on the bus to argue that courage informs *dissident practices of the marginalised* who '*publicly* contest prevailing arrangements of power by means of oppositional democratic practices' (1997: 75; emphasis added). What would courage mean, and how would it express itself in closed spaces like prisons that are structured to occlude what Hannah Arendt calls the 'space of appearance' (1958: 199)? How would prisoners make their protest 'visible' and their bodies bear 'witness' to the truth of the power of the state, endowing the body's 'wordless testimony' with the power of speech/act?

The spectacle of starvation/death

In *Remnants of Auschwitz*, Agamben reflects on the act of *witnessing*. Agamben argues that one of the reasons driving a prisoner in a camp to survive was 'the idea of becoming a witness' (1999: 15). Agamben quotes one such witness, a camp survivor: 'I firmly decided that, despite everything that might happen to me, I would not take my own life ... since I did not want to suppress the witness that I could become' (Agamben 1999: 15). If the testimony of the survivors of Auschwitz represented what the body remembered, the hunger-striking prisoners held their bodies out in defiance to speak through the spectacle of pain. Margaretta D'Arcy was one of the 'Armagh Eleven' imprisoned for demonstrating in front of Armagh prison on International Women's Day in 1979 to draw the world's attention to women political prisoners in jails.[1] D'Arcy had studied and worked in English theatre. She went to India in 1969 to study the use of folk theatre in political agitation. Arrested and imprisoned with her family in Assam, she gave a 'notice' of hunger strike to the government to obtain the release of her children (D'Arcy 1981). Upon her return to England, D'Arcy became active in the organisation Women Against Imperialism. In her prison memoir, D'Arcy wrote about her experience of incarceration in Block A of Armagh Prison, where women Republican prisoners were on a no wash 'dirty protest' in solidarity with the Irish Republican Army (IRA) men in the Long Kesh/Maze Prison. D'Arcy reflects on the complex relationship between organisations such as Women Against Imperialism and the Republican movement and between feminists in the movement and women who shared the views of the conservative Catholic Church, which also played out in the discussions among women political prisoners. What propelled the women's protests forward, however, was the conviction that they were equal partners in a war that the Republicans were waging. Their 'special' treatment in courts and prisons was because of their political activities, and they wanted to be considered 'prisoners of war' (Loughran 1986).

In his book on the H Block hunger strikes in Maze Prison and its ramifications for the Republican movement in Northern Ireland, Liam Clarke writes of the 'no wash' protest by women prisoners in Armagh and 'the women's determination to persist' (1987: 113). The protests, he writes, 'played an important part in raising the temperature of the overall prison struggle', but 'uniquely', it played a role in 'uniting' what he calls 'the feminist left with the Catholic right'. This unity was achieved 'through the powerful images of outraged Irish womanhood, forced immodesty and bodily violation' (Clarke 1987: 113). In 'utilising dirt', in particular 'intimate and inherently sexual body fluids' like menstrual blood, the women were confronting the 'essentialist ideals' of Irish womanhood, which endured in 'the male dominated republican movement' and the 'patriarchal Catholic Church' (Burns 2013: 29). Referring to the women's 'no wash' protest in Armagh and the emaciated body of a sick prisoner, Pauline McLaughlin, the journalist and playwright Nell McCafferty wrote in *The Irish Times* that 'Armagh was a feminist issue': 'Shall we feminists record that she [i.e. Pauline McLaughlin] is inflicting the condition on herself in case any question of moral dereliction arises against us? The menstrual blood on the walls of Armagh prison smells to high heaven. Shall we turn our noses up?' (McCafferty, cited in Clarke 1987: 113). Writing about the impact of the dirty protest on the women prisoners, D'Arcy refers to Pauline McLaughlin as 'an ever present spectacle': 'a nineteen year old girl who looked like an old woman of ninety. Hair falling out, teeth falling out, emaciated skeleton body' (D'Arcy 1981: 85). Her continued presence in prison, thought D'Arcy, was like a 'warning', 'set up with callous calculation' by prison authorities, that this is how they would all end up if they persisted with the protest (D'Arcy 1981: 85).

In a way, Pauline McLaughlin epitomised 'permanent starvation' as a constant condition of prison life. D'Arcy writes: 'There was a bare minimum of food. ... Hunger pangs never left us. I had never expected this feeling of permanent starvation' (D'Arcy 1981: 81). The first hunger strike in 1980 in the Long Kesh Prison, more commonly referred to as Maze Prison or simply the H Blocks, ended in an 'ambiguous' agreement between the British authorities and the Republican prisoners regarding their status as political prisoners. Mary Doyle, one of the three women prisoners in Armagh who went on hunger strike in support of the demands put forth by the male prisoners, despite the opposition of the 'H-block leadership', reported in an interview that women were 'determined to participate' since they felt that they had an 'equal stake' in the demands being met (Clancy 2011). Public attention was, however, riveted to hunger strikes by male prisoners. In her film *Silent Grace* (2001), which narrates women's experiences of the dirty protest and hunger strike of 1980, Maeve Murphy draws attention to the 'last ditch attempt' by women prisoners to draw attention to prison conditions (Cantacuzino

2004). The journalists were, however, 'all camped out in Belfast's Europa hotel where the story was fixed on the male prisoners. ... War is after all about men' (Cantacuzino 2004). Megan O'Branski sees the 1981 protests as a mode of turning the 'abject body' into a weapon – rolling back the emasculation that imprisonment and abuse brought with it. The weaponisation of the body, she argues, was 'a proactive attempt to reclaim the masculine body through the narrative of the hard man' (O'Branski 2014: 97–98).

The analogy of war was also invoked by Bobby Sands while defending the decision to take recourse to a second hunger strike in Maze Prison, which began on 1 March 1981. The night the fast was announced officially, it was clear that those:

> who went on hunger strike were engaged in an operation of major importance to their IRA comrades in jail and outside it; they must be prepared to die and those who did not must be prepared to accept the death of others rather than give in. On the second day of the hunger strike the end of the dirty protest was announced, halting its slow attrition and concentrating all the prisoner's hopes on the four hunger strikers. The attitude of the Northern Ireland Office, fresh from one hunger strike victory and convinced, as Margaret Thatcher was later to say, that the IRA was playing its last card, was emphatic. 'If they insist and carry it on', Humphrey Atkins said, 'they will die'. (Clarke 1987: 139)

In the film *Hunger* (2008), directed by Steve McQueen, on the dirty protest and hunger strike in Maze Prison – a film with prolonged silences with visuals that produced somatic impact – there is an almost twenty-minute long sequence of dialogue between Bobby Sands and a priest, Father Dominic Moran. In communicating his own and the IRA leadership's position on the hunger strike, Father Moran is sceptical of the hunger strike. What would it lead to, he asks, 'mindless dialogue?' Sands insists that it is the *prisoners* who constitute the frontline in the war and explains the 'new' strategy: 'the last time there was a flaw ... everyone went on strike together and when the weakest died, sooner than expected, the strike lost steam. This time the strategy would be different – the strike would be consecutive – someone dies – we replace them'. The priest is sceptical: 'Why should you care, you are already dead, right?' Failure would mean many dead men, families torn apart, the whole Republican movement demoralised. Sands is adamant that the priest should expect a new generation, more determined, more resilient. Accusing him of ignorance, Sands says: 'there is a war going on and you talk like a foreigner'. Significantly, the priest is not convinced by the idea of a hunger strike as a 'pre-designed strategy for negotiation'. In any case, he believed that a hunger strike was suicide – a position that Sands contests ideologically: 'You call it suicide, I call it murder. We are both Catholic *and* Republican.' Sands is accused by the priest of 'eulogising murder', of losing touch with reality, and not understanding what 'life' was: 'You don't know what life is. In years in the prison, you are not normal, there is nothing normal [about you] – the republican movement will walk into a corner. ... What would you achieve by dying? ... The future of the republican movement is in the hands of a set of men who have lost all touch with reality.' It is at this point that Sands makes an emphatic statement about the 'political' nature of his protest, which arose from a *desire for freedom*: 'My life is a real life, not some theological exercise. A desire for freedom, an unyielding love for that belief. ... Putting my life on the line is a good thing. I am clear on all the repercussions.' Sands's statement is also designed as an emphatic challenge to Margaret Thatcher's description of the hunger strike as the 'last card' chosen by the 'men of violence', who when 'faced with the failure of their discredited cause' had turned 'their violence on to themselves through a hunger strike to death ... work on the most basic of human emotions, as a means of creating tension, stoking the fire of bitterness and hatred.'

The film details the waning of life and emaciation of Sands's body as the strike progresses. Yet, even as the body weakens with hunger, the power of hunger as protest is reinforced through the modalities of 'representation' and 'reiteration', making 'a spectacle' of starvation and bringing 'shame' to the oppressors. In the course of the hunger strike, Sands is elected a Member of Parliament, bringing into effect what Ellmann calls a 'double representation': his body standing in to represent the Fermanagh county, his 'starving body' representing his 'bondage to the nation'. Indeed, Ellmann argues that it was only when Sands was elected to Parliament that the 'world's press swarmed into Belfast to represent his starving body to the nation' (1993: 17). A leaflet issued during Sands's election campaign asked voters to 'lend' their votes to 'save a life': 'the reader [of the pamphlet] should not stand by and let prisoners die. ... Bobby Sands was only "borrowing" the votes for one election. ... The blanketmen and the women prisoners are BORROWING this election in an attempt to illustrate your support for the prisoners and your opposition to the British government' (Clarke 1987: 143).

The hunger protest in Maze Prison began on 1 March 1981 and resulted in the death of ten prisoners. In a manifestation of the power of 'reiteration', hunger strikes were not synchronous, and the deaths did not coincide. By ensuring that there was a 'steady stream' of coffins emerging from the prison, the protesters forestalled the ascription of 'personal pathology' to the deaths. Lucy Fiske writes:

> Deaths from the hunger strike were carefully timed to ensure a steady stream of coffins emerging from the prison. The British government may have been able to manage a single death, perhaps being able to 'spin' the death as a suicide and evidence of an individual's personal despair, which was notable because of its exceptionality. However, coffins emerged day after day, exemplifying the problems hidden from view by the prison walls and calling into question the legitimacy of the state. (2016: 120)

The 'queue of corpses' emerging from behind the closed walls of the prison had a reiterative effect as outrage accumulated incrementally to shake the 'moral legitimacy of the British state' (Feldman, cited in Fiske 2016: 120). The power of reiteration assumed by the dead bodies distorted and destabilised the 'reiteration of power' (Mills 2000: 271) through which the state kept the prisoners in a state of subordination. The hunger protest not just enabled the prisoners to disrupt the power of subjection held by the state but also unsettled the conditions in which their subordination could be renewed and reinvoked.

In the Indian context the legacy of hunger strikes in prisons as an idiom of protest was located in different ideological strands of Gandhian *satyagraha* and socialist revolution. In their specific ways the *satyagrahi*s and the revolutionaries interrupted the colonial paradigm of prison discipline by refusing to participate in the affirmation of the penal truth of colonial power. Gandhi's hunger fast was an influential, non-violent protest form. Based on the distinction between individual and collective protests, it was steeped in a higher morality intended to invoke empathy in the aggressor. *Upvaas*, as Gandhi called his individual fasts, were bound by the norms of *satyagraha* and the religious idiom of purification. All his fasts, however, took the form of a 'war of positions' between him and the colonial government. While it would have to eventually act against Gandhi to shore up its authority, the government had to carefully choose a time when this would generate the least possible disturbance. The government wanted, moreover, to avoid, as far as possible, endowing Gandhi with a martyr's halo. A dead Gandhi could be a greater challenge for the colonial state than an alive one. While a hunger fast within the framework of *satyagraha* gave centrality to its spiritual aspects and intended to arouse empathy in the oppressor, for the socialist revolutionaries it emanated from the 'cult of self-sacrifice'. The desire to embrace death was witnessed in both the revolutionary nationalist traditions – the Irish Republicans and the HSRA prisoners, several of whom, including Terence MacSweeny in 1920 and Bobby Sands in 1981 among the Irish Republicans, and Jatin Das of the HSRA in 1929, courted death in prison. Both these movements, while aspiring for independence and 'nationhood', espoused violent resistance against a repressive state but adopted hunger as 'passive and non-violent resistance' within the prison.

Yashpal, a member of the HSRA, who was arrested for possessing explosives and attempting to murder Lord Irwin by bombing the train he was travelling on, recounts his experiences in Malaka Jail in Allahabad. Upon reaching the jail in a police lorry guarded by a dozen armed policemen, Yashpal was approached by an ironsmith to be fitted with handcuffs and chains. He resisted. He was a political prisoner – a *rajnaitik kaidi* – he would not be chained. Yashpal went on hunger strike in protest, and on the fifth day, the jail superintendent, an English man and a civil surgeon in Allahabad, admonished him for taking recourse to a hunger strike, which was a punishable offence. The biggest trauma for a prisoner, writes Yashpal, was the feeling that people outside had no information about them, or even worse, they were not interested in them. The jail officials loved to torment them: 'you thought you were a martyr and a *deshbhakt* – no one cares about you'. Yashpal elaborates on what an *anshan* meant to a revolutionary – it was not a spiritual exercise of purification, nor an exhortation to God. It meant generating *public* sympathy for their demand of political prisoner-hood and hatred for their adversary – the colonial government – among the people. However, this could be achieved only if news of their *anshan* would percolate outside, which was often not possible given the impermeable security in prisons. In such conditions it was important that those on hunger strike were able to communicate to the '*sarkar*' that despite their sufferings, their spirit remained indomitable (Yashpal 1961: 157–161).

The hunger strike by HSRA prisoners culminated in the death of Jatin Das on the sixty-fourth day while being force-fed. The demands of the HSRA prisoners were grounded in their self-perception as 'political', claiming the basic requirements of diet, labour, reading, and association. The death of Jatin Das had reverberations, and other HSRA prisoners implicated in different conspiracy cases against the government resolved to follow in the footsteps of Das and issued public statements.[2] The newspaper *The Tribune*, printed from Lahore, carried a photograph of Jatin Das's body draped in a shroud being carried out of his cell on the front page of its 15 September 1929 issue. The photograph was taken at the entrance of Borstal Jail on the evening of 13 December 1929, according to Das's younger brother Kiron Das, who had been permitted to live in the prison with Das and take care of him. Kiron Das mentions that after the picture of the 'dead hero' was taken, 'the bier was bedecked with garlands and flowers' and taken through the streets of Lahore, attracting unprecedented crowds of people. *The Tribune* had consistently supported the national movement and had been reporting the ongoing hunger strike in Lahore prison. At a time when photographs were rarely printed in newspapers, a half-page photo essay on 'Lahore's Tribute to Jatin' was printed on 17 September 1929. The photo depicted 'a sea of people walking with the bier in Lahore's Anarkali Bazar and women decorating his bier outside the jail' (Bharti 2019). The body of Jatin Das was handed over to his family, but it was the Bengal Congress that took the responsibility of transporting the body from Lahore to Kolkata. In the course of the long journey, the train stopped at numerous stations, where people swarmed to take a look at the body. The death of Das, according to Kama Maclean, 'caused a sensation in the press and all the way back to Calcutta' (Bharti 2019). A two and a half-minute news clip of Pathé News shows a 'rare view' of

Jatin Das's funeral procession in Lahore on 13 September 1929. Ironically, the clip opens with the statement 'India – the Empire's Greatest Problem today', with the subtitle 'Fanatical hordes "martyrize" Jotindra Nath Das agitator who dies after hunger strike of 61 days'. The silent news clip shows the funeral procession that *The Tribune* had described as 'a sea of people'. Large numbers of people thronged the long stretch of the route taken by the funeral procession, standing on parapets and moving with the bier, with banners and flags.³ A 'mammoth' public meeting was held after which Durga Bhabi, a revolutionary, took Das's body by train to Calcutta. Large masses of people turned up at every station, and in Calcutta 'an unprecedented crowd of 600,000 followed his coffin to the crematorium' (Dogra 2020).

On 13 September 2019 *The Tribune*, printed from Chandigarh, reprinted the photograph of Das's dead body with a commemorative feature article. This article claimed that the photograph, when printed ninety years back, had shaken the 'conscience of the Indian masses'. Kama Maclean, author of the book *A Revolutionary History of Interwar India* focusing on Bhagat Singh and HSRA, was cited in the article as follows: 'Das's death created a major impact on nationalist politics, as indicated on the first page of The Tribune [1929]. After this, the British stopped handing over the bodies of revolutionaries to their kin. Subsequently, the bodies of Bhagat Singh, Rajguru and Sukhdev were secretly cremated at midnight on the banks of the Sutlej' (Maclean, quoted in Bharti 2019).

The bodies of hunger strikers became a 'part of exchange' (Grant 2019) between the Irish Republicans and the Indian nationalists in the 1920s. Kevin Grant, in his study of the hunger strike as 'the last weapon' for those who resisted the British Empire, writes of the shared inspirations and methods of protest that were transmitted across countries, from the suffragists to the Irish Republicans and the Indian nationalists. Das was anointed 'the Indian Terence MacSwiney' after his death. Mary MacSwiney sent the following cablegram to Calcutta's mayor: 'Family Terence MacSwiney unites patriotic India in grief and pride on death of Jatin Das. Freedom will come' (Grant 2019: 141). A condolence message was similarly sent by Eamon de Valera, a Sinn Fein leader. Grant sees these messages as the recognition of the 'power of the hunger strike', and the 'solidarity' that 'familiarity' with suffering and a common enemy brought:

> This familiarity was on their own cultural terms rather than on those of Indians with whom they were united by a common enemy. They were moved nonetheless by the visceral, common experience of starvation, of a body wasting and a mind wandering away. They may also have shared a belief, confident or just bitterly hopeful, in the effect of hunger in protest on the British liberal conscience … they all recognised the power of starvation as the last weapon with which to turn the British regime's violence upon itself. (Grant 2019: 141)

The custodial state and the science of torture

In addressing the hunger strikes in prisons in India, the colonial state followed the broad patterns that had emerged in Britain while addressing concerted resistance in prisons by the suffragettes. In 1909, in a case involving force-feeding a suffragette prisoner, the judge ruled that 'force feeding was the duty of the prison officials to preserve the health and lives of those in custody' (Smith 1984). The decision to forcibly feed the suffragettes in prison was met with public indignation, leading to the enactment of the Prisoners (Temporary Discharge for Ill Health) Act 1913, commonly known as the 'Cat and Mouse Act'. By the end of the 1920s, when the HSRA prisoners went on a hunger protest in India, three patterns of state response to hunger strikes had emerged in Britain: forcible feeding, temporary release under the Cat and Mouse Act, and letting the prisoner take his own course. While the first two options were exercised in the case of suffragettes and conscientious objectors, the third was applied to Irish Republican prisoners, letting the protest run its course, leading to the deaths of some. The colonial government's policy on hunger strikes in India was based on the premise that concessions to the strikers should be resisted; to keep the prisoners alive, they should be forcibly fed, and if the process of forcible feeding would endanger life, death from 'inanition' was preferable. Prisoners on hunger strike were liable to disciplinary action. This would include isolation from other prisoners. A mass hunger strike would be considered a mutiny to be punished by whipping and other penalties.

Forcible feeding was based on the principle of 'safe custody' – the idea that it was the state's duty to protect those in its custody on the grounds of both humanity and policy. This duty was buttressed by the force of legal sanction from the instructions issued to jail superintendents to feed forcibly whenever necessary to save a life. The principle of 'safe custody' became prevalent among prison officials to legitimise force-feeding. It is significant that most jail officials at this time belonged to the Indian Medical Service (IMS). By the end of 1929 a 'scientific' method of feeding hunger-striking prisoners had evolved, addressing the body and mind of the prisoners. In actual practice it was a systematic method of torture under the garb of altruism, to break the resistance of the hunger striker. Within the prison, forcible feeding became another front where the hunger-striking prisoners resisted the efforts of the state to take over their bodies. The narratives of hunger-striking prisoners reveal that force-feeding constituted moments of confrontation between hunger-striking prisoners and jail officials. Bejoy Kumar Sinha, a revolutionary prisoner in the Andaman Cellular Jail, noted that when forcible feeding was resisted, the fluid often entered their lungs, leading to the death of some (Sinha 1988: 17–37). It also often led to 'reverberations' across prisons, triggering hunger strikes in prisons on the mainland so that events in the island prison in the Andamans did not remain insulated from public scrutiny. In his memoir, *Kala Pani*, L. P. Mathur recalls that the second hunger strike in Andamans in 1937 led to a chain of strikes in prisons in the mainland – in Alipur, Berhampur, and Deoli. While preparing for the strike, prisoners trained themselves to resist forcible feeding and 'court death'. Mathur suggests that since courting death became difficult due to 'the great care and precaution' taken by the jail medical staff, revolutionaries who had stayed away due to their chronic bad health decided to join the strike since they were more likely to die due to starvation and during force-feeding. Ironically, force-feeding also made it possible to prolong hunger protests (Mathur 1985). In his book *Sinhavalokan*, Yashpal writes that the prisoners detested the process, but the feed energised the body for further fasting. A new strategy was, therefore, devised by the superintendent to break the strike. He ordered all the paraphernalia for forcible feeding to be arranged for a hunger striker. After having effectively raised expectations, the superintendent would examine the pulse of the prisoner and decide that the prisoner did not need any artificial feeding (Yashpal 1961).

Conclusion

The spectacle of death conjured by hunger protests in prisons disturbed the state's field of power. By refusing to participate in its rituals of ruling, hunger fasting presented the possibility of politics of a different kind. Quite like Kafka's hunger artist, through the performance of hunger within prisons, the prisoners confronted the public with the spectacle of endurance and the courage to overcome their fear of mortality. In doing so they reconstituted the prison as a 'critical' public space, which made their 'powerlessness' complex (Sassen 2011). Through what Kraidy calls creative insurgencies, the hunger strikers turned 'despotic bodies' of those who exercised power over life and death into 'degraded grotesque bodies', corroding dominative power, even when not completely dismantling it (2016: 5–6). The 'hunger artist' in prison could transform hunger into dissidence, rolling back their marginalisation through the power of representation and reiteration. Prisons as a site of affirmation of state power have persisted, and hunger strikes in prisons have attracted punitive responses from the state. In India hunger strikes are construed as 'attempt to commit suicide', punishable under Section 309 of the Indian Penal Code (IPC). Perhaps the longest such attempt to establish penal control over a self-starving body was seen in the sixteen-year-long hunger strike by Irom Sharmila against the Armed Forces Special Powers

Act (AFSPA) in Manipur. From November 2000 to August 2016, Sharmila was kept in a hospital under the watch of the state police. Charged under IPC for refusing to eat until the AFSPA was withdrawn, she remained in the 'custodial care' of the state where her hunger protest played out as a curious annual 'cat and mouse' ritual. Every year, immediately after completing her detention, Sharmila would declare her intention to go on a fast again and would promptly be sent back to the 'hospital prison' for another year – the paraphernalia of nasal feeding reinstalled to keep her body alive. This sequence of release, imprisonment, and force-feeding was carried out as a perennial cycle, widely reported across the world, till she declared her intention to give up her protest to enter 'public life'. While the state denied Sharmila the power to choose death over what she considered living under an unjust law, her fast disrupted the order of the state by democratic iterations of what Scarry calls the 'reanimation of the practice of self-rule' (1987: 4). Countries such as Israel have laws that provide for force-feeding hunger-striking prisoners. Most such prisoners are behind bars for being a threat to national security, and their hunger strikes have led to protests in the streets of Palestine (Gross 2015). The responsibility to 'save life' has been presented as justification for force-feeding in Guantanamo Bay by shackling prisoners into a 'restraint chair'. At the peak of the hunger strikes in 2005, almost thirty detainees were being force-fed each day (Rosenberg 2013). In 2013 almost two-thirds of the detainees in Guantanamo Bay went on a hunger strike, forcing President Obama to mention it in his national security speech (Nocera 2013).

The hunger fasts by IRA prisoners and the socialist revolutionaries in India spawned an empathetic public who questioned the moral authority of the state. The fasts produced 'reverberations' – persistent and prolonged *effects*. Some of these took the form of dissident 'irruptions' within the domain of the state, and others of 'replication' on a public stage. The dissident articulation of what the 'duty to save' meant in the code of medical ethics interrupted the medico-legal carceral regimes of the custodial state. Debates over the ethics of the 'duty' to feed irrupted in the public domain in the context of the hunger strikes in Maze Prison. The question being raised was whether the custodial interests of the state and those of doctors employed by the state were the same. In her prison memoir, Margaretta D'Arcy wondered whether the British Medical Association had:

> considered the implications of their members in the prison service having to work with such a system in the name of humane care? Has it considered, for example, the lack of trust between doctor and patient that must inevitably develop under such conditions: particularly if the patient is deliberately taking part in a politically motivated protest against the system, and the doctor is an official of that system? (1981: 84)

Deaths in prison due to hunger strikes in Northern Ireland presented 'ethical and emotional difficulties to prison doctors' (Smith 1984: 210). The *ethical* problems were 'temporarily resolved in Britain' in 1974 when following the refusal by a prison doctor in Brixton to force-feed a prisoner, the Home Secretary left the decision to 'individual doctors' (Smith 1984: 210). Since 1974 it has become an 'accepted practice' in Britain '*not* to force feed', and it was 'never seriously considered in Northern Ireland' (Smith 1984: 210). The *emotional* problems persisted, however. Smith writes of the 'dreadfully draining' experiences of some of the doctors who cared for the Maze hunger strikers, 'to sit watching those men die'. Significantly, what troubled the doctors was the *publicity* – 'this whole grisly scene was enacted in the brightest of limelight with journalists and film crews from all over the world and even the Pope's envoy arriving' (Smith 1984: 210). In November 1992 the World Medical Association's Declaration in Malta recognised the 'conflict of values' faced by doctors when hunger strikes occur in a 'setting where people are detained', including prisons and immigration detention centres.

The higher morality accorded to hunger protests in prisons, which made the 'suffering' body a site for staging dissidence, have endured through hunger protests in the 'public'. A range of issues from development projects and environmental concerns to corruption have elicited large-scale mobilisation through what have largely been individual 'fasts'. Hunger fasts have also been a common mode of protest by students on university campuses (Munsi 2020). While fasts in public places are sometimes seen as a 'politics of comment' (Morris-Jones 1963), a 'saintly idiom' of politics enacted by exemplars, as a 'politics of insurgent citizenship', they make way for a continual opening of the 'public world of appearance' essential for installing enduring structures of the public space.

Notes

1 'Dolours Price, Ann Bates, and Dolores O'Neill were to be in prison over 20 years or for ever, Mairead – 14 years, Sinsead – 12 years' (D'Arcy 1981: 83).
2 File no. 244/30&KW, H(P), NAI, p. 29.
3 The Pathé News archive is known today as British Pathé. This clip can be accessed at https://youtu.be/pn-B4AkcB2k?t=5.

Bibliography

Agamben, Giorgeo. 1999. *Remnants of Auschtwitz: The Witness and the Archive.* New York: Zone Books.

Anderson, Patrick. 2010. *So Much Wasted: Hunger, Performance, and the Morbidity of Resistance.* Durham, NC: Duke University Press.

Arendt, H. 1958. *The Human Condition*. London and Chicago, IL: University of Chicago Press.
Arnold, David. 1994. 'The Colonial Prison: Power, Knowledge and Penology in Nineteenth Century India.' In *Subaltern Studies*, volume VIII, edited by D. Arnold and D. Hardiman, pp. 148–187. Delhi: Oxford University Press.
Bharti, Vishav. 2019. 'The Tribune Photo That Shook the British Empire.' *Tribune News Service*, 13 September. www.tribuneindia.com/news/archive/punjab/the-tribune-photo-on-jatin-das-shook-british-empire-831659. Accessed on 4 November 2020.
Burns, P. 2013. 'Rethinking the Armagh Women's Dirty Protest.' In *Theory on the Edge*, edited by N. Giffney and M. Shildrick, pp. 29–37. New York: Palgrave Macmillan.
Cantacuzino, Marina. 2004. 'The Forgotten Protestors.' *Guardian*, 9 February.
Clancy, Emma. 2011. 'Ireland: The Armagh Women's Hunger Strike Remembered.' Green Left 878, 11 May. www.theguardian.com/film/2004/feb/. Accessed on 19 March 2021.
Clarke, Liam. 1987. *Broadening the Battlefield: The H-Blocks and the Rise of Sinn Fein*. Dublin: Gill and Macmillan.
D'Arcy, Margaretta. 1981. *Tell Them Everything*. London: Pluto Press.
Dogra, Bharat. 2020. 'Recalling the Sacrifice of Brave and Exemplary Jatindra Nath Das.' *The New Leam*, 13 September. www.thenewleam.com/2020/09/recalling-the-sacrifice-of-brave-and-exemplary-jatindra-nath-das. Accessed on 6 November 2020.
Ellmann, Maud. 1993. *The Hunger Artists: Starving, Writing, and Imprisonment*. Cambridge, MA: Harvard University Press.
Fiske, Lucy. 2016. *Human Rights, Refugee Protest and Immigration Detention*. London: Palgrave Macmillan.
Foucault, Michel. 1985. *Discipline and Punish: The Birth of the Prison*. Harmondsworth: Penguin.
Goffman, Erving. 1961. *Asylums: Essays on the Social Situation of Mental Patients and Other Inmates*. New York: Arthur Books.
Grant, Kevin. 2019. *Last Weapon: Hunger Strikes and Fasts in the British Empire, 1980–1948*. Oakland: University of California Press.
Gross, Judah Ari. 2015. 'Knesset Passes Controversial Force-Feeding Bill for Prisoners.' *The Times of Israel*, 30 July.
Guha, Ranajit. 1977. 'Knowing India by Its Prisons.' *Frontier* 11(37): 15–29.
Holston, James. 2008. *Insurgent Citizenship: Disjunctions of Democracy and Modernity in Brazil*. Princeton, NJ, and Oxford: Princeton University Press.
Kafka, Franz. 1922. 'A Hunger Artist.' https://docs.google.com/file/d/0Byq6h70zkproSjVoSVNxLXdjT1k/edit. Accessed on 16 November 2020.
Kraidy, Marwan M. 2016. *The Naked Blogger of Cairo: Creative Insurgency in the Arab World*. Cambridge, MA: Harvard University Press.
Loughran, Christina. 1986. 'Armagh and Feminist Strategy: Campaigns around Republican Women Prisoners in Armagh Jail.' *Feminist Review* 23(1): 59–79.
Maclean, Kama. 2015. *A Revolutionary History of Interwar India: Violence, Image, Voice and Text*. London: Hurst and Company.
Mathur, L. P. 1985. *Kala Pani: History of Andaman and Nicobar Islands*. Delhi: Eastern Book Company.
McCafferty, Nell. 1980. 'It Is My Belief That Armagh Is a Feminist Issue.' *Irish Times*, 17 June.

Mills, Catherine. 2000. 'Efficacy and Vulnerability: Judith Butler on Reiteration and Resistance.' *Australian Feminist Studies* 15(32): 265–279.

Morris-Jones, W. H. 1963. 'India's Political Idioms.' In *Politics and Society in India*, edited by C. H. Philips, pp. 133–154. London: George Allen & Unwin.

Munsi, Urmimala Sarkar. 2020. Asserting 'Freedom': Building Resistance in Student Communities through Consumption Strategies.' In *Food Power: Expressions of Food-Politics in South Asia*, edited by K. Mukhopadhyay, pp. 169–180. Delhi: Sage.

Nocera, Joe. 2013. 'Is Force-Feeding Torture.' *New York Times*, 31 May.

O' Branski, Megan A. 2014. '"The savage reduction of the flesh": Violence, Gender and Bodily Weaponisation in the 1981 Irish Republican Hunger Strike Protest.' *Critical Studies on Terrorism* 7(1): 97–111.

O'Neill, D. J. 1984. 'The Cult of Self-Sacrifice: The Irish Experience.' *Eire-Ireland* 24(4): 83–105.

Rosenberg, Carol. 2013. 'U.S. Military Force Feeding a Third of Guantánamo Hunger Strikers.' MiamiHerald.com, 26 May. www.miamiherald.com>americas>article2349411. Accessed on 19 March 2021.

Sassen, Saskia. 2011. 'The Global Street: Making the Political.' *Globalizations* 8(5): 573–579.

Scarry, Elaine. 1987. *The Body in Pain: The Making and Unmaking of the World*. New York: Oxford University Press.

Sinha, Bejoy Kumar. 1988. *In Andamans: The Indian Bastille*. Delhi: People's Publishing House.

Smith, Richard. 1984. 'Deaths in Prison.' *British Medical Journal* 288: 208–212.

Sparks, Holloway. 1997. 'Dissident Citizenship: Democratic Theory, Political Courage, and Activist Women.' *Hypatia* 12(4): 74–110.

Swinney, George. 1993. 'Irish Hunger Strikes and the Cult of Self-Sacrifice.' *Journal of Contemporary History* 8: 421–437.

Thatcher, Margaret. 1981. Speech at Stormont Castle Lunch, Belfast. Thatcher Archives. www.margaretthatcher.org/document/104657. Accessed on 4 November 2021.

Yashpal. 1961. *Sinhavalokan*. Lucknow: Viplav.

4

Of quiet resistance: *Shy Radicals*, divergent world-making, and the poetics of statecraft

Anika Marschall

In this chapter I examine the arts-based movement *Shy Radicals: The Antisystemic Politics of the Militant Introvert* (2017), founded by Hamja Ahsan. *Shy Radicals* is first a manifesto publication by Ahsan, in which he creates the figure of the introvert militant, the shy radical, who opposes what he terms 'extrovert supremacist culture'. In his poetic satire, Ahsan performs a divergent kind of world-making, which connects the activist concepts of neurodivergence, modernist statecraft, and performative writing to galvanise radical social transformation. The manifesto *Shy Radicals* works as a vessel through which Ahsan himself takes on the role of a political campaigner, engaging with autonomous groups and spaces and offering a new vocabulary for the Left – particularly, a vocabulary of *quiet* resistance.

Ahsan is a British Bangladeshi artist and independent curator born in 1981, whose *Shy Radicals* movement challenges issues of racism and ableism. By imagining this revolutionary movement as an alternative nation state for 'shy people', Ahsan seeks to reclaim forms of mental health diagnosis and medical models of mental disability as different ways of being. Moreover, *Shy Radicals* blurs boundaries between reality and creates a symbolic framework and vocabulary. *Shy Radicals* draws on historical movements such as the Black Panthers or the *Hikikomori* phenomenon in Japan, cites known public figures such as Audre Lorde and international films such as *Heathers*, and references geopolitical conflicts such as the Israel–Palestine conflict and the Scottish independence movement. Ahsan envisions the state of Aspergistan as a space to rethink and contest notions of citizenship, classicism, the welfare state, and the diagnostic and charity culture around disabilities. Controversially, Ahsan stirs the question and potential of political extremism throughout his writing. He mixes the language of constitutional legislation, oral history, film curation, and identity politics to provide an alternative, critical, embodied lens on representation and prefigurative politics. Critiquing prevalent and exclusive 'left echo-chambers' (Hall 2019: 14), *Shy Radicals* also questions what type of personalities can actually run for Parliament, shape public debate, and, more generally, who gets to sit in meetings where future policies, plans, and political decisions are crafted

(Bayly 2015) – arguably, not those in fear of public speaking or identifying as on the autistic spectrum. Ahsan's performative statecraft project and the fictional territorial space of Aspergistan provide refuge and an alternative set of rights, granting asylum to all those suffering the violence of loudness and persecution in liberal 'extrovert-supremacist states'.

Putting in dialogue the emerging geographic and feminist theories of 'quiet activism' (Horton and Kraftl 2009; Askins 2015; Pottinger 2017) and disability studies (Bumiller 2008; Hilton 2017; Rodas 2018), this chapter critically investigates how the activist concept of neurodivergence enters aesthetic representation, activism, and everyday politics. The chapter examines how Ahsan's *Shy Radicals* views the modernist form of statecraft as a creative form of world-making with the potential to uphold progressive human rights protection and good public services, which need a more liberal kind of co-opting. This binary is not new for Left aesthetics of resistance, but *Shy Radicals* provides new insights into structural violence and essentially provides new formations of 'we', being, as theatre-maker Milo Rau has put it, 'realistic in an unrealistic manner' (Rau and Wolters 2014).

By introducing parts of Ahsan's story, who came of age under the Prevent campaign in the UK and discrimination against Brown Muslims, I situate his work on *Shy Radicals* more carefully in its contemporary political context. Second, I identify *Shy Radicals* as a performative script, which politicises the relational and acoustic space between different bodies. The politicisation and policing of acoustic spaces can impose pernicious violence on to some bodies and minds more than others, irrespective of their neurological dispositions. Consequently, this chapter is based on a performance studies lens and driven by my call to work towards a more inclusive future Left politics. The issue of acoustic violence and the work of *Shy Radicals* are understood as part of a wider neurodiversity movement, prompting me to discuss 'quiet activism' (Askins 2014; Pottinger 2017). Finally, I argue that Ahsan's imaginary Aspergistan, despite reinvigorating the much-discussed critique of the nation state, creates new forms of and platforms for quiet political action which move beyond 'left echo-chambers' (Hall 2019: 14), including reading, listening, crafting and quietly being with.

Shy Radicals

Ahsan is an activist, writer, curator, and artist. He is a campaigner for prisoners, human rights, and civil liberties under the War on Terror, and was shortlisted for the Liberty Human Rights award for his Free Talha Ahsan campaign. His work is driven by radical Leftist zine-making culture, and in 2013 he co-founded the DIY Cultures Festival. Ahsan describes citizenship as conditional, coming with different protections and entitlements for different categories of people. Ahsan's human rights campaign for his detained brother, who was held without trial for six years and placed in solitary confinement in the US, shows that certain markers determine who is fully recognised as an inherent part of the body of the nation and whose political membership to this community is denied or not fully recognised. These markers are evidently drawn along racial and also neuro-normative lines and have been further transformed through the securitisation of the state – especially in regard to the monitoring of Muslim activism through the UK Prevent campaign.

Bogumilla Hall analyses that Ahsan is of a generation who has come of youth in the UK, in an austerity state, which is 'also a security state, whose violence affects disproportionately minority citizens and noncitizens of color' (Hall 2019: 2). These intersectional structures of oppression have culminated in the so-called War on Terror post-9/11 and the 2014 and 2016 Immigration Acts under Theresa May as Home Secretary, when British Muslims were criminalised and surveilled, and required to 'prove their national belonging' through increased civic participation and commitment to 'British values' (Hall 2019: 2). Hall describes this, poignantly, as 'racialized disciplining into "good citizens"' (2019: 2). Hall asks how the artists and activists of Ahsan's generations' political 'engagements relate to those of previous generations, in particular, the radical black movement of the 1970s and 1980s?' (2019: 2). These contemporary engagements include not a mere confronting of the state but bypassing it and 'carving out spaces of mutual help, solidarity, and care' (Hall 2019: 3). In doing so, Ahsan and his generation employ a plethora of practices to seek epistemic justice: 'campaigns at universities to challenge racism inherent in higher education, the campaign of Grime musicians and fans in support Jeremy Corbyn, ... community work of black feminists, and the DIY spaces of Muslim and black art-activists' (Hall 2019: 2). They 'depart from the narrow language of civil rights, and think through an alternative framework of decolonial transformation' (Hall 2019: 3).

Problematically, 'loud', outspoken dissent and campaigning are often seen as crime – and the idea of a 'good citizen' seems to be one who is 'quiet', docile, and grateful, one who has the duty to report signs of radicalisation and of dissent. Hall argues, therefore, that activism, citizenship, and migration cannot be seen apart. Protest and campaigning remain important tools to resist state violence, detention, and deportations. Ahsan's work makes evident the political importance for artistic practices and movements which speak of the disillusionment with the liberal state as a guarantor of rights for all.

With *Shy Radicals*, Ahsan reimagines the hostile environment in the UK against Muslim communities and Brown people and envisions the body politic anew as one that is nurturing and protective for quiet, shy, and neurodivergent people. As a young racialised activist, he departs from a politics of recognition, street protest, and rights claims to one that questions the multiple exclusions on which citizenship relies, articulating a radical, decolonial, and *quiet* vision of social justice. While Hall sees a rise in identity-based claims for retribution and a decline in social justice narratives since the 1990s (2019: 9), Ahsan, without putting one against the other, puts both 'rights talk', that is, engaging in the very idea of state projects, and everyday politics, as in community healing, reclaiming minorities' lives, stories, and ways of being, centre stage in *Shy Radicals*.

Shy Radicals reclaims and subverts the nation state framework and envisions its very own radical nation state project. In *Shy Radicals* Ahsan plays with form and style, including speculative fictions, legal styles, oral history interviews with fictional prisoners, and drawings. The publication and movement oscillates between fact and fiction, dystopia and utopia; it is undecidable but resonates enough with the political world we inhabit today to affect myself and others. Ahsan's vocabulary is particularly striking, and the term 'extrovert supremacy' is even slowly entering university curricular and discussion panels on neurodiversity movements. The opening chapter of his book functions as the draft constitution of Aspergistan, including sixty poetic, constitutional articles of 'Shy-ria law'. It enfolds a very ambiguous nature, moving from disillusionment with the nation state to co-opting its frame and starting the creation of autonomous spaces for individualised self-expression, small-scale exchanges, and reciprocity. Subsequently, Ahsan briefly describes the phenomenon *Hikikomori* in Japan, which details how young adults withdraw from society and seek isolation. What follows is the 'New Lexicon of Democracy', which is written as a comic manual to guide you through twenty-six *Shy Radicals* communication tactics, reminding reversely of some of the bodily signals used by the Occupy movement in the early 2010s, such as the infamous human microphone. Ahsan's shy hand and body gestures include, among others, curling up on the floor, staring up at the sky, biting nails, the 'Rodin position' in which one mimics his famous sculpture *The Thinker*, slouching, and taking deep breaths in and out (Ahsan 2017: 39–46). Upon meeting Ahsan, he likely will ask you to pose with a curling fist in front of your mouth, so he can take a picture for his social media account.

Shy Radicals includes a fictional interview with Amy Littlewood, a political prisoner who is being held for thirteen years in 'company confinement' and who refuses her Australian citizenship in favour of seeking refuge in Aspergistan. She is presented as a symbolic figure of the movement and calls out the defunding and disappearance of public libraries and conservation areas. Other parts of the book include examples of political allies, brief fictional and personal notes from shy people and their personal struggles, suggestions for films from around the world, which could be programmed in a film festival for shy people, and dealing with questions of silence and separatist struggles. Ahsan closes the manifesto with a demand for financial reparations and the information to donate to his bank account and Patreon side.

Ahsan's thought experiment presents a deeply felt work of imagination, which develops a rich symbolic framework. He redefines national symbols and cultural images, and, for example, he envisions the national anthem of Aspergistan to be the sound of your own body when holding a seashell up to your ears:

> Article 22. The flat of Aspergistan consists of a black flag punctuated thusly '…' The ellipsis will be represented as three dark blue circles symbolizing silence and the depths of the ocean. The flag will never be publicly hoisted. The flag may be used only by citizens wishing to silently indicate their request for quiet, solitude, and personal space. It will be the shared responsibility of citizens to respect the wishes of the flag bearer. (Ahsan 2017: 22)

> Article 24. The national anthem is the sound of a seashell, which may be accessed on a twenty-four-hour basis by citizens via the holding of the shell to the ear. Non-citizens outside the current territory of Aspergistan may also access the anthem in this manner. (Ahsan 2017: 23)

Shy Radicals is also an artistic response to the dismantling of public places where you can be quiet, sit in solitude, dwell, and just be – most of all, public libraries, which are probably very dear to many of us: 'Article 32. The state shall guarantee twenty-four-hour access to all public libraries, museums, laboratories, book shops, tea and coffee houses, archives and cathedral within its sovereign territory' (Ahsan 2017: 24).

Closely examining the rhetoric and very first words of this draft constitution, it becomes clear that it references the US Constitution. However, Ahsan does not call into existence one people alone but a plural of peoples. In doing so, he sets foot on a slightly different path, towards a pluralistic, progressive political project – a nation state serving a manifold of different peoples across the globe:

> We, the peoples of Aspergistan, embody the shy people's republic of Aspergistan – the sanctuary, beacon and homeland of oppressed Shy, Introvert and Autistic Spectrum peoples – and understand that our nation's crowning principles will serve as a bulwark against the hegemony of the Extrovert World Order, marking a decisive step toward the fraternal and sororal collaboration and co-existence of all Shy Peoples in an autonomous worldwide union. (Ahsan 2017: 14)

Further, this peek into Ahsan's statecraft is telling because it speaks of its contemporary Left discourse by critically acknowledging more fluid gender and sex relations – that there are different forms of collaboration, including both fraternity and/or sorority. Politically, while he later lays claim on specific territories, here he speaks of an 'autonomous worldwide union', which suggests that at the heart of *Shy Radicals* we find a radical Leftist ideology seeking to undo and dismantle the very idea of the nation state and borders altogether. What sparks my interest as a performance scholar most of all, though, is the notion of embodiment. Aspergistan is first and foremost *embodied* in its people.

While at first glance a literary work, I aim to position *Shy Radicals* within the so-called social turn, the shift away from an artwork contemplated by audiences and towards a more interactive and participatory encounter between artwork and audiences. Ahsan, more often than not, presents the work in autonomous spaces, explaining his approaches in audience discussions, performing readings, and showing exhibitions. *Shy Radicals* is being studied in different university programmes in the UK and the US and also offers some suggestions as to how to change current curricula and make them more inclusive for neurodivergent and shy students. Since the publication of *Shy Radicals* in 2017, it has been translated into Italian and transformed into different exhibitions, that is, commissioned by the Centre for Contemporary Arts in Glasgow and the Ljubljana Biennal of Graphic Arts in 2019. Inspired by the book's serious activist gesture, the UK Autism Arts Festival has included a programme where people can wear different-coloured fashion to identify how comfortable they are with speaking to others. Crucially, during the COVID-19 lockdown in 2020, Ahsan set up a phone helpline for people not used to staying by themselves at home. *Shy Radicals*, I argue with Claire Bishop, is a socially engaged artwork, rather than a 'discrete, portable, autonomous work of art that transcends its context' (2004: 54). It builds a stage for possible future scenarios, for imagining otherwise. Thus, I argue that *Shy Radicals* is not a literary work alone but performative in that it creates a counternormative geography of acoustic refuge from violence and social exclusion.

Acoustic violence

Jenny Schrödl writes about contemporary German theatre, saying that acoustics play a crucial role because they spread 'across space and [have] the capacity to affect and involve people physically and emotionally, they seem particularly fitted not only to representing violence but also, or especially, to producing it and making it productive as a factor of effect' (2012: 80). While she lists silence and not speaking alongside a plethora of acoustics such as music, voices, and noises, I do want to stress that silence and not speaking is very different from the quietness Ahsan is seeking in *Shy Radicals*. It is noteworthy that in 'its volume and power, the discourse around autistic silence ... threatens in real terms to overwhelm the articulations of the more than 80 percent of autistic people who do speak, ... who write, sign, or express themselves nonverbally' (Rodas 2018: 37). *Shy Radicals* is seeking a radically utopian, anti-violent world for 'those presumed to be without words or language' or presumed to have nothing to say (Rodas 2018: 38). Nonetheless, Schrödl's argument is persuasive, that there is a connective tissue between violence and acoustics because acoustics – no matter the volume and no matter the neurological disposition of the listener's body – are affective and effective, and impact human (and more-than-human) bodies and their emotions. Therefore, both sound and silence bear the potential of bodily, emotional, and mental harm. They are expressive and performative forces; they index a political subject acting in and of themselves.

> Acoustic phenomena may, firstly, inflict physical and psychological injury and, as such, have a very insistent and direct effect. Excessive volume, constant exposure to sound, noise, yelling, or, indeed, silence can cause physical and psychological harm; for example, in the form of sudden hearing loss, stress-related illness, pain, anxiety, or depression. Secondly, acoustic phenomena may exert a far more subtle and indirect influence on the body and soul: we might think here of techniques of manipulation, conversion or seduction; for example, by means of musical atmospheres. ... The last form of injury inflicted by acoustic phenomena is symbolic harm. Voice, not-speaking or particular forms of hearing can attack, undermine or constitute people's status, identity, power relationships, and so on. (Schrödl 2012: 88)

In *Shy Radicals* Ahsan invokes images of all three forms of acoustic violence: for example, he presents a directory of helpful services, including a state-funded emergency programme which rescues people from harmful situations, imagining first aid kits with 'favourite tea bag, a yipped black hoodie, comfort blanket and selection of used books (donated by charities). In extreme situations of company confinement, a professionally designed rescue operation consisting of temporary sensory deprivation, kidnapping and hooding was provided' (2017: 132).

The productive friction between acoustics and violence necessitates an instant, embodied relationality between voicer, sound-maker, silencer, and the listener. It is important to mention here, especially when dealing with *Shy Radicals*, that this relationality also could be minimalist and mean your own body's palpable presence in space, hearing your own body making sounds, and breathing. While alive, we are always already soundful. In Roland Barthes's infamous words, what becomes audible are 'the tongue, the glottis, the teeth, the mucous membranes, the nose' (Barthes 1977: 183). This attention to the audible body does not take centre stage in *Shy Radicals*, but it is what Schrödl links to theatre's paradigm of liveness. I would add that this liveness, then, is not just the mode of perception or an atmosphere created by and through theatre, but, crucially, performative liveness is about the living, breathing being; it is about life itself that we begin to acknowledge and recognise in this instant. When reading *Shy Radicals*, it might not necessarily be the case that we notice and listen to our own bodies sounding. However, when it enters the realm of social engagement through Ahsan's touring readings, discussions, exhibitions, and generative artworks, the live communal gatherings highlight *Shy Radical*'s performative potential.

I am invested in Ahsan's *Shy Radicals* and in his continuous fight against marginalisation and exclusions of stateless and shy people, and like him I do not believe in a romantic notion of turning one's back on the state. I would position my privileged self as somewhat more of a pragmatist: I think that sometimes even more radical art projects need to hijack neoliberal funding regimes, capitalist logic, and extractivist culture to gain social currency, public recognition, and to create more sustainable, durable projects in the arts (see also Marschall 2018). What compels me to present *Shy Radicals* in this chapter, while contributing to the discussion about the future of the Left, is my drive to further a more inclusive society where people with different neurological dispositions assert their place and make demands for inclusion. The media scholar Xinghua Li observes a contemporary 'volume politics', which she believes 'is largely inherited from the modernist age when only the privileged could make loud sounds … and the oppressed could only whisper' (2011: 31). In regard to the book cover of Foucault's *Fearless Speech* (2001), which portrays him shouting into a loudspeaker, Li problematises that this 'volume politics' still 'dominates the leftist imagination of a revolution. … Yet the Anglo-American political world has gradually entered into a different historical stage – a stage when pluralistic voices from various social groups are not only allowed but even encouraged' (2011: 31). *Shy Radicals* equally problematises this volume's politics and prompts us to envision political agency through acts of quiet resistance.

Quiet resistance

Shouting, chanting, arguing, placard-waving, stamping, clapping, singing, demonstrative activists demand to be seen and heard. Being activist is often associated with grandiose, iconic gestures and fanfare, and an 'unconditional state: an identity, mindset, standpoint or self-aware commitment' (Horton and Kraftl 2009: 17). A collective activist identity can often be presupposed and thus inflexible, enforcing an ideal that goes way beyond the reach even of those deeply committed (Brown and Pickerill 2009). The term 'quiet politics' or 'quiet activism' (Pottinger 2017: 217) has recently been used in the field of human geography and social movement theories to describe a set of practices that mark themselves as *other* than traditional forms of activism and politics, presumably loud politics. Some of these practices include yarn-bombing, seed-sharing, and creating friendships between displaced peoples and locals in small communities. Albeit not loud in volume, these actions are 'purposeful rather than passive expression of quietness' (Pottinger 2017: 217). For the geographer Laura Pottinger, 'quiet activism' is a 'form of engagement that emphasises embodied, practical, tactile and creative ways of acting, resisting, reworking and subverting' (2017: 217). The label 'quiet' makes not only explicit how actions are performed at varying and low volume but also pertains to a 'visible, tactile, temporal and scalar' dimension of actions. To Pottinger, it is 'characterised by qualities of gentleness, slowness, subtlety and subversion' and 'extends the political realm beyond the cognitive and verbalised' (2017: 216).

The notion of quietness permeates recent discussions in social movement research, geography, and the arts, and likewise, a plethora of contemporary publications in performance studies suggest that an interrogation of the audible and the politics of listening is urgently needed (Collins 2012; Wake 2014; Hamdan 2016; Marschall 2017; Thomaidis 2017). Pottinger summarises, poignantly, that:

> [a]cademic theorisations of political activism (action on behalf of a cause) tend to overlook the everyday embodied repetitions and practices of care that make modest, yet purposeful, contributions to progressive social and environmental goals. While traditional accounts champion and romanticise antagonistic, vocal and demonstrative forms of protest, geographers have begun to expand the category of activism to include small, quotidian acts of kindness, connection and creativity. (2017: 215)

With *Shy Radicals*, Ahsan performs such quiet activism. Pragmatically, it is a literary work which can be and is presumably more often than not read alone, in silence, perhaps in a safe place, where one has time and refuge to sit down and imagine and not keep up a protective guard as much. Beyond that and from a more political viewpoint, *Shy Radicals* particularly asks, how can citizenship, nationalism, and the state be reimagined to be more homely to neurodivergent people? Culturally, *Shy Radicals* asks us to reimagine neurodivergent people as civic dissenters, subversives, and revolutionaries.

Kye Askins, in her article 'Being Together', draws on a participatory research methodology to write about a befriending scheme which pairs refugees, asylum seekers, and local residents in the North East of England – Newcastle-upon-Tyne. She considers that 'there is a particular quiet politics of encounter being enacted, attached to desires to belong in the local area, enabled and mutually co-produced through everyday geographies' (2015: 471). Her lens is based on a particular urban refugee community and the specifics of place and territory, arriving and/or being in a place together and not (yet) being literate in hegemonic languages. While this quiet politics, I argue, resonates and produces productive friction for analysing *Shy Radicals*, the latter certainly divests from thinking too closely about a particularly placed community facing forced displacement and different political stakes, i.e. persecution, survival, and exile. Instead, Ahsan envisions a global movement, seeking and drawing connections between people living and rooted in different places all over the world. Nonetheless, he also expresses the desire to belong and imagines a place and geography for being together otherwise. In a similar vein Askins references Elspeths Probyn's *Outside Belongings* (1996) to think through this desire to 'long to be', highlighting the emotional dimension of attachment and 'being part of something bigger, forming social bonds with others at some place' (2015: 472), which goes beyond a locality or geographic position. Importantly, the desire to belong does not come from a position of powerlessness (Hyndman 2010: 456).

Askins further problematises the idea of diversity in regard to befriending others within a larger political discourse around migration, inclusion, and minority communities:

> *meaningful* encounters are *also* about how people come to recognise simultaneous similarity, developing new relations that shift pre-existing stereotypes through some appreciation or experience of connection or commonality (Parekh 2000). That is not to flatten out diversity, or collapse into a simplistic universalism, but to hold both 'same' and 'not-same' within notions of identity constructions. With regards to community cohesion, a 'transformative politics of encounter' (Askins 2008) incorporates a radical openness to the simultaneity of difference and similarity, to deconstruct dominant discourses that essentialise minorities as only different. (2015: 473)

I think Askins's reflection on the potential to connect with others, despite and because of racialised, politicised, migratory difference and similarities, offers some resonances for *Shy Radicals*. Ahsan equally speaks to and of shy, introverted, and autistic spectrum people. This worldwide community champions a 'new kind of interconnectedness' and has utilised 'virtual communication channels that allow for easy self-expression, immediate exchange of information, and freedom from some of the intrusiveness of face-to-face interactions' (Bumiller 2008: 981).

In an often limiting way, autism is commonly understood in terms of otherness, something *other* than or *divergent* from social and behavioural norms. Of course, these norms depend on 'cultural context and time period, as well as [on] gender, race, class and sexuality' (Schalk 2018: 62). The theatre scholar Nicola Shaughnessy cautions that a discussion of 'autistic poetics … risks exoticizing the otherness of autism, celebrating differences that also present considerable difficulties to the person with a diagnosis for whom communication and social interaction are considered "disordered"' (Shaughnessy 2013: 323). Kristin Bumiller points out that people diagnosed with autism make up a relatively small percentage of people living with other disabilities, but the overall number has been 'escalating' up to three, four times as many compared to thirty years ago, and has even been seen as a 'public health crisis' (Bumiller 2008: 967), which seems in need of managing and containment. Autism is a neurological dis/ability with varying degrees of consequences for social functioning. People with autism

> experience their environment differently, particularly in terms of how they process sensory information or social knowledge. That is, when people with autism manifest differences that are socially recognized (and therefore disabling), it is often a consequence of the unusual manner in which their bodies perceive reality (Grandin 1995). For example, autistic persons may actually hear noises as louder or with enhanced frequencies, recognize atypical patterns of visual information from faces or pictures, and register unusual tactis sensibilities like feeling soft touch as painful (Williams 1992). (Bumiller 2008: 974)

From a feminist perspective, Bumiller writes specifically about the neurodiversity or autism rights community who struggle 'for a collective sense of identity' and have allied at times with civil rights campaigns, gay liberation movements, and disability rights advocacy, rather than subscribe to 'any single political affiliation or ideology' (2008: 968). In order to claim certain rights to education and public services, people must be medically diagnosed as autistic, a diagnosis which 'in its actual application is so broad' that it 'sets the stage for confusing and ambiguous social constructions of identity in other forums' (Bumiller 2008: 969).

Autism Network International, founded in 1993, has formed a new movement which critiques the authority of the medical profession to define them (Chamak 2010: 106–108) and seeks to affirm difference by 'mov[ing] beyond the framework of normalcy' (Bumiller 2008: 971), and away from cultural stereotypes of ableism, gender, and race. Some members prefer to be known as a distinct cultural group, 'separate from the normal life of neurotypicals' (Bumiller 2008: 970), and even more recently, some members have advocated to be recognised as a minority group by the United Nations. As Bumiller convincingly points out, the 'crucial issue is not the critique of the social construction itself but how such essentialist constructions affect people as they form their identities, seek support, and attempt to find a place in their social worlds' (2008: 973). Importantly, and this connects to what Ahsan is performing in *Shy Radicals*, the crux is the efforts to normalise disability. Normalisation occurs in cultural contexts 'in which disabled people become worthy of charity or respect when they fit into acceptable social categories such as innocent children, employable adults, and participants in normative heterosexual relationships' (Bumiller 2008: 975), following the standards and social conventions of non-disabled communities. Therefore, Bumiller argues for a shift 'from simple demands for inclusion to a utopian vision of a society that values human diversity' (2008: 979).

> As a group whose identity is based on their failure to conform to social norms, people with autism are likely targets of social discrimination, and resistance to this discrimination is essential for participation in society. The existence of a neurodiversity movement in itself is evidence of the desire of autistics to reframe their social challenges in political terms. As political actors, ... in their quirkiness they contribute to a culture of citizenship that fosters equality without sameness. Furthermore, the autistic person can be taken as representative of a certain kind of cosmopolitan way of being: without fixed loyalties in either the social or political realm and engaging the state only for the purpose of creating hospitable conditions for the expression of her or his own sensibilities. (Bumiller 2008: 980–981)

For Bumiller, 'thinking about political engagement for people with autism brings a new dimension to these discussions [about deepening democracy], especially considering the particularities of mind–body communication and their implications for social interaction' (Bumiller 2008: 984). Crucially, this includes 'a political *will to engagement* that requires commitment', which makes quiet political actions 'more than implicit' (Askins 2015: 475). However, at times this will to action can be compromised by an 'affective dissonance', whereby you might feel overwhelmed facing global, large-scale challenges of inequality, injustice, and extraction, but at the same time, you might feel 'capable of doing *something*' (Pottinger 2017: 220). This *something* counts, not despite but because of its ephemeral, fragile, subversive critique, which might even go under the radar (Mann 2015). This *something* does not merely count as opposite to loud, demonstrative activist action, but it counts 'as active embodied stances, capable in their own right of preserving desired ways of living' (Pottinger 2017: 220). However, this *something* might also make possible 'activist self-critique' and, thus, make Left activism more accessible and 'influence the political mainstream rather than existing on the political fringe' (Chatterton and Pickerill 2010: 480).

A quiet political action means an 'unassuming praxis of engaging with others, in which new social relations are built' (Askins 2014: 354). A quiet politics 'crucially must recognise that encounters between different groups can draw upon and reiterate socially constructed difference, but that they also have the *potential to shift* how we see and how we feel about our others' (Askins 2015: 473). As I have discussed elsewhere, theatre and socially engaged arts hold the potential to create spaces for sensing commonalities, where relationships become political just by bringing communities together and by asking us to be with another, where, more specifically, relationships become 'quietly political' (Marschall 2021). Aesthetic encounters in and through theatrical frames can help nourish a sense of belonging and an emotional attachment to a different community and space. With their commitment to the lives, bodies, and sensualities of participants, some performative practices are especially equipped to deal with quiet togetherness and produce a lasting sense of belonging. Nicola Shaughnessy and Melissa Trimingham's research investigates the potential of performance art and its sensorial multimodalities to imaginatively engage with autistic states of being and overcoming an aesthetic–non-aesthetic binary (Shaughnessy and Trimingham 2016). Communal gatherings certainly will gain more importance for neuroscientists, as they 'increasingly recognise the importance of what lies outside the body/brain – not only the material world in all its rich potential of sight, sound, smell and touch ... but, crucially, other people' (Shaughnessy and Trimingham 2016: 296).

Both Pottinger and Askins unpack specific forms of making – a refugee-befriending scheme and a seed-swap event in the UK – and deal with the notion of activism, questioning implications of what it means to be active or activist and what representational registers inhibit from recognising other actions as activist. However, I intentionally reword their focus and instead want to emphasise the notion of resistance in light of Ahsan's *Shy Radicals*. While indeed *Shy Radicals* makes, does, and is activist through various quiet actions, the notion of resistance offers a slightly different lens, pertaining to the quotidian nature of living through everyday systemic violence rather than focusing solely on taking activist steps towards a future change. 'To resist' invokes a more pacifist, defensive register than, for example, 'to counteract' through an organised opposition, but it also implies that there is already an oppressive, violent force acting on someone, which, problematically, is by definition not them or even implicated in them: Ahsan explicates this as the 'global Extrovert-Supremacism' (Ahsan 2017: 14). Clearly, Ahsan, working activist and writer himself, is well aware and here plays with invoking different registers, an othering narrative, and the technocratic power of language, too.

Aspergistan: autism poetics as statecraft

Drawing on different performative and literary practices, including legal texts such as constitutions, comics, interviews, and maps, I argue that Ahsan is a cultural producer, who participates in forging some idea of a different kind of nation state of Aspergistan by mocking and reclaiming it performatively. I will take inspiration from what Chiara de Cesari has argued in regard to Palestinian artists setting up a national museum and non-governmental organisation (NGO)-organised biennials. For Cesari, such artistic experiments 'constitute a kind of artistic practice that does not just represent or imitate the social world: they are artistic practices that purport to *produce* new social arrangements – in particular, a set of new "state" (art and cultural) institutions under conditions of statelessness' (2012: 82). Further, de Cesari identifies these artistic practices as 'a tactic of *anticipatory representation*, which calls into being, by representing them beforehand, institutions that do not yet (fully) exist' (2012: 82, emphasis added).

I find it particularly striking that Ahsan introduces the notion of statelessness as one of the pertinent issues of the neurodivergent movement. I have analysed elsewhere that we find a dramaturgy of statelessness in contemporary artistic interventions, which perpetuates a White, citizenist gaze upon migrants moving towards Europe in search of safety, refuge, and humanity, notwithstanding that there are many more people internally displaced (Marschall 2016). Internal displacement is put centre stage in *Shy Radicals*, both as metaphor and as everyday lived reality by neurodivergent people. Whereas many Left critiques of the nation state focus on the harms it causes, including environmental and capitalist extraction, oppression and domination of people, and the marginalisation of cultures, Ahsan reimagines the nation state as possible space for neurodiverse refuge, asking 'what else can be said and done with the state – as a material formation, as something imagined, and in the movement between the two?' (Cooper 2020: 1).

Ahsan reimagines the nation state in the form and shape of Aspergistan as a refuge, protective, democratic, and progressive and thus affects social movement activism, discourse, cultural, and political practices. Different forms of cultural representation make this imagination possible: anthems, flags, national sports teams, commemorations, ceremonies, and so on. It is not my aim to dismiss Left critique of the nation state, but I have written this chapter in the hope that an imagining with and through *Shy Radicals* can tackle the oppressive forces states employ to control racialised and ableist colonial relations in regard to sound policing and forms of making noise, making yourself heard, and working productively as a 'good citizen'. To culturally participate in forging a radically different nation state, for a radical anticipatory representation, we need to grapple with different modes of seeing and knowing the state (Cooper 2020: 10), and I would add we need to grapple with different modes of hearing and speaking of communities at its margins.

Ahsan's imagination of Aspergistan is not simply a disembodied narrative, but it has material shape and travels to and through different communities in the form of a book, or rather performative script. This cultural expression has an inherent political dimension in itself and is also accompanied by forms of collective mobilisation, the historic Disability Rights Movement (DRM), and new *Shy Radicals* fan communities. It is important to note that Ahsan's writing practice takes root in zine-making culture and, therefore, functions in line with a feminist and anarchist reading, appears inherently subversive, and is championed by a communal, democratic, and non-profit ethos (Hall 2019: 12). Thus, as Hall and de Cesari have analysed for different but related cultural projects, *Shy Radicals* bears a prefigurative dimension: it asserts difference, creates an inclusive platform, redefines what activism means, and enacts an archive for memorising and disseminating knowledge about past communal struggles, i.e. the racialised surveillance of neurological difference (Hilton 2017). For the zine-making culture in the UK specifically, Hall has shown how young, racialised makers search for a new kind of political action 'that moves beyond traditional, hierarchical and formulaic "left echo-chambers"' (Hall 2019: 14) and breaks away 'from the rigidity of traditional [radical] organiz[ing in the 1970s and 1980s] ... [and] the class of "professional" activists, and make[s political action] more accessible for ordinary people' (Hall 2019: 15).

In his more than twenty-five-year-old opinion piece in *Monthly Review*, James Charlton maps the historic development and socio-cultural successes of the DRM as well as his own experience of engaging in Left politics and activism in the US context (Charlton 1994). He describes his experience of the latter as a person with disability as 'frustrating and disturbing' (Charlton 1994: 77), while he underlines that the culture and identification with and of the DRM community had shifted from self-pity and helplessness towards 'dignity, anger and empowerment' (Charlton 1994: 77). The belief Charlton expressed more than twenty-five years ago still holds true today for me: 'that the most important political issues concern class, race, and gender. These overarching considerations should be the primary focus for our work on the political Left. However, other issues demand attention and support from the Left. These include environmental protection, gay and lesbian rights, and disability rights' (Charlton 1994: 79). Further, Charlton reflects on the position of the DRM within the overall movement for social change, referring to the persistent use of discriminatory language and holding political meetings in buildings, which are inaccessible to people with disabilities, and/or who cannot participate due to a lack of interpreters. 'For many, probably most leftists and progressive activists, disability politics has been an afterthought at best. Many leftists would argue that the DRM has limited political significance and little relation to the question of political power. This view is not only wrong but arrogant' (Charlton 1994: 79).

In response to the rise of pro-fascist governments in India, the Brexit campaigns and elections in the UK, and Trumpism in the US, Larne Abse Gogarty writes at the end of 2016 (which still reads convincingly, writing this six years later) that rather

> than sink into nihilism or attempt to produce a left populism that cynically seeks to capture this moment through promoting a nostalgic nationalism, we need a movement and art that are full of expressive feeling, material and emotional solidarity, as well as unrelenting refusal to acquiesce or become useful to our enemies in any way. (2017: 119)

Shy Radicals certainly is full of expressive feeling, material, and emotional solidarity, and refuses to be useful to our enemies in both an ideological and a playful way. The writing and generative work of Ahsan pertains to different bodies and bodily vulnerabilities. It asks us to listen and respect, to recognise and care for a plurality of voices – loud and quiet.

References

Ahsan, Hamja. 2017. *Shy Radicals: The Antisystemic Politics of the Militant Introvert*. London: Book Works.

Askins, Kye. 2008. 'Renegotiations: Towards a Transformative Geopolitics of Fear and Otherness.' In *Fear: Critical Geopolitics and Everyday Life*, edited by R. Pain and S. Smith, pp. 235–248. Aldershot: Ashgate.

Askins, Kye. 2014. 'A Quiet Politics of Being Together: Miriam and Rose.' *Area* 46(4): 344–360. doi.org/10.1111/area.12138_5.

Askins, Kye. 2015. 'Being Together: Everyday Geographies and the Quiet Politics of Belonging.' *ACME: An International E-Journal for Critical Geographies* 14(2): 470–478.

Barthes, Roland. 1977. 'The Grain of the Voice.' In *Image, Music, Text*, pp. 179–189. New York: Hill & Wang.

Bayly, Simon. 2015. 'We Can't Go on Meeting Like This: Notes on Affect and Post-Democratic Organization.' *Performance Research* 20(4): 39–48. doi.org/10.1080/13528165.2015.1071036.

Bishop, Claire. 2004. 'Antagonism and Relational Aesthetics.' *October* 110: 51–79.

Brown, Gavin, and Jenny Pickerill. 2009. 'Space for Emotion in the Spaces of Activism Emotion.' *Emotion, Space and Society* 2(1): 24–35.

Bumiller, Kristin. 2008. 'Quirky Citizens: Autism, Gender, and Reimagining Disability.' *Signs: Journal of Women in Culture and Society* 33(4): 967–991. doi.org/10.1086/528848.

Cesari, Chiara de. 2012. 'Anticipatory Representation: Building the Palestinian Nation(-State) through Artistic Performance.' *Studies in Ethnicity and Nationalism* 12(1): 82–100.
Chamak, Brigitte. 2010. 'Autisme, handicap et movement sociaux.' *ALTER: European Journal of Disability Research* 4: 103–115. doi.org/10.1016/j.alter.2010.02.001.
Charlton, James I. 1994. 'The Disability Rights Movement and the Left.' *Monthly Review* 46(3): 77–80.
Chatterton, Paul, and Jenny Pickerill. 2010. 'Everyday Activism and Transitions towards Post-Capitalist Worlds.' *Transactions of the Institute of British Geographers* 35: 475–490.
Collins, Rebecca. 2012. 'On Being Audience: Modalities of Theatrical Speech and Listening.' *Activate* 2(1): 1–11.
Cooper, Davina (ed.). 2020. 'Introduction.' In *Reimagining the State: Theoretical Challenges and Transformative Possibilities*, pp. 1–15. London and New York: Routledge.
Gogarty, Larne Abse. 2017. 'Usefulness in Contemporary Art and Politics.' *Third Text* 31(1): 117–132.
Grandin, Temple. 1995. *Thinking in Pictures: And Other Reports from My Life with Autism*. New York: Doubleday.
Hall, Bogumila. 2019. 'Coming of Age in the "State of Emergency": Race, Religion, and Political Imagination among Britain's Youth of Color.' *American Behavioral Scientist*: 36(11): 1–17.
Hamdan, Lawrence Abu. 2016. *[inaudible] A Politics of Listening in 4 Acts*. Berlin: Sternberg.
Hilton, Leon J. 2017. 'Avonte's Law: Autism, Wandering, and the Racial Surveillance of Neurological Difference.' *African American Review* 50(2): 221–235.
Horton, John, and Peter Kraftl. 2009. 'Small Acts, Kind Words and "Not Too Much Fuss": Implicit Activisms.' *Emotions, Space and Society* 2(1): 14–23.
Hyndman, Jennifer. 2010. 'Introduction: The Feminist Politics of Refugee Migration.' *Gender, Place and Culture: A Journal of Feminist Geography* 17(4): 453–459.
Li, Xinghua. 2011. 'Whispering: The Murmur of Power in a Lo-fi World.' *Media, Culture and Society* 33(1): 19–34.
Mann, Joanna. 2015. 'Towards a Politics of Whimsy: Yarn Bombing the City.' *Area* 47(1): 65–72. doi.org/10.1111/area.12164.
Marschall, Anika. 2016. 'The State at Play? Notions of State(less)ness in Contemporary Interventionist Performances.' Critical Stages 14. www.critical-stages.org/14/the-state-at-play-notions-of-statelessness-in-contemporary-interventionist-performances. Accessed on 22 February 2024.
Marschall, Anika. 2017. 'To Speak the Truth, the Whole Truth and Nothing but the Truth: About Political Performances of Listening.' *Platform* 11(1): 67–87.
Marschall, Anika. 2018. 'What Can Theatre Do about the Refugee Crisis? Enacting Commitment and Navigating Complicity in Performative Interventions.' *Research in Drama Education: The Journal of Applied Theatre and Performance* 23(2): 148–166.
Marschall, Anika. 2021. 'Between Tokyo and Frankfurt: Akira Takayama's "Theatre 2.0", Migratory Encounters and Urban Solidarity in the Contemporary City.' *Research in Drama Education* 26(2): 205–223. doi.org/10.1080/13569783.2020.1838892.
Parekh, Bhikhu. 2000. *Rethinking Multiculturalism: Cultural Diversity and Political Theory*. London: Palgrave.

Pottinger, Laura. 2017. 'Planting the Seeds of a Quiet Activism.' *Area* 49(2): 215–222. doi.org/10.1111/area.12318.
Probyn, Elspeth. 1996. *Outside Belongings*. London: Routledge.
Rau, Milo, and Nina Wolters. 2014. 'What Is to Be Done?' TDR/*The Drama Review* 58(1): 2–3.
Rodas, Julia Miele. 2018. *Autistic Disturbances: Theorizing Autism Poetics from the DSM to Robinson Crusoe*. Ann Arbor, MI: University of Michigan Press.
Schalk, Sami. 2018. *Bodyminds Reimagined: (Dis)ability, Race, and Gender in Black Women's Speculative Fiction*. Durham, NC: Duke University Press.
Schrödl, Jenny. 2012. 'Acoustic Violence in Contemporary German Theatre.' In *Destruction in the Performative*, edited by A. Lagaay and M. Lorber, pp. 79–98. Amsterdam and New York: Rodopi and Brill.
Shaughnessy, Nicola. 2013. 'Imagining Otherwise: Autism, Neuroaesthetics and Contemporary Performance.' *Interdisciplinary Science Reviews* 38: 321–334.
Shaughnessy, Nicola, and Melissa Trimingham. 2016. 'Material Voices: Intermediality and Autism.' *Research in Drama Education* 21: 293–308.
Thomaidis, Konstantinos. 2017. *Theatre & Voice*. Basingstoke: Palgrave Macmillan.
Wake, Caroline. 2014. 'The Politics and Poetics of Listening: Attending Headphone Verbatim Theatre in Post-Cronulla Australia.' *Theatre Research International* 39(2): 82–100.
Williams, Donna. 1992. *Nobody Nowhere: The Extraordinary Autobiography of an Autistic*. New York: Times Books.

Part II

Theatre

5

Acting politically: Making performance in the eye of history

Adrian Kear

'History has its eyes on you', as Lin-Manuel Miranda and Christopher Jackson's brilliant song from *Hamilton* affirms. 'History has its eyes on me.' However, how does history see? How does history see us when we are ourselves historical beings living in and through the very storm of history? How do we see ourselves historically? Theatres of the Left have been concerned with investigating the visual construction of historically lived experience since Brecht, seeking to deploy performance as a critical optic through which to examine and make visible the political relations at play in the contemporary social formation and historical conjunction. This chapter provides a sustained account of what Brecht called 'the crucial technical device' of historicisation (2015: 140), demonstrating its centrality to practical theatre-making methodologies and the creation of new horizons for acting politically. It explores the continuation of the Brechtian method of opening up ways of seeing historically in contemporary performance practice, and in the political theatre of Anna Deavere Smith in particular. The chapter offers a detailed exposition of her work, *Notes from the Field* (2019), outlining how it historicises the emergence of the Black Lives Matter movement theatrically and situates its performative exposition of structural and systemic racism in the context of exposing the deep-seated continuities and connections between the contemporary social formation and the historical inequalities and injustices of segregation and slavery.

Of course, *Hamilton* itself raises these questions by suggesting that recasting the eyes of history – reframing who gets to be seen as a historical actor and re-functioning the aesthetic-political apparatus of appearance by which they are seen – changes the very nature of seeing historically. By insisting on Black, Latino, Asian, and First Nation actors being seen as foundational to the constitution of America, *Hamilton* challenges and destabilises the hegemonic historical narrative of nation formation by creating an image of the historically lived reality of racial co-presence and grounds this in the materiality of the theatrical apparatus. As image theorist Georges Didi-Huberman argues, 'seeing perpetually changes the nature of what is seen as well as the constitution of the one who sees it' (2018: xvi), demonstrating the performative co-production of historical forms of visibility, ways of seeing, and political modes of subjectivation. For Didi-Huberman, perhaps inadvertently reprising the line from *Hamilton*, 'history has eyes just as a hurricane makes its eye' (2018: xxiv). He regards the eyes of history, forged in the 'relative calm' at the epicentre of history's events – 'in the very eye of history' (2018: xxiv) – as having binocular heuristic clarity and historiographic focus. This chapter argues that the critical function of this optical apparatus – seeing through the eyes of history – is mobilised methodologically in the creative practices of contemporary theatres of the Left to deconstruct the political operation of the social and historical events that they might otherwise be seen to merely represent.

In his book *The Eye of History*, Georges Didi-Huberman elaborates how looking at and through the eyes of history enables the practice of seeing to 'both deepen and critique historical knowledge' at the same time as ensuring the historicisation and critique of forms of visuality and modes of visibility (2018: xxv). Although primarily concerned with the matter of photographic images and the material conditions of their emergence as partially torn from the fabric of lived historical experience, Didi-Huberman recognises that through the materiality of their very production, 'images *participate in a gesture*' of historicity by indexing the act of their making within them. Accordingly, he sees making an image as 'a gesture that transforms time' and acts 'in and on history' to render visible not only that which is seen but also the social production of its conditions of visibility (2018: xxvii). While Didi-Huberman is at pains to stress that this is not the same thing as acting directly in the sense of taking direct action or participating in political activism, it is also clear that the trajectory of the gesture is towards becoming act, towards its codification within an apparatus of action and logic of dramatisation. As Sruti Bala contends, gesture 'is situated between image, speech and action; no longer image but not yet act' (2018: 15). It is still to be condensed and contained by the codification of what Bertolt Brecht named *gestus*: 'the gesture of a gesture' (Puchner 2002: 15) within a specifically theatrical mode of presentation. For Brecht, *gestus* is demonstrative and denaturalising, bringing the immediacy of gesture under the control of the theatrical operation. It forms part of the aesthetic dynamics of estrangement, breaking open the mimetic closure of the gap of representation to show the material relations and social reality underlying its manifestation. The theatrical transition of gesture into *gestus* thereby not only contributes to the aesthetic mode by which theatre seeks to regulate and limit uncontrolled mimesis, but it also serves to demonstrate 'that what we took to be natural was, in reality, social' – the historical product of human actions and social relations which remain 'equally capable of turning it into something else' (Jameson 1990: 84). As such, it offers a way of seeing and acting, politically.

Throughout *The Eye of History*, Didi-Huberman turns to Brecht as his touchstone reference for his argument that '*art shows politics*; it exposes it in every sense of the word' (2018: 104). This emphasis on exposure, with its photographic resonance, recalls Walter Benjamin's insistence that 'the epic dramatist makes use in a new way of the great ancient opportunity of the theatre – to expose what is present' (Benjamin 1973: 267). For Benjamin, likewise channelling Brecht, the political task of performance is not to 'reproduce' the historical situation by means of representation but rather to 'discover' it – to allow its historicity to be seen – through an aesthetic of critical exposition that seeks to historicise the contemporary by uncovering its conditions and demonstrating their contingency. He contends that, in performance, the interruption of a scene or sequence of action does not simply offer a dramaturgical 'stimulant' but operates as 'an organizing function' of the aesthetic of critical distancing (*verfremden*) (1973: 266). This constitutes performance as an art of interruption – the interruption of the everyday lived experience of history and the apparent continuity of social conventions and ideological formations – in order to create an 'eye' on its operation formed in its 'very eye'. Cutting across the normative frames of naturalistic action and teleological narration, interruption suspends dramatic time and displaces the representational 'drama of history' to create an image, a freeze-frame compression that Benjamin describes as revealing 'the dialectic at a standstill' (1973: 12). The image formed within such a temporal disjunction operates as a *gestus* exposing the historical conditions and social relations underscoring the dramatic situation, enabling the effective historicisation of events on stage. The example Benjamin gives is of a stranger interrupting a scene of domestic violence at a crucial moment (a woman is 'just about to grab a bronze sculpture to throw it at her daughter'). His entrance freezes the action and constructs a critical relation to it, enabling a new way of seeing the everydayness of 'present day existence' (1973: 267). The stranger's interruption is, in micro, a demonstration of the intervention made by the epic dramatist and politically engaged spectator: the initiation of complex seeing and its implication of critical thinking. The dialectical image thereby 'bears within it, upon it, the very conditions of its own gesture' (Didi-Huberman 2018: xxvii), creating a viewpoint for seeing historically.

Didi-Huberman centres Brecht's theatrical conception of the image as demonstrative in order to explain that 'the eyes of history ... reveal something of the space and time that they see' (2018: xxxv). This suggests that the theatre – as the space of seeing par excellence (*theatron*) – serves to explicate the processes by which 'seeing could both deepen and critique historical knowledge' and contribute to the 're-temporalizing of our way of looking' (2018: xxxvi). The political potentiality of theatre is seen to correspond to its historicising operation. Accordingly, theatre for Brecht functions as an 'art of historicization' that, interrupting the seemingly seamless continuity of narrations to show their social construction, 'restores the essentially critical value of all historicity' (Didi-Huberman 2018: 59). Such a re-functioning (*Unfunkionierung*) of performance as a critical operation on the social puts the 'crucial technical device' of historicisation to the service of exposing the social relations of production of the specific historical conjunction (Brecht 2015: 140). It is, therefore, important to recall the specific historical conditions that Brecht's aesthetics sought to uncover and to caution against regarding theatricality as essentially or necessarily producing reflexive critical practice.

In this context, Bishnupriya Dutt usefully situates Brecht's concern with the development of *gestus* 'against the experience of National Socialism's use of overt gestures and hyperperformativity', suggesting that his aesthetic of interruption 'deliberately focused on countering the dangerous consequences of being drawn into a vortex of totalitarian mimetic frenzy' (Dutt 2021: 524). Putting acting at a distance from the representation of an action or into partial suspension can be seen as an attempt to break open the 'mimesis of mimesis' of fascist theatricalisation, whose 'monotonous repetition of words and gestures' seeks to foreclose critical intervention (Adorno and Horkehiemer 1979: 185). So, for Brecht, the notion of *gestus* as a deliberate re-functioning (*Unfunkionierung*) of the repetitive gesture enables it to become a critical intervention into the mimesis reflex, detaching it from its immediate context and demonstrating that 'in every sentence and every gesture there is [a] decision to be signified' and a political choice to be made (Brecht 2015: 62, 185). Dutt explains that this allows both the actor and the spectator 'to focus on the gaps between mimetic and gestural expressions' (2021: 524) and thereby begin to open up the gap between reality and representation otherwise foreclosed by the mimetic operation.

The prising open of this gap is central to both the aesthetic critique of representation and the possibility of making a political intervention into the social situation, which is thereby placed 'in quotation'. The quotation itself demonstrates 'that the action is intended to achieve a purpose in the world that the gesture, the agent of action, must use as a means to achieve that purpose' (Brecht 2015: 23). For the actor, then, acting politically means acting in a way that places acting in suspension, rendering it quotation, in order to prise open the space of an emergent *gestic* action to counter the hegemonic modes of theatricality and representation. Brecht sees quotation as a mode of interrupting the historical formation, for, first and foremost, as Benjamin explains, 'quoting a text implies interrupting its context' (1973: 19).

Acting as quotation requires the actor to adopt a critical position in relation to the action and their acting, producing a form of 'third-person' acting that enables the actor to hold both the text and their acting 'at a distance on stage and allowing its ventriloquism to designate itself' (Jameson 1998: 54). Nonetheless, this procedure is not entirely self-referential as it necessarily involves the citation of existing historical material – the gesture or text being 'quoted' that still appears within the space of the recognisable 'quotation' and continues to provide the 'substance of the quote' (Jameson 1998: 54) – even as this material is opened up to dialectical seeing. For the audience, the actor's performance 'interrupts the context into which it is inserted', producing a disjunctive experience that invites them to take a critical position on a dialectical image which 'counteracts the illusion' of the self-evidence of history (Benjamin, cited in Buck-Morss 1989: 67). The framing of acting as quotation, in this respect, not only enables the mimetic operation of theatre to be disrupted – so that, as Brecht contends, historical social reality can be demonstrated to be the result of contingent human action (praxis), and therefore capable of being transformed by praxis – but also creates the space to recognise that the specific bodies, voices, histories, and social identities of the performers themselves might interrupt the culturally constructed gestures and historical narratives they are ostensibly performing. Put simply, the performers' 'third-person' presence itself destabilises the mimetic closure of representation and draws the audience's attention to its citational operation.

Hamilton itself is a good case in point. The casting of actors of colour to play all the historical figures in the musical – representing their otherwise unmarked Whiteness by inverse association with the material presence of the non-White actors performing the work – breaks open the narrative of the foundation of America as an explicitly ideological formation. The actors' work – the work of acting – exposes the gap between presence and representation through the critical deployment of bodies, gestures, and voices, drawing attention to the history being performed as itself being a narrative construction. Their work in performance indexes the unacknowledged labour of the workers of colour who do not necessarily appear in the historical narrative as specific historical individuals such as Washington and Hamilton but whose presence (and exploitation) is nonetheless essential to the history being represented. While the actors appear to re-enact one of the foundational moments of American history, they do so by placing it in quotation through their voices and interrupting its context through their performative presence and embodied gesture. At the same time, the overt theatricality of the musical theatre form – its self-knowing artificiality – serves to reinforce the sense of the agency of the performers in deploying their specific voices, bodies, histories, and heritage to interrupt and destabilise the historical narrative they are themselves performing. The theatrical event allows the performers to hold the story at a distance on stage and thereby to show it as an imaginary construction, utilising ventriloquism, quotation, and citation to enable its deconstruction. In this way we see 'the migration of history into the work's very form' as theatre and recognise acting as a social as much as aesthetic labour (Jameson 1990: 187), precisely to the extent that it appears as a counteracting of the representation of history as a singular narrative and completed teleology. Acting politically, in this context, appears as a reopening of historical perspective and performative possibility by showing the constitutive absences structuring the social formation by virtue of their visible presence and overt theatricalisation.

'History has its eyes on you', *Hamilton* reminds us. Yet it also reminds us that the task of learning to see with 'the eye of history' is a theatrical challenge specifically, foregrounding how theatre constructs ways of seeing and being seen historically. Acting and spectating, with their focus on the framing of historically lived experience through the political codification of visibility and speech, remind us that 'we make history, and we make histories, because we are historical' (Ricoeur 2004: 284). In other words, acting reanimates the possibility of history being imagined, and practised, otherwise – precisely by resuscitating the political potential archived within it. By placing the historical figures being represented in quotation, the performers of *Hamilton* adopt a position in relation to the action, which enables the historical exclusions, omissions, and missed opportunities it contains to be made visible again and seen not simply as theatrical but as 'genuinely historical' (Benjamin, in Buck-Morss 1989: 249). In this repurposing of history as immanent potentiality, *Hamilton* suggests that theatre's performative historiography rests at least in part in the recovery of the remaindered possibilities covered over by the chance of history's violent unfolding. The song *History Has Its Eyes on You* itself stages a scene of Washington's own prehistory – the story of Washington before he became Washington mirroring Hamilton before he becomes Hamilton – which also, of course, at the same time reflects the history of the racial-capitalist imperial settlement before it is sedimented as 'History'. Accordingly, the protagonists are not the only ones who 'have no control who lives, who dies, who tells your story'. We are all subjects of history, because we are historical subjects. Whereas Washington and Hamilton's duet places them together but separately in the eye of history, appearing in the calm of the centre of the storm, other stories circulate around them, reverberating in the bodies and voices of the performers. 'History has its eyes on you', the song concludes. And by association, it also has its eyes on us, spectators but also social actors and the potential remakers of historical relations. In this respect, as Ricoeur tellingly suggests, 'the presumed meaning of history is no longer dependent on [the historian] but on the citizen who responds to the events of the past' (2004: 500) and seeks to determine redressive action and possible future direction.

The dialectical seeing opened up by the theatrical interplay of presence and representation creates space for the imaginative construction of what Ariella Azoulay calls 'potential history' (2019: 43). Drawing on Benjamin's conception of the dialectical image emerging in the 'flash' of the discontinuous experience of history and offering a mode of recovering its potential political alterity – the capacity for things to have been otherwise, and to be otherwise – Azoulay regards 'potential history' as offering 'a space wherein violence ought to be reversed' and 'different options that were eliminated are reactivated' in order to counter 'the imperial movement of progress' (2019: 43). Critically, this space is conceived theatrically as 'a form of being with others, both living and dead, across time, across the separation of the past from the present' in order to decolonise an intrinsically ideological conception of history as teleological and irreversible (2019: 43). For Azoulay, the space and time opened up by 'potential history' – a theatrical space and time, enabling the reanimation of dialectical seeing – serves to reconnect 'history and politics' as the ground of civic, social responsibility (2019: 43). She echoes Benjamin in suggesting that, far from being fixed, past actions can be recovered and resuscitated in order to trouble the narrative temporality of 'progress' and draw attention to the political tension between the lived experience of 'people's worldly active life' and the 'operative actions' of the 'imperial apparatus' that attempts to consign such struggles to the past (2019: 43). Benjamin's concern with the reanimation of the remaindered potentiality of historical materials (1978: 99), neatly recast by Azoulay as 'potential history', suggests that history remains the source of redressive future action: 'because the past has been a future it always retains the trace of the latter's power' (Düttmann 2002: 22).

Azoulay describes 'the practice of doing potential history' in explicitly Brechtian terms as 'rehearsing disengagement' (2019: 43). The principle of distancing (*Verfremdung*) is apparent in the strategies of defamiliarising and disrupting the ideological effects of imperialism's narrativisation and naturalisation of history as 'the motion of progress' that she suggests. These include: the *reiteration* of 'existing statements that were made obsolete by imperialism' (2019: 44); the *quotation* of texts performed or written under conditions of 'imperial violence'; and the *restaging* of 'moments of resistance to imperial power' regarded as failures or deemed futile in order to demonstrate their continued resonance and potential repurposing and reanimation (2019: 44). For Azoulay, 'rehearsals of disengagement' serve as creative investigations of performative historiography that aims to 'retrieve a world' in which the colonial-capitalist settlement 'was not yet accomplished' and 'could not be taken for granted' (2019: 44), thereby showing imperialism as a historical ideological formation, not simply a given historical condition. As rehearsals function by subjecting texts to a transformative process, opening up their incompletion to discover alternate meanings, contexts, and urtexts, the dynamic of restaging is itself directed to recovering 'modalities of protest, erased by imperial power' so that they might be re-functioned aesthetically and 'emerge again as competing valid options' (2019: 44). Rehearsals also imply the co-presence of performers whose embodied agency challenges and changes the direction of the text and its representational logic. The reiteration of gestures and detached quotation of texts thereby situates actors as the political as well as aesthetic subjects of the rehearsal process, crediting them with 'the assertion of the gesture in civil society ... as a form rooted in the materiality of bodily performance' (Dutt 2021: 519). Effectively, the formalisation of rehearsal discovery into repeated performance concretises the transition from ephemeral protest to practised resistance. Yet the key to potential history, for Azoulay, lies in the rejection of 'imperialism's conceptual apparatus altogether' and the avoidance of a 'temporality that asks us to seek new solutions for a better future' (2019: 44). It is therefore to hold open the space of rehearsal as a moment of temporal suspension and political refoundation.

This suggests that the practising of theatre might be usefully reconceived as continuous critical enquiry and creative investigation rather than simply a space for the composition of discrete works or performance outcomes. It implies the re-functioning of theatre as a site of learning and unlearning, as a mode of investigating ideas and positing possibilities, as a practice of generating and testing historical ways of seeing. Accordingly, for Brecht, the years spent in exile from 1933 to 1948 – without a theatre, without actors – proved a crucial opportunity to forge a performative approach to the rehearsal of disengagement and the practice of critical spectatorship as the ground of political action. During this period, Brecht developed a detailed method of observing, analysing, and archiving the materiality of everyday life, seeking to document the fabric of historically lived experience in his journals in order to construct a horizon of possibility for action and actors to come. His systematic recording of journalistic articles and propagandist image materials, explicated by Didi-Huberman in *The Eye of History*, works as a practice of assembly and quotation that attempts to unpick and prise open the 'mimesis of mimesis' of fascist theatricality and imperialist fantasy. As an exercise in curating potential history, Brecht attempts to invest in the absence of theatre to rehearse a theatre of material presence and political possibility – a theatre without theatres, designed to resist hegemonic theatricality. In the process, he effectively recasts the work of the actor and acting from the domain of representation (as a discrete function and skill set) to the space of presentation (as a political task and critical orientation). This means that the actors' work and training – their practising of rehearsal as an expanded cultural field – 'consists in acting in such a way' as aesthetic-political subjects that they are 'oriented towards knowledge' (Benjamin, cited in Didi-Huberman 2018: 54) and the production and circulation of distributed social critique. As Didi-Huberman puts it, 'in order to know we must take a position' (2018: 3); 'in order to know, we must know how to see' (2018: 24). Accordingly, the art of observation is positioned as central to acting as a process, and to the construction of the distance that is necessary for the actor to be able to show. Distancing (*Verfremdung*) is essential in pointing to the gap between the act of showing (presentation) and what is shown (representation), thereby enabling the production of a spectatorial dialectic of seeing. For Brecht, 'to distance is to show' (Didi-Huberman 2018: 58), which is why historicisation is not only a 'crucial technical device' in the actor's repertoire and training (2015: 140) but, as Roland Barthes has pointed out, 'a general exigency of thought' (1957: 98). The actor's production of embodied thought – manifested in gesture, voice, and ensemble interaction – necessitates their taking a position on the contemporary moment being observed, and altering the existing configuration of discourses, images, and relations in order to expose their ideological construction and political operation. Acting as distancing thereby operates as a rehearsal of disengagement that 'dismantles and reassembles history in order to show its political content' (Didi-Huberman 2018: 104) and recover its potentiality. It reframes acting as acting politically.

For Brecht, taking a position in relation to the action was the key to the actor's work in enabling the spectator to construct their own. By adopting a stance (*Haltung*) on the material investigated and presented, the actor facilitates a critical and political relation to the historical situation. This is why Brecht calls acting an 'art of historicization'. By breaking narrative continuity and creating disjunctive juxtapositions, the actor's work – the work of distancing – consists in knowing 'how to handle one's visual or narrative material like a montage of citations referring to real history' (Didi-Huberman 2018: 58) and being able to insert the materiality of their own – and the audience's – embodied, lived experience of contemporary history into the gaps created. As Didi-Huberman explains, 'to take a position is to desire, to demand something, to situate oneself in the present and to aim for a future' (2018: 3) – to go beyond the reality currently experienced by enabling its historicisation. The 'crucial technical device' of historicisation (Brecht 2015: 140) enables the actor's work to be refashioned neither as a merely representational practice nor the simple presentation of embodied presence, but as an active prising open of the gap between presence and representation. This, then, determines not only the political content but the formal organisation of the performance (Benjamin 1969: 148). For Brecht, taking a position or adopting a stance (*Haltung*) was the key to the actor learning to be able to hold open the eye of history and to historicise the contemporary. It enables the actor to rehearse disengagement from the action, opening up a space of disidentification through the work of aesthetic distancing. Rather than being indissociable from the role they embody or portray, the actor stands alongside the representation and opens up its gaps in order to demonstrate both their ideological construction and the need for a refoundation.

To this extent, acting politically produces an alternate image of the actor as contesting the frame and regime of representation through a practice of counteracting and de-representing what the actor otherwise appears to represent. Accordingly, Brecht saw the development of *Haltung* as core to the actor's work in training and rehearsal as well as being a mode of performance, creating a framework for them to investigate the reality of the representation's construction rather than subsuming themselves into the reality being represented. Fredric Jameson argues that this constitutes the core of the Brechtian intervention, developed as an underlying methodology of practice across all modes of his aesthetic thinking. Jameson contends that the rigorous deployment of the concept of *Haltung* suggests that 'there existed a Brechtian "stance" [*Haltung*] which was not only doctrine, narrative, or style, but all three simultaneously; and ought better to be called, with all due precautions, "method"' (1998: 132). This method is designed to systematically dismantle what Alain Badiou calls 'the intimate and necessary links joining the real to semblance, links resulting from the fact that semblance is the true situating principle of the real' (2007: 48). *Haltung* as method exposes this gap within the real and 'renders visible the brutal effects of the real's contingency' (Badiou 2007: 48). Taking a position is therefore not only an acting technique but a coherent critical-aesthetic method through which the actor, acting politically, is able to demonstrate that semblance (ideological, political, cultural) is not coextensive with the real, and that what is constituted as historical 'reality' operates as a political construction.

At the time of Brecht's exile, the practice of taking a position on contemporary history would have been experienced as an immediate political necessity. In the midst of an historical situation that showed, as Benjamin argued, 'that the state of emergency in which we live is not the exception but the rule', the demand to 'bring about a real state of emergency' that would acknowledge and accelerate 'the struggle against Fascism' was acute. For Benjamin, this required 'a concept of history that is in keeping with this insight' and the development of a lived cultural-political practice of dialectical seeing (1969: 257). In this context, the method of *Haltung* offered a framework for resisting totalitarian mimetic theatricality and countering its operation through the suspension of acting as a mimetic procedure altogether (Dutt 2021: 524). The task of the actor in rehearsing detachment and disengagement from their interpellation in the situation 'is not so much the development of actions as the representation of conditions' (Benjamin 1969: 150). By constructing a critical relation to the action, the actor seeks to reveal the historical conditions of the political situation and their own imbrication within it: 'he [sic] shows his [sic] subject by showing himself [sic], and he [sic] shows himself [sic] by showing his [sic] subject' (Benjamin 1969: 153). For Benjamin, it is the actor's adopting a position in relation to their role that enables the audience to 'adopt an attitude vis-à-vis the process' (1982: 266) – the aesthetic-political process of the rehearsal of disengagement and the performance of detachment – by which the conditions revealed to them show 'the dialectic at a standstill' (Benjamin 1973: 12). *Haltung* as aesthetic-political method is designed, then, not only as a mode of presentation and technical operation but the construction of a historical way of seeing the social that enables theatre to 'expose what is present' and thereby to historicise the contemporary (Benjamin 1982: 267).

While it is important to stress the precise historical conditions giving rise to Brecht's development of the methodology of *Haltung* as the actor's aesthetic-political responsibility for taking a position or 'adopting a stance' on the historical situation they occupy and that occupies them, it is equally crucial to note in concert with the knowledge of 'the tradition of the oppressed' within which Benjamin grounds his philosophy of history (1969: 257) that variations of the fascist-imperialist 'state of emergency' from which it emerged continue to be experienced as lived historical reality. In this context, it is worth recalling that the Brechtian practice of disassembly and reassembly of historical materials within a reimagined chronology – designed to demonstrate the ideological formations and deformations that constitute them – gravitates towards and 'swirls around an inaccessible knot of *real* – the eye of history, the eye of the hurricane' (Didi-Huberman 2018: 168). The methods developed in Brecht's exilic journals and anticipatory actor-training theory might therefore remain useful as a resource for making performance in times of crisis. Furthermore, tracing their reappearance in contemporary acting practices enables a timely re-examination and critical explication of the continuing significance of acting politically in the eye of contemporary history.

Anna Deavere Smith's virtuoso solo performance, *Notes from the Field* (2019), provides an exemplary investigation of these dynamics in the context of the racist colonial-capitalist formation of the US. *Notes from the Field* offers a compelling articulation and impassioned voicing of the experience of the current and continuing 'state of emergency' – the state of emergency of structural and systemic institutional and ideological racism drawn attention to by the Black Lives Matter social movement – from the perspective of people of colour who have lived and are living through it. This extraordinary documentary theatre work is the product of over 250 interviews conducted by Deavere Smith over a seven-year period of sustained research and inquiry into what she calls the 'school to prison pipeline' that subjectivates young Black men, in particular, through the racialised dynamics of educational exclusion, criminalisation, and incarceration. That the extended period of investigation is coextensive with the emergence of the Black Lives Matter movement enables the work to become interanimated by and interconnected with its social, historical, and political context. Consequently, it operates not only as a documentary theatre practice but as a persuasive document of contemporary history, tracing the continuities and convergences between the current moment of crisis and the historical experience of colonial-capitalist exploitation in the US. In drawing clear lines of connection between Black Lives Matter and the Civil Rights Movement, *Notes from the Field* outlines the contemporary social formation's continuation of the divisions, dispossessions, and injustices of segregation and slavery. The work consistently historicises the Black experience of exploitation, degradation, and confrontation within White social institutions as effects of the structural antagonism that continually reproduces racialised logics of othering and objectification as socially sanctioned violence.

As Achille Mbembe has explained, racist violence does not interrupt the smooth functioning of state democracy but is intrinsic to its operation, to the extent that 'democracy, the plantation, and colonialism are all part of the same historical matrix' (2019: 23). The tendency of modern democracies has been to contract out the 'originary violence' of this formation and locate it in exteriorised spaces such as 'the camp and the prison' in order to codify its alterity and constrain its latent capacity for re-emergence as social disruption, political protest, and potential revolution (Mbembe 2019: 27). Deavere Smith's account of the systematic reproduction of the 'school to prison pipeline' confirms the historical materiality of this 'radically stigmatized' space as internal to the US system of governmentality and essential to its biopolitical operation (2019: 34). It is worth recalling that biopower, according to Michel Foucault's explication of the term, refers to the myriad ways in which division is made between lives that matter and lives that are deemed not to matter and the mechanisms through which the boundary between them is perpetually reinscribed. Importantly, this is not conceived as merely a repressive regime but the active production of lived relations constructed by the operation of power within the field of living beings – 'of which it takes control and in which it invests itself' (Mbembe 2019: 71). For Foucault, the ensemble of capillary activities that constitute biopower as the interpenetration of biological life and political apparatuses enables the subdivision, categorisation, and hierarchisation of both forms of life and groups of population, which, as Mbembe notes, he 'refers to using the seemingly familiar term, "racism"' (2019: 71). Yet for Mbembe, the terms biopower and biopolitics are insufficient to account for the historical divisions determining the differentiation between 'those who must live and those who must die' (2019: 71), not least because they do not recognise the 'contemporary forms of subjugation of life to the power of death' which have been optimised by colonial capitalism to create 'new and unique forms of social existence in which vast populations are subjected to living conditions which confer upon them the status of the living dead' (2019: 92). The terms he proposes instead, necropower and necropolitics, are intended to demonstrate how in the 'displaced topographies of cruelty (the plantation and the colony)' (2019: 92) and their contiguous successor spaces (the prison and the ghetto), there exists an inversion of the priority of life and death, 'as if life was merely death's medium' (2019: 38). Political sovereignty is here designated as 'the capacity to define who matters and who does not' and the power to determine 'who is *disposable* and who is not' (2019: 80). Disposability is in this respect the necropolitical effect of the colonial-capitalist world order, whose epistemic violence produces racialised groups of human beings as material to be worn out, used up, and discarded, as having lives that are presumed not to matter outside of their economic function and social instrumentality (Vergès 2021: 76).

Francois Vergès argues that the persistence of the social formations resulting from the colonial-capitalist deformation continues to structure the contemporary field and to produce 'a politics of disposable life' (2021: 16) – of gendered and racialised injustice and structural violence – even 'when the regimes associated with these phenomena have disappeared' (2021: 15). Deavere Smith's *Notes from the Field* makes a similar argument through constructing diagonal connections between the contemporary situation and the inheritance of the necropolitical logics of slavery and segregation. The performance works in the mode of verbatim theatre, with Deavere Smith performing the words spoken by her interviewees as recorded and acting all eighteen 'characters' in the show herself. In her actorly vocalisation of their words, Deavere Smith does not attempt to simply *imitate* her subjects' tone and mode of speech but rather to enable their voices to resonate through her own virtuosic acting. To the extent that this mode of performing inevitably deploys a degree of mimicry-mimesis in order to embody another voice and presence, it does so in order to open up acting practice to difference and distance and to re-function it into a formal theatrical *gestus*, 'in which an actor's body is trained to encode historical resistance' (Diamond 1997: 39). Deavere Smith's expert performance augments her subjects' experiential accounts theatrically, ensuring her acting functions to reverberate their acts of resistance by asserting their significance as a gesture of resistance in civil society. In performing their words and consolidating their gestures, Deavere Smith *takes a position* alongside her research subjects as 'characters', allying her acting to their historical actions and visibly adopting a political stance on the material co-produced and seemingly co-performed with them. The effect is an extraordinary reverberation of the contemporary political-aesthetic potentiality of the methodology of *Haltung*.

The section of *Notes from the Field* re-examining 'The Death of Freddie Gray' at the hands of the Baltimore police in 2015 exemplifies Deavere Smith's approach to putting aesthetic practice to the service of critical enquiry and the documentation of historical resistance. The section begins with a short video clip of Freddie Gray forcibly being taken into custody, taken on his mobile phone and offered as eyewitness footage of the arrest by a young videographer, Kevin Moore. This was the last moment Freddie Gray was seen before his arrival at the police station with three cracked vertebrae, a crushed larynx, and an effectively severed spine. Deavere Smith portrays Kevin Moore on stage as a theatrically doubled figure framed by both his constant speaking and continually being filmed. Her verbal delivery is animated and intense, stretching vocal dexterity to capture the shape and texture of his west Baltimore accent and authenticate the embodied evidence he presents. The otherwise slightly incongruous playing of a young man by a middle-aged woman wearing an oversized hoodie with the caption 'Copwatch' printed on it is framed by her always talking directly to a camera operated by an on-stage videographer who follows her movement around the stage. The video is itself relayed live, creating the impression that Kevin's verbal testimony is itself a reflection and redoubling of the testimony of the visual image. In keeping with this, the character notes that his role in the scene of Freddie Gray's arrest was to ensure the capture and circulation of images because 'somebody has to *see* this' (Deavere Smith 2019: 14) – history has to have its eyes on it. It is precisely this operation of refocusing the attention of the eyes of history by reframing and restaging the dialectical images generated within its very eye that Deavere Smith's performance purposefully enacts by standing alongside them. 'It's a movement', Kevin/Anna says; 'and it ain't gonna stop' (Deavere Smith 2019: 14).

The performance itself is directed towards supporting this movement. Arresting the frenetic motion of the stage, Deavere Smith sits calmly at its centre and shifts the tone of the narration. 'Eye contact': it sounds like a heading but functions performatively as a caption, condensing and containing the 'whole story' narrated (Deavere Smith 2019: 14). At the moment she says it, the screens framing the stage flash up a triptych of images from a street mural showing the face of Freddie Gray with figures from the Civil Rights Movement, past and present, moving in solidarity behind him. In the foreground a young Black man – conceivably Kevin – is walking along the street in front of the wall on which it is painted. Staring out from the image, the eyes of Freddie Gray make contact with the audience and hold us in their gaze, even as the figure in the street resolutely looks away. 'Eye contact', we're told, is the 'whole story' of the murder; because Freddie Gray made eye contact with the police officers involved, they maintained they had 'probable cause' to apprehend him and 'do whatever' thereafter, as Kevin puts it. It acts as the moment of interpellation into a racialised matrix of criminalisation. 'Just a glance. The eye contact thing … it's like a trigger. That's all it takes here in Baltimore, just a glance' (Deavere Smith 2019: 14). Here on stage, the moment of eye contact is reopened and repositioned as a theatrical relation of seeing and being called upon to see. Here, its gesture of resistance is reanimated and redirected so that the theatre might act as a moment of recognition and re-subjectivation in the eye of history. In this space the act of making the image makes apparent the fact that 'images demonstrate: they rise up, and sometimes make us rise up too' (Didi-Huberman 2018: xxii).

The impression of the performance being interanimated by social protest and political uprising is confirmed in the next scene, which presents Deavere Smith embodying the figure of Allen Bullock, an eighteen-year-old Black Lives Matter protester facing charges of rioting in the wake of the murder of Freddie Gray. The scene opens with projected images of the windscreens of a Baltimore city police car being smashed by a man wearing baggy jeans and a pair of Timberland boots. This man is Allen Bullock. Anna Deavere Smith sits in a large, leather, high-backed chair in front of the screens also wearing a pair of Timberland boots. Her vocal embodiment of the character's testimony – explicitly framed as such, being recorded in a swanky lawyer's office – is even more remarkable for being delivered seated, its containment and localisation enabling the audience to see the work of the actor in a politically focused way as taking a position in relation to the action, character, and narration. The actor's micro-gestures, described in the stage directions as 'hand gestures of the time, probably specific to Baltimore' (Deavere Smith 2019: 18), are distinctive and yet denotive of a lived historical experience that extends beyond the representational depiction of a single character towards the presentation of a connection linking 'the gesturing bodies to resistance' (Dutt 2021: 519). The narration itself focuses on Bullock's resistance to being interpellated by the police into the role he is presumed to occupy as a young Black man. He refuses to 'even look the police way' – that is, to compliantly look down or look away – and either ignores them completely or takes the decision to 'look back' enigmatically without being drawn into the kind of confected scene of confrontation a direct 'hard and straight' stare would imply (Deavere Smith 2019: 18). Here, in the doubled space of Deavere Smith's performance, the act of looking the police in the eye appears as a mode of facing down the eye of the storm, defiantly looking back at the eye of history. Bullock disengages from his role in the drama of policing – 'runnin' from them' being outlined as his preferred strategy, because they 'don't like it when you run from 'em' (Deavere Smith 2019: 20) – and in so doing offers an awareness of his own acting in this scenario and acknowledgement that the beatings that follow act to reincorporate him into it, re-interpellating him as a racialised subject within this scene of subjection. The character's double-consciousness of his own acting within and against a lived historical racial formation is redoubled by Deavere Smith's adopting a position of active distance from and non-participation in the apparatus of dramatic representation as likewise operating as a mode of subjectification and normalisation. She appears as the actor within the theatrical mise-en-scène, but at the same time her acting demonstrably points to both the character's contestation of the role of racialised 'actor' in a colonial regime of representation and her own rehearsal of disengagement from its structures.

In this context the deployment of the methodology of *Haltung* works to rearticulate and recalibrate a constantly interrupted yet continually repeated gesture of defiance – 'looking ba[ck]' – (Deavere Smith 2019: 18) – so as to re-accentuate it as a calculated act of resistance. By opening up the gap between the actor and the character, Deavere Smith foregrounds the political potential of the gap between the social actor's mode of appearing within a racialised regime of representation and their resistance to this ideological construction. The gap between presence and representation essential to the theatrical operation of *Haltung* is thereby used to redouble the Black subject's resistance to their subjectification and objectification within a racialised frame of seeing and appearing. Deavere Smith's construction of an actorly *gestus* to stand alongside the historical image of Allen Bullock draws attention to his narration's exposure of interpellation as a form of violence while at the same time directly implicating representation itself in the 'epistemic violence' of racism. As Achille Mbembe explains, 'in racist contexts, "to represent" is the same thing as "to disfigure"', manifesting theatre's participation in 'a play of shadows' that constructs the other as a 'phobic object … first discovered through the gaze' (2019: 138–139) and repeated endlessly through the representational injunction to 'relive the traumatic scene … being reproduced in the reality of the present' (2019: 170). In *Notes from the Field* this 'theatre of appearing' (Mbembe 2019: 170) is disrupted by the political agency of the actor in perpetually opening up the space between the subject and its representation – a space that the racialised subject of representation continually observes as 'the spectacle of his [sic] own duplication' and experiences as 'the capacity to become separate from himself [sic] and objectify himself [sic] while at the same time becoming a subject' (Mbembe 2014: 98). In occupying that space theatrically as a site of political dissonance and aesthetic dissemblance, Deavere Smith's rehearsal of disengagement from the structures of racialised representation enables a dislocation of 'the fictive double referenced by the shadow' (Mbembe 2014: 99) and the construction of a potential history of self-presentation.

Notes from the Field stages some of the overwhelming weight of evidence testifying to the historically lived experience of racism and racial violence in America, and to the role of representation and image construction in perpetuating as well as contesting that history. Anna Deavere Smith's extraordinary performance grounds these testimonies in the materiality of theatre as a space of seeing and hearing, constructing an aesthetic-political apparatus of visualisation and a Brechtian method of critical distancing to frame the historicity of the images and stories presented. Her acting, conceived as acting politically, is designed to enable her interviewees' words to resonate through being interanimated by her voice, enabling them to find a place on stage as at once specific, doubled, and multiplied. The intersecting and overlapping of multiple voices through a central, single performer works dramaturgically to produce a compelling theatrical argument demonstrating the interconnectedness of the lived historical experience of racism and its reproduction within the racialised regime of representation governing the social formation. Composed through montage, the argument works through and across the singularity of the accounts assembled, breaking down any residual sense of isolation or anomaly to build a sense of resonance and reverberation that accumulates to enable a presentation of the historical situation in its specificity. The form of the work itself, opening up the gaps between actor and character and exposing the tension between presence and representation, augments its production of a dialectic of showing and seeing that seeks to historicise the contemporary and demonstrate its theatricality.

Yet, perhaps the theatrical construction of potential history requires as much investment in imaginative possibility as it does the rehearsal of critical and political disengagement. Deavere Smith appears to focus on such a transformative leap of faith in her performative re-enactment of Pastor Bryant's funeral oration for Freddie Gray. She focuses on connecting two moments of resistance form the earlier episodes that are linked together in this extraordinary speech. Firstly, looking out to the audience, she recalls that 'in a subtlety of revolutionary stance', Freddie Gray decided to do 'something that black men were trained – taught – know *not* to do. He looked the police in the eye' (Deavere Smith 2019: 25). Standing in the eye of history, he decided to look history in the eye. And so, secondly, 'he stopped running' (Deavere Smith 2019: 25), refusing to conform to the role ascribed to him historically. He decided to take a stand, to adopt a stance, and to refuse the role of the shadow by appearing in the eyes of history not as a doubled, contorted figure but as a political actor, acting politically. In Pastor Bryant's eulogy, this moment of re-subjectivation is likened to the resurrection of Lazarus, with Jesus lifting his hands up to touch the casket. These words, this action – explicitly referencing the Black Lives Matter gesture of 'hands up, don't shoot' – elevate the gesture so it acts as consciously political *gestus*. The epideictic mode of the funeral speech here becomes performative, as the audience are implicated in the instruction to 'Get up' (Deavere Smith 2019: 27). Although initially framed as Jesus's statement to Lazarus, the phrase is repeated and reanimated in the contemporary context as a historical injunction to re-subjectivate Black cultural identity and to mobilise it politically. As *gestus*, its repetition interrupts the normative state of the situation – depicted by Pastor Bryant as a state of resigned acceptance that must be redirected as political resistance – to make an intervention 'in the break of colonial-capitalist time' (Schneider 2018: 306), which historicises its operation and deconstructs its organisation. Deavere Smith's re-enactment of his address underscores this point directly, making theatre 'in the break' between act and actor, event and representation, and opening the space between them as a site of performative intervention and potential history. 'This is not the time for us to have no respect for our legacy and for history! … He said, "I need you to get up". … get yourself up! … get up! … Get your black self up and *change* this city!' (Deavere Smith 2019: 27). The Pastor's words have the young man in the casket rise up to form an image – an image forged in the eye of history, an image enacting an historical uprising. The image rises up and it invites us to rise up too. 'No justice!' it silently exclaims; 'No peace!' the audience vocally replies. 'No justice!' in the eyes of history; 'No peace!' in history's eye. 'No justice!'; 'No peace!' all repeat.

References

Adorno, Theodor, and Max Horkheimer. 1979. *Dialectic of Enlightenment*, translated by J. Cumming. London: Verso.
Azoulay, Ariella. 2019. *Potential History: Unlearning Imperialism*. London: Verso.
Badiou, Alain. 2007. *The Century*, translated by A. Toscano, Cambridge: Polity.
Bala, Sruti. 2018. *The Gesture of Participatory Art*. Manchester: Manchester University Press.
Barthes, Roland. 1957 (2002). 'Brecht, Marx and History.' In *Ouevres complètes, Volume 1, 1942–1961*. Paris: Le Seuil
Benjamin, Walter. 1969. *Illuminations: Essays and Reflections*, translated by H. Zohn. New York: Schocken Books.
Benjamin, Walter. 1973. *Understanding Brecht*, translated by A. Bostock. London: Verso.
Benjamin, Walter. 1978. *Reflections*, translated by E. Jephcot. New York: Schocken Books.

Benjamin, Walter. 1982. 'The Author as Producer.' In *The Essential Frankfurt School Reader*, edited by A. Arato and E. Gebharddt, pp. 254–269. New York: Continuum.
Brecht, Bertolt. 2015. *Brecht on Theatre: The Development of an Aesthetic*, edited and translated by John Willett. London: Bloomsbury Methuen Drama.
Buck-Morss, Susan. 1989. *The Dialectics of Seeing: Walter Benjamin and the Arcades Project*. Cambridge, MA: MIT Press.
Deavere Smith, Anna. 2019. *Notes from the Field*. New York: Random House.
Diamond, Elin. 1997. *Unmaking Mimesis: Essays on Feminism and Theatre*. London: Routledge.
Didi-Huberman, Georges. 2018. *The Eye of History: When Images Take Positions*, translated by S. B. Lillis. Cambridge, MA: MIT Press.
Dutt, Bishnupriya. 2021. 'Performing Gestures at Protests and Other Sites.' In *The Oxford Handbook of Politics and Performance*, edited by S. Rai, M. Gluhovic, S. Jestrovic, and M. Saward, pp. 517–530. Oxford: Oxford University Press.
Düttmann, Alexander García. 2002. *The Memory of Thought: An Essay on Heidegger and Adorno*, translated by N. Walker. London and New York: Continuum.
Jameson, Fredric. 1990. *Late Marxism: Adorno, or, the Persistence of the Dialectic*. London: Verso.
Jameson, Fredric. 1998. *Brecht and Method*. London: Verso.
Mbembe, Achille. 2014. 'Requiem for the Slave.' In *The Divine Comedy: Heaven, Hell and Purgatory Revisited by Contemporary African Artists*, pp. 96–105. Berlin: MMK.
Mbembe, Achille. 2019. *Necro-Politics*, translated by S. Corcoran. Durham, NC, and London: Duke University Press.
Puchner, Martin. 2002. *Stage Fright: Modernism, Anti-Theatricality and Drama*. Baltimore, MD: Johns Hopkins University Press.
Ricoeur, Paul. 2004. *Memory, History, Forgetting*, translated by K. Blamey and D. Pellauer. Chicago, IL: University of Chicago Press.
Schneider, Rebecca. 2018. 'That the Past May Yet Have Another Future: Gesture in the Times of Hands Up.' *Theatre Journal* 70(3): 285–306.
Vergès, Françoise. 2021. *A Decolonial Feminism*, translated by A. J. Bohrer. London: Pluto.

6

Theatre of the streets: Of working-class strikes, protests, and democratisation of life

Bishnupriya Dutt

Moloyashree Hashmi, in a discussion at the time of pandemic, exclaims, 'If we don't do theatre in these times of crisis, if we cannot reach our audience or be where the present struggle is – what the hell are we doing?'[1] Her position highlights the urgency of the pandemic situation and its aftermath, and addresses the plight of millions of people in India, who she refers to as 'our audience' and who, in the wake of the lockdown – vulnerable, anxious, and in distress as part of an unprecedented reverse migration – tried to find their way home. Subsequently, they returned and, in response to a two-day strike on 26 and 27 November 2020, showed a remarkable consciousness and mobilisation and consequently brought live theatre back to the streets. Hashmi and her team with face shields were once again out on the streets performing their street plays. The strikes and the protest against the draconian laws passed by the Indian Parliament in September 2020 aimed to drastically reform the economy and to open up markets in industrial and agrarian sectors to private players, and brought back protests of an unprecedented scale as well as street theatre as a strategic mediation.[2]

This chapter intends to associate the present protests with the heralding of neoliberal reforms since the 1980s when movements and street theatre actively engaged with these issues and, in many ways, proved effective in stalling specific laws. Two such significant moments in street theatre history were in 1988 when Jana Natya Manch (Janam) performed its *Chakkajam (Strike)*, and in 1995 when Anamika Haksar directed the play *Gaon Se Sehar Tak (From the Village to the City)*. Both these plays were micropractices that dealt with the issues at hand but also used innovative and experimental idioms and forms and, most importantly, were effective in the field and realised their objectives. I look at the significance of the sites, which in popular parlance is referred to as the street theatre practice, implicated in collaborating with Left politics, political parties, and trade unions. The reference to the 'street' indicates its locations, namely industrial areas, factory premises, labour or union offices, slums, bustees, and places outside the gentrified neighbourhoods. Simon Charlesworth, in his *A Phenomenology of a Working Class Experience*, reads such locations as the mnemonics of such practices:

> Obviously, the lives of different class groups are situated in different spaces and take place through different sites. In the sites that groups use, they assimilate the space through their own dispositional schemes and they thus establish conditions in which their own locations will have value; that is, participants will collude to establish criteria of appreciation favourable to their own products. (2004: 220)

The reference to the 'working class', however, is more in line with Alain Badiou's challenge of how to read the Marxist category of the proletariat in today's context as 'universal' and 'generic' rather than 'particular' and not substitute a mere collection of identities for the saturated generic identity of the working class and 'find the political determination that integrates the identities, the principles of which are beyond identity' (Badiou, quoted in Dean 2018: 254). Jodi Dean, in response, prefers to characterise the generic subject of communism and, thus, the working class as 'people engaged in struggle' but cautions against other ideologies, such as populism and democracy, who also speak in the name of the people. She elaborates that the '"people" thus has a powerful legacy as a name for that political subject which strives for emancipatory egalitarianism' (Dean 2018: 255).

Street theatre in this context has been and continues to be the most radical genre of political theatre in India, with a long history of engagement and efficacy at the grassroots level of its practice. This chapter does not aim to look back with nostalgia at a bygone practice but highlights its significance in the current scenario when the basic premises of the culture of labour are being eroded and weakened. Its continued existence stands out against the growing Right-wing populism and majoritarian religious cultures, which is devastating India. I explore this double bind, which flags the need for such practices and the threats that it faces in its very existence, and try to understand the historical and contemporary paradigm in this context.

Vijay Prasad, in a recent series of lectures on the communist movement in India (Prasad 2020–2021), draws the historical legacy of the current protests to a long genealogy of workers and peasant movements originating in the robust anti-colonial nationalist popular struggle under the leadership of the communists and the socialists. He regards this history as a long and continuous people's struggle in colonial and postcolonial times, which compelled the state and governments to implement principles of socialist measures and a protectionist economy for the sake of the people who barely manage to survive. Since liberalisation in the 1980s and the unfolding of neoliberal economic policies, which is the purview of this particular chapter, the state and vested interests have had to deploy a long line of negotiations and manipulations, and, as the current scenario illustrates, unleash violence to ensure shifts towards the unbridled run of neoliberal capitalism. These are heavily contested sites, and the resistance is remarkable and has been the greatest opposition the Narendra Modi government has faced since its return with an overwhelming majority to the Indian Parliament in 2019. They are organised as strong sites of resistance for survival against a ruthless capitalist system and to safeguard the minimum condition of a dignified life to live.

Simon Charlesworth traces how the destruction of industries and corrosive cleansing for the laissez-faire economy systematically weakened 'the culture of labour that had been at the heart of the ethics of the people, a way of life of their form and respect of care' (2004: 49). What theatre does in close collaboration with the trade unions and the Communist Parties, then, is that it fulfils the needs of social mediation through cultural interactions, which would relate their participation in civil society, initiating a political process that enables them to defend themselves as subjects of injustices. The vibrant public domain that emerges performs the crucial role of combining the civic and community lives of large sections of the people who otherwise are increasingly excluded from civil society. Dean regards the struggle led by the Communist Parties as one that encompasses more than only demands for 'shorter working days, safer working conditions and higher wages. They saw these struggles as the political process of the subject of Communism' (Dean 2018: 257).

The inherent characteristics of the street theatre practice can then be read as what Janelle Reinelt and Shirin Rai in the introduction to their book, *The Grammar of Politics and Performance*, categorise as a fall back to a key form of political theatre of the twentieth century where 'clear strategies of intervention into contemporary political struggles through various theatre works … sought to create and represent a mass political subject, a capitalism resistant sociality' that 'appealed to its audiences in terms of collective address' (Rai and Reinelt 2015: 8). This also includes those works that could be easily subjected to critique for their propagandist nature, and Rai and Reinelt indicate how new performance scholarship has preferred to reject such practices on grounds of being replete with messages '(let alone didactics), settled meanings, direct political polemics – all of these seen as being alternately crude and heavy handed or insulting and oppressive for audiences who need emancipation from discursive engagement perceived as harangue' (2015: 8). In this regard I would like to argue that a new field has opened up at protest sites with innovative performance activism emerging from the site itself, engaging with the issues at hand and improvising rather than pre-empting the responses (Dutt 2015, 2017, 2021; Roy 2016; Arora 2019a, 2019b, 2020). Moreover, it is also important to retrieve older genres of protest theatre practices that have a longer dedicated engagement with the sites themselves, which are not, as Dragan Todorovic describes in this volume, hyper-sites of protests without leaders or formulated programmes. With their durational and iterative work in the field, neglecting such practices deprives the rich field of the existing political theatre of one of its most significant practices.

Janam and *Chakkajam*: a successful strike and theatre active in mobilisation

In 1988 *Chakkajam*, the play devised by Janam for the eight-day industrial strike in Delhi, was a defining moment for Janam, particularly due to the growing proximity between the Communist Party of India (Marxist); its affiliated trade union, CITU; and Janam. The group was also reconstituting itself through workshops in colleges and universities, and younger members from Left students' organisations were now joining Janam. With a number of its senior and founder members leaving, Safdar Hashmi was leading the group into a new path, and *Chakkajam* was devised and performed as part of the mobilisation leading to the eight-day strike called by the Left trade unions in November 1988. From its inception as a group of idealistic young theatre-makers who wanted to perform in the streets with inexpensive material ensuring mobility to visit varied sites and exclusively for the common people, Hashmi, in an interview in 1988, stated, 'We just wanted to make revolutionary theatre which would help Trade Union Movement, inspire the workers and the union' (Hashmi 2013: 31).

The strike had been called by the Left trade unions in response to the Industrial Relations Bill, which aimed to inaugurate neoliberal economic conditions pertaining to industries and reform labour codes. A clause in the bill particularly targeted the trade unions by empowering local governments to deal with them and make preventive arrests, as well as abolish labour tribunals that sorted out labour disputes at the local level (Deshpande 2020: 43–44). The call for strike included, besides the withdrawal of the bill, the raising of minimum wages from Rs 562 to Rs 1,050 ($6.81 to $12) and a dearness allowance of Rs 2 as per the rise in the price index of the country. It also demanded the reduction of working hours from sixteen to twelve hours (Deshpande 2020: 182). Included in the larger list of demands were also improvement of living conditions, creating permanent jobs for permanent work, and demanding abolition of the contractual system. These were typical, legitimate demands by trade unions. The 1988 strike was preceded by growing labour unrest with successful twenty-four hours strikes in 1986 and a seventy-two-hour strike in 1987. Delhi, never a strong industrial hub, however, had five important textile mills (Delhi Cloth Mill Ltd (DCM), DCM Silk, Swatantra Bharat Mills (SBM), Ajudhia Textile Mills, and Birla Mills). Half of the working class in Delhi worked in these mills, while the other half worked in the medium-scale (250 in 1988, including flour mills) and small-scale (thirty) industries. The workers were mostly migrant workers, and Delhi had a less organised trade union movement. Therefore, 1988 was seen as an important watershed moment for trade union strategies. In the wake of neoliberalism, the textile mills were already downsizing their labour force, and other arbitrary anti-worker measures were coming up systematically.

Janam's participation focused on mobilisations prior to the strikes with a new play, *Chakkajam*, literally meaning a strike that was devised for the moment. The play-making process came up through workshops and improvisation. Safdar Hashmi came to the rehearsals with short sketches and scenes that were finalised, added, or dropped in discussion and collaboration.[3]

In the opening scene of *Chakkajam*, a young couple singing a love song, in a parody of Hindi film renderings, with human bodies posing as trees, was a new way of talking about the strike. As the police stopped the troupe from any overt political propaganda in the play, they decide instead to do a love story, and the opening song ensures a joyous beginning with its audience

Figure 6.1 *Chakkajam*, 21 November 1988, at the Artists Rally in support of the seven-day industrial strike (photo by Safdar Hashmi)

laughing and enjoying the scene. The love song is followed by a strict interrogation of Jogi, the prospective groom, by the girl; Aasho's parents refuse their daughter permission to marry Jogi, who, as a worker in the factory, does not earn enough to make ends meet. Low salaries clearly show that a decent living is impossible, and the living conditions are deplorable and full of squalor. Aasho's father urges Jogi to join the upcoming strike and union activities if he is to survive, marry Aasho, and live a decent human existence. The mention of joining the union and participating in the strike alerts the policeman who comes wielding a stick, and the actors hurriedly agree to change the scene to express their admiration for the prime minister who had recently given a speech eulogising liberalisation and urging workers to sacrifice their rights and lives for the good of the country (read the capitalists). In the prime minister's scene, two actors with two local *gamchas* (towels used by common people) hold the ends to create a frame, which is a television. A masked man appears in the frame (on TV) and reads out the speech with intonations and cynicism in its rereading. Everyone knows who the masked man is; he needs no introduction. Both the prime minister and the policeman symbolise autocratic power. One episode makes a similar parody of the policeman, who starts dreaming of the accolades he will receive from his superiors and maybe even a promotion as he has managed to control the actors and turn them pro-establishment. While he thinks of rising higher, the actors form steps with their bodies, and he physically climbs the bodies to go up one step at a time to the highest level, but the actors, once he is up, move away, and he falls unceremoniously to the ground. Such subversive scenes and episodes create the scene breakers.

One of the main aspects of Janam's pro-trade union stance is that it was always in a self-critical mode, challenged with the question of the women workers and the apathetic stance of trade unions, even the Left ones, to the women's question. A number of working-class, women-oriented plays such as *Aartanad* (*Cry of Anguish*, 1995) and *Aurat* (*Woman*, 1979) brought out these issues very strongly, and in the final episode of *Chakkajam*, the women's issue is flagged. The women trying to enter the factories become part of the warring groups, those who want them to go to work and to join the strike. The women are ready to join the trade union movement if their specific demands are taken into consideration. Moloyashree Hashmi, as Parvati, is one such woman who comes in angry with a child in her arm as she has been forbidden entry by the management as she is with the child. In the ensuing commotion we learn that she has nowhere to leave her child behind, and she needs the wages and work.

Moloyashree Hashmi, in the context of Janam's street theatre style, also emphasises that these interceptions come up in most of their plays, and they refuse to shy away from the contradictory positions male comrades hold in relation to their woman counterparts. Hashmi's acting in these spaces and in these roles is powerful and embodies the struggle as well as the vulnerability of the women workers who find it difficult to get their voices heard. Known for her powerful roles, she holds strong postures and gestures. As she says, 'we do not characterise or try to be the protagonist in any way but we are in the character and hold these postures, particularly the torso and other bodily stances establish our presence and what we are playing' (Hashmi 2021). Lines are then delivered and projected clearly across to the audiences in the crowded streets. There is intense labour involved in getting seen and straining the vocal cords to be heard above the street noises as a large number of people are gathered around.

The first performance of *Chakkajam* happened in front of the Labour Commission Office on Mall Road and continued with many shows leading up to and during the evenings of the eight-day strike. They performed twenty-nine times in sixteen days (2–21 November 1988). On the eve of the strike, a large procession was organised to make the citizens of Delhi aware of the forthcoming strike and its demands. *Chakkajam* was performed during the procession, followed by meetings and interactions with people (the middle classes) who generally keep away from working-class areas or their struggles.

Deshpande gives a vivid description of the strike days and picketing by the workers. Workers waited outside the gates where the owners' henchmen, protected by the police, stood, and the trade unions and activists standing in between the two groups shielded them from the gates while shouting slogans for the strike. Within a couple of hours, it was clear that the workers were not going to enter the gates, and the trade union and other political activists would merge with the workers who moved into an ever-expanding space of human bodies. Safdar Hashmi himself was there with the trade union leaders as a committed party activist. The eight-day strike was an enormous success, work came to a stop, and at the end of it wages were increased from Rs 562 to Rs 750 with 85 p Dearness Allowance (DA) in lieu of the rise in the price index (Deshpande 2020: 207).

Anamika Haksar and *Gaon Se Sehar Tak*: raising social and economic consciousness

Even though they were somewhat apparent in the late 1980s in India, the inauguration of neoliberal reforms took on a more ominous and dangerous shape by the mid-1990s. In this context and against the backdrop of exploitative industrial practices that were recruiting workers on unfair contracts, one of the most innovative directors of her times, Anamika Haksar, came forward to explore street theatre practices. Graduating from the Russian

Institute of Theatre Arts (GITIS) in the USSR, she cites a socialist ethos ingrained in her training that propelled her in 1995 to find means to connect with ordinary people (Haskar 2021). She worked with the trade union in a steel utensil manufacturing industry in Vazirpur, located in the older parts of Delhi in Chandni Chowk. Two horrifying incidents of murder had fanned discontent among the workers and created a volatile atmosphere. Feeling ill-equipped to create theatre in these circumstances, Haksar started by compiling economic, social, and personal data of the workers in the steel factories over a period of three months in association with the trade union. Haksar duly realised that the workers were unaware of the unfair terms of their unemployment and contracts. However, what was also important for a relevant theatrical performance to emerge was the knowledge of their backgrounds and where they belonged. She came to know that most of the workers were migrants who came from villages and were landless labourers compelled to come to the city to work for survival and livelihood amid the poverty and starvation that awaited their families. In the social strata, they also belonged to the lowest caste and class groups, and she remembers how one worker had confessed that it was only in the city that no one asked him his caste identity, and it did not affect interactions.

Haksar's training in the USSR provided her with a model of how to evolve the text and performance to create innovative strategies and artistic interventions. Her protagonist, a migrant worker, comes to the city to seek work. The city scenes are presented stylistically on cardboard, and they pass by him till he arrives at the factory, where he seeks employment in the most miserable possible terms. The factory, as depicted in the play, is an improvised space represented by a backdrop painted in the Russian constructivist style of revolutionary art with wheels, screws, and various parts of the machine. The factory owner arrives with a mask and headgear made out of steel scraps, a grotesque figure reminiscent of the demons of the folk performances and familiar to the workers who came from the village, laughing in a typical style and performing menacing gestures as an incarnation of the devil. He also drinks a red liquid from a bottle through a straw, symbolising that he is sipping the blood of the workers. Haksar talks of the constant exploitation, oppression, and frequent bootlegging, where the workers would be thrown out at the drop of a hat. Other symbols of authority were the policeman who would be carrying a huge eye mounted on cardboard and the local minister who would be carrying a grotesque face mounted like the eye on a stick. In one episode Haksar describes how the workers would perform not only the burden of their labour but also the diseases which afflicted them and left marks on their bodies. The men would often develop tuberculosis or lung diseases or toxicity working with metal and furnaces, while the women, restricted from using toilet facilities, developed kidney and gall bladder problems.

Haksar talks about how before the performance, the actors would walk around with posters depicting these scenes in cartoons, followed by fifty laughing children on their trail. These scenes in the factory and related issues would be highlighted through short sketches intercepted by memories of home – small, perfectly etched models of huts, bullock carts, trees, and nature with poems, songs, and music – which created a contrasting scenic scape as a relief but did not romanticise it. These were, as Haksar points out, culled out of the memories and given a metaphoric theatrical expression from their earlier conversations during the survey. A parallel trajectory would also show the women waiting in the villages, eager for the men to come back with money and other small luxuries, but what returned was, in this instance, a lifeless and dead body. The play, however, ended on a positive note, with the five actors creating choreography with sticks, collaborative and collective bodies, energised and gaining momentum and emerging rebellious. It did not require slogans or direct propaganda; it was a mise-en-scène of life, the oppression, and opening up ways to struggle and fight and resist and dissent.

Initially, Haksar worked with two of her student actors from the National School of Drama, Vijay Kumar and Ritu Talwar, but for a longer run took a radical step when she recruited local actors, mostly those in the union, and slowly initiated five local activist actors into the roles and the play. Working late into the night when they could be free from work, they prepared all the roles – the mother Munia, the workers, the owners, the policeman – each actor playing multiple roles. Haksar also notes how they brought their own ideas to the play. The worker coming into the city now wore bells on his feet as he got near the city. His feet dance in anticipation and in the hope of a new life and possibly less hardship. The role of the mother was taken up by one of the woman activists, Sarita Sahi, who, in Haksar's account, comes forward to find a new source of communication and agency.

The play had about forty shows reaching out to about 20,000 to 40,000 audiences in the locality but was also taken to other places and cities after its first run. Performed in front of the factories during lunchtimes, the sons of the owners tried to disperse or threaten the actors. Haksar also talks about how after many shows, the workers/audiences would come up wanting to join the party, and Haksar says that directing them to the trade unions was also a way to understand the role theatre can play and even its limitations. She emphasises the point that the play was to raise consciousness regarding working-class rights and issues, such as minimum wages and hours, and labour protection laws that existed. It was meant to mobilise the workers and would or would not lead to direct resistance, but it imparted to them a sense of their own identities. It reflected on them, through embodied gestures, an understanding of oneself as a human being who finds his/her dignity in political consciousness.

Haksar did not do much street theatre thereafter, but *Gaon Se Sehar Tak* subsequently had a life of its own; not only was the play taken to many other sites, but it was also readapted by the participants to focus on other issues that were emerging. In time the basic framework was retained but changed completely from the original version. Haksar continued to be in touch with many of the people she had come to know, developed lifelong friendships, and later, in her film *Ghode ko Jalebi Khilane Le Ja Riya Hoon* (*Taking the Horse to Eat Jalebis*, 2018), cast them in their own roles as they developed into the characters, to play themselves or people they knew very closely.

Critical debates and social citizenship

From the effective protest campaigns and mobilisations around strikes, such as in 1988, or subsequently against aggressive neoliberal reforms and laws, to the present situation, things have changed considerably. While the long-term engagement and reiterative nature are critical factors, and these performance practices have carved out for themselves strategic spaces on the streets, and among those who inhabit these spaces, at the same time, the street theatre activists are aware of the systematic weakening of the premises on which they operate as India hurtles towards its neoliberal destiny amid inequality, poverty, and the growing division in society. The working-class consciousness and a culture of labour rooted in trade unions and street theatre contrast with the cultural practices gaining ground, identified as growing Right-wing populist cultural practices with distinct communal overtones. As wide-scale unemployment, exploitative practices, and contractual and temporary migrant workforces are replacing the older economic relations, the working-class cultural practices, which I have tried to focus attention on and historicise, are under threat. This crisis situation is also what brought Janam and other activists to the streets in support of the workers' strike and the ensuing farmers' protests in the face of the new labour codes.

Caution in celebrating working-class culture and consciousness has always been prevalent in academia, resulting in a vibrant debate that is important to cite in this context to understand the tension between the two modes of cultural consciousness. Dipesh Chakrabarty's influential work *Rethinking Working Class History, Bengal 1890–1940* argued that it would be a fallacy to perceive the working classes in India through universal categories of class formations. In retrospect, Chakrabarty argued, the Indian working classes never developed a working-class consciousness, which a working-class cultural practice would address, as it was subsumed in pre-capitalist relationships and a culture characterised by the absence of notions of 'citizenship', 'individualism', and 'equality' before the law. In this context, according to him, 'the master slave dialectics reproduce itself far more often than the phenomenon of the rule of the citizen' (Chakrabarty 2000: xiii). Chakrabarty's working class and their cultural preferences are, rather, invested in an overwhelming socio-religious belief system, which is guided by primordial and community loyalties so that the working class culture would be more inclined towards communal riots or religio-cultural celebrations than any engagement with issues of class struggle and transformative cultural practices based on social or economic critical rationality, provoking debates pertaining to a modern political consciousness (Chakrabarty 2000). For the working class to even choose to watch and respond to street theatre requires a degree of class consciousness, an understanding of the issues at hand, and an impetus towards being and acting (Dean 2018: 26). This, in turn, entails prioritising the harsh economic conditions of their lives over a socio-religious belief system that tends to eclipse the socio-economic reality.

Following culturalist formulations, such as that of Chakrabarty's, a vibrant debate ensued in academia in the 1990s. These formulations were countered by historians adhering to a more Marxist and economistic interpretation by citing rich empirical research on working-class life and protests in the colonial period to make links with contemporary forms, presenting a visionary future for Left politics (Chakrabarty and Das Gupta 2019: 18). This was undoubtedly what provided a lifeline to the street theatre genre, but what is also evident is the setback the working-class movement is facing in recent times, particularly with the neoliberal measures taken for reforming the economy. Nair, in the introduction to Chakrabarty's book, writes: 'As a political subject on whom many revolutionary hopes were mistakenly pinned, as a unified economic category, whose foundational exclusions were exposed; as a site of a more ambiguous "consciousness" than class alone – a fatal preoccupation with working-class consciousness may have led to a certain blindness' (2019: 22).

From the theatre practice perspective, what is critical is to acknowledge the growing polarisation and tensions between these two modes of working-class practices, those being mobilised around communal lines and those that are trying to bring back critical issues around capitalist exploitation and neo-liberalisation, and urging for a claim to the democratisation of life, indicating egalitarianism and citizenship as a legitimate demand. In this context how do we revert back to the sites and the workers with all the present complications without falling back into either the older celebratory notion of agitprop, which inspires transformative politics, or looking at the

Right-wing mobilisation on the grounds of religious identities and assuming that populism is the order of the day with no other alternatives or options?

In view of the examples and case studies I have laid out, I would like to offer an alternative perspective, which does not celebrate a working-class culture but takes into consideration the changing scape of labour practices and hence a more grassroots reorientation of the theatre practices. Partha Chatterjee offers a paradigm shift in recent times in India, where he argues that there is a growing divide between civil society and middle-class citizens who inhabit civil society, enjoying the rights of a modern citizen, as compared to what he describes as a political society, which includes large sections of the rural population and the urban poor. If the workers or audiences that street theatre has been addressing belong to Chatterjee's political society, they also have the formal status of citizens, but they do not relate to the organs of the state in the same way that the middle classes do. 'Those in political society make their claims on government, and in turn are governed not within the framework of stable constitutionally defined rights and laws, but rather through temporary, contextual and unstable arrangements arrived at through direct political negotiations', writes Chatterjee (2011: 219). The structural exclusion of political society can be attributed to the lack of social and material conditions and the compromise on an egalitarian promise.

These political strategic negotiations of the political society, however, do require visibility and mediations. Nivedita Menon argues that 'if we accept this understanding, then it is clear that the struggle to reclaim and produce meaning will have to be waged in this uncomfortable realm, that of the political society' (2011: 217). This would entail, she says, 'to unhitch Chatterjee's notion of "political society" from its link in his argument to the welfare function of government and relocate it as the realm of struggles to produce an alternate common sense – alternative that is, to the common sense of civil society' (2011: 217). Chatterjee offers, in his article 'Theatre and the Publics of Democracy', a proposition – an important mediating and strategic role for the theatre operating in the political society – that combines an economical theatre with a pedagogic purpose, but also is popular. His recommendations echo the role which street theatre has been performing for many decades now (Chatterjee 2016).

According to Chatterjee, the fact

> that theatre performance can address only small numbers at a time means that it has the opportunity to deal not with large heterogeneous publics but with small and relatively homogenous groups. There is no pressure here to spread the net wide to catch a disparate collection of views and interests and thus to simplify the dramatic representation of a complex social or political reality.
> (2016: 213)

The major characteristics which Chatterjee specifies are the genre characteristics of what we have been defining as street theatre through its practices and examples. These are variable texts, addressing particular segments of the publics – the same set of actors addressing different sets of publics, who respond differently, focusing on concerns that 'resonate in the immediacy of a specific encounter between the actors and audiences' (Chatterjee 2016: 215). The pertinent features are those which can be seen as locationality and the cumulative results of many encounters advocating issues of social and political reality. All these can be easily applied to the street theatre experiences.

The complex social and political reality, which Chatterjee elucidates as an ideal form of democratic theatrical strategy in spaces beyond civil society, is where the practices of street theatre have evolved, developed, and reinvented themselves constantly. If these social realities are related to the site and the abysmal poverty all around, they also reflect the fragile structures of inequalities. The subjects of the plays remain situated at the various intersections of exclusion and discrimination ingrained in the social structures of violence, and so do the audiences they reach out to. It is this vulnerability that makes its appearance in the plays through the women protagonists, who at these intersections of various identities possibly suffer the most. Through these plays and performance activism, we see how such subordinations are structured within a system of capitalist production (work), social reproduction (home), and motherhood.

In this context I have highlighted the role of Parvati in *Chakkajam* as the recurring woman protagonist who symbolises the plight of the women at the intersections of class and other identities such as caste and religion. In an astute move the play refuses closure merely on account of an impending strike and its outcome. Similarly, Haksar, through cultural activities, created a local leader in the activist Sarita Sahi. As she started handing over organisational and even artistic responsibilities to the activists, Sarita Sahi came forward to take up those jobs. As a marginal entity hitherto in the trade union activities, particularly in times of strikes and growing discontent, the theatre activities brought her to the foreground in sites where otherwise her presence would not have been visible. What Parvati in the play highlighted, Sahi underlined these issues in real circumstances.

The presence of the women in situ of a strike, both as imagined characters but also in reality, is a provocation, which, while highlighting the need for political action, such as demands for minimum wages or workers' rights, also shows that there is no simple resolution. This is rather a long struggle for the democratisation of daily life and for egalitarian possibilities. Elaine Aston refers to such theatrical strategy as encouraging an act of rebellion – it allows an affective mode of popular engagement – which reanimates 'political source of desire' – in an ongoing mode. It allows one to point towards the failure of addressing structural differences of a socio-economic system, which then prevents any vestiges of a democratization but also as a stoic symbolic presence to 'claim spaces to remember'. (2020: 90)

I would argue that such theatrical strategy breaks the way the working class is perceived within a binary of hopelessness and escapism or as a populist majoritarian cultural practice. It even offers an alternative possibility of democratisation through reclaiming participation in civil society. This democratisation is undoubtedly based on what Niraja Gopal Jayal would read as investing in social citizenship, economic, and social rights rather than legal or civic rights, and encourages us to explore how structural inequalities ultimately make citizenship a mirage. She reads it as a historical lacuna between '"substantive democracy" and formal procedural democracy. Substantive democracy is considerably more demanding than procedural democracy, rendering the former always a "work in progress"' (Jayal 2013: 5).

The structural inequalities, reflected in the inequitable material distribution of wealth, are worsening with despicable economic conditions and the falling GDP, and with the pandemic added to this, the situation has reached a crisis point. Street theatre made a comeback at the end of 2020 and the beginning of 2021, 'connecting the past struggles for dignity and economic justice in the workplace to present abject conditions experienced by poorly paid workers' (Aston 2020: 109), as symbolised by the women workers, echoing a continuity of maladies that have plagued issues of social citizenship in the past and continue to do so in the present.

Moloyashree Hashmi and two other actors in their new play *Ansune Afsane* (*Unheard Stories*, 2019) sit in the middle of the street reading out letters written by workers (based on actual correspondences) to the management or the government on various issues, including recent terminations, violation of contracts, and also how the minimum conditions of social rights are being compromised. Hashmi, in a change of role, plays a loyal worker who is grateful to the management for giving her job back after a miscarriage. Her younger colleague, who is pregnant, urges her to join union activities to demand rights, including those of maternity leave, but Hashmi refrains. Hashmi is apathetic to the struggle for rights under an organised movement until she sees the body of a dead worker, who could have been the son she had lost in the miscarriage.

Similarly, in another play, *Kis Aur Ho Tum* (*Which Side Are You on?*, 2020), Hashmi comes on as the spirited elderly 'piece worker'[4] negotiating employment terms with the contractor to secure better rates and some rights that could stop the exploitation of the women workers of the unorganised sectors, who work from home and belong to the most precarious and exploited in the workers' hierarchies. The women embody the gesture of two types of inequalities, the material on the one hand and the cultural and symbolic on the other. Inciting the need to address these issues in an affective mode, they, at the same time, urge one another to convert affect into a political desire.

Conclusion

Street theatre in Delhi has a long history and legacy of activist practice, and I highlight its ongoing role since the 1980s when neoliberal economic measures started unravelling. The history of performance activism in these sites counters the perception of the lacuna in labour cultures in India and also offers strong resistance to the new mass cultural celebrations in communal lines. It has offered critical interventions and ideological steer towards the radical potentiality of egalitarianism and social citizenship based on the equitable distribution of wealth. It is the theatre which continues to respond to injustices and exploitations at economic, social, and political levels and is driven by a concern for the suffering of others rather than the subject-self (Tomlin 2019). What is unique in this context is that the street theatre responds to its working-class subjects by what Jodi Dean, in the context of Left cultural practices, would regard as 'recognising it in the crowd and thereby making the crowd something more than it is. It gives the crowd a history, letting its egalitarian moment endure in the subjective process of people's struggle' (2018: 259). This is exactly what the street theatre interventions of Janam and Haksar intended. They recognise in the working class, in the crowds, not only subjects but also co-creators with whom a dialogue is possible to create a different political and theatre history and practice. In this context the street theatre becomes a site of radical political desire and imagination in contrast to the populist cultural sites where the masses are instrumentalised for Right-wing agendas. In contrast, Left-wing agendas, as I have tried to lay out through these examples, aims at a radical political practice which extends the 'collective desire for collectivity after the crowds go home' (Dean 2018: 261).

Notes

1 Moloyashree Hashmi's quote was part of a conversation held (online) on 12 June 2020 on 'Theatre and the Political in the Age of the Global Pandemic' as part of the project Cultures of the Left. www.youtube.com/watch?v=KxJLiigb6s8
2 The laws abolished protective measures for workers and farmers and are framed within typical neoliberal language and a sledgehammer approach. 2.5 million

workers went on strike on 26 November 2020, and farmers marched in protest to the capital, mainly from Punjab and Haryana, and set up camps in key borders such as Singur, Tikri, and Ghaziabad. The farmers' protests still continue six months on.
3 Sudhanva Deshpande, in *Halla Bol: The Life and Death of Safdar Hashmi* (2020), has provided a day-to-day account of how the play was devised and how each episode came up. I have, however, conducted detailed interviews of Moloyashree Hashmi and Ayesha Kidwai, two of the actresses in the play, on 21 January and 2 January 2021 respectively (online).
4 Piece workers in the informal sectors are those paid by each piece they deliver.

References

Arora, Swati. 2019a. 'Walking at Midnight: Women and Danger on Delhi's Streets.' *Journal of Public Pedagogies* 4: 171–176.
Arora, Swati. 2019b. 'Be a Little Careful: Women, Violence and Performance in India.' *New Theatre Quarterly* 35(1): 3–18.
Arora, Swati. 2020. 'Walk in India and South Africa: Notes towards a Decolonial and Transnational Feminist Politics.' *South African Theatre Journal* 32(2): 14–33.
Aston, Elaine. 2020. *Restaging Feminisms*. London: Palgrave Macmillan.
Chakrabarty, Dipesh. 2000. *Rethinking Working Class History in Bengal, 1890–1940*. Princeton, NJ: Princeton University Press.
Chakrabarty, Dipesh, and Ranajit Das Gupta. 2019. *Some Aspects of the Labour History of Bengal in the Nineteenth Century: Two Views*. Delhi: Oxford University Press.
Charlesworth, Simon J. 2004. *A Phenomenology of Working Class Experience*. Cambridge: Cambridge University Press.
Chatterjee, Partha. 2011. *Lineages of Political Society*. Delhi: Permanent Black.
Chatterjee, Partha. 2016. 'Theatre and the Publics of Democracy: Between Melodrama and Rational Realism.' *Theatre Research International* 41(3): 202–217.
Dean, Jodi. 2018. *Crowds and Party*. London: Verso.
Deshpande, Sudhanva. 2020. *Halla Bol: The Life and Death of Safdar Hashmi*. Delhi: Leftword.
Dutt, Bishnupriya. 2015. 'Performing Resistance with Maya Rao: Trauma and Protest in India.' *Contemporary Theatre Review* 25(3): 371–386.
Dutt, Bishnupriya. 2017. 'Protesting Violence: Feminist Performance Activism in Contemporary India.' In *Performance, Feminism and Affect in Neo-Liberal Times*, edited by E. Diamond, D. Varnay, and C. Amich, pp. 105–116. London: Palgrave Macmillan.
Dutt, Bishnupriya. 2021. 'Performing Gestures at Protest and Other Sites.' In *The Oxford Handbook of Politics and Performance*, edited by S. Rai, M. Gluhovic, S. Jestrovic, and M. Saward. Oxford: Oxford University Press.
Hashmi, Moloyashree. 2021. Online interview, 12 January.
Hashmi, Safdar. 2013. 'The People Gave Us So Much Energy.' Interview by Eugene van Erven. In *Theatre of the Streets: The Jana Natya Manch Experience*, edited by S. Deshpande, pp. 18–65. Delhi: Janam.
Haskar, Anamika. 2021. Online interview, 19 January.

Jayal, Niraja Gopal. 2013. *Citizenship and Its Discontents*. Delhi: Permanent Black.
Kidwai, Ayesha. 2021. Online interview, 2 January.
Menon, Nivedita. 2011. *Recovering Subversion: Feminist Politics beyond the Law*. Delhi: Permanent Black.
Nair, Janaki. 2019. 'Introduction.' In *Some Aspects of the Labour History of Bengal in the Nineteenth Century: Two Views*, by Dipesh Chakrabarty and Ranajit Das Gupta, pp. 16–24. Delhi: Oxford University Press.
Prasad, Vijay. 2021. 'A Short Course on Indian Communism (1920–1947).' Tricontinental Institute, October 2020–January 2021. www.youtube.com/watch?v=eGQ7feqYrJo&feature=youtu.be. Accessed on 24 February 2024.
Rai, Shirin M., and Janelle Reinelt. 2015. *The Grammar of Politics and Performance*. London: Routledge.
Roy, Anupama. 2016. *Citizenship in India*. Delhi: Oxford University Press.
Tomlin, Liz. 2019. *Political Dramaturgies and Theatre Spectatorship: Provocations for Change*. London: Methuen.

7

The Cheviot and its legacies: Dramaturgies of the Left in Scottish theatre

Trish Reid

In the autumn of 2015 a major revival at Dundee Rep Theatre of John McGrath's (1935–2002) and 7:84 Scotland's celebrated socialist history play *The Cheviot, the Stag and the Black, Black Oil* (1973; hereafter *The Cheviot*) was rapturously reviewed by the Scottish press. After a successful run in Dundee, the production toured Scotland the following year to equally positive reviews. A further tour, co-produced with the National Theatre of Scotland (NTS) and Live Theatre Newcastle and scheduled for 2019 into 2020, was cut short only as a result of the COVID-19 pandemic. As well as applauding the vitality of Joe Douglas's direction and the energy and skills of the ensemble cast, critics found time both to affirm the legendary status of the play and also to stress its continuing political relevance for Scottish audiences. In her five-star *Scotsman* review, Joyce McMillan was effusive and described *The Cheviot* as 'arguably the single most important show in the whole history of Scottish theatre' and its content as 'almost frighteningly relevant today' (McMillan 2015). Neil Cooper, writing in *The Herald*, similarly characterised it as 'one of the defining plays of twentieth century Scottish theatre' and 'a vital statement on the world we live in now' (Cooper 2015). The return of *The Cheviot* to Scottish stages after a long hiatus was cause for widespread celebration, not least because, despite its status as a seminal Scottish production – it received an unusual amount of exposure through the original tour, a televised version for the BBC's *Play Today* in 1974, and the publication of the text by Methuen – *The Cheviot* has been seldom revived. Indeed, apart from Douglas's production, the only major restaging was by 7:84's musical offshoot *Wildcat* at the Edinburgh Fringe in 1991.

In this chapter I do not so much wish to question the continuing relevance of *The Cheviot* for Scottish audiences as to suggest that the criteria against which its relevance is being judged have shifted substantially in the almost half-century since the original 7:84 Scotland production. As Janet Wolff has noted, the value of analysing the 'determinants and mediators of cultural production is not to prove that they are always operative in the same way and with the same force' but rather to shed light on 'the variety of factors which come into play with more or less efficacy at different times' (1981: 140). Two key and related factors ensured the play's renewed relevance, I want to argue. First, the pernicious effects of neoliberal capitalism – especially since the financial crash of 2008 – that have been widely critiqued and to which the play now appears to speak directly. Second, the ascendancy in the years since the original production of a form of civic Scottish nationalism that does not, as Ben Jackson notes, 'primarily demand independence for Scotland in order to defend a threatened ancestral culture' but instead emphasises 'that independence is the most effective way to promote the agenda of the left in a neoliberal era' (2002: 2). In 1998, summarising the various campaigns for a devolved Scottish Parliament that had come to fruition in a positive referendum result a year earlier, Lindsay Paterson observed that 'at its most rational, the debate has been about good and effective government, how best to manage the affairs of Scotland, and more widely, the UK and Europe' (1998: 2). He also suggested, however, that devolution would never have gained traction had it simply been about good government, concluding that 'the emotional fuel on all sides has come from some version of politicised national identity' (1998: 4). This 'emotional fuel', he argued, was drawn largely from a 'radical current' on the Left, which 'gained its sustenance, not from the Labour movement, but from a wholesale shift towards nationalism in Scottish intellectual culture' (1998: 76–77). My intention is to lay the groundwork for my argument by locating *The Cheviot* within this developing intellectual culture. By way of context, however, and because it will be helpful to readers unfamiliar with McGrath and his work, I want to begin by providing a précis of McGrath's career, followed by a summary account of 7:84's place in Scottish theatrical traditions of the Left. I will then consider the significance of 'history' in the Scottish theatre tradition and in Scottish culture more broadly before comparing the Dundee Rep revival with the original production of McGrath's play.

A theatre of the people

Celebrated for his lifelong commitment to a consciously Left-wing and populist theatre, John McGrath was among the most influential and inspirational British theatre-makers of the late twentieth century. Born into a family of Irish Catholic descent in Merseyside, he completed two years of national service before gaining a scholarship to study English at St John's College, Oxford. There he met his future wife and artistic collaborator, the Scottish actor Elizabeth MacLennan, and was part of an outstanding group of theatre- and film-makers that included Giles Havergal, Alan Bennett, Ken Loach, and Ariane Mnouchkine. Between 1960 and 1965 McGrath wrote and directed for television at the BBC, most notably creating the long-running police show *Z Cars* with Troy Kennedy Martin in 1962. Thereafter, inspired by the oppositional politics of the late 1960s, and especially events in Paris in 1968, he renewed his commitment to making working-class theatre for working-class audiences. Importantly for McGrath, the ambition to create such theatre raised questions of form as well as content. He remained disdainful of the revolutionary pretensions of realist theatre of the kind championed at the Royal Court in the 1960s, describing it as 'the elaboration of a theatrical technique for turning authentic working-class experience into satisfying thrills for the bourgeoise' (1981: 11).

McGrath's commitment to the popular audience was evidenced in 1971 by his founding, with MacLennan and her brother David, of the 7:84 Theatre Company. Its name 'derived from a statistic published in *The Economist* in 1966, indicating that 7 per cent of the population of Great Britain owned 84 per cent of the capital wealth' (DiCenzo 1996: 83). In 1973 7:84 split into English and Scottish branches. Thereafter, McGrath scored his greatest critical successes in Scotland, most famously with *The Cheviot*, which was later televised in 1974 as part of the BBC *Play Today* series and consequently made accessible to a larger audience. McGrath outlined 7:84's new approach in a set of lectures at Cambridge in 1979, which were published as *A Good Night Out: Popular Theatre, Audience, Class and Form* (1981). Subsequently, his ideas became influential, particularly for fringe and Left-wing theatre-makers. Like Dario Fo in Italy and Joan Littlewood in England, McGrath drew on popular performance modes, acknowledging their long traditions of irreverence and critique, but he also utlised them purposefully as a set of conventions to re-enliven the practice of epic theatre. Gramscian notions of the dynamic potential of popular traditions, the role of the organic intellectual, and, most importantly, in the context of *The Cheviot*, the tension between peripheral and dominant cultures coalesce in McGrath's work which consciously draws on popular culture but reinscribes it as part of a political project. As Janelle Reinelt notes, McGrath's theatre 'constructs and is constructed by Brecht's conception of the poplar' insofar as it draws on popular and folk forms – in this case popular British forms – but also in the way it conceptualises and addresses its audience (1994: 177). In *A Good Night Out*, McGrath reasserts his belief in the existence of a 'working-class audience for theatre in Britain which makes demands, and which has values, which are different from those enshrined in our idealized middle-class audience' (1981: 4). His unflinching commitment to bringing work to this audience, which he argues 'defines itself locally rather than nationally', and to wilfully eschew the constituency of the bourgeois theatre and its stages, are among his most significant achievements (1981: 32). While acknowledging the value and influence of Brecht's example, especially in promoting formal experimentation, McGrath has reservations about certain aspects of his practice. In particular, he struggles with the dynamics of a pedagogic theatre, which he sees as hostile to the working-class audience: 'Pedagogics, after all, is the art of passing *down* information and judgements, the art of the superior to the inferior' (1981: 40). On the other hand, as Reinelt notes, McGrath 'praises Brecht for being willing to put out information in a direct and sometimes complicated fashion, assuming that the audience will comprehend it' (1994: 180).

In the Scottish context, *The Cheviot* exists within a long tradition of political theatre of which McGrath was a student and in which he consciously located his own work. As a result of this focus, 7:84's work in recovering key plays of the first half of the twentieth century for new audiences actively contributed to the construction and consolidation of a visible tradition of Left-wing populist theatre in Scotland. This activity reached a high point in the company's 1982 Clydebuilt Season, which was staged in venues across Glasgow and which included revivals of George Munro's *Gold in his Boots* (1947), Joe Corrie's *In Time o' Strife* (1927), Ewan MacColl's *Johnny Noble* (1945), and, most famously, a revised version of Ena Lamont Stewart's *Men Should Weep* (1947) directed by Giles Havergal at the Glasgow Citizens'. This last production established Stewart's play as a Scottish classic and also triggered renewed interest in Glasgow Unity Theatre – the company that had originally commissioned and produced it and that is now considered one of the most important companies in the history of Scottish theatre. The effort to revive interest in the plays consisted not only in the productions themselves but, as Adrienne Scullion observes, 'the publication of a number of core plays, printed in volumes that included other primary sources such as contemporary reviews, interviews, and photographs' (2002: 216). This material not only facilitated greater critical engagement with the plays and their contexts, but its collection also helped jump-start the newly established Scottish Theatre Archive at the University of Glasgow. Thereafter, as Scullion notes, scholarly engagement with it 'helped shape a critical orthodoxy within Scottish theatre studies that prefers a history of working class and broadly naturalistic drama and theatre' (2002: 215–216). In what amounts to an acknowledgement of their canonical status, both *Men Should Weep* and *In Time o' Strife* were revived in major productions by the NTS in 2011 and 2014, respectively. The NTS production of Corrie's play, which focuses in a realist mode on the struggles of a Fife mining community during the General Strike of 1926 and was written to raise money for the strike fund, was later performed in the chamber of the Scottish Parliament. Such an outcome would doubtless have satisfied McGrath, who argued for their continuing relevance. 'These pieces', he wrote, 'have been ignored; they've been cut out of the theatrical history – it seemed to me that this was completely wrong, that this is the way the working class loses its history, its self-awareness; it loses, if you like, a cultural richness' (2002: 135). Finally, with *The Cheviot*, 7:84 Scotland also modelled a touring practice that was to have a significant impact on where theatre took place in contemporary Scotland and who was considered its legitimate audience. The use of community centres, social clubs, and village halls – initially across the Highlands but later throughout the Lowlands as well – established touring as both a viable prospect and also an obligation for Scottish companies. In this way, as Linda Mackenney notes, 7:84 revived a practice developed by Left-wing companies in the first half of the twentieth century: 'Joe Corrie's Fife Miners Players, who toured village concert halls, cinemas and music-hall theatres in the 1920s [and] Glasgow Unity who toured throughout Scotland in the 1940s' (1996: 66).

In 1996 McGrath also updated Sir David Lyndsay's satirical morality play *Ane Satyre of the Thrie Estaitis* (1554) for *Wildcat* at the Edinburgh International Festival, adding a fourth estate, the 'Meeja' (media) and the arch-villain Lord Merde, an Australian international media tycoon. *Thrie Estaitis* is among the oldest surviving Scottish play-texts, and in it we first encounter the playful and vivid combining of popular forms with the political intention that McGrath was to draw on in his own work: it shifts freely between performance styles and genres, combining elements of farce, biting satire, didacticism, and high-moral seriousness. McGrath's *Satire of the Four Estates* (1996) serves to remind audiences and historians, then, that a tradition of political playwrighting that engaged directly with the political issues of its day in the presence of large and socially diverse audiences was more than four hundred years old.

In spite of his support for the plays produced by Left-wing companies in the twentieth century, McGrath eschewed realism in his own practice, preferring the distinctive mix of epic and popular influences found in *Thrie Estaitis*. *The Cheviot* is exemplary in this regard. Its chronological scope is broad, covering two hundred years of Highland history from the infamous Clearances in the eighteenth century to the present day. The theme of profit before people is a constant throughout the piece, which is structured in three sections broadly in alignment with the play's title. The first recounts the brutal forced eviction of crofters from their ancestral land to make way for Cheviot sheep, the farming of which offered the prospect of lucrative incomes to landowners. McGrath is clear-eyed in the latter part of this first section about the way in which displaced Highlanders were culpable in advancing the interests of imperialist expansion abroad, where native peoples like the Highlanders before them found themselves 'defeated, hunted', and 'treated like scum of the earth, their culture torn out with slow deliberation and their land no longer their own' (2015: 114). *The Cheviot*'s second section deals with a different invasion in the form of Romantic nineteenth-century tourism, which both fetishised and 'othered' the Highland landscape and its remaining people while appropriating and reshaping it for hunting, shooting, and fishing. The most emblematic of these new estates was Balmoral, which was purchased by Queen Victoria and Prince Albert in 1852. The processes of depopulation in the previous century had, of course, paved the way for the refiguring of the Highlands as an empty wilderness, a refiguring that underpinned the new tourism and continued to do so in the following century. McGrath uses statistics to drive this point home: 'In 1755 the population of the seven crofting counties was more than 20 per cent of the population of Scotland ... in 1851 it was 13 per cent ... yesterday it was 3 per cent' (2015: 134).

McGrath's third and final section – the Black, Black Oil – brings the play to its 1973 present day and the exploitation of the oil fields discovered in the North Sea in the 1960s, off the coast of Aberdeen. It shows how profits were siphoned off to and by large, mostly American-controlled oil companies, and the Scottish landscape was scarred by the building of refineries while control of revenues, extraction, and distribution remained outside Scotland. 'In fact', as Graeme MacDonald notes in his commentary in his student edition of the text, 'the control – and squandering of North Sea oil remains one of the most controversial issues in modern British politics' (2015: 55). The televised version of *The Cheviot* included testimony from working-class Aberdonians, who were struggling to pay rent as a result of inflation in the local economy. In summary, then, the first two sections of *The Cheviot* detail a history of the repeated displacement of indigenous Highlanders, while the final contemporary section urges the audience to apply the lessons of that history in resisting a new invasion and further displacement by oil companies and their interests.

Performing histories

While the anti-capitalist politics of its creators are evident throughout, formally, *The Cheviot* is unusual in comparison with other Scottish historical dramas of the period, such as Stewart Conn's *The Burning* (1971), Bill Bryden's *Willie Rough* (1972), and Hector MacMillan's *The Rising* (1973), which tended to favour conventional plotting and character development. The 1970s saw a resurgence in the Scottish history play and an interest in Scottish history more generally, which accompanied a rise in nationalist sentiment. 'History', it should be stressed, has long had a problematic and exaggerated significance in Scottish culture. A quick glance, as David McCrone observes, 'at the "Scottish" shelves in any major bookshop reveals that much of Scotland seems to be "over", for they are weighed down with accounts of the country's past' (2001: 129). For centuries, key figures and events in the nation's past have been circulated, distorted, sentimentalised, and mythologised in a process of representational overload that has, according to some critics, effectively replaced a meaningful focus on the present. This fixation on figures such as Mary Queen of Scots, Bonnie Prince Charlie, and William Wallace contributed to a profound pessimism among twentieth-century Scottish intellectuals, and subsequently, a consensus of sorts emerged about the roots of the Scots' predilection for highly selective and sentimentalised accounts of their own history. Since the Treaty of Union in 1707, the argument goes, Scotland has lacked real political agency and has turned instead to over-inscribed historical narratives for a sense of cultural identity. Scottish culture has become distorted and stunted in the process. The most influential and powerful expression of this line of thinking is Tom Nairn's *The Break-Up of Britain* (1977) in which he argues that the 'oddity of the Union' had 'posed grave cultural and psychological problems in Scotland – problems recognisable ... through a characteristic series of sub-national deformities, or neuroses' (1977: 118). Nairn is especially scathing about sentimentalised and sanitised representation of Scottish life – particularly rural life – that exist at some remove from the harsh realities of urban Scotland. He is also suspicious of popular forms that he sees as escapist. Nairn famously labels these tropes 'the vast tartan monster' (1977: 162). Continually producing fantasy versions of Scotland and Scottishness, he contends, the monster leaves little room for progressive representations of the nation.

With the benefit of hindsight, Nairn's arguments appear overly pessimistic. McGrath's work in *The Cheviot* and elsewhere demonstrates that popular forms can be crucial, integral, and beneficial to progressive dramaturgies. Complex and innovative, McGrath's play utilises the oral performance traditions of the ceilidh – a celebratory Gaelic form of entertainment involving song, dance, and storytelling – that it enriches with tropes such as the double-act and the satirical sketch drawn from popular commercial forms including music hall, variety, and pantomime. A hallmark of his approach is the combination of recognisable commercial songs with new satirical lyrics and traditional Gaelic folk songs, which are mostly delivered with sincerity and in the mode of lament. As Ian Brown and Sìm Innes have argued, this first dramaturgical strategy involves 'the ironic and subversive use of tunes to encourage alternative readings of both the music and the politics' that underwrite them (2015: 218). McGrath also borrows elements from the armoury of agitprop, including a portable pop-up set designed by the artist and playwright John Byrne that is now on permanent display at the Victoria and Albert Museum in Dundee, the inclusion of factual information delivered in direct address, and representations of real historical figures. All of this is organised in short scenes, with actors playing multiple roles.

In his important study *Performing Histories* (2000), Freddie Rokem usefully described actors who nightly re-enact past events as 'hyper-historians', who 'serve as a connecting link between the historical past and the "fictional" performed here and now of the theatrical event' (2000: 13). In the case of *The Cheviot*, these 'hyper-historians' are especially conscious of the role they are playing. For example, one effect of the self-consciously jolly dramatisation of Scottish history in the play – the here and now of the theatrical event – is, as Drew Milne observes, that comedy 'intervenes in the tendency to lament and mourn the past that is constitutive of a backward-looking nationalist sentiment' and instead directs the audience's focus towards learning the lessons of this history (2002: 319). McGrath's political stance is palpable in the structuring of the narrative and the selection of narrative material. The company revisits history neither with disinterest nor to mourn its failures but rather to ascertain its lessons and to publicise them. Accounts of battles lost are balanced with specific examples of resistance. In relation to the Clearances, for example, the audience learns that the people of Knockin, Elphin, and Coigeach made 'a stout resistance [to the evictions], the women disarming about twenty policemen and sheriff-officers, burning the summonses in a heap, and ducking the representative of the law in a neighbouring pool' (McGrath 2015: 97). Similarly, when, in the second section, the Duke of Sutherland tries to enlist men to fight the Russians in Crimea, nobody volunteers. 'It is the opinion of this country', an old Highlander explains, that 'should the Tsar of Russia take possession of Dunrobin Castle, we couldn't expect worse treatment at his hands than we have experienced at the hands of your family for the last fifty years' (McGrath 2015: 152–153). In this way the utopian potential of drawing attention to historical resistance punctuates the narrative.

Key aspects of *The Cheviot*'s impact relied on the careful handling of transitions of tone from satirical swipe to straightforwardly sincere political assertion:

Enter SNP employer.

SNP employer: Not at all, no no, quit the Bolshevik haverings. Many of us captains of Scottish industry are joining the Nationalist Party. We have the best interests of the Scottish people at heart. And with interest running at 16 per cent, who can blame us?

MC2: Nationalism is not enough. The enemy of the Scottish people is Scottish capital, as much as the foreign exploiter.

Drum roll (McGrath 2015: 155)

There is a note of tension, certainly, in McGrath employing nationalist rhetoric – the 'Scottish people' – precisely in the moment of dismissing nationalism as a political solution. It is this note of ambivalence, I will argue later in this chapter, that Douglas exploits in his 2015 revival. Nonetheless, the thrust of *The Cheviot* works consistently to expose the economic and political forces that have decimated the Highlands across successive generations as contingent, not inevitable, and, therefore, the play is typically and rightly understood as an unusually effective and influential example of socialist theatre. As Baz Kershaw observes in *The Politics of Performance* (1992), it 'crystallised a form of cultural production that became increasingly important in the 1970s' (1992: 167).

Socialist nationalism?

In *The Cheviot*, historical material is presented in a dynamic dialectic with contemporary events so that history is used primarily to shine a light on the present and, in particular, to emphasise the extent to which current attitudes represent a falling away from ideological clarity and rigour. This was a common theme across the Left in Scotland in the late 1960s and early 1970s, where a rejuvenated intelligentsia was beginning to organise and align itself with the cause of socialist nationalism. In November 1967, much to the chagrin of the British political establishment, the Scottish National Party (SNP) candidate Winnifred Ewing won a by-election in Hamilton, Lanarkshire, with a 38 per cent swing from Labour. This event signalled the arrival of the SNP as a credible electoral force and triggered a good deal of soul-searching on all sides. In response, two key publications appeared in the following year: Tom Nairn's article 'The Three Dreams of Scottish Nationalism' in the *New Left Review* (1968) and the first issue of the magazine the *Scottish International Review*. Nairn's article is worth considering in some detail here because the arguments he expounds in it and later develops in *The Break-Up of Britain* (1977) were to provide a powerful scaffolding narrative for Scottish intellectuals of the Left who wished to make a case for independence.

For Nairn, the resurgent bourgeois Scottish nationalism of the 1960s is nothing more than 'the late reflorescence of a dream, the hope of an identity, to which [the Scots have] clung, obscurely and stubbornly, across centuries of provincial stagnation', in the absence of real political power or agency (1968: 4). The single 'most important trait' of this dream, he insists, is its 'vast, impossible dissociation from the realities of history' (1968: 4). He sees the present moment as 'the third phase in the dream-psychology' in which imaginative compensation effectively replaces meaningful historical recovery (1968: 4).

According to Nairn, the first 'tormented vision Scotland was subjected to' was the Calvinist Reformation of the 1560s (1968: 5). He notes that this 'Reformation struck Scotland long before there was any significant mercantile or capitalist development' and, consequently, unlike other European Reformations, cannot be said to have been initiated by a rising bourgeoisie. Instead, Nairn observes that the Scottish 'religious revolution derived its power and character precisely from its historical isolation' at some distance from the Weber-Tawney model (1968: 5). He concludes: 'because it could not be the veiled ideology of a class, the Scottish Reformation was bound to be an abstract, millennial dream – in effect, a desperate effort at escape from history, rather than a logical chapter in its unfolding' (1968: 5). In the aftermath of the Treaty of Union with England in 1707, the 'strange, truncated condition of Scotland ... made it natural to search for effective substitutes for the lost national identity. The Kirk was indeed such a substitute' (1968: 6). Along with the legal system, the Church of Scotland (the Kirk) was specifically preserved from the dissolution of the state, and, consequently, it became a main vehicle through which a separate national identity was maintained.

By Nairn's account, the second phase in the creation of Scotland's dream-psychology was not, as one might expect, the Enlightenment, in which Scotland attained greater eminence than any nation apart from France, but Romanticism. 'It is difficult to exaggerate', he insists, 'the importance of Romanticism for Scotland. While the Enlightenment was only an episode, Romanticism entered her soul' (1968: 7). In the collection of states that was to become Italy and Germany, Romanticism fed into the formation of national identity, but in the constitutional limbo that was Scotland, Nairn argues, it simply acted as another substitute for it. Particularly in the work of Sir Walter Scott, he observes that nostalgia was substituted for real experience. This commentary on Romanticism's sinister hold over the Scottish imagination brings Nairn up to date:

> From this fertile soil has grown the myth-consciousness of modern Scotland, expressed in her Nationalism. Nationalism is her third dream. It is basically a dream of redemption. For the Scots, national existence must represent that magic, whole reality of which they have been cheated by history – in it, their maimed past will be redeemed, in more vivid colours than a history can ever provide. (1968: 8)

Nairn understands the national consciousness of industrial Scotland – he is writing in the late 1960s – as essentially schizophrenic. On one side is the debased Romanticism of a popular culture fixated on tartan and bagpipes, whisky and haggis, Calvinism and a celebration of the Scottish martial contribution to the British Empire. On the other is the 'ethereal tartanry' of the intelligentsia, which ostensibly rejects debased popular images of Scotland but ultimately reproduces them at a more refined level (1968: 9). As David Daiches pointed out some years earlier, sentimentality had 'lodged itself more deeply in Scotland than elsewhere, because of the division between the Scottish head and the Scottish heart that history had already produced' (1964: 82).

Unsurprisingly, Nairn condemns the SNP as bourgeois nationalists of the kind that completed the transition from feudalism to capitalism in Europe or that enabled non-European peoples to liberate themselves from their imperial conquerors. Nevertheless, there are two reasons why the nationalist aspirations of the Scots should be supported, he concludes. First, because they represent 'a blow against the integrity of British imperialism [and] a destructive factor of change in the reactionary equilibrium of UK politics', and second, because they would result in 'some transfer of power to a smaller arena' (1968: 16). Instead of supporting the SNP, however, Nairn urges Scottish socialists to develop their own brand of nationalism in opposition to the bourgeois nationalism of the SNP. He closes his article with the following challenge in the form of a question: 'Is it really impossible that Scotland, which has dwelt so long and so hopelessly on the idea of a nation, should produce a liberated, and revolutionary nationalism worthy of the name and the times?' (1968: 18).

As mentioned above, 1968 also saw the launch of the controversial and influential literary magazine the *Scottish International Review*, which was published quarterly from January 1968 to May 1971 and then monthly until its final issue in March 1974. Funded by the Scottish Arts Council, the *Scottish International*, as it came to be known, published poetry, short fiction, and critical essays by some of the most important writers of the time. As the title implies, its founding editor Bob Tait intended the magazine to provide a platform for Scottish work to be understood and promoted in international contexts. Along with other small magazines that emerged in the 1970s, such as *Radical Scotland* and *Cencrastus*, the *Scottish International* served as an outlet for increasingly heated debates about Scottish culture and politics, which, as Ben Jackson notes, 'resonated far beyond their initially rather selective readerships' (2002: 10). It was into this charged arena that *The Cheviot* emerged. Its first public outing was in Edinburgh at the 'What Kind of Scotland?' conference organised by the *Scottish International*. McGrath recalls in his introduction to the play's text delegates including 'politicians, union men, writers, social and community workers, academics, and ordinary people who cared about the future of Scotland' (2015: xi). The play was presented as a rehearsed reading and very much a work in progress. McGrath continues:

> It was the best thing we could have done. The audience at the end rose to its feet and cheered, then poured out advice, corrections, support, suggestions of great practical value, facts, figures, books, sources, and above all, enthusiasm.

Not because we'd been 'good' or 'clever' – but because, what we were struggling to say was what they, and masses of people in Scotland, wanted said. (2015: xi)

This anecdote, which has been widely circulated in accounts of *The Cheviot* and which locates the play's genesis within a specific political context, is an example of the fusion of radical and nationalist agendas that have shaped narratives of the Left in contemporary Scotland. In the late 1960s and 1970s, as Rory Scothorne has shown, and partly in response to Nairn's call to arms, 'the radical left in Scotland developed a set of narratives about itself, Scotland and the British state through which it could make sense of and justify its engagement with the politics of Scottish autonomy' (Scothorne 2018: 1). A number of features of this socialist nationalist project chime strongly with McGrath's aims in *The Cheviot*. For one thing, the conviction that Scotland has a complex cultural inheritance of its own, which requires a distinctive analysis of Scottish society and its histories from a Left-wing perspective, is embodied in the play's content and historical reach. For another, the importance of creating a sense of an alternative dream of Scottish identity, located in the present but more amenable to socialist appropriation, is achieved in *The Cheviot* by relating histories full of sadness and righteous anger with what Milne describes as 'vitality and festive energy' (2002: 323). In this way McGrath sought to sow or revive the seeds of collective agency in communities that had suffered most from capitalist exploitation. By his own account, theatre cannot aspire to '*cause* a social change' but instead can 'articulate the pressures towards one' (2015: xxx).

Inheritances

It is undeniable that *The Cheviot*'s influence on subsequent generations of Scottish theatre-makers has been significant. This is partly because, as Adrienne Scullion has stressed, 'work undertaken by theatre scholars on Scottish theatre from the late 1970s and into the 1980s, when the subject area was new, was particularly influential in scoping the locus of study and in establishing a critical rhetoric' and because populist and working-class political traditions were given particular emphasis by these scholars (2002: 218). Political ambition aside, however, *The Cheviot* became important as a stylistic influence embodying, as it did, a kind of pronounced folk populism that came to be seen as emblematic of a distinctively Scottish theatre tradition. In his 'Director's Note' in the published text of *Black Watch* (2006), John Tiffany contends that 'John McGrath and 7:84 changed the face of Scottish theatre with *The Cheviot, the Stag and the Black, Black Oil*' (2007: xi). In the post-devolutionary period, its influence can certainly be seen, in the formal organisation if not necessarily the ideological bent, of Tiffany's acclaimed production of Gregory Burke's *Black Watch*, Keiran Hurley's *Rantin* (2013), David Greig's *The Strange Undoing of Prudencia Hart* (2014), and Lee Hall's *Our Ladies of Perpetual Succour* (2015). The success of these productions undoubtedly paved the way for Douglas's 2015 revival, but the status of Dundee as a 'yes' city, that is, one in which the majority of voters had supported Scottish independence in the 2014 referendum, was also a factor in the timing of the revival.

In the years following 1999, mainstream nationalist discourse was notable for an absence of explicit ideological controversy. The question of whether independence was a means or an end remained unanswered, and indeed, as Ben Jackson notes, in order to reassure a cautious Scottish public, many nationalist politicians were at pains to 'downplay how radical a break independence would be from the economic and social status quo under the Union' (2002: 178). However, the mobilisation of independence supporters during and in the aftermath of the 2014 referendum and the surrounding rhetoric revitalised a nationalist movement both strongly committed to a popular vote in favour of a sovereign Scottish nation and also wedded to the idea of independence as a decisive rupture from the existing political and economic models of the UK. It was in this context that Douglas's revival was created and received. In 2015 the Scottish Independence referendum was still fresh in the mind of the Dundee audience. The city had voted 'yes' to independence by a higher margin than any other constituency in Scotland, and because of its unrelenting focus on the absence of agency among ordinary Scottish people, the democratic deficit in a specifically nationalist context seemed a major theme of McGrath's text. This was gleefully foregrounded in Douglas's staging.

Unlike the original, which toured extensively to small community venues in the Highlands and Islands, Douglas's revival was a main-stage production in a major Scottish theatre. This fact alone distances it from the original and from McGrath's lifelong antipathy towards bourgeois stages. No doubt restricted by available funding streams, the following year it embarked on a tour of mid- to large-scale venues across the country. To stress continuity with the past and its grievances, the auditorium at the Rep was rearranged in Graham McClaren's design, and a section of the audience was placed around tables on stage where a bar served whisky. Some of the action unfolded in the auditorium as though it were one of the village halls in which the original had been performed. The set was adorned with lampshades to emphasise the homespun aesthetic. A ceilidh band played traditional tunes as the audience arrived. In this way, the production evidenced nostalgia for a particular mode of theatrical production as much as for a theatre of ideological clarity and rigour. A small number of references were added to make the play more topical, but essentially McGrath's script remained intact, although it was delivered with contemporary emphases. Early in the show, for instance, the young female Scottish actor Jo Freer asked the women in the audience to stand. After they had done so, she delivered a speech cataloguing the punishments inflicted on women who resisted the authorities during the eighteenth-century Highland Clearances. Greer's listing of the whippings, head injuries, and sexual assaults suffered by women for defending their homes directed particularly, if not exclusively, to the women in the audience conjures a slightly different form of solidarity, more explicitly linked to the Me Too movement than the international socialism of McGrath's original. While the reviews of the show commented on the undiminished impact of the play's focus on the recurring economic exploitation of the Highlands and the social and political impact of that exploitation, McGrath's explicitly internationalist reading of Scottish history – which is a central dramaturgical strategy of the play – was not much commented upon. This is, I want to suggest, because the play has been effectively co-opted for the cause of contemporary Scottish nationalism, for bolstering popular belief in our progressive potential, maliciously stifled as long as we remain in the Union.

Recent voting patterns in England for Brexit and for a Conservative government at Westminster have served only to strengthen this narrative. In 2016 Scotland voted to remain in the EU, and in 2019 Westminster held an election in which the Conservatives gained an eighty-seat majority; the Tories won six seats of the fifty-nine available in Scotland, while the SNP won forty-eight. Some of this SNP success was undoubtedly built on gaining votes in Scotland's traditional Labour heartlands by shifting to the Left on social policy, but Labour was also the author of its own demise. In the 2015 Westminster election the party suffered its worst ever electoral defeat in Scotland, losing forty of its forty-one seats. The referendum campaign of 2014 had forced Labour, probably against its better instincts, to declare openly for the Union, and to share a platform with the Conservatives. Many of the 45 per cent who had voted 'yes' for independence, a large proportion of them Labour voters, switched to the SNP. Whether they will remain loyal to the SNP is another question.

As the above results make clear, the gap between Scottish and British politics has a radicalising potential, although commentators tend to agree that this has yet to be realised. Successive SNP administrations at the Scottish Parliament in Edinburgh have tended to favour stability and Centre–Left initiatives over radical change, in an attempt to quiet the anxieties of those sections of the electorate who fear the scale of the disruption that would follow independence. As Scothorne notes, the invention in the late 1960s of a pro-independence radical 'tradition required a close, critical engagement with

Scotland's past, present and future [that] laid the foundations for the better-known resurgence of Scottish cultural and historiographical work which occurred over the following decades' (2018: 5). The stories about Scotland, including *The Cheviot*, that gained traction – of a Left-wing nation where the people were sovereign – reflected the radical Left's attempts to justify its own emotional engagement with what was, in truth, not a particularly radical project or at least with a nationalist project that has yet to prove itself radical.

Bibliography

Brown, Ian and Sím Innes. 2015. 'Parody, Satire and Intertextuality in the Songs of *The Cheviot, the Stag and the Black Black Oil.*' *Studies in Theatre and Performance* 35(3): 204–220.

Cooper, Neil. 2015. 'Theatre Review: *The Cheviot, The Stag and The Black, Black Oil* Dundee Rep.' The *Herald*, 14 September.

Daiches, David. 1964. *The Paradox of Scottish Culture: The Eighteenth-Century Experience.* Oxford: Oxford University Press.

Dicenzo, Maria. 1996. *The Politics of Alternative Theatre in Britain, 1968–1990: The Case of 7:84 (Scotland).* Cambridge: Cambridge University Press.

Dicenzo, Maria. 2006. 'John McGrath and Popular Political Theatre.' In *The Companion to Modern British and Irish Drama*, edited by M. Luckhurst, pp. 419–428. Oxford: Blackwell.

Jackson, Ben. 2002. *The Case for Scottish Independence: A History of Nationalist Political Thought in Modern Scotland.* Cambridge: Cambridge University Press.

Kershaw, Baz. 1992. *The Politics of Performance: Radical Theatre as Cultural Intervention.* London: Routledge.

Mackenney, Linda. 1996. 'The People's Story.' In *Scottish Theatre since the Seventies*, edited by R. Stevenson and G. Wallace, pp. 65–72. Edinburgh: Edinburgh University Press.

McCrone, David. 2001. *Understanding Scotland: The Sociology of a Nation.* London: Routledge.

McDonald, Graeme. 2015. 'Commentary.' In *The Cheviot, the Stag and the Black, Black Oil*, by John McGrath, pp. 17–71. London: Bloomsbury.

McGrath, John. 1981. *A Good Night Out: Popular Theatre, Audience, Class and Form.* London: Methuen.

McGrath, John. 2002. *Naked Thoughts that Roam About.* London: Nick Hern Books.

McGrath, John. 2015. *The Cheviot, the Stag and the Black, Black Oil* (*Student Edition*). London: Bloomsbury.

McMillan, Joyce. 2015. 'Theatre Review: *The Cheviot, The Stag, and The Black, Black Oil.*' The *Scotsman*, 14 September.

Milne, Drew. 2002. 'Cheerful History: The Political Theatre of John McGrath.' *New Theatre Quarterly* 18(4): 313–324.

Nairn, Tom. 1968. 'The Three Dreams of Scottish Nationalism.' *New Left Review* 1(49): 3–18.

Nairn, Tom. 1977. *The Break-Up of Britain: Crisis and Neo-Nationalism.* London: Verso.

Paterson, Lindsay. 1998. *A Diverse Assembly: The Debate on a Scottish Parliament*. Edinburgh: Edinburgh University Press.

Reinelt, Janelle. 1994. *After Brecht: British Epic Theater*. Ann Arbor, MI: University of Michigan Press.

Rokem, Freddie. 2000. *Performing Histories: Theatrical Representations of the Past in Contemporary Theatre*. Iowa City, IA: University of Iowa Press.

Scothorne, Rory. 2018. 'The Radical Current: Nationalism and the Radical Left in Scotland, 1967–1979.' *H-Nationalism*, 25 May, pp. 1–8. https://networks.h-net.org/node/3911/discussions/1862513/left-and-nationalism-monthly-series-%E2%80%9C-%E2%80%98radical-current%E2%80%99. Accessed on 24 February 2024.

Scullion, Adrienne. 2002. 'Glasgow Unity Theatre: The Necessary Contradictions of Scottish Political Theatre.' *Twentieth Century British History* 13(3): 215–252.

Taxidou, Olga. 1996. 'Epic Theatre in Scotland.' In *Scottish Theatre since the Seventies*, edited by R. Stevenson and G. Wallace, pp. 164–175. Edinburgh: Edinburgh University Press.

Tiffany, John. 2007. 'Director's Note.' In *The National Theatre of Scotland's Black Watch*, by Gregory Burke. London: Faber and Faber.

Wolff, Janet. 1981. *The Social Production of Art*. London: Macmillan Education.

8

Between the Right and the Left: Staging political, emotional, and social polarisations on the Canadian stage

Yana Meerzon

In the 2018 documentary *Fahrenheit 11/9*, Michael Moore blames the US oligarchy for allowing the rise of Trump and points at Trump's skilful manipulation of media that, in its hunt for 'a hot story', has created a phenomenon of Trump(ism).[1] He demonstrates that populists such as Trump are always ready to exploit the divide between the language of the educated Leftist elite and the needs of the underprivileged. In her book *For a Left Populism*, Chantal Mouffe engages with similar effects of populist rhetoric, arguing that the time has come for the Left to reclaim its political weight using strategies of populist performance. In its objective to reconstruct the peoples – the collective we of 'the workers, the immigrants, and the precious middle class' (2018: 24) – the new Left must fight for 'the radicalization of democracy' (2018: 24). It must use affect to mobilise this new collective subject. Using strategies of populist performance rooted in the processes of collective identification and affect (2018: 72–73), artists need to speak from the place of concrete problems that 'people encounter in their daily life', so they can offer 'a vision of the future that gives them hope' (2018: 76). The questions I would like to ask in this chapter are: is theatre – political or activist – a type of media which can truly produce such profound intellectual and emotional impact on its audiences? Does it have to be populist? What does this term – populist performance – really signify? And finally, would a documentary theatre piece, which takes place in a designated theatre space and preaches to the educated and to the converted, serve such purpose? Or is it only a mass protest or performance activism that can mobilise the political agenda of the Left? The response cannot be homogeneous or out of context. Each political project, I argue, needs to imagine its own means of performance-making and reception pertinent to the questions, expectations, and experiences of its target spectatorship. Sometimes, putting forward a provocation to those who already consider themselves open-minded can serve as political incitement, specifically if such provocation makes these audiences confront their own biases.

One such project is *The Assembly* (2018) written by Alex Ivanovici, Annabel Soutar, and Brett Watson of the Montreal company Porte Parole[2] and directed by Chris Abraham. A rare example of bringing together the so-called 'political extremes', including representatives of the political far Right and far Left, into a space of a single theatre performance, *The Assembly* proved to be both a commentary on what we would identify as a political status quo of the widely liberal-minded English Canadian audiences and a provocation. It made many of us feel uncomfortable within the tenants of our soft liberalism, as (paradoxically) we would recognise the ideas and the concerns articulated by both the characters of the far Right and the far Left as our own. In many cases, including myself, this discomfort led to questioning our/my political stands, beliefs, and assumptions, and essentially writing this chapter.

Enthused by interviews with political supporters of Donald Trump, which Ivanovici and Watson conducted in 2016, *The Assembly* focuses on the political, economic, and cultural polarisation of today's world. The play begins with a scripted re-enactment of a dinner party that took place in Montreal in December 2017. In this section, four actors play four Canadian citizens, who gather at a dinner table to discuss the issues of immigration, polarisation, and free speech, and whose statements were recorded, transcribed, and edited to create a dramatic script. In its second part *The Assembly* presents a so-called 'long table', which features audience members who voluntarily take the actors' places to participate in this debate. It closes with the characters back on stage writing a letter to Trump's supporters. Tightly choreographed, *The Assembly* interrogates the political impact of public gatherings when one's agency is made visible through their physical appearance on stage. It uses the aesthetics of Brecht's *learning play* to steer thoughts and emotions, but it provides neither recipes for moral, political behaviour nor reconciliation. It does ask the major question of our time: 'In the absence of good leadership, what choice do we have?' (Timson 2018). A theatrical platform for political debate, *The Assembly* forces the Left and the Right to face each other and to put their ideologies on trial through dialogue. Interested in the politics of ordinary people or *the experts of everyday* (Roselt 2008: 63–65), it creates a theatrical response to the rise of extremism and tribalism today, and thus it turns the tables on to its audiences. *The Assembly* 'puts the responsibility and focus on ordinary people to explain and defend their views and to interact with those who don't share them. It pushes us all further down that fast-moving conveyor belt of political discourse where we can choose to understand each other a little more or get even more outraged' (Timson 2018). To examine how a theatre project can use the aesthetics and the strategies of populist performance to steer political emotions and debates, I situate my observations within Judith Butler's arguments on the performative power of assembly (2015).

On the performative power of the assembly: Judith Butler vs Porte Parole

According to the Oxford English Dictionary, the word 'assembly' refers to (among others) 'a group of people gathered together in one place for a common purpose; a group of people elected to make laws or decisions for a particular country or region, such as *National Assembly*; [and] the action of gathering together as a group for a common purpose'.[3] To this already complex definition of the word 'assembly', I add a category of a temporal/spatial happenstance or political chronotope (Bakhtin 1981) in which, according to Judith Butler, the performative power of a public gathering is manifested (2015: 22). This power lies with the structure of the assembly, that is, with the 'expressive freedom' of people, who exercise their political autonomy and will through spontaneous or improvisational and voluntary appearance in a large group (2015: 22). Butler interprets this act of appearance as a type of speech act, expressed not through our linguistic statements or acts but through the gesture of our bodily arrival and presence, or embodied manifestation of the self, within the space of this public gathering. In Butler's reading of the performative power of the assembly, linguistic performativity and bodily performativity overlap, although they are neither distinct nor identical to each other:

> If performativity has often been associated with individual performance, it may prove important to reconsider those forms of performativity that only operate through forms of coordinated action, whose condition and aim is the reconstruction of plural forms of agency and social practices of resistances. So, this movement or stillness, this parking of my body in the middle of another's action, is neither my act nor yours, but something that happens by virtue of the relation between us, arising from that relation, equivocating between the I and the we, seeking at once to preserve and disseminate the generative value of that equivocation, an active and deliberately sustained relation, a collaboration distinct from hallucinatory merging or confusion. (2015: 9)

This gesture of bodily performativity informs the politics of the assembly, that is, it allows one's expressive freedom to be manifested and interpreted within the context of one's own historical and biological time and also as cultural specificity. To Butler, therefore, the impact of the assembly is not necessarily in the language and discourse it produces but in the performative gesture of bodily attendance and appearance. This gesture of bodily appearance is already political. Like the illocutionary power of a speech act, in which the action is expressed and performed through making a linguistic statement, the body that appears in the public space acquires a special power of expression. By appearing in the space of gathering, the body performs its power through the act of arrival and through its own materiality or lived experience, which informs this materiality. Even before we begin to talk, the materiality and the semiotics of our arrival into the space of visibility create the performative gesture of resistance and protest.

At the same time, Butler acknowledges that not all gatherings are made equal because not all people can make their bodily presence visible or available in a public space. This statement brings Butler's argument to the second major ingredient that makes up the assembly, which is 'the public' and 'the people'. To Butler, both the bodies that appear in the public space of the assembly and those who reach it remotely or via a proxy constitute and add to the idea and the practice of 'the people' – the word is used here both as a linguistic stand-in for living human creatures and as a discursive category of the language of legislation and politics. To Butler, bodies create the assemblies, which

> already signify prior to, and part from, any particular demands they make. Silent gatherings, including vigils and funerals, often signify an excess of any particular written or vocalized account of what they are about. These forms of embodied and plural performativity are important components of any understanding of 'the people' even as they are necessarily partial. (2015: 8)

The performative power of the assembly, therefore, rests with Butler's thesis that

> acting in concert can be an embodied form of calling into question the inchoate and powerful dimensions of reigning notions of the political. The embodied character of this questioning works in at least two ways: on the one hand, contestations are enacted by assemblies, strikes, vigils, and the occupation of public spaces; on the other hand, those bodies are the object of many of the demonstrations that take precarity as their galvanizing condition. (2015: 9–10)

Historical materiality and concreteness of the bodies that come together into this public sphere make the assembly performative but also politically viable. The strength of the speech act of appearance generated by the assembly lies in the fact that

> it is *this* body, and *these* bodies, that require employment, shelter, healthcare, and food, as well as a sense of a future that is not the future of unpayable debt; it is *this* body, or *these* bodies, or bodies *like* this body or these bodies, that live the condition of imperiled livelihood, decimated infrastructure, accelerating precarity. (2015: 15)

Although Butler's focus remains on the assembly that takes place in the space of an unstructured *agora* – 'an open space serving as an assembly area and a place for commercial, civic, social, and religious activities',[4] in which peoples' political statements are made visible – her theoretical approach can be used in the analysis of a political theatre project, which borrows the structures of a public assembly to empower the artists and to make the political stands of their subjects visible and audible. Documentary theatre – to which *The Assembly* by Porte Parole belongs – uses mechanisms of political performativity similar to those theorised by Butler.

The Assembly: making the engine work

Driven by the unsettling discrepancy between Trump's skyrocketing popularity in 2016 and the media's attempts to draw an unbiased, although worrisome, picture of the President to come, Porte Parole decided 'to drive to the States to interview Trump's supporters' (Dunlevy 2018). To the company's surprise, the story they eventually shaped was not about Trump but about the polarisation of people who lost their ability to listen to each other. *The Assembly*, as its title indicates, came to interrogate the idea of performative plurality, and it used the theatre stage for ordinary people to negotiate their personal politics. Initially, in its geographical scope, the project focused on North America, although it has also aspired to move beyond this geopolitical bubble. In 2019 it was devised and presented as *The Assembly – University of Maryland* in Maryland and toured across Canada. The French language version, *L'Assemblée – Montréal*, featured four women who discussed the national identity of Quebec, affordable living, and feminism. Its German version was to open in Dusseldorf during the Theatre der Welt festival (summer 2020) and later in Lithuania in 2022. The COVID-19 pandemic put a temporary pause on this work,[5] and so in this chapter I examine only the English language version of this play, which I saw live in Ottawa, at the English Theatre National Arts Centre (NAC), in March 2020.

Situated in the space (Figure 8.1), which reminded me of an oversized meeting room, with an oval table centre stage, with mikes, papers, food, and drinks placed in front of each participant sitting around it, *The Assembly* spoke to Butler's theory of *a bodily speech act*. Each entrance of a new participant emphasised the material appearance of a new political body in the designated and specifically arranged space of the debate. Each entrance was slightly choreographed to imitate an 'I–song' or an opening number of a protagonist in a musical performance, with a special spotlight directed at the newcomer. As the participants gathered around the oval table centre stage, their faces were immediately projected on to large TV monitors surrounding it. This way, each of their facial expressions or gestures acquired special meaning by zooming in on each participant's body and face and projecting them on to the screens. The performance commented on the devices of popular media to present public gatherings as highly essentialised performative modes of social and political behaviour.

Figure 8.1 *The Assembly* by Alex Ivanovici, Annabel Soutar, and Brett Watson, directed by Chris Abraham, a Porte Parole Production. Actors featured in the photo (left to right): Amélie Grenier, Christina Tannous, Alex Ivanovici, Brett Watson, Pascale Bussières, and Nora Guerch (photo credit: Maxim Côté – www.flickr.com/photos/porteparole/46175357261/sizes/l)

Despite this heightened theatricality and visual allusions to mass gatherings used by media as tactics of populist politics and rhetoric, the performers remained only stand-ins for those real people whose political opinions they were called to articulate. The scripted part featured Valerie (played by Tanja Jacobs), who identifies as an '"alt-right" woman in her 70s' and who prefers Katie Hopkins or Pamela Geller, 'hated and vilified by everybody' (Ivanovici *et al*. 2018: 18), to present her on stage; Shayne (played by Jimmy Blais), who presented himself as a queer, Jewish anarchist; Hope (played by Ngozi Paul), who spoke of herself as 'a woman of colour with "liberal tendencies"'; and James (played by Sean Colby), a young Conservative activist.

The power and the truth of these peoples' experiences were manifested in the gesture of their on-stage presence, even if they appeared in this public space only via proxy – that is, as enacted by the professional theatre performers. For example, focusing on the questions of truth and authenticity in the work of documentary theatre, Porte Parole had to negotiate the use of the names of this play's characters. On several occasions the participants agreed to keep their identities and names intact. Thus, Valerie entered the fictional space of *The Assembly* under her real name – Valerie Price, the

Figure 8.2 *The Assembly* by Alex Ivanovici, Annabel Soutar, and Brett Watson, directed by Chris Abraham, a Porte Parole Production. Actors featured in the photo (left to right): Sean Colby, Tanja Jacobs, Jimmy Blais, and Ngozi Paul (photo credit: Maxim Côté – www.flickr.com/photos/porteparole/32303551178)

leader of the largest grassroots alt-Right organisation in Canada, ACT! for Canada.[6] Hope spoke as a Jamaican immigrant, who came to Canada to work as an accountant, but James used a pseudonym as he did not feel safe disclosing his identity on stage (Ivanovici *et al.* 2018: 21).

The dialogue the performers spoke was a verbatim recording of the conversation that took place in December 2017, with snippets of interviews the company conducted with the participants before and after it. Ivanovici and Watson moderated the discussion, helping participants navigate this onerous political encounter. Freddie Rokem identifies the actors engaged in the re-enactment of historical events or historical figures as 'hyper-historians' (2000: 13). In documentary theatre the performers of real or historical people also become the channels of historical energies:

> The actors serve as a connecting link between the historical past and the 'fictional' performed here and now of the theatrical event; they become a kind of historian, what I call a 'hyper-historian', who makes it possible for us – even in cases where the reenacted events are not fully acceptable for the academic historian as a 'scientific' representation of the past – to recognize that the actor is 'redoing' or 'reappearing' as something/somebody that has actually existed in the past. (2000: 13)

The Assembly of Porte Parole builds on this double energy of enacting history on stage – it brings the historical figures of Valerie, Shayne, Hope, and James re-enacted by the performers, and thus it engages the performative power of a speech act as the power of truth and as the power of bodily appearance. In other words the actors impersonate the everyday people, who despite the fact that they do not stand in the historical spotlight, like country leaders do for example, still take on the functions of historical figures and players. In the production these people (the subjects of the interviews in this case) acquire special historical significance as their testimonies serve as a kind of proof of truth to the historical momentum of our time.

The actors who enact the original members of the assembly lend their own bodies to these people's, and thus a double performativity takes place. As this meeting unfolds, tension builds, and disagreement rises:

> Valerie is especially in your face. She went to a Trump inaugural party in New York, describing it as 'the best night of my life,' and sees Black Lives Matter as 'anarchy.'
>
> On the other hand, Shayne, Valerie's polar opposite, mimicking her hero Trump, makes a crude misogynist remark to her, calls her a Nazi and states flatly that 'if you're a white supremacist, your death will save my life.' The conversation makes you realize we just don't have ways to talk about our polarization that don't further inflame or separate us.
>
> It also underscores that though these are not the people committing murderous acts, their words and beliefs give air to the deadly ideological framework around such acts.
>
> As young conservative James puts it, 'Even though a lot of Canadians won't admit it, there are a lot of people here that are sympathetic toward Trump'.
> (Timson 2018)

This drive for double performativity characterises each step of this project's making, during the period of interviewing the subjects, the time of editing data and writing the script, and on stage when actors enact their characters, and it brings Butler's ideas of the performative power of the assembly forward. This double performativity takes on one more layer of transformation when the subjects themselves – Valerie, Shayne, Hope, and James – come to see this play in the theatre. Their reactions, as the Porte Parole team recollects, varied from somewhat timid to outraged, with some members of the group asking the company to retract their statements or change them.[7] In this act of double performativity, an actor/hyper-historian – someone who watches history and evokes it through the performance at the same time – is born. As Rokem points out:

Performing history means to reenact certain conditions or characteristic traits inherent in such historical events, presenting them to the spectators through the performance, but it can never become such events or the historical figures themselves. In order to understand the notion of the actor as a hyper-historian when performing history, we have to examine how the aesthetic potentials of the actor's body as well as emotions and ideological commitments are utilized as aesthetics materials through different kinds of embodiment and inscription. (2000: 13)[8]

In *The Assembly* this performative power of re-enactment and public appearance is mobilised once again in its second part, when the actors step off the stage and invite audience members to step on to it themselves. This second section runs unstructured and unsupervised. It often reveals the audiences' own political attachments and biases based on emotions and affections generated by what they just heard and saw on stage. In this performative gesture of taking an exit, the actors create a new performative space for appearance, participation, and demand; thus, they provide a new theatrical space for Butler's political performance to take place.

When spectators/volunteers step on to the stage or rather arrive at the space of this gathering, they become a part of the assembly. In this gesture of arrival and appearance, spectators/volunteers begin to exercise the power of a bodily speech act, as it is in the visibility of the bodies that the freedom of appearance is mobilised (Butler 2015: 8). By stepping into the space of the performance, spectators enact their right to free expression and help in creating another new public space for political debate. This new space builds upon and refers to the scripted performance we just witnessed, and it is as temporal, ephemeral, and unique as any other political manifestation can be. Spectators/volunteers speak for themselves and share their personal political assumptions, reactions, and beliefs, but in the process of participation, they also re-enact the past that just happened in front of them. This way, they become the new hyper-historians of our collective theatrical experience. In this gesture of public appearance, the historical time is archived, and the political power of the present is reinforced.

These multiple temporal and performative modalities of *The Assembly*, as well as its participatory and performative structures, approximate this theatre project to Butler's reading of the political power of the assembly in a public sphere. Power of assembly, Butler explains, is rooted in the gesture of bodily enactment – by the act of coming together, people already express their political stance; so the power of assembly is rooted within the freedom of people's will to perform and enact an act of gathering, and it mobilises 'a plural form of performativity' (2015: 8). This gesture of appearance or 'parking of my body in the middle of another's action' is by default relational, as it points at the unbreakable bond of the plural 'we'.

'If performativity has often been associated with individual performance, it may prove important to reconsider those forms of performativity that only operate through forms of coordinated action, whose condition and aim is the reconstitution of plural forms of agency and social practices of resistances' (2015: 9).

Translated into the language of theatre, the materiality and the semiotics of one's appearance in a public gathering contribute to the performative gesture of the 'aesthetics of resistance', as identified by Peter Weiss, who asserts that art and culture, documentary theatre in particular, can serve as a catalyst to new modes of political action – the action of the Left – and to new forms of political, social, and cultural being (1971: 41). The makers of *The Assembly* echo Weiss's thoughts, and so they state:

> We are building *The Assembly* one episode and one performance at a time, upon the conviction that we must assemble, in person, as often as possible in today's world in order to demystify the human behaviour which makes us so polarized. You, our audience, are an important part of this process. By being present in this space, you signal that you still value the live encounter. By choosing theatre as a medium of entertainment, you express your appetite for witnessing people face off against one another before your very eyes. Perhaps most importantly, you expose yourself to the unnerving fact that human beings can don a political perspective as if it were a role they were playing in the theatre (Ivanovici et al., 2020)

To Jillian Keiley, an artistic director of the English Theatre National Arts Centre (NAC), Ottawa, at the time, and who programmed this play for its 2019–2020 season, polarisation, fake news, and alternative truth, on which Trump's administration stood for four years, are not just a local phenomenon, symptomatic for one country. It is a global disease of contemporary politics, which has profound echoing in Canada. By inviting Porte Parole on to the NAC main stage, Keiley asked her audiences difficult questions of compliance and conformism:

> The conversation [on stage] makes [us] realize – one of the critics wrote – [that] we just don't have ways to talk about our polarization that don't further inflame or separate us. It also underscores that though these are not the people committing murderous acts, their words and beliefs give air to the deadly ideological framework around such acts. (Timson 2018)

The production speaks directly to the inflammatory power of language and bodily appearance: by giving the right of speech to the radical Right and the radical Left, it wants to provoke, unsettle, and make people take sides. It also speaks of discomfort within the interlocutors, who were triggered by the altercations between Shayne, who uses hate speech and death threats to condemn neo-fascists, the alt-Right, and Trump's supporters (Ivanovici et al.

2018: 41–47), and Valerie, who wishes to save her country (2018: 30), and who speaks on behalf of Canada's poor but against immigration, and specifically against Islam (2018: 92–93). In both cases, however, it is the fear – the fear of the other and the fear of the new (2018: 68–73) – that predetermines personal positionality of each actor/actant, to use Bruno Latour's phrasing (2005), and thus it drives the actions and the dialogue of the characters.

It is not surprising, therefore, that within several short years of its run, *The Assembly* steered both high praise and harsh criticism, to the extent that one polemical review – 'The Assembly Aims to Illuminate, but Only Simulates Today's Divisive Politics' written by Kelly J. Nestruck and published in October 2018 in the Canadian national newspaper *The Globe and Mail* – has made it into the production's own dramatic canvas.

The Assembly: under the spotlight

The Toronto run of *The Assembly* opened in October 2018, the night before the fatal shooting in Pittsburgh's synagogue that left eleven people dead. A forty-six-year-old Robert Bowers, a White supremacist, was found guilty of this hate crime and convicted of murder, with prosecutors seeking the death penalty. Trump condemned Bowers's actions as 'pure evil' and stated that 'there must be no tolerance for antisemitism in America or for any form of religious or racial hatred or prejudice' (Trump, cited in Buncombe 2018). By the time these righteous statements had been made, 'the President's language, frequently aggressive and mocking of people who disagreed with him', had created an environment in which hate speech and hate actions had been legitimised (Buncombe 2018).

Realising the impact of Trump's divisive language and actions on his supporters and opponents, Porte Parole decided to fold them into the dramaturgy of *The Assembly*. It comes as no surprise that the critic Kelly J. Nestruck, sensitive to the impact a political performance can make on its public, condemned the project for its recklessness when toying with political provocation. He reviewed the play within the context of Pittsburgh's shooting and blamed the director Chris Abraham for turning 'extremism into entertainment'. Nestruck wrote: 'this documentary theatre project has resulted in a comedy about how naively Ivanovici and Watson curated their panel and how incompetently they controlled it – but the false balance isn't that funny when it ultimately leads to them handing over their platform to a virulent Islamophobe' (2018).

Nestruck's emotional reaction illustrates the kind of polarisation and its effects to which the play refers and which it can stir. It also proves that the language of populism, divisiveness, and schism, on which Trumpism is based, can corrupt anybody, even the most open-minded people. An attentive reader of new scripts, Nestruck compared *The Assembly* to 'the idealized assemblies of ancient Greece where democracy and theatre were born', and to such politically charged plays as Ayad Akhtar's *Disgraced* (2012), in which 'characters with varying viewpoints gather around a table, usually for dinner, drink a lot, and then explode about the issues of the day' (2018). At the same time, Nestruck hesitated 'about the ethics of simulating [drama – YM] in the real world as fodder for a verbatim play' (2018). He accused the company of being irresponsible for bringing these polarisations on to the stage:

> Valerie (played by Tanja Jacobs), the panelist who inevitably dominates the proceeding, is an older white woman who helped found a group that describes itself online as 'concerned about the triumphalist brand of Islam that seeks to erode our cherished Western principles of free speech and equality with the goal of eventual Islamic supremacy in the West.' ... At the other end of the table, there's Shayne (played by Jimmy Blais), who self-describes as queer, Jewish and anarchist. He gives a rather eloquent description of anarchy as an extreme form of democracy, but his main talking point is that nazis should be killed, because nazis ultimately want to kill him. 'If you value your life, stop being a nazi,' he says. (2018)

Figure 8.3 *The Assembly* by Alex Ivanovici, Annabel Soutar, and Brett Watson, directed by Chris Abraham, a Porte Parole Production. Actors featured in the photo (left to right): Ngozi Paul and Jimmy Blais (photo credit: Maxim Côté – www.flickr.com/photos/porteparole/32303550648)

In 2020, however, Nestruck admitted the shortcomings of his emotional response and prefaced the Ottawa run of the show with the following: 'I had a, well, strong reaction to *The Assembly* when I saw it in Toronto, but that's kind of the point of the show – which has evolved and, since it includes a participatory segment, is able to incorporate critiques of itself' (Nestruck 2020). Indeed, in the Ottawa version, the performer Tanja Jacobs read Nestruck's review on stage, which served as a transition between a scripted part of the performance and a participatory one. This way, the history of this work's reception entered its dramaturgical canvas and approximated *The Assembly* to Brecht's political theatre.

Like Brecht's epic theatre, *The Assembly* insists on the gaze of irony to be cast at every participant of this project, including the hosts, the guests, and the spectators/volunteers. In the conversation that I conducted with Porte Parole in May 2020, Annabel Soutar spoke at length about the fact that as privileged and educated artists or academics, we often do not know the other side. The conversations that the company conducted with Trump's supporters, which led to making this production, brought them to a series of questions, such as: how can we – the people of liberal convictions – start approaching the other, especially if this other is on the opposite of our side of the political spectrum? And what do we need to do to better understand how this other side operates? In the end, as the 2020 US elections demonstrated, Trump and his politics continued to be braced by a great number of voters, in fact by millions, and those who thought otherwise took them over only by a thin margin. As we know only too well, Trumpism is not truly gone with Trump's loss of the elections; it continues to evolve and strive in every corner of the world that has become even more divided and polarised. For Porte Parole, the first step in reclaiming the Left is to cast a long look at what makes the Right and to better understand what fears the Right faces, what ideals it upholds, and what utopias it cherishes.

To illustrate this point, *The Assembly* includes excerpts from an interview with the US conservative citizens Danielle Bernard and her husband (Ivanovici *et al.* 2018: 65–67). Fear is the underlying feeling that this family lives with: it is a fear of a murky economic future and losing one's job, a fear of political instability, and of an invasion of their lifestyle by something or somebody who they have never met before. Similarly, fear of being taken advantage of – economically and politically – marks Valerie's discourse. Shayne senses this weakness and blames Trump for using this fear to his advantage: Danielle 'was very honest about her fears – Shayne states – and that was exactly the rhetoric that Trump's electoral campaign was playing at' (Ivanovici *et al.* 2018: 71). Recognising the power of fear – the fear of the other and of the unknown – that defines many conservative minds is the first step that Porte Parole invites us to take. In this, it follows Brechtian tradition – to diagnose the social disease and to bring it on to the stage to steer the anger and the debate and to give the audience a chance to identify this illness as their own.

The second strand of the theatrical lineage that can be identified within the performative fabric of *The Assembly* is the political theatre of 1960s Quebec, which flourished in the wake of its nationalism. This theatre relied on the traditions of agitprop and collective creation and used *joual* – the language of the French-speaking working class in Montreal – to create its work. In its style, the 1960s theatre of Quebec was 'committed to populism', which was based on a shared belief that political performances 'should take place among the people, in community centres, union halls, schools and the work place' (Filewod 1987). The work of Françoise Loranger (1913–1995) exemplifies this practice. Her two-act satire *Médium saignant* (1970)[9] can be seen as a historical precursor to *The Assembly*. Set in the style of an impromptu municipal council meeting, *Médium saignant* focuses on political polarisation of Quebec caused by its language debates. The play evokes a so-called St-Léonard Conflict of 1968, which was caused by Bill 22 passed by the government of Quebec.[10] Created in the style of agitprop theatre, *Médium saignant* used a theatrical convention of an assembly – almost à la Butler – to depict people's fear of nationalistic tendencies in the highly polarised political atmosphere of Quebec and their 'profound mistrust of federal politics and politicians' (Charlebois 2019).

Likewise, Porte Parole does not shy away from bold political statements, and it does not retreat from the issues of over-representation, specifically when it applies to Valerie and Shayne. A version of Valerie's speech that she gave at one of the gatherings of ACT! for Canada finds its way into the show but is left without a proper political rebuttal.[11] Nestruck finds this dramaturgical oversight highly problematic because Hope and James – both of moderate political convictions – have a lesser stage presence in the play. Their arguments are either underdeveloped, weakly formulated, or do not represent a stable platform. This seems to be specifically problematic in the case of Hope, who is 'the only person of colour at the table, [and] is a self-described moderate liberal accountant who keeps her cool remarkably' (Nestruck 2018). The performance misses an opportunity to bring the conversation of systemic racism and xenophobia into its special focus, which in the wake of the Black Lives Matter movement, when this chapter was being written, appears not only as a political oversight but a serious flaw in the political fabric of this work, which sets to examine, critique, and condemn populism as the basis for hate and polarisation. This oversight instigates anger in the auditorium: 'One black audience participant hit it on the head when she told Jacobs that Valerie's voice was well-represented – and asked her to consider instead, "Who's not at the table?" … The absence of a Muslim voice in the play is particularly egregious given that Ivanovici, Watson and Soutar allow Valerie extra time' (Nestruck 2018).

The rebuttal – in the eyes of the creators of this project – comes in the form of a long table when the audience is given a chance to appear in the public space and speak. Joining the debate, the spectators make their own performative gesture or speech act: they come to (dis)agree with the offered opinions and thus become new agents of this political event. The power of provocation that *The Assembly* offers is exactly in this performative gesture of appearance: leaving the long table in the hands of the audience challenges the power of a spotlight and offers a chance for everyone to try it on.

Conclusion: on truth and reconciliation of *The Assembly*

To bring this theatrical event to a tentative conclusion, *The Assembly* invites its four characters to compose a letter addressed to Trump's supporters. The letter must end with a series of questions, which Hope constructs, including 'What do you intend to do to make this world a better place?', 'to make America great again?' (*Ivanovici et al.* 2018: 95) The production closes with an open ending: the company refuses to provide their moral verdict and thus makes the audience accountable for our personal politics. Moreover, the project finds both the people on the stage and those in the auditorium equally guilty of bad judgement and personal bias. It implicates the audience or even makes us responsible for the politics of populism. By extension, *The Assembly*, one might argue, also mobilises Butler's notion of 'the people' (2015: 3), which she identifies not 'as a given population' but as a collective of individuals 'constituted by the lines of demarcation that we implicitly or explicitly establish' (2015: 3). To Butler, recognition of those 'who count as people' (2015: 5) must become the major aim of radical democracy: 'democratic politics has to be concerned with who counts as "the people", how the demarcation is enacted that brings to the fore who "the people" are and that consigns to the background, to the margin, or to oblivion those people who do not count as "the people"' (2015: 5). Such new 'politics of recognition', to paraphrase Charles Taylor, must go beyond the already established groups of non-inclusion; in fact, it must break the paradox of recognition (Butler 2015: 6), when the groups of inclusion and non-inclusion evolve in parallel, if not in direct dependency from each other. This new politics of recognition can be built within the public space of the assembly, in which the well-established lines of demarcation partly dissolve.

Theatre performance, which stages political polarisation, turns into Butler's space of a public assembly. Through manifestation and clash of different political beliefs on stage, it rehearses the devices of new recognition, and it reflects today's political delineation that makes 'the people'. Moreover, it invites the people on stage and those off stage to acknowledge their personal positions of difference; it makes me recognise the other within my own self and position. A volunteer's body, which appears on stage during the long table section, turns into a signifier or a stand-in for many other bodies in the auditorium. By recognising my own self reflected within the body of a volunteer on stage, I see my politics enacted in a new space of difference and protest. The invitation remains open, and thus the choice of appearance and of the protest remains with each of us.

Notes

1 *Fahrenheit 11/9* – written, directed, and narrated by Michael Moore; produced by Michael Moore, Carl Deal, and Meghan O'Hara; cinematography by Luke Geissbühler and Jayme Roy. Midwestern Films, Briarcliff Entertainment, 6 September 2018 (TIFF).
2 Porte Parole is a Montreal-based theatre company, which was founded in 2002 by playwright Annabel Soutar and actor Alex Ivanovici. The company's mandate is to 'produce original documentary plays about Quebec and Canadian contemporary life that inspire diverse audiences to think critically together about current social issues' (https://nac-cna.ca/en/event/artists/21573#jillian-keiley).
3 'Assembly', from lexico.com/definition/assembly.
4 'In ancient Greek cities, an *agora* was an open space serving as an assembly area and a place for commercial, civic, social, and religious activities. Use of the agora varied in different periods. Located in the middle of the city or near the harbor, it was often enclosed by public buildings, covered areas containing shops, and stoas for protection from sun and bad weather. The highest honor for a citizen was to be granted a tomb in the agora' (Merriam-Webster: www.merriam-webster.com/dictionary/agora).
5 Between summer 2020 and spring 2021, the company developed three digital editions of *The Assembly*. The first one – 'Épisode 0: Les arts vivants doivent-ils se réinventer à l'ère de la distanciation sociale?' – featured four prominent artists from Montreal, who came together to discuss the effects of social distancing on live theatre in Quebec. The second and the third editions were dedicated to the questions of polarisation and economic survival in the times of COVID-19. The second episode featured prominent figures of Quebec's political, economic, and academic scenes; whereas the third one included prominent economists and politicians from English Canada.
6 ACT! for Canada stands 'on guard to defend Canada and the Canadian people against all enemies, foreign and domestic who, through stealth or outright aggression, seek to undermine the freedoms, economic prosperity, traditional values and heritage of the Canadian nation and peoples' (www.actforcanada.ca).

7 This demand was rather surprising to the Porte Parole team, as during their rehearsal and interview process Porte Parole followed ethical protocols of working with their subjects, and asked the participants to sign consent forms to be recorded during the interview as well as their statements to be used in the production (Ivanovici *et al.* 2018: 9–10).
8 In this chapter I am working with the assumption that the time of our present is an evasive time frame, which is both experiential (i.e. belongs to the present moment, to the now) and historical (i.e. will turn into the past as soon as this present moment passes). The further away we are from this present moment, the more diverse the lens of our analysis and comprehension becomes. In these assumptions I am following Walter Benjamin's arguments, who studied this interdependency between present and past in his famous essay 'On the Concept of History' (2006).
9 Tibor Egervari, Professor Emeritus of University of Ottawa, was the first one to suggest this connection, and hence I would like to acknowledge his help in researching and writing this chapter. *Médium saignant* premiered at the Comédie-Canadienne on 16 January 1970. It was directed by Yvan Canuel with costumes by Janet Logan, lights by Yves Gélinas, and set by Jean-Louis Garceau. It featured Jean Duceppe, Gabriel Arcand, Hélène Loiselle, Carmen Tremblay, Jean Brousseau, Roger Garand, Rolland Damour, Raymond Roger, and Madeleine Langlois, among others.
10 The Bill made 'French the primary language in public administration, public enterprise, the workplace, business and education' (CBC News 2014).
11 Valerie Price. 'Freedom of Speech, The Lifeblood of Democracy', 30 March 2014. www.youtube.com/watch?v=Ji-UkHDJdPU.

Bibliography

Bakhtin, M. M. 1981. *The Dialogic Imagination: Four Essays*, translated by C. Emerson and M. Holquist, edited by M. Holquist. Austin, TX: University of Texas Press.

Benjamin, Walter. 2006. 'On the Concept of History.' *Selected Writings*, Volume 4, transcribed by H. Zohn. Cambridge, MA: Harvard University Press.

Buncombe, Andrew. 2018. 'Pittsburgh Shooting: Names of 11 Victims Released as Donald Trump Accused of Saying Things to "Bring Us into Conflict with One Another".' *The Independent*, 28 October. www.independent.co.uk/news/world/americas/pittsburgh-synagogue-shooting-latest-victims-names-robert-bowers-a8605376.html. Accessed on 20 February 2024.

Butler, Judith. 2015. *Notes toward a Performative Theory of Assembly*. Cambridge, MA: Harvard University Press.

CBC NEWS. 2014. 'Looking back at 40 Years of French as Quebec's Official Language.' CBC NEWS, 31 July. www.cbc.ca/news/canada/montreal/looking-back-at-40-years-of-french-as-quebec-s-official-language-1.2724050. Accessed on 20 February 2024.

Charlebois, Gaetan. 2019. 'Médium saignant.' *Canadian Theatre Encyclopedia*, 26 February. www.canadiantheatre.com/dict.pl?term=M%E9dium%20saignant. Accessed on 20 February 2024.

Dunlevy, T' Cha. 2018. 'Theatre: Porte Parole Reminds Us – Polarization Goes beyond Trump.' *Montreal Gazette*, 9 November. https://montrealgazette.com/entertainment/theatre/theatre-porte-parole-reminds-us-polarization-goes-beyond-trump. Accessed on 20 February 2024.

Filewod, Alan. 1987. 'The Ideological Formation of Political Theatre in Canada.' *Theatre Research in Canada-Recherches Theatrales Au Canada* 8(2): 254–263. https://journals-lib-unb-ca.proxy.bib.uottawa.ca/index.php/tric/article/view/7372/8431. Accessed on 20 February 2024.

Ivanovici, Alex, Annabel Soutar, and Brett Watson. 2018. *The Assembly*. Unpublished manuscript.

Ivanovici, Alex, Annabel Soutar, and Brett Watson. 2020. 'Playwright's Note.' National Arts Centre, March. https://nac-cna.ca/en/event/notes/21573. Accessed on 20 February 2024.

Keiley, Jullian. 2020. 'The Assembly – Montreal: Artistic Director's Notes.' National Arts Centre, March. https://nac-cna.ca/en/event/notes/21573. Accessed on 20 February 2024.

Latour, Bruno. 2005. *Reassembling the Social: An Introduction to Actor–Network Theory*. Oxford: Oxford University Press.

Mouffe, Chantal. 2018. *For a Left Populism*. Brooklyn, NY: Verso.

Nestruck, Kelly J. 2018. '*The Assembly* Aims to Illuminate, but Only Simulates Today's Divisive Politics.' *The Globe and Mail*, 31 October. www.theglobeandmail.com/arts/theatre-and-performance/reviews/article-review-the-assembly-aims-to-illuminate-but-only-simulates-todays. Accessed on 20 February 2024.

Nestruck, Kelly J. 2020. 'What's on Stage across Canada Feb. 25 to March 1.' *The Globe and Mail*, 25 February. www.theglobeandmail.com/arts/theatre-and-performance/article-whats-on-stage-across-canada-this-week. Accessed on 20 February 2024.

Porte Parole. Series: *The Assembly*. https://porteparole.org/en/play-series/the-assembly/. Accessed on 20 February 2024.

Rokem, Freddie. 2000. *Performing History: Theatrical Representations of the Past in Contemporary Theatre*. Iowa City, IA: University of Iowa Press.

Roselt, Jens. 2008. 'Making an Appearance: On the Performance Practice of Self-Presentation.' In *Experts of the Everyday: The Theatre of Rimini Protokoll*, edited by M. Dreysse, F. Malzacher, and R. Protokoll, pp. 45–68. Berlin: Alexander Verlag.

Taylor, Charles. 2019. 'The Politics of Recognition.' In *Multiculturalism*, Volume 15, pp. 25–74. Princeton, NJ: Princeton University Press.

Timson, Judith. 2018. 'Our Leaders Are Failing, So It Is Up to Us to Stop the Bigots and Haters and Stay Civilized.' *Toronto Star*, 29 October. www.thestar.com/life/opinion/2018/10/29/our-leaders-are-failing-so-it-is-up-to-us-to-stop-the-bigots-and-haters-and-stay-civilized.html. Accessed on 20 February 2024.

Weiss, Peter. 1971. 'The Material and the Models.' *New Theatre Quarterly* 1: 4–43.

9

The indiscreet charm of Left nostalgia: Reeking redolence in the contemporary

Ameet Parameswaran

Yearning for a past, whether in melancholic or nostalgic mode, holds a complex and controversial place in Left imaginations and aesthetics. Wendy Brown (1999), drawing on Walter Benjamin's writing on 'Left melancholia', makes a powerful critique of what she marks as the Left's cathexis on ideas and sentiments linked to the past. Left melancholia, for Brown, makes it impossible for the Left to engage politically with the present, making it impossible for the Left to be affirmatory. Brown argues that the Left 'is thus caught in a structure of melancholic attachment to a certain strain of its own dead past, whose spirit is ghostly, whose structure of desire is backward looking and punishing' (1999: 26). Enzo Traverso (2016), on the other hand, foregrounds the significance of the events at the end of the twentieth century to reframe Left melancholia as a historical phenomenon in the contemporary. Highlighting the end of the Cold War with the fall of the Berlin Wall and the twenty-first century 'born as a time shaped by a general eclipse of utopias' (2016: 5) charged with a new kind of disillusionment, Traverso argues that 'melancholy still floats in the air as the dominant feeling of a world burdened with its past, without a visible future. The West, the East, and the South: the former "three sectors" of world revolution have become three realms of wounded memories' (2016: 45). Rather than conceptualising melancholia as a refusal to engage with the present, for Traverso, Left melancholia results from a condition where mourning is, in fact, impossible – 'communism is both a finished experience and an irreplaceable loss, in an age in which the end of utopias obstructs the separation from the lost beloved ideal as well as a libidinal transfer toward a new object of love' (2016: 45). What for Brown is a 'conservative tendency' for Traverso could be seen 'as a form of resistance against demission and betrayal' (Traverso 2016: 45). In this scenario, for Traverso, 'successful mourning' would, in fact, be an 'acceptance of lost socialism replaced by accepted capitalism' (2016: 45). Traverso argues that '[i]f a socialist alternative does not exist, the rejection of real socialism inevitably becomes a disenchanted acceptance of market capitalism, neoliberalism, and so on. In this case, melancholy would be the obstinate refusal of any compromise with domination' (2016: 45). According to Traverso, therefore, Left melancholia is a productive phenomenon, 'an enabling process' as 'it means to rethink socialism in a time in which its memory is lost, hidden, and forgotten and needs to be redeemed' (2016: 20). Moving away from the pathological framing of melancholia derived from Freud, Traverso thereby explores how Left melancholia is not a 'lamenting [of] a lost utopia, but rather rethinking a revolutionary project in a nonrevolutionary age. This is a fruitful melancholia that, one could say with Judith Butler, implies the "transformative effect of loss"' (2016: 20).

Alastair Bonnett (2010), on the other hand, unpacks the alternate modality of looking back, the complex history of nostalgia as a productive, dangerous, transgressive phenomenon that has had an integral place in Left and radical imaginations. Looking at four areas of radicalism – early English socialism, anti-colonialism, anti-racism, and the avant-garde – Bonnett foregrounds the messy, 'unkempt' forms of attachment such as nostalgia as a critical response and reaction to alienation and deracination in modernity. Further, as nostalgia is a significant product of modernity, Bonnett foregrounds the complex relation between nostalgia and politics, wherein nostalgia cannot be looked at only through the prism of the instrumentalisation of politics. For nostalgia 'quietly rebel[s] against the politicization of life, against the idea that things are only of value if we can find a place for them in a political ideology' (2010: 10).

Taking forward Bonnett's foregrounding of nostalgia, the present chapter explores the potentialities and contradictions of Left nostalgia in South Asia as it is imagined and materialises through the space-time of theatre. I analyse the popular and acclaimed theatrical performance *Mathi* (*Sardine*, 2013) by the young director Jino Joseph with the group Malayala Kalanilayalam Nadakavedhi, Kuthuparamba, Kannur in north Kerala. Performed widely as part of festivals and otherwise,[1] *Mathi* has at its centre the eponymous tiny oil sardine that is deemed to 'reek' and which in Kerala was often regarded as the staple food of the poor. The narrative centres around a fisherman, Rafeeq, who consciously sells the local *mathi*[2] and no other fish, only for him to lose his world of sociality due to the changing relations of labour and commodification of fishing under globalisation. I explore how the production, with the trope of melancholy of the lost lifeworld, materialises a conspicuous nostalgic world through theatre, wherein *mathi* that is cooked centre stage for the whole duration of the performance and offered to the audience at the end for consumption becomes a metonym of (the lifeworld of) Rafeeq.

Two interlinked aspects of the production come across as contradictory to Bonnett's larger perspective. Firstly, unlike the macro-history of the defeat of the Left, in this context, the Left has a dominant presence in terms of ideology as well as holding power within parliamentary democracy. While on the national level the Left has ceded its place considerably even as a strong opposition in recent times, in Kerala, in the last two decades, the Left has been more dominant than ever.[3] Secondly, in his analysis of nostalgia, Bonnett centres sites of radical nostalgia that are inconspicuous, arguing that one will 'learn more about the connections between nostalgia and radicalism from difficult encounters and repressed allegiances than we will do from less fraught situations' (2010: 1). *Mathi* is definitely not an unacknowledged site of nostalgia as the production is often framed as a nostalgic yearning for a 'village life' and 'the goodness and harmony of a [different] time' in the advent of changes brought about by globalisation (www.jinojoseph.com/work/matthi/). In fact *Mathi* becomes troubling precisely in its indiscreetness, materialising through theatre a different temporality from the present as a palpable experience in the present. Bonnett, in his analysis, does highlight the centrality of nostalgia within Left and radical imaginations in the Global South. He identifies nostalgia in the Global South as linked to anti-colonial movements and offers a reading of postcolonial theory as a radical imagination that has at its heart a nostalgia for the anti-colonial movement. While such macro-perspectives are significant, it becomes a limiting framework when seen in the light of the complex history of Left movements in India, wherein Left movements and practices are indelibly linked to but also distinct from the discourse and practices of nationalism. *Mathi* offers ground to understand the contradictions of nostalgia, and it troubles by indicating the Left's implication in the rationalisation of life and the development discourse of the contemporary neoliberal regime. Bonnett's argument about the relationship between nostalgia, modernity, and politics is critical here as he writes that

> Modernity may be the time of politics but a great deal of modern life is not experienced as a political choice. It does not feel like a political choice to not have time to see one's family, or know one's neighbours, or have incessant traffic noise grinding in our ears. Politics can appear ineffective, even meaningless, when pitted against these remorseless features of modern existence. If we also accept that nostalgia is itself a kind of rebellion in and against the instrumental rationalities associated with purely political judgement, we are left with a view of politics as a site of anxiety and disappointment. Perhaps though these characteristics are also a testament to its necessity. Politics gestures towards a redemption from modernity at the same time as it offers us bigger and better modernities. It is a troubling combination but it is one that we moderns seem to need. (2010: 11)

Mathi conspicuously stages a nostalgia by grasping the world at a reconfigured scale – the micro-scale of the body, both that of Rafeeq as well as that of *mathi*. In doing so it foregrounds an alternate temporality, an excess, charged with the undervalued ethos of the Left challenging the conceptualising of value solely through the lens of political efficacy. What might be the excess induced by nostalgia beyond the politicisation of life, and what would be its contradictions, dangers, and potentialities to offer a different becoming?

The reeking trace in globalisation

Hailing from an agrarian family and professionally untrained in theatre, Joseph reminiscences that he grew up watching commercial theatre performed as part of local religious festivals, moving on to do amateur theatre for schools and colleges, and is, in his own words, engaged in an 'extreme form of rural theatre'.[4] Jino Joseph's reminiscence about how he came about writing the play foregrounds the valuation of the subjective everyday experience of the material culture of the region and conviviality. In an interview Joseph details how he came about creating the performance. Joseph says, 'I had written and directed, for schoolchildren, a play named *Porotta*, which won a state-level competition.' *Porotta* is a popular food item in Kerala, and the experimental play was on the education system.[5] Joseph continues:

> one day, when I was eating porotta and *mathi* curry in Wayanad, a colleague joined me and said I must have a 'Mathi' for my porotta; he meant I should write a new play called 'Mathi' to complete the dish. That's when I became interested in the subject, because the bond we share with mathi in Kerala is unique – the fish has a distinctive smell, it's healthy, incredibly tasty.
> (Mazumdar 2018)

The performance *Mathi*, just under two hours in length, follows an episodic structure and is devoid of what one would reckon as a well-developed narrative or characterisations. The major part of the performance is simply an experience of a space-time cathected to *mathi* and a sociality based on friendship that it engenders: the cooked *mathi*, its taste and smell, envelops and creates the atmosphere in which the charming world of Rafeeq, his sister Kunjami, and Rafeeq's friends materialises. Within this world, they are seen as engaging in Leftist protests, rehearsing Left political theatre, falling in love, and joking and playfully interacting with each other. *Mathi* is always at the centre of the stage action – as it is continuously cooked, tasted from the pan as it is frying, shared, and eaten throughout the performance by the characters.

While such a world is presented for almost three-quarters of the performance, without giving an inkling of the historical process, this world is suddenly declared as lost. In dramatic and swift declarations, the new order of the post-1990s corporatisation and changing labour relations are laid out. The cheap and local *mathi* fishing and trade has become corporatised and linked to the global fisheries market, with the *mathi* from Mangalore now imported to Kerala while the fish from the state is being exported to different places. Rafeeq's friends have all left Kerala looking for jobs, and his lover announces her impending departure to another state to find work, her comportment coming across as a final probing for him to understand and respond to the changes. Having lost what he deems to be his lifeworld, and it seems unable to or possibly unwilling to adjust to the times, Rafeeq commits suicide. The roles of the narrator and Rafeeq interchange, with the narrator now coming on to the stage and Rafeeq interacting with him from the outside space of darkness. A new migrant working class from outside Kerala are now engaged in construction jobs and other hard labour, while the democratic cultural organisation, with theatre at its heart, has lost its collective ethos. This is emblemised in the transformation of the figure of the political theatre activist Chandran *mash* who used to lead their political theatre work and also entertain them with his drunken singing and revelry. Chandran *mash* has now transformed into a man dressed in a glossy shirt and, rather than being called *mash* (a term literally meaning male teacher, used endearingly), is called 'sir' (indicating power hierarchy) by the new migrant labourers who are being deployed to conduct cultural events for him. Chandran sir tells the migrant labourers that they should hold up whatever political flags he tells them to hold up and starts practising theatre with them. Rafeeq reminiscences with the narrator about their own theatre rehearsal. He says, 'remember, in our play we had asked whether we should behead the landlord. Now, whom should we behead?' He requests that the narrator gives a kick to Chandran *mash* for his sake, and the narrator goes on to do the same with the popular song '*Pulayaadi Makkalkku…*' written by P. N. R. Kurup, playing in the background, only to be beaten up badly by the workers and dumped on the ground with the casteist slur '*pulayaadi mone*'.

Before moving into the specifics of the staging, it is important to mark the framing of the discourse of loss as a result of labour migration. Globalisation and the development discourse that drives the contemporary moment create an experience of space-time as a disjuncture wherein the scales such as nation, region, domestic, and the body are territorialised and re-territorialised in relation to each other in multiple ways. In the case of the south Indian region of Kerala, the outward migration, especially to the Gulf from the 1980s, and the diasporic community play a critical role to the extent that scholars would argue that the remittance is possibly the most important factor offering an economic base and contributing to poverty alleviation over the years (Zachariah and Rajan 2016).[6] The fact that the protagonist is a Muslim makes it more critical as Muslims, in 2014, constituted 41.3 per cent of the total emigrants from Kerala (Zachariah and Rajan 2016: 67). In the case of *Mathi*, the loss is clearly posited in this context of outward labour migration and the contemporary space of Kerala being the site of inward labour immigrants from other parts of the country, since the labour rates in Kerala are comparatively higher than in other parts of India. This framing of loss, with the stress on seeming cultural rootedness, is clearly emerging from the perceived anxieties and crisis in modernity in globalisation based on language and culture. In the context of globalisation, Devika has argued that region under globalisation cannot be simply viewed as oppositional to nation, as 'unique' and 'fixed sorts of material culture' identified with a region, because 'the net result of the intensification of the processes of globalization has been to mix up social identities, national affiliations, cultural allegiances and geographical locations in myriad ways, yet the [linguistic-based regional] "Malayalee" does persist, in ever-newer forms' (2007: 30). The strategy of nostalgia, on the one hand, evades engagement with the processes of change and the real world of migrant labour in the contemporary. The migrants who have come to the state are also seen as alienated, forced to perform for the 'sir'. In that sense their cultural practices become a mere extension of the labour relation and its hierarchies. Yet, on the other hand, a nostalgia cathected to *mathi* emerges that instead of simply marking a specific space-time of essentialised community, or a fixed place of Kerala/village in the past with specific contours that bestow it authenticity, reconfigures the scale to the level of the body. This specific drawing on region in the process is closer to what Bose and Varughese would argue about the region as an assemblage. Drawing from Grosz's framework, Bose and Varughese argue that region needs to be seen as 'being incessantly de-/re-territorialised, resists fixed genealogies and identities and provides multiple entryways into it; as an assemblage it brings together and connects diverse fragments but also creates ruptures' (2015: 7). The central element of this reconfiguration is the specificity of *mathi* as linked to the region, as opposed to the new export–import regime.

The primary strategy followed by Joseph in his recent plays is isolating one figuration and, through what might come across as an obsessive one-point focus on the subjective realm and lifeworld of that figuration, opening a constellation beyond the processes of historicisation or even proper characterisation.[7] The opening sequence sets up *mathi* as this single-point focus in an abstract manner. While foreboding music is playing, Kunjami and Sheeba are seated centre stage beside a small cooking gas cylinder. In an exaggerated manner, in a 'slow motion' rhythm,[8] they smile and pour oil into the pan and place *mathi* into the pan once the oil is hot. In the background we see a group of bare-bodied men, climbing in pairs on to one another, creating verticality and pulling out a long coir. The gestures indexing catching fish through nets are accompanied by the sound of chanting, ending in the creation of a fish form shaped out of the coir. The men then let go of the coir, ending the choreography in laughter, and a peppy popular tune starts playing alongside the foreboding music. We see the men lined up as a group, moving together with only their bare backs visible to us. Finally, they break into a flowing dance – their bodies now in full view of the audience. The sequence ends with a door drawn to the frying pan and the coir in the spotlight.

A narratorial male voice from outside the stage says:

> Dear all ... this is *mathi*! Let's start with the hot spicy smell that you are deeply inhaling into your nose right now. *Mathi* – as you can see, the cheap and small fish that is frying in the pan in front of you is *mathi*. *Ayyayyo*, I am not saying this to make fun of you. But some things are like that! It seems that some things are understood only when they are explained – that's the sole reason why I am saying this. If someone has felt slighted by this ... we can sort it out ... afterwards! As I was saying, *mathi* ...

By this time, he starts coughing and says, 'Kunjami ... Kunjami ... the *mathi* is burning'.[9] The narrator suggests how the reek of *mathi* 'pollutes' the people associated with it, indexing the logic of caste and class.

The next long sequence sets up all the basic ingredients of this nostalgic world. Kunjami enters the stage and starts frying the fish, reading through a magazine. The long sequence is drawn out as an interaction with the lively narratorial voice from outside. This narratorial voice is that of an older man, invisible till the death of Rafeeq, at which point he climbs on to the stage. Throughout the performance, the narratorial voice casually interacts with the characters on stage, sometimes prodding the unfolding of the conversations and actions with casual questions, suggestions, and interjections. In Kunjami's conversations with the narrator, it comes across that Kunjami is cooking *mathi* for a theatre rehearsal that is supposed to happen later in the evening and is terribly irritated as Rafeeq is late, without having any information of where he is. Amid the conversation, Kunjami says that she does not have to cook *mathi* and comments that it is not that she is getting paid for cooking *mathi* for the people coming to their place after the protest procession and threatens that she would stop making *mathi* and even 'strike'. After a while, Sheeba also appears on stage, asking for Rafeeq. When Sheeba asks the young boy Appu to go and get water from the Panchayat well, Kunjami comments that 'there is law in place against child labour'. The narratorial voice and Sheeba wonder where the young Kunjami is getting the ideas of struggle from. Sheeba takes up the magazine, goes through it slowly, and declares that she has found out what Kunjami is referring to. Sheeba exclaims, 'aah! this is the reason!' and reads aloud, 'There was a time when the farmers' struggles and protests used to overflow from lane to lane. From the southern hilltop, Chirunkandan loudly said, "Imperialism down-down"' with Sheeba holding a pose with a raised fist to embody the slogan. Chirukandan was one of the four who were hanged to death by the British on 29 March 1943 for participating in the iconic Kayyur struggle that is marked as a significant moment in the rise of the communist movement in the region. Her sloganeering is echoed from off stage, and suddenly it becomes a full-fledged protest march as the marchers flood the back of the stage through the revolving doors, moving in line and sloganeering as Sheeba joins them. As the protesters move on, Rafeeq finally appears, dressed in a blue lungi and yellow shirt with red pockets, indexing the flashy theatricality, and riding a bicycle. Rafeeq tries to make it up to Kunjami by giving her nuts and chatting her up, and the conversation swiftly moves to her *mathi*-making for the theatre rehearsal (see Figure 9.1). In the interaction between Rafeeq, the narrator, and Kunjami, Rafeeq says that steaming tuber and frying *mathi* are 'great cultural activities' and that through this work, she will become the 'world-famous Kunjami'. The narrator picks on this and responds, 'that's nice ... World-famous Kunjami! Under the leadership of the Cultural Forum – Kunjami's statue will be unveiled, *pushparchana, kuttayottam, padayatra.*'[10]

While later in the chapter I will analyse these 'exaggerated' claims about the value of the work that raises the issue of what indeed might be the valuation of gendered work for a cultural organisation, here I will focus on the central strategy of the performance to present Rafeeq as a figure emerging in a metonymic relation to *mathi*. As he enters the stage for the first time, Rafeeq is even introduced by the narrator with the coinage *Mathi*-Rafeeq. *Mathi*-Rafeeq in the performance is a staging of what Una Chaudhuri has termed as zooesis, referring to 'the discourse of animality in human life' and its effects that 'permeate our social, psychological, and material existence' (2003: 647). In a dramatic sequence Rafeeq elaborates on his relationship with *mathi*-trading as he stands on top of the bicycle, giving a speech. He starts off at a fast pace throwing in one after the other the big words generally used in speeches: 'globalisation, global warming, chlorofluorocarbon,

Figure 9.1 Rafeeq and Kunjami interacting, with *mathi* being fried on stage (courtesy of Jino Jospeh)

global terrorism, democracy, tsunami, dengue, democracy, Jesus! Between all of these, it is *mathi* that I have to talk about: Tasty, healthy, economic is equal to *mathi*.' We come to know that the choice to sell *mathi* is a choice that is taken up by Rafeeq as a conscious refusal to sell other 'big' fishes, and, Rafeeq says, 'I am forced to ask my friends, if *mathi* was priced at 300 rupees, then all the executives would have bought and eaten *mathi*.' In the initial sequence, as people have assembled for rehearsal, one of them asks Rafeeq why he did not attend the meeting of the cultural forum or the protest procession. Rafeeq retorts that selling local *mathi* is also a form of struggle; it is 'a struggle of small fish against big ones'. At various points, the fish is anthropomorphised. Rafeeq tells Kunjami that when he is deep in the sea, he can hear *mathi* converse with each other, and that; they are like his friends. Further, Rafeeq is especially taken in by their struggle before death. The phrase that fish sellers use to highlight the freshness of the fish to woo customers is 'flopping fish', one that is not yet dead, a phrase that in the production Rafeeq himself uses while selling fish. But, at another point, Rafeeq frames the same flopping of *mathi* differently, as an intense struggle and resisitance, and effort to escape on their part even after they get caught in the fishing net, declaring that 'no other fish does that'. In this struggle *mathi* is marked as having a collective spirit and a spirit of not giving up (see Figure 9.2).

Yet this coinage of *Mathi*-Rafeeq is not simply because he is engaged in catching and selling fish or the anthropomorphising approach. The significant aspect that also links them is the smell of *mathi*, which the audience also smells during the whole duration of the performance. In the early part of the performance, Rafeeq himself moves between the audience seated in the front

Figure 9.2 Members of the cultural organisation listening as Rafeeq is on the bicycle in one of his ruminations about *mathi* and life (courtesy of Jino Joseph)

with a *mathi* to see their response to the rank smell. Even in the first interaction we witness Kunjami saying to Rafeeq, 'you are reeking'. Rafeeq retorts that it is not reek; it is instead a 'smell, a reeking smell'. Here, the English word 'smell' is used in performance, where in everyday usage the word smell as a loanword from English to Malayalam indicates 'fragrance'. He goes on: 'Some smells are like that ... in our clothes, in our breath, in whatever we touch or hold ... and even if we die, those smells will be here around.'

In another scene the narrator raises the question to the people assembled for rehearsal that 'every [written] complaint that Rafeeq has submitted has been settled', and the theatre activist responds to everyone's laughter, '[it's because] he and every one of his complaints have a reek ... the file, the shelf and even the office in which the complaint was kept has a reek', with the narrator concluding about the smell with the description, '[starting] mildly, mildly and then intensifying, reek', a description that in Malayalam also plays on associations of a (percussion) rhythm that starts slowly and intensifies. Here, smell is critical in intimating an experience distinct from the hegemony of the scopic regime in modernity that constitutes itself by denigration and diminution of the olfactory sense (Chalmers and Chaudhuri 2004). As an external force, enveloping and taking over, spreading from one's body to everything else, beyond one's control and finally lingering as a trace, smell is at the heart of memory and assertion of what has been lost. As indicated, the idea is that some smells simply linger after we pass on; the intense smell of *mathi*, for Rafeeq, is indeed a trace, an assertion even after death, that 'it was here'. Once Rafeeq hangs himself, the metonym is concretised as we see first a huge *mathi*, of Rafeeq's size, hanging in the same place where he hanged, and substituted by a huge skeleton of a *mathi* for the final sequences. In this sense the smell of *mathi* becomes part of Rafeeq and his lifeworld and, in fact, standing in for it transforms from a metonymy to a synecdoche. In the entire performance, the Rafeeq and *mathi* relationship is conspicuously excessive. This excessiveness is openly admitted as in the case when the voice tells Rafeeq, 'why are you trying to insert *mathi* into everything?' Rafeeq retorts, 'of course I will do that' and breaks into another set of statements about *mathi*. What allows this conspicuous excess is a specific articulation of possibilities of theatricality to stage the trace.

Playfulness, theatricality, and the retake of nostalgia

About the spectatorial reaction at the end of the performance, Joseph notes:

> usually, in Kerala, the audience run on to the stage to taste the fish. In Delhi, after the play, one lady came asking for some fried mathi to be packed for her child. Mathi represents celebration. It connects people in a way nothing else does, and that's why we announce at the beginning of the play that it's not a drama; it's a slice of life. Life is being enacted. (Mazumdar 2018)

This extremely positive response to the production needs to be analysed in relation to the world constituted through the production. The statement that 'it's a slice of life. Life is being enacted' might, on a surface reading, suggest an approach of realism. What is critical in the production is that so-called life is manifested through a space-time based on a distinct conceptualisation of theatricality. While nostalgia is the trace that lingers on even after something has passed away, this trace itself is recognised or activated through a foregrounding of theatricality, whereby the reek in its staging is transformed into fleeting redolence.

One of the obvious strategies that stands out in the theatricality of the production is the exaggerated slowing down of gestures in a varied manner throughout the performance, what the written play-text records in its description as 'slow-motion'. Scene after scene, one sees the process of frying the fish, checking it periodically, tasting it, turning it around, eating small pieces even as it is being shallow fried in the pan, and licking the oil from the bottom of the pan. However, as I noted previously, right at the start of the performance, one sees exaggerated actions played in slow motion by Kunjami and Sheeba of putting the fish into the frying pan, and the performance ends with the same actions. The slowing down and exaggeration, a conspicuous display of theatricality at work, is what defines the group/crowd sequences, even in the cases when the protagonists are shown engaging in everyday activities such as protests and hard labour of the immigrants working at construction sites. Even in the scenes of love between Rafeeq and Sheeba, we see Rafeeq moving towards Sheeba in slow motion and interacting in slowed-down and heightened gestures. These are, on the one hand, theatrical strategies drawn from global theatrical practices that have widely percolated in the vernacular: slowing down and repetition of the same actions are often used to highlight abstractions of experience, such as in the stylised opening sequence of fishermen at work, or the slowed-down sequences depicting hard labour by the new immigrant labourers. Yet the instances of the everyday acts slowed down clearly come across as embodied citations of the experience of the slow-motion technique in films. However, unlike the logic of iconisation of the masculine body that popular films undertake with slow-motion shots of heroes and their comportment, in *Mathi* they come across more as a playful celebration of the possibilities of theatricality rather than the iconisation of masculine figures. Further, this is also not the Brechtian unmasking of theatricality. Instead, the slow-motion sequences foreground a specific theatricality of what is deemed as life itself and the conceptualisation of theatre as a mode of foregrounding and extending this theatricalisation of life.

The nostalgia staged through theatricality is not a fixed place that is perceived to be lost. As Svetlana Boym has argued nostalgia is 'a yearning for a different time' rather than a return to a place (2001: xv). Unlike elements of mainstream feudal nostalgia, especially indexed with the agrarian landscape, older *tharavad* (ancestral homes), or temples, nothing in the representational space, in fact, gives it a specificity of a place per se. The stage has nothing specific apart from the two small huts of Rafeeq and Kunjami and that of Sheeba, whose small windows are on either end of the stage. Expect some short scenes, such as when Rafeeq, who is outside, interacts with Sheeba while she is at the kitchen window of her hut, no significant actions happen inside the huts; they are simply indexing a space. The stage space otherwise is an open space where theatre, protests, cooking, and social interactions can take place, with multiple revolving doors at the back that allow staging of certain crowd sequences such as the protest procession. This spatial configuration also results in a collapse of the distinction between the public and the private realm. Bonnet highlights the 'disjunction between the two worlds of nostalgia – the public and the private' (2010), foregrounding that

> while in the public realm nostalgia is rebuked, within the personal realm it tends to be tacitly indulged. We do not expect the treasured objects, the valued images, that we use to personalize our homes and 'work stations' to be sneered at ... For, however sentimental they may appear to others, they speak not only of a shared humanity but also of a shared vulnerability, an emotional range that includes love, loss and loyalty. It is, conversely, the spaces that fail to convey nostalgia that 'offend': the blank wall, the empty desk, the absence of signs of depth and connection. (2010: 6)

While the audience is seemingly immersed and trapped in the subjective world of Rafeeq, this is not an exploration of a private realm as everything (including the private) seems to be public in the world of *Mathi*. Partly it has to do with the absence of bourgeois individualised spaces in the case of the poor both as a physical possibility as well as the larger idea of shared intersubjective relationships in place of individualised subjectivity. The frame of the narrator, outside the space interacting with the characters on stage in an informal manner, makes the world on stage a presentation one is interacting with rather than simply observing. Even though the performance seems to be a subjective exploration of Rafeeq's lifeworld, by the end of the show, one has no inkling of Rafeeq or Kunjami's parents or their past. While the name and dressing indicate their religious location as Muslims, distinct from the strategies of claiming authenticity in a formal way by deploying 'native'/'indigenous' performance structures as done by the 'theatre of the roots'[11] movement, there is no reference to religious rituals or performance traditions.

While the theatre scenes of rehearsal embody familiar Leftist slogans and poems against caste discrimination from the 1970s (though none of them being iconic per se), and some famous popular songs, the irresistible smell and taste of *mathi* in its materiality also offers a break from the seriousness of the performance. For instance, in one of the theatre-within-the theatre sequences, the protagonists are rehearsing a play that depicts oppression and violence by the Brahmin landlord towards peasants that ends with the murder of the landlord by one of them. The actor who plays the Brahmin embodies the character in an exaggerated manner, accentuating the gesture of wearing the sacred thread and exaggerating the stylised bodily comportment and accented Malayalam associated with Brahmins. While others are taking their time to say their lines, the smell of *mathi* frying on the side is irresistible to him, and he keeps breaking off from the postures he is supposed to hold on to, often failing the rehearsal itself. While others are acting, he simply sits down alongside Kunjami, talking to her, checking and tasting the fish and the oil, only to be scolded by the others to get back to embodying the Brahmin again. The rehearsal is the only context where we see an invocation of a traditional performance as we see Teyyam (a figure from a popular ritual-healing performance of north Kerala) appearing in the murder scene of the landlord. In a range of practices including political theatre, the Teyyam figuration, decontextualised from the tradition itself, has often been deployed symbolically to capture heightened emotional moments, especially indexing moments of rage and violence.[12] In the rehearsal the seriousness of this citation is immediately undercut by playfulness. After the rehearsal of the scene, everyone else quickly sits down excitedly to eat the fried *mathi*, while the performer wearing the Teyyam costume is in a fix as he cannot sit down and eat wearing the huge, bulky, unmanageable costume. Kunjami quickly joins Teyyam, taking his headgear, and putting it on her own head, she breaks into a dance with him.

Playfulness runs through every action and statement in this nostalgic space-time. Earlier, we saw the claims of the excessive efficacy for Kunjami's cooking efforts that undercuts the seriousness of the claims of her contribution to the cultural organisation. When Rafeeq expresses his love to Sheeba in poetic lines, Sheeba lovingly says, 'wonderful! You spoke just like the teacher in my tutorial class', highlighting the fascination with flowery language. At one point, between the conversations of Kunjami, Rafeeq, and the narrator, when Kunjami says Rafeeq's smell has an 'organicity' to it, they tease her saying she is using high-flying words. Kunjami responds, 'I heard it being used by my teacher, and just tried it.' In another sequence Rafeeq makes Kunjami sit beside him at night and talks about his experiences of going to the sea and catching *mathi*. The scene builds as if it is one of an intimate sequence that reveals to us the subjective world of Rafeeq. Kunjami patiently listens for a while as he talks about how he listens to the *mathi* in the sea conversing among themselves, only to abruptly retort at the end, 'go and sleep'. While generally, such an undercutting of seriousness is associated with postmodern sensibilities of deconstruction that celebrate the experience of hybridity and fragmentation, the performance strategy in *Mathi* draws from the everyday conception of theatricality – at its heart filled with playful humour. Theatricality, here, is posited as an attempt to embody this claim for small, everyday pleasures of sociality based on friendship.

At various points in the play, when Rafeeq makes a mistake or misses doing something, he requests a 'retake', and the narrator at one point tells Rafeeq, 'you can't do retakes in life' but goes on to give him a second chance. After his suicide, when the narrator first encounters his body in the dark, he tells him to 'ask me for another chance Rafeeq ... we can do it differently ... [please] ask for one more chance'. The performance ends with a repetition or retake, taking us full circle, and the sequence plays back some of the dialogues that we have heard in the performance. On the darkened stage, ghostly figures appear behind Kunjami frying the *mathi*; all (except Rafeeq) come out of their ghostly figuration as the characters we have seen before the loss. Kunjami and Appu bring one *mathi* to the front of the stage and offer it to the audience, declaring '*mathi*' (see Figure 9.3). The stage is lit once again, and to the background of peppy songs, we see the characters once again inhabiting the space-time of celebration; some perform abstract actions with the coir of catching *mathi*, the narrator, in a corner, slowly holds the gesture of a raised fist, while Sheeba fries *mathi* centre stage. Rafeeq appears in a window from backstage, looking on to the

Figure 9.3 Celebration or the 'retake' of life towards the end of the performance (courtesy of Jino Joseph)

stage and giving a gesture of thumbs up to the song with the lines, 'will tell you a story now, the story of *mathi*. It isn't a big matter, but a small one. The *mathi* flopping around like the flopping in the heart … this has a smell … smell of reek … the smell of flopping humans.'

Conclusion

Mathi, its irresistible smell and taste, attempts to engender sociality based on conviviality and friendship as bodies sit around the frying pan, tasting the oil and spices, checking and turning the *mathi* around in the frying pan, eating directly out of the pan, and feeding each other small pieces of *mathi*. Nostalgia is the reek that lingers on in the present even after something has passed away or been lost. In this sense it troubles and is something that cannot be controlled or erased in the rationalisation of developmental politics. Yet rather than going back to a pre-fixed or authentic space-time, this trace is recognised by means of a theatricality that foregrounds a retake, the possibility of once again-ness with a difference. It does work with the trope of Malayalee people, foregrounding a troubling frame based on anxieties arising from a space-time of Kerala when Malayalees have become diasporic and immigrant labour has taken over due to globalisation. Yet, the trace of the production itself after its consumption raises a peculiar challenge about the need to pause and think about a different conception of the sustainability of life. Rather than folding back to a feudal nostalgia or that of a Left nostalgia anchored on moments of assumption of power by the Left in Kerala and its genealogy, *Mathi* foregrounds a Left ethos wherein micro-scale is critical. While the production does not set out any alternative, the staging makes manifest those forms of work and processes – cooking, theatre rehearsal, friendship – that are not recognised or are devalued and invisibilised within the narrative of development and rationalising political processes. These are presented as work, yet simultaneously pleasurable, fleeting, and that can be subjected to retakes. While at the heart of the staging is melancholia and loss, what the performance as celebration of theatricality posits is a distinct anti-productive space-time, a 'romantic anti-capitalist' space-time of the working class, as Ridout (2013: 6) calls it. It replaces the rhetoric of lack that drives the development discourse with an affective space-time contentedness in sociality based on friendship at the scale of the body. It registers the lingering reek of Left ethos through a theatricalisation of life that demands to transform the world democratically by imagining and engaging in retakes that could go beyond the framing and the limits of the performance itself.

Notes

1 *Mathi* received the Kerala Sangeetha Nataka Akademi Awards in 2013 in three categories, including 'Best Play' and 'Best Script', as well as the Kerala Sahitya Akademi Award, and in the festival of Mahindra Excellence in Theatre Awards, conducted in New Delhi, it bagged four awards in 2015.
2 Throughout the chapter I have italicised the term *mathi* for the fish, and used capitalisation of the first letter in the instances where it refers to the title of the production.
3 It has been coming to power every alternate five years, and in fact recently, breaking this pattern, the Left came to power for a second consecutive term in 2021.
4 Jino Joseph records: 'I grew up watching commercial drama staged in churches and temples during festivals every year. I used to sit in front of the stage, on the floor, to watch those plays. In those days our source of movies was Doordarshan, which aired a new film every Sunday evening, and we waited for it every week. The hangover from those films and plays inspired me to write scripts for plays and direct them when I was in school. Later I joined Government Brennen College, Thalassery, which had a good artistic culture. There was no funding, but our teachers were welcoming of experimental plays. I wrote small plays for schoolchildren and directed short plays for colleges, which won several awards at youth festivals.' About the amateur group itself, Joseph highlights: 'There are no big organisations supporting us and it's a collective initiative by people who are not trained in theatre. The actors are not professionals – some are students, others are auto-drivers. The central character is played by Ranji Kankol (Best Actor awardee), who is a sculptor. He was selected for his body language and appearance' (Mazumdar, 2018).
5 *Porotta*, made of *maida*, is an extremely popular flaky textured flatbread in Kerala.
6 In their study Zachariah and Rajan have shown how remittances are '1.2 times the revenue receipt of the Kerala Government and over five times the amount that the state gets from the centre as revenue transfer' and are '1.5 times the government's annual expenditure' (2016: 71).
7 Even in a more recent production *Nona* (Lie 2018) that undertakes a frontal critique of the Hindutva Right wing, Joseph seems to work with a vision that isolates the figuration and obsessively follows it. In the case of *Nona* it is the 'other' side, that of the functioning of Hindutva figures and their grotesqueness, that is explored.
8 The term 'slow motion' is used in the published play-text to describe the actions (Joseph 2014).
9 All the quotations from the performance are taken from the video documentation of the production at the META Theatre Festival, New Delhi, in 2015. The translations are all mine.
10 *Pushparchana* refers to the floral offering, performed in temples as well as for venerating people. *Kuttayottom* refers to the group running as a social event, and *padayatra* is a journey undertaken on foot, here referring to the political

action where the politicians move around the state interacting and campaigning with people.
11 'Theatre of the roots' refers to the state-driven discourse in the post-independent period wherein a new theatre aesthetic as distinct from realism and Western theatre was articulated by important theatre practitioners by engaging with performance forms and structures that are deemed to be native/indigenous. For more on theatre of the roots and its critiques, see Dharwadker (2005) and Mee (2008).
12 Teyyam is a northern Malabar ritual-healing form of performance where a person from the lower caste community embodies the deity for the duration of the performance. The immensely popular performance of Teyyam, where caste boundaries are troubled, holds significant political significance in the region. The important theatre director K. N. Panikkar made use of Teyyam figuration and its aesthetics as a central element in his plays and performances, and currently the figure is used along with forms such as Kathakali to index a Kerala identity in popular representations.

References

Bonnett, Alastair. 2010. *Left in the Past: Radicalism and the Politics of Nostalgia.* London and New York: Continuum.
Bose, Satheese Chandra, and Shiju Sam Varughese (eds). 2015. *Kerala Modernity: Ideas, Spaces, and Practices in Transition.* Hyderabad: Orient Blackswan.
Boym, Svetlana. 2001. *The Future of Nostalgia.* New York: Basic Books.
Brown, W. 1999. 'Resisting Left Melancholy.' *Boundary 2* 26(3): 19–27.
Chalmers, Jessica, and Una Chaudhuri. 2004. 'Sniff Art.' *TDR/The Drama Review* 48(2): 76–80.
Chaudhuri, Una. 2003. 'Animal Geographies: Zooësis and the Space of Modern Drama.' *Modern Drama* 46(4): 646–662.
Devika, J. 2007. '"A People United in Development": Developmentalism in Modern Malayalee Identity.' CDS Working Papers 386. Trivandrum: Centre for Development Studies.
Dharwadker, Aparna Bhargava. 2005. *Theatres of Independence: Drama, Theory, and Urban Performance in India since 1947.* Iowa City, IA: University of Iowa Press.
Joseph, Jino. 2014. *Mathi.* Thrissur: Kerala Sangeetha Nataka Akademy.
Mazumdar, Arunima. 2018. 'Packed like Mathi.' *The Hindu Business Line,* 23 January. www.thehindubusinessline.com/blink/watch/packed-like-mathi/article7137389.ece. Accessed on 25 June 2021.
Mee, Erin B. 2008. *Theatre of Roots: Redirecting the Modern Indian Stage.* Calcutta: Seagull.
Ridout, Nicholas. 2013. *Passionate Amateurs: Theatre, Communism and Love.* Ann Arbor, MI: University of Michigan Press.
Traverso, Enzo. 2016. *Left-Wing Melancholia: Marxism, History, Memory.* New York: Columbia University Press.
Zachariah, Kunniparambil Curien, and S. Irudaya Rajan. 2016. 'Kerala Migration Study 2014.' *Economic and Political Weekly* 51(6): 66–71.

10

Staging revolution: Utpal Dutt's *Kallol* (1965) and the question of 'spectacular' aesthetics in Calcutta's Leftist theatre practice

Trina Nileena Banerjee

Introduction

From the late 1950s onwards, the celebrated Marxist playwright and director Utpal Dutt's (1929–1993) aesthetic and political language deeply influenced the shape and direction of much of India's progressive theatre practice. However, this influence did not develop without its share of controversies. In Calcutta of the 1960s, both the form and content of an ideal revolutionary theatre were under debate. The widely pondered question was: what should a *true* 'people's theatre' look like? This chapter will revisit one aspect of these debates among Leftist theatre critics, practitioners, and activists in Calcutta: the politics of stage design in Utpal Dutt's plays from this time. The ethics and politics of 'spectacular' staging in Dutt's plays were widely debated. Some critics sought to impose the imperatives of aesthetic austerity on Dutt's vision of a popular urban revolutionary theatre. The creation of an underground coal mine in *Angar* in 1959, followed by the overwhelming presence of the ship *Khyber* in *Kallol* (1965), simultaneously stunned audiences and incensed certain critics. Dutt was accused of trying to overwhelm people with formal tricks and technical brilliance (Mukhopadhyay 2010: 94). Besides, such aesthetic and financial extravagance was seen as antithetical to the notion of an authentic 'people's theatre'. How were these controversies related to the larger ideology of Leftist theatre in Bengal? How did Dutt formulate his own notion of theatrical form in relation to his politics as a playwright, dramaturg, and director? How were Dutt's international political and artistic influences, which ranged from Piscator and Brecht to Okhlopkov and Eisenstein at this time, responsible for shaping his vision of a revolutionary stage of this magnitude, quite unprecedented in the Calcutta of the time? Was the monumentality of *Khyber* merely physically spectacular, or was it embedded in an international history of revolutionary aesthetics?

Dutt's essays and other writings from the time bear witness to the growing breadth of his intellectual and theatrical vision, as well as the expansiveness of his international exchanges that had been widened through obsessive reading and travel. In her memoirs the veteran actress Sova Sen (Dutt's wife and comrade) meticulously records their travels from the early 1960s onwards – to Russia, Germany, and England, among other places. These are journeys marked by one primary intent: watching as much theatre as possible, especially in the cities of the former Soviet Union and the German Democratic Republic (GDR). At one point in her reminiscences, Sen describes, in painstaking detail, the experience of watching Nikolay Okhlopkov's production *Ocean* at his Mayakovsky Theatre in Moscow in October 1962:

> As soon as we sat down in the auditorium, we noticed that *there were no stage curtains*. But something like a thick blue curtain was lying on the floor of the enormous, open stage. Slowly, the lights in the auditorium (which was full) began to be dimmed. Suddenly we noticed that six or seven people dressed as sailors had picked up the corners of that massive blue curtain. They stood at the different corners of the stage holding that piece of cloth. The blue fabric began to move a little. Gradually, the movement of the cloth picked up speed and soon it felt as if the whole stage was being shaken by the roughest of sea waves. I cannot explain how magnificent it was! Then, we found that a ship's lights were shining in the great distance. We sat watching, mesmerized.[1] (1993: 62)

Less than a year before this, in an essay on stage design written in December 1961, Dutt wrote:

> As soon as I have a theatre and an audience, *I shall get rid of the curtains*. Then the wings, the border etc. Then I shall remove anything that looks like a painted scene. *I shall fill up the stage floor with platforms of various sizes; put stairs everywhere randomly*. Actors will be forced to use the stairs whenever they walk. ... To indicate a storm, I shall use Craig's striped, black curtain or Brecht's grey curtain with the lightning painted on it. To indicate water, I shall use twenty dancers in blue costumes. For fire, I shall wave around Uday Shankar's red ribbons. (1998: 78)

How did this astonishing range of influences, international political conversations, and capacious aesthetic tendencies find ground in the cultural and political context of Calcutta in the 1960s? What was really at stake in the discursive and ideological conflicts around Dutt's 'excessive' stage design? How were his intentions and vision understood or misunderstood within his own context? More broadly, what were the *ideological tensions* between an avowedly minimalist Leftist aesthetic and an alleged tendency towards visual excess? What was the relationship of these tendencies with the demands of Left politics and the motivating concern with the representation of the 'masses' in a people's theatre? The larger aim of this chapter is to explore the relationship of the popular theatrical representation of revolutionary history in *Kallol* to its visual design, that is, not to see this debate as one where content militates against form but where the shape of each is deeply imbricated in the other. We shall begin by discussing two earlier productions that critically shaped Dutt's theatrical language in the years that led up to the making of *Kallol*, as well as his travels during the early 1960s that had a considerable impact on his subsequent scenographic practices.

Angar (*The Burning Coal*, 1959)

The Minerva Theatre in North Calcutta was taken on a hundred-year lease by the Little Theatre Group on 3 July 1959 (Dutt 2005: 451; Sen 1993: 42; Mukhopadhyay 2010: 45).[2] Dutt first staged his play *Angar* at Minerva on 31 December 1959. An unprecedented success, *Angar* narrativised the lives of coal mine workers who are brutally exploited by a ruthless management bent on maximising profits at any cost. Dutt based the play on a series of incidents that took place at the Baradhemo and Chinakudi coal mines in Bengal in the late 1950s. Numerous workers were injured or killed because of the colliery management's criminal negligence. *Angar* included striking visual and sonic landscapes of the coalmines. Inside the coal mine, a netherworld of darkness, soot, and danger become visible to an urban audience unfamiliar with this life of precarious labour:

> [*Pithead. The wheels are turning up above – trolleys carrying buckets full of coal are sliding and stopping. From some moving cars, an exhausted worker or two steps out – round helmets on their heads, with lights fitted on them; some are carrying sacks, others pickaxes and shovels. There is a small fire burning downstage. A few workers are huddling around it. We see Sanatan amongst them. There is a poster on the wall: 'We demand punishment for the murderers of Dinu Mukherjee! Join the union!'*]. (Dutt 1994: 91)

The scene immediately drives home an atmosphere of workers' solidarity and simmering rage but also an ominous state of affairs: a sense that darkness is slowly closing in even as the miners prepare for organised resistance. The mines have filled up with gas, often bursting into small fires in places. We learn that a few days ago, an explosion took away the life of a senior worker. The sense of precarity and danger hanging over the scene is enhanced by the gloom solidified by Tapas Sen's light design and the mechanised soundscape:

> *The sound of an enormous explosion. In the darkness, we see some searchlights, lanterns and smoke. We hear the sound of several sirens, and the bells of the fire engine ringing.*
>
> *The light shines. We see the state of the pithead – it seems to have been ravaged. The big iron machines have been crushed, there is no sign of the glass*

window of the lamp room, only half of a signboard containing the Sheldon Company's name is hanging over it. From the pit a thick, dark column of smoke is climbing towards the sky. A barbed wire fence circumscribes the dangerous area. ... A siren howls in pain as it comes to rest near the officers. The rescue team enters, fastening their uniforms. (Dutt 1994: 117)

We have a sense of an almost cinematic visual landscape, a space split up by light and darkness, smoke fading out, scenes of chiaroscuro and machinic sounds violently punctuating the tentative human efforts towards survival. Despite the meticulous scenography which created stage history, later in his career Dutt became critical of the political content of *Angar* and especially its despairing ending. This retrospective disapproval could be understood in relation to his admiration for the fundamental tenets of Socialist Realism, including the rejection of pessimism in the literary or artistic depiction of working-class life. While critical of repressive figures such as Andrei Zhdanov, Dutt was respectful of the core of Socialist Realist ideology: the celebration of the labour and revolutionary struggles of the working classes as well as a faithful, concrete depiction of proletarian reality. Perhaps the crux of the Socialist Realist imperative was the productive tension between the need for a concrete, materialist representation of reality and the pull towards a utopic revolutionary future: an idea that inspired Dutt. Eisenstein's *Battleship Potemkin* (1925) remained one of the most significant international influences on Dutt's artistic life as well as a model for the writing of *Kallol*, as we shall go on to see.[3]

Despite Dutt's many reservations about a play which he began to see as defeatist and insufficiently revolutionary, *Angar* faced virulent attacks from mainstream newspapers, which alleged that the play had fabricated the incidents of injustice against coal miners and was politically motivated to stir up trouble against the authorities. The ruling Congress party in Bengal was so incensed by its staging that Minerva was attacked several times in the next few years by hired goons bent on stopping *Angar*. Dutt had perhaps expected this turn of events from the staging of a play with such incendiary content. What he had not foreseen were the ideological attacks and severe criticism from within the Leftist camp. Dutt was accused of excessive concentration on formal tricks and stage gimmicks aimed at creating an overwhelming visual spectacle intended to draw audiences to the theatre for all the wrong reasons. Such a bid for popularity was deemed befitting of commercial theatre producers, but the serious 'people's theatre' was meant to appeal to its audience solely through the force of its revolutionary political content. Dutt writes:

> What astonished me, however, was that some leaders of the *Indian Peoples Theatre Association* began to criticise the play with the sharpest of invectives. Their main objection was the dominance of formal elements in the play. They

claimed that the force of acting had been swept away by mechanized techniques. On the other hand, Hemanga Biswas[4] banged tables in support of *Little Theatre*. He was convinced that we had destabilised the world of commercial theatre with our success, without compromising even a little bit on political content. (Dutt (2005) 1977: 452)[5]

Dutt was committed to creating a revolutionary theatre that could serve as *popular entertainment* for the working classes. He quite openly declared his willingness to unhesitatingly use all the well-known and allegedly 'commercial' devices of coincidence, fast-paced narrative, thrill, suspense, melodrama, and grand spectacle.[6] In truth, the popularity, as well as the scenographic brilliance of *Angar*'s ending remains iconic in the history of Bengali theatre. The play ends with the deliberate flooding of the mine by the ruthless owners of the colliery. This inhuman and gut-wrenching scene was depicted by Dutt by means of a magnificent stage set representing the underground tunnels of the coal mine. The illusion of actual flooding was created by the technical brilliance of the light designer Tapas Sen. The last scene of the play begins with the entrapped workers still looking for a means of survival inside the collapsed mine:

> *The insides of the chasm filled with intense darkness. Three or four tunnels meet here. We see six cap lamps and a torch dancing in that darkness. The lights advance towards us. Seven creatures are desperately looking for a way out. The first one to reach the stage is Mostak, a pickaxe in his hand.* (Dutt 1994: 134)

The scene is designed to give the audience a sense that the mines were spread out far behind and all around the performance space. The ubiquitous darkness, as well as the distant and unpredictable movement of lights, deliver a sense of deep despair, hopelessness, and claustrophobia. Perhaps it is this slowly building, visceral sense of entrapment that Dutt, along with his designers Sen and Guha Roy, methodically engendered in his audience that led to the unprecedented impact of the final scene of the play. The stage directions from this final scene of workers drowning proceed thus:

> *Everyone pricks up their ears to listen. Drip-drip: the sounds of water drops begin to fill up the air. Inside the tunnel, every drop, every sound is magnified by reverberations into something terrifying.* (Dutt 1994: 142)

Here, Dutt builds up the terror merely with the simple sound of drops of water – which, echoing, create a terrifying soundscape. Those who accused Dutt of being merely spectacular – because of Tapas Sen's visionary lighting of the last scene – surely missed the extraordinarily chilling sonic build-up towards the brutal climax. Realising from the rising sound of water that they are about to die, the workers each decide to write a letter to leave behind for their loved ones:

Staging revolution 185

Figure 10.1 Still from Utpal Dutt's *Angar* (1959)
(photograph by Sambhu Banerjee)

(Sanatan reads aloud his letter to 'the people of the world').

His voice is drowned by the tremendous roar of the waves, yet Sanatan goes on writing rapidly ... He quickly gathers the letters together and puts them in the box with the gunpowder. He puts the box away with utmost care inside a crack on the wall of the mine. Now the waves seem to be roaring inside the tunnel itself, the reverberating sound fills up the space. ... The three of them start singing. (Dutt 1994: 144)

Amid the hullabaloo around this scene, few paid attention to Dutt's use of a minutely designed soundscape to create a visceral atmosphere of terror and claustrophobia. Ravi Shankar's music added to the poignance of this tragedy. Sen writes of how Shankar created fourteen original full-length pieces of background music for the play (1993: 46).

However, what was Dutt's intent in creating such an intricate design? The spectators at Minerva included urban middle-class and working-class inhabitants of Calcutta, most of whom had encountered the news of the recent mining disasters in newspapers printed in the city. Like numerous other news items in the daily newspapers, these would have left very little impact on a metropolitan audience. Dutt tried to recreate the visceral, embodied experience of entrapment in order to bring home the brutality of what had been done to the workers at the coal mines. While most audiences found this last scene of drowning heart-rending and awe-inspiring, sharp criticism arose from a certain rank of Leftist critiques. Arup Mukhopadhyay, Dutt's biographer, writes of the time: 'Their primary complaint was that *Angar* has deplorably drowned its noble subject matter by having indulged its audience in cheap formal thrills' (Mukhopadhyay 2010: 94). There were some important positive reviews of the design as well and some prominent figures, including the celebrated film director Satyajit Ray, came to Dutt's defence.

The Bengali monthly magazine *Desh* published a review that said: 'The entire technical apparatus of the colliery and the infrastructure of the coalmines along with the incisive use of chiaroscuro has taken shape in front of us in such a concrete way – it would not be wrong to say that such a thing has never been witnessed on stage in this country before' (Mukhopadhyay 2010: 94). Many of the same criticisms of his stage design arose a few years later when Dutt staged *Kallol* at the Minerva, but by then Dutt's own scenographic practice had undergone a sea of change: he had become bolder rather than more circumspect in his stage experiments.

The politics of Dutt's stage design: Okhlopkov, *Titas*, and beyond (1959–1965)

What came in between these two landmark productions, that is, *Angar* and *Kallol*, were Dutt's extensive travels across the Soviet Union and the former GDR. In September of 1962 Dutt travelled abroad for the first time with his wife, Sova Sen. The Soviet government had invited him to travel to Tashkent and Moscow. This was followed by his first tour of GDR. Dutt's biographer writes of the critical significance of this trip for Dutt's intellectual and artistic life. His meeting with various theatre directors in the USSR and GDR, as well as watching plays at some of the best-known theatres of the world, bolstered his wide reading into the histories of the theatres of Europe and the Soviet Union. Among the plays that Dutt saw was the Berliner Ensemble production of Brecht's *Three Penny Opera*, *The Lower Depths* at the Maxim Gorky Theatre, and a production of Tolstoy's *The Living Corpse* at the Pushkin Theatre in the Soviet Union.

Sova Sen's memoirs *Smarane Bismarane: Nabanna Theke Lal Durgo* (*Reminiscences: From Nabanna to Lal Durgo*) are the richest and perhaps the only direct source for an account of these travels. For example, Sen's memoirs have a brief but detailed account of the couple's visit to Rostock while in the GDR:

> We travelled into the sea a little distance on a motor launch and saw enormous ships – they were being built, being repaired, huge metallic cranes were picking up loads. The sailors were looking at us, talking amongst themselves, and then

there was another group painting the ship. Ships from so many countries were standing there in numerous rows. (1993: 57)

The image of the monumental ship, and the chaos of activity surrounding it, was to appear very soon in Dutt's work. Perhaps the most striking experience of this journey was Dutt's meeting with Nikolay Okhlopkov in Moscow, followed by an evening at the Mayakovsky Theatre to watch his play *The Ocean*. If we return to Sova Sen's description of the stage in *The Ocean*,[7] we will find once again the image of the rough, chaotic waters of the sea and a ship's lights in the distance. About Okhlopkov's meeting with Dutt, Sen writes: 'We discussed for a long time the particularities of his directorial style, his methods, and his many experimentations with stage design. He, too, was attracted to us because of Utpal's deep knowledge of Soviet theatre and the many discussions they had on various subjects' (1993: 61). Okhlopkov, who was once Meyerhold's student, had a deep impact on Dutt's subsequent work and especially on his stage design, bringing a new fluidity and multidimensionality to Dutt's visual and spatial conception of the stage.[8]

Dutt's next directorial work *Titas Ekti Nodir Naam* (referred to as *Titas* in the rest of the chapter), after he returned to India, was based on a novel by Adwaita Mallabarman. It told the story of a subaltern fishing community on the banks of the river Titas in Brahmanbaria, Bangladesh, and premiered on 10 March 1963 at the Minerva Theatre. Arup Mukhopadhyay writes: 'It was in this play that Dutt used the particular modes of stage design that he had witnessed in Moscow in the maestro Okhlopkov's work' (2010: 98). In staging the play Dutt had to keep in mind the riverine landscape of Bengal and the life of a community that was deeply entwined with the river that sustained it. The fluidity of the stage witnessed in the dark and flooded mines of *Angar*'s coalfields, as well as Okhlopkov's ships and oceans witnessed in Moscow, was to return again here: in the form of the river Titas. In *Titas* Dutt used, for the first time, the ramp that became a hallmark of his plays at Minerva: an enormous catwalk that came up from the middle of the audience seats and joined the stage. Sen describes in detail how this ramp was used in *Titas*:

> The foremost attraction of this play was the absolute novelty of its stage design. A path ascended the stage from the middle of the audience seats. In the very first scene, a group of women came up this path to the stage carrying lit lamps and trays of flowers for a ritual. Once on stage, they danced to celebrate this ritual. Each of us had to dance. (1993: 69)

A ramp that split the barrier between the audience and the actors was a recurrent feature in Okhlopkov's stage design. In his 1973 essay for *The Drama Review*, Gail Lenhoff gives a detailed diagrammatic account of

Okhlopkov's various experiments with the ramp. He writes: 'Okhlopkov fixed his attention on one central issue: how to destroy the barrier that any stage, no matter how it is altered, creates between the actor and the spectator' (1973: 93). Lenhoff writes that when, in 1930, Okhlopkov was made the head of the Realistic Theatre in Krasnaya Presnya, he was left to work with the smallest stage in Moscow and an auditorium with a seating capacity of merely three hundred. Obviously, this auditorium was meant for intimate and small-scale chamber plays, but Okhlopkov dismantled the stage and replaced it with movable platforms.

Remember here Dutt writing in 1961, '*I shall fill up the stage floor with platforms of various sizes; put stairs everywhere randomly*. Actors will be forced to use the stairs whenever they walk' (Dutt 1998: 78). The resonance is remarkable, especially because Dutt understood that the moving platforms came to Okhlopkov's work from his teacher Meyerhold's 'constructivist scaffoldings', as Gail Lenhoff calls them (1973: 93). These design innovations in Dutt's work had a politico-aesthetic lineage, and Dutt was conscious of his embeddedness in these international histories. Okhlopkov's first directorial work at the Realistic Theatre in 1931, which was a production of Stavsky's *The Start*, introduced the stage ramp, which appeared in different ways again in his productions of Gorky's *The Mother* (1932) and Alexander Serafimovich's *The Iron Flood* (1933). Lenhoff writes:

> a small stage was erected in the centre of the auditorium; along the upper half of the hall wound a ramp half-surrounding the audience. A circular bridge lifted the action over their heads. All these ramps were not bare scaffolding, as they would have been in Meyerhold's direction, but were decorated with sunflowers, foliage and fruit trees. The critics were bewildered. (1973: 93)

The critics were similarly bewildered by *Titas* and its stage design in Calcutta in 1963, even though it did not cause the kind of controversy that *Angar* and later *Kallol* did. However, each of these times, it seemed that they were unable to politically and aesthetically situate Dutt's scenographic innovations. Some of them diagnosed his interventions as Brechtian. An exasperated Dutt writes of the critical vacuum and misreading he encountered after *Titas*:

> If the actors ascend the stage from the midst of the audience, then inevitably these recently literate critics will write: 'We witnessed some Brechtian methods in this production.' Brecht had never left the stage to go into the audience. This was done by Edmund Jones in the 1930s and *Okhlopkov in Moscow in the 1960s*. (quoted in Mukhopadhyay 2010: 98)

What bothered Dutt in these contemporary critiques was the absence of any robust historical understanding of his scenographic politics. Dutt was deliberately placing his experimentations within an international tradition of Leftist theatre aesthetics, where various (sometimes even contradictory) lineages of imagining the performance space were coming together: from Brecht and Piscator to Meyerhold and Okhlopkov. Looking at revolutionary scenography as a worksite of the cultural Left demands that a global intellectual and political history of stage design in post-independence India be written while critically considering the embeddedness of metropolitan theatre buildings such as Minerva and Star Theatre within a repressive history of colonialism. The architectural site of the colonial theatre itself was symbolic of both censorship/repression and political courage/resistance, an idea that Dutt takes up passionately six years later in his play *Tiner Talawar* (*The Tin Sword*, 1971). Dutt was understandably frustrated at the limited nature of the criticism he received, including the strident claim that what was spectacular could not be 'people's theatre'. Indeed, there were many ways of being spectacular on stage – some of which demanded sensory density rather than opulence – several of which belonged to Leftist international traditions of stage design and scenography.

Kallol (*The Waves*, 1965): a monumental battle

Despite Dutt's sharply critical response to the attacks on *Angar*'s 'excessive' stage design, almost the exact same controversy arose during the staging of *Kallol* six years later. Amid intense political uproar on the question of the historical accuracy of the plot, the nature of the play's stage design also provoked bitter debates. Yet there was intense excitement among the general audience about the grandeur of *Kallol*'s scenography (see Figure 10.2). *Kallol* was first performed at the Minerva Theatre in Calcutta on 29 March 1965 (Sen 1993: 42–45). The play was based on the incident of a naval mutiny against the British by the sailors of the ship *Khyber* in the year 1946. In the play Dutt wished to recover an alternative history of India's struggle for independence through a systematic dismantling of the ruling party's 'bourgeois' version of it. The point was counterpropaganda, upholding the 'communist' version of that same history.[9]

As mentioned earlier, in defending *Kallol* against accusations of historical inauthenticity, Dutt invoked Eisenstein's 1925 classic *Battleship Potemkin*, arguing that the failed revolt of Potemkin found historical fruition in the successful October Revolution of 1917 (Dutt 2009: 64). Fitting perfectly as it did into the Socialist Realist mode of envisioning historical art, this argument was not the only reference to *Battleship Potemkin* to be found in contemporary discussions around *Kallol*. Eisenstein's 1925 film about the 1905 Russian naval mutiny hovers all around Dutt's imagination of the imperial battleship *Khyber* constantly. *Potemkin* is a political, formal, and aesthetic

Figure 10.2 Still from Utpal Dutt's *Kallol* (1965) (photograph by Sambhu Banerjee; courtesy of the Utpal Dutt Foundation)

prototype that shapes many of the play's concerns. For example, in speaking of the music of the play, singer and music director Hemanga Biswas writes:

> Dutt's contribution towards creating the music of the play was no less. He has an incredible collection of revolutionary music from the world over. In consultation with him, I used the music of three famous naval mutiny songs from around the world in the context of this Indian naval mutiny. They were the song of the rebellion of the naval officers of the battleship Potemkin from 1905 – 'Potemkin has reached Odessa', 'Aurora' – the song of the rebellious sailors in Petrograd of 1917 and another song that came from the German naval mutiny of 1918 – 'Red flag on the waters of a Blue Sea.' Besides this, of course, we used the song that belongs to the oppressed all over the world – the 'Internationale'. The music was immensely successful. (1986: 6)[10]

Important clues about the scenography can be derived from the brief reminiscences of the stage designer Suresh Dutta, who built the grand structure of the ship *Khyber* for the stage at Minerva. The influence of Moscow was paramount in Suresh Dutta's theatrical vision at this time as well. In 1961–1962 Dutt won a scholarship from the Indian Department of Education to study puppetry under the renowned Soviet puppeteer Sergei Obraztsov. Obraztsov helped found the Moscow Puppet Theatre in 1931 and served as its head. This theatre later came to be called the Sergei Obraztsov State Academic Central Puppet Theatre. Dutta writes:

> I had returned from Moscow in 1961. I had been deeply influenced by the modes of theatre practice I had witnessed there. The scientific methods of doing theatre work in that place, the process of doing 'table work' – all this had changed my conception of theatre fundamentally. ... I witnessed similar scientific methods in the creation of theatre once again while working for *Kallol*. (1986: 12)

Tapas Sen introduced Suresh Dutta to Utpal Dutt, where the text of *Kallol* was read to him. He liked the play immensely. After this, Dutta writes that Utpal Dutt showed him some pictures, which he gives us no details about. He then goes on to write:

> I told him [Utpal Dutt] that I want to see an actual warship. This was especially because it was necessary in several scenes of the play to show the interiors of the warship. So, I needed to see an actual ship and its interiors from up close, and in detail. Consequently, the three of us went to see a ship – Tapas Sen, I and another person. I came back and made a drawing of the ship as needed in the play. Dutt was pleased with my drawing and asked me to begin work on the stage. (1986: 12)

Dutta describes in some detail the process of building the ship *Khyber* for the Minerva stage. He speaks of how despite limited financial resources, there was a lot of moral strength, commitment, and unity in the Little Theatre Group, which often compensated for the lack of money. Dutta writes that he first made a model of the ship based on his initial drawing. Since the play was to be staged at Minerva, it was important for him to map out exactly how much support he would have from the architecture of the stage and to build the ship accordingly. The model was based on these calculations. He then started working on the construction and assemblage of the actual ship. He writes:

> I don't remember everyone's name, but there were 20/25 carpenters and shifters. With this team, it took us twenty days to make the stage. There were a couple of workers called Rangu and Sudha, their contribution was unforgettable. In those days, the whole thing had cost us Rs. 15000. ... Each element, part and instrument that went into the making of the ship was systematically numbered, and we worked according to those numbers. At this time, we had very little idea of how it would all come together and what the final ship would look like. [...] On the day on which all the work was completed and only the painting of the ship was left, I asked Utpal Dutt to leave me the stage for one night so that I could set it all up. Dutt agreed. All through that night I kept calling out the numbers one by one and my colleagues on the team kept arranging the pieces accordingly. When we saw the final result, we were all overjoyed. I had been able to apply fully what I had learnt in Moscow. (1986: 12)

Suresh Dutta writes of Utpal Dutt's delight the next morning on seeing the *Khyber* for the first time on the Minerva stage. The actors began to work with renewed enthusiasm on this new set, and within a few days, Dutt asked him to finish painting the ship. He describes how, as the final look of the ship emerged after its painting, he himself was overcome by its sheer grandeur:

> I finished painting the ship within one night, with the help of my collaborators. I remember when it was finished, how astonished I was myself. The stage appeared before my eyes in all its expansiveness. We were all stunned. I have never done this kind of work ever again in my life. (1986: 12)

The playwright Anal Gupta writes in his reminiscences:

> This was the beginning of the *Kallol* era in Bengali theatre. The grand architecture of an immense, floating warship on the stage. The unforgettably significant, meaningful use of light. The revolutionary inflections of the music constantly reminded one of *Battleship Potemkin*. The unprecedentedly innovative use of maps and charts. The use of entirely new methods in the movement of the actors. In sum, what could be called 'total theatre'. With the staging of *Kallol*, the Calcutta audience had the taste of an entirely new experience. To put it simply, in terms of staging and technologies of the stage as well, *Kallol* created a new era. (1986: 10)

A densely layered account of the staging of *Kallol* appears in the reminiscences of Bishnupriya Dutt, Utpal Dutt's daughter and a theatre scholar in her own right. In an interview with me recorded in August 2022, Dutt said:

> I think it was *Kallol*. … What Nirmal Guha Roy (the set designer of many of Dutt's plays, including *Angar*) used to do was … he would put up a rough replica – not a model – of the real set design of whichever play was coming up, so that the actors knew what they were going to do. If there was a screen there, he would put up the screen. If there was going to be ramp in the middle, which was very important for Minerva, he would put that in. The actors kept their stuff there, they also had a lot of makeshift props … so he would put things in their right place. It didn't look like the ultimate set would be, but it really helped in the choreography, blocking, working with the actors together, giving them a sense of the space but also the size and height of objects … What I remember most distinctly about *Kallol* was the ramp, which my father had already set up during the rehearsals.[11]

The famous catwalk/ramp returns in Shantanu Ghosh's description of the play:

> We were astonished to see the catwalk and apron outside the proscenium in *Titas Ekti Nodir Nam*. Before *Kallol*, we were unable to imagine that one could accomplish so much so perfectly on a stage. Just as we could not imagine the three-dimensional steps of *Ferari Fouj* or the changing colours of the underground coalmines in *Angar*. (1986: 20)

However, the production generated a debate around its stage design that seems eerily familiar. Sadhan Guha summarises these criticisms quite thoroughly in his essay on *Kallol*:

A question was raised by some workers of the progressive theatre movement. Would it be possible to reach rural audiences with such an extravagant staging? Could we take the play to them? Suffice it to say that the theory of people's theatre had been entirely simplified in this question. (1986: 18)

Guha goes on to argue that if any politically conscious theatre group from the villages had invited the play to be staged, it would be easily possible for the team to find simpler ways to create the stage set-up. He suggests that a bamboo framework could be created for the ship *Khyber*, which could be stuck on a paper background to reconstruct the setting for the play. He admits that the 'total effect' of the Minerva stage may not be achievable in these situations, especially because of the limited availability of electricity in the villages. Nonetheless, he argues that with organisational dexterity, the play could be staged anywhere, even though the glamour of the Calcutta stage might be missing. He also gives examples of how *Kallol* was successfully staged in Siliguri and Alipurduar – both small towns in the north of Bengal.

In sum, however, Guha's argument runs antithetical to Dutt's larger vision of a total political theatre bringing together entertainment with revolutionary intent and content with form. Guha reiterates that it was the subject matter of *Kallol* that was important to its making. It is the content and not the form of the play, he argues, that should be considered in any political assessment of its revolutionary and transformative potential. In arguing thus, Guha recreates that exact division between content and form that Dutt had so vigorously dismissed as 'bourgeois' and anti-political during his defence of *Angar*. Dutt's vision of the form of a 'total' political theatre, as well as the critical importance of design and scenography to this vision, is hard to miss in any careful perusal of his writing. In an essay called 'The Language of Theatre', written in the autumn of 1962, Dutt writes:

> There is no great dividing wall between colour and music. Actors' bodies can move in a way that creates imageries of the words in the play; it is possible to structure stage design and lights in a way that reflects the words and music before our eyes. And again, it is possible to dress the words and music in a way that resonates with the scenography. If such a unity can be achieved, we might be able to create a unique language that belongs only to the theatre. (1998: 116)

Conclusion

The criticisms of Dutt's stage design were based on two primary arguments. The first was economic: the financial extravagance was seen as antithetical to Leftist politics. A related and pragmatic reason was the impossibility of travelling with a technically complex show in a country like India, where the rural masses had no experience of proscenium theatre and in places with no access to auditoriums or electricity. The other reason was more moral and a little bit more nebulous. It was the belief that the 'people's theatre' must engage its audience purely through political content and that technical spectacle appealed to the baser instincts of the audience, like shock and awe, much like in the shallow commercial theatres of Calcutta. In truth, however, the 'people's theatre' in Bengal, even in the mythical days of the staging of *Nabanna* (1944) in late colonial India, had never managed to entirely break through the urban–rural divide. Regional histories of the Indian People's Theatre Association (IPTA) from other parts of India in the 1940s tell a different story, while in Bengal the IPTA split down the middle in 1946 on the question of the indispensability of the revolving stage for *Nabanna*. Hence, the mythical claims of the minimalism of the iconic Left theatre of the 1940s are not borne out by the actual historical facts of the matter. The contradiction between the urban form of proscenium theatre, with its architectural roots deeply embedded in the history of colonialism, and the political content intended to revolutionise the rural masses was far from historically resolved. In her article on the IPTA in Bengal in the 1940s, Malini Bhattacharya writes in considerable detail about the problems that *Nabanna* faced in the few shows that were attempted in the rural hinterland. It seems clear that these problems far exceeded the question of the indispensability of the revolving stage[12]: 'in its performances outside Calcutta, the IPTA activists confronted a totally new kind of audience, which though politically aware, found the *Nabanna* type of play quite unfamiliar as a cultural form' (1983:11).

Perhaps the question, then, was not so much about the greater or lesser spectacular play but the architecture and politics of proscenium theatre itself, as well as the impossibility of a uniform dramaturgical and scenographic language for the 'people's theatre' in a country as diverse as India. In truth, what was actually popular among the rural masses was the *Jatra*, a melodramatic and musical form with its roots in folk performance, which Dutt began to experiment with in the 1970s and 1980s. Despite these historical complexities, the legend of the minimalist jute curtain[13] from *Nabanna* acquired such a symbolic and ideological force that it was strong enough to return to haunt Dutt during the staging of both *Angar* (1959) and *Kallol* (1965). Some of his worst critics, by his own admission, were the then members of the IPTA, who swore by the legendary austerity of *Nabanna*'s stage design and saw it as the unique hallmark of the people's theatre. Some of these critics were deeply concerned about the financial extravagance that they perceived as essential to the kind of stage design Dutt was espousing.

While a simple conclusion to such a knotty problem seems difficult to arrive at, it is pertinent to note that the contours of this debate on 'excess' in the theatre resonate with the strain of asceticism that has often dominated

Left ideological discourse in India, and especially Bengal, in the past. In another context Dutt had once written: 'Temperance and moderation in everything is the petty-bourgeois way of life; but it is inherited from the bourgeois, and is positively dangerous when they pass it off as a proletarian ideal' (Dutt 2009: 85).

It seems to me that the note of puritanical moral fervour in the demand for formal restraint has roots in a larger ideological and discursive tendency of certain sections of the Indian Left rather than in any actual analysis of the historical complexities of formulating an aesthetic for the people's theatre in the subcontinent. Dutt, on the other hand, was, in his work at the Minerva theatre, radically re-envisioning the political potential and architectural possibilities of the colonial proscenium, enlivened through spectacular, even melodramatic, 'excess'. His vision resonated urgently with his political comrades in the GDR and the Soviet Union. Never one for outright dismissal, Dutt argued repeatedly in his essays about the importance of historicising and contextualising artistic practices. At Minerva, Dutt was looking for an alternative historical legacy for the proscenium – perhaps one embedded in the international revolutionary history of people's struggles in the twentieth century. Here, the ramp began to aesthetically witness the subaltern community's coming together – in *Titas*, in *Kallol*, and in many plays afterwards. His rebellion against the ideological weight of the colonial theatre and his celebration of anti-colonial resistance in Bengal found forceful expression in his later play *Tiner Talawar*.[14] The stage itself, as in Okhlopkov, broke down into many fragments and extended far beyond itself in Dutt's work: always excessive, always unapologetic in its celebration of revolutionary spectacle.

Notes

1 This and all subsequent translations from Bengali are mine.
2 The members of LTG, including its director Utpal Dutt, had felt that a space for regular rehearsals and performances was necessary for the group to be able to function professionally, a privilege then available only to the producers of the commercial stage in Calcutta. Since the owner of Minerva Theatre was unwilling to give out the hall on lease to a theatre group, the legal document was drawn personally in Utpal Dutt's name.
3 *Potemkin* appears repeatedly in Dutt's writing when he defends the climax of *Kallol* against accusations of historical inaccuracy: 'To us, the end of the RIN mutiny is the beginning of a revolutionary process ... that is why, larger than the fact of surrender, is the truth of revolutionary transition and that in theatrical language is symbolised in *Khyber*'s refusal to surrender. *Khyber* refuses to surrender for precisely the same reason that Eisenstein's *Potemkin*

does, though in factual history it did. *Potemkin*'s mutiny ended in victorious October 1917; therefore, the precise moment in history when the sailors of *Potemkin* raised their hands in surrender cannot be considered in isolation, as an absolute be-all and end-all of time' (2009: 64). In this passage Dutt is not far from the Hungarian Marxist philosopher Georg Lukács's interpretation of the theory of Socialist Realism, for whom the originality of a work of art only enhanced its capacity to reflect reality. Max Rieser elaborates on Lukács's views on Socialist Realist art thus: 'Sometimes one might be deluded into thinking that the work is not such a reflection (of reality) because no single element of it is comparable to any element of reality. However, *we must compare the total impression of the work of art with the total impact of reality to render a fair judgment.* ... The work of art, according to Lukács, *may also show a new order of things replacing the old one and have a propaganda effect in doing so,* as have all genuine works of art' (1957: 237–248, 238–239; italics mine).

4 Hemanga Biswas (1912–1987) was a veteran singer and composer, member of IPTA, and the music director of *Kallol* (1965).
5 Indeed, there was a lot riding on the commercial success of *Angar* for the Little Theatre Group. Dutt later wrote: 'In the 1150 shows of *Angar*, I don't ever remember a seat being empty in the auditorium. The Minerva office filled up with letters, hundreds of letters from overwhelmed audience members. Gradually, all the ridiculous criticism around 'form' died down. Despite many shortcomings, *Angar* brought to the stage a critical narrative of struggling workers and their resistance' (Dutt 2005: 453). The play was a resounding success.
6 In *Towards a Revolutionary Theatre*, Dutt wrote: 'There is the other theatre, the so-called *avant-garde*, which mouths a lot of politics to empty seats but must necessarily distort the entire terminology of politics, because every work commonly used and understood by the masses is a revolting cliche to them. ... The revolutionary theatre addresses the working masses and must adjust its pitch, tone and volume accordingly, and to hell with the so-called critics who find our plays naïve, melodramatic and loud' (2009: 81–82).
7 Near the beginning of this chapter.
8 Sova Sen writes: 'Okhlopkov is known all over the world for his experimentation. Starting his life as an actor and as the favourite student of Meyerhold, he gradually established himself as an accomplished director. ... On the next day, the 20th of October, we saw Okhlopkov's production of Ostrovsky's *Thunderstorm* at the Mali Theatre. Here, Okhlopkov had used lightning on stage, along with the sound of thunder, as a kind of poetic symbol' (1993: 62).
9 Dutt writes of the time when the play was staged: 'I was arrested on the day of the ceasefire at my house and detained without trial in Presidency Jail, and attacks on my play *Kallol* mounted to awesome proportions. One day, all newspapers, excluding *The Statesman*, refused to print our advertisements. That they were acting in concert and under instructions from the Congress and police chiefs was obvious to all. But that did not stop the play. The theatre printed posters in hundreds and thousands, and trade unions and peasant associations volunteered to plaster the cities and villages of Bengal with them.

If anything, *Kallol*'s popularity increased and the courage of my colleagues, who played on with plainclothes policemen following them round and constantly watching the theatre, made my life in prison bearable' (2009: 52).

10 The influences coming out of the Soviet Union on the play were many. For several artistes participating in the making of *Kallol*, Soviet influences as well as reception were of crucial importance. Biswas writes: 'The Soviet poets Yevgeny Dolmatovsky and Anwar Alim Zhanov were full of appreciation for the play. Dolmatovsky even invited us to Moscow to stage the play. Besides this, he also wrote about *Kallol* in the Moscow publication – "Literaturnaya Gazeta". My boss at the Calcutta office – V. Makutin asked me to arrange a translation of this essay. Professor Niren Roy translated this essay from Russian and it was published in the brochure/programme for the play in its subsequent shows' (1986: 7).

11 Interview with Dr Bishnupriya Dutt, at Kallol, 16 August 2022 (Kolkata).

12 It had been argued that a play as episodic as *Nabanna* in its structure could only work in terms of pace and dramaturgical structure on a revolving stage, which would be impossible to find in the villages.

13 In a passage from an essay called 'Drishyo Sojja' ('Stage Design'), written in December 1961, Dutt's response to the critics becomes clear: 'If you are going to act in front of a single-coloured curtain, what would be the difference between recitation and acting? … And the second reason for using the jute curtain adds up to this: one ends up rebelling against the stage itself in trying to rebel against the commercial distortions of the stage. If we deny tradition all together, what will we stand on? Further, this becomes tantamount to acceding to the traditional dominance and supremacy of the actor just as it was in the commercial theatre. Stage design was neglected before; now it is abandoned altogether. The actor was primary before, now he becomes the only factor. … I want to argue that the great Indian People's Theatre Association is mistaken in this matter. In trying to free the erstwhile commercial stage, they have been imprisoned by its limitations themselves. This is not how the Bengali stage can be reformed. No, there is no question of doing away with stage design. Rather, it must be strengthened and advanced to such a degree that its significance equals that of the actors. We must preserve the grandeur of the stage in order to progress with it. Denying its significance will not solve the problem' (1998: 79).

14 I am grateful to Bishnupriya Dutt for pointing out the importance of the colonial legacy of theatre buildings such as the Minerva in this context.

Bibliography

Bhattacharya, Malini. 1983. 'The IPTA in Bengal.' *Journal of Arts and Ideas* 2: 5–22.

Biswas, Hemanga. 1986. 'Uthilo Somudro Kallol.' *Epic Theatre: Kalloler Kuri Bochhor*, Numbers 1–5. Kolkata: People's Little Theatre.

Dutt, Utpal. 1994. *Angar. Utpal Dutta Natak Samagra Prothom Khondo*. Kolkata: Mitra and Ghosh Publishers.

Dutt, Utpal. 1994. *Kallol. Utpal Dutta Natak Samagra Dwitiya Khondo*. Kolkata: Mitra and Ghosh Publishers.
Dutt, Utpal. 1998. 'Angik.' In *Utpal Dutta Gadyo Samagra*, pp. 68–74. Kolkata: Dey's Publishing.
Dutt, Utpal. 1998. 'Drishyo Sojja.' In *Utpal Dutta Gadyo Samagra*, pp. 75–81. Kolkata: Dey's Publishing.
Dutt, Utpal. 1998. 'Theaterer Bhasha.' In *Utpal Dutta Gadyo Samagra*, pp. 113–119. Kolkata: Dey's Publishing.
Dutt, Utpal. 2005. 'Little Theatre O Ami.' In *Utpal Dutt: Ek Samagrik Abolokan*, edited by N. Saha, pp. 439–463. Kolkata: Utpal Dutta Theatre Festival Committee.
Dutt, Utpal. 2009. *Towards a Revolutionary Theatre*. Kolkata: Seagull.
Dutta, Suresh. 1986. 'Kalloler Mancha.' In *Epic Theatre: Kalloler Kuri Bochhor*, Numbers 1–5, pp. 12–13. Kolkata: People's Little Theatre.
Ghosh, Shantanu. 1986. 'Kallol.' In *Epic Theatre: Kalloler Kuri Bochhor*, Numbers 1–5, pp. 19–20. Kolkata: People's Little Theatre.
Guha, Sadhan. 1986. '"Kallol" Sothik Orthei Kallol.' In *Epic Theatre: Kalloler Kuri Bochhor*, Numbers 1–5, pp. 16–18. Kolkata: People's Little Theatre.
Gupta, Anal. 1986. 'Sesh Juddho Shuru Aaj Comrade, Salvo!' In *Epic Theatre: Kalloler Kuri Bochhor*, Numbers 1–5, pp. 9–11. Kolkata: People's Little Theatre.
Lenhoff, Gail. 1973. 'The Theatre of Okhlopkov.' *The Drama Review* 17(1): 90–105.
Mukhopadhyay, Arup. 2010. *Utpal Dutt: Jibon O Srishti*. New Delhi: National Book Trust India.
Rieser, Max. 1957. 'The Aesthetic Theory of Social Realism.' *Journal of Aesthetics and Art Criticism* 16(2): 237–248.
Sen, Sova. 1993. *Smarane Bismarane: Nabanna Theke Lal Durgo*. Kolkata: M.C. Sarkar & Sons Pvt. Limited.

11

Love in the time of revolution: Exploring the political theatre of Utpal Dutt

Mallarika Sinha Roy

The following excerpt is from the penultimate scene of *Sannyasir Tarabari* (*The Crusade*, 1972), the play-text of Utpal Dutt's 'Jatra-play'[1] on 'the myth of a patriotic struggle'. The myth refers to the eighteenth-century Sannyasi-Fakir Rebellion in northern Bengal against the British East India Company headed by Governor General Warren Hastings. It was a militarised conflict, in the wake of the devastating famine in Bengal in 1770, between the monastic governance system and the East India Company's rapacious system of tax collection (Pinch 2006; Chatterjee 2013). The stage direction in Dutt's *Natak Samagra* is:

> [Prison. Enter Rennell, followed by Ramananda in chains. He is encircled by British soldiers; their guns aloft]. (1997: 447)

The scene progresses mainly through exchanges of dialogue between Ramananda Giri (a warrior ascetic) and Rennell (an English Captain) on the nature of revolutionary violence and identifying the enemy of the people of Bengal. Devi Chaudhurani (a woman warrior ascetic) enters to pay respect to Ramananda, while Rennell retreats to the background. The romantic tension between Ramananda and Devi Chaudhurani, articulated in several previous scenes, drives their conversation. Ramananda refuses to acknowledge that he had once harboured romantic feelings towards Devi as he declares himself a heartless exterminator of enemies – becoming a steel sword of revolution. Rennell enters the conversation again at this point:

Rennell:	Are you finished?
Devi:	Yes.
Rennell:	There was no response, was there? I knew it. He does not listen, to anyone.
Devi:	The steel sword has no ears; how would he listen? It falls as swiftly as it rises. It does not know how to stop. (Exit)
Rennell:	I was wondering, if I were a scoundrel like Warren Hastings, I could have broken your resistance. I could have tortured Devi

	Chaudhurani. You would have agreed to proclaim non-violence to save her.
Ramananda:	(smiling) Do you take me for such a weak person?
Rennell:	Is love a weakness? I do not think so. What I do think, is, in your entire life Devi Chaudhurani is the only ... the only ... how does one express? Brightest bloom – beauty – fruition.
Ramananda:	Devi Chaudhurani is no one special in my life. I am an ascetic; I do not allow anyone to grow their roots in my existence.
Rennell:	Please refrain from such naiveté. Not to this world-weary Rennell.

(Dutt 1997: 452)

This excerpt introduces different layers of the politics of emotion. As it confirms, despite his denial, Ramananda cannot not hide his love for Devi from Rennell, who occupies the tenuous connecting space between a sophisticated English gentleman and a pitiless colonist. Rennell refrains from torturing Devi, affirming a glimpse of humanity within the colonial system. Rennell's reference to Warren Hastings as a 'scoundrel' underlines that he is well aware of the brutality of the Company Raj and that he chooses not to resort to such violence. The internal conflict of Rennell opens up the tension within the discourse of colonialism, which finally morphs into a subtler form of violence in the final act of the scene. Rennell poisons Ramananda inside the prison, disallowing him to be a martyr in the public eye, and succeeds in crushing the rebellion through deceit.

It is interesting to note that the deceitful colonist articulates that love is not weakness, while the emotionally exhausted revolutionary could barely suppress his desperation for an escape through martyrdom. It is equally interesting that Dutt prefers male characters to represent doubt, suicidal thoughts, and emotional vulnerability – the personal crises of a revolutionary – after committing an act of revolutionary violence or as protagonists who are vulnerable in front of a historic betrayal. Both Major Rennell and Ramananda Giri are excellent examples of this crisis, and such representations beg the question of whether Dutt is also hinting through the dynamism between love and violence at a historical crisis in Bengali masculinity. It is Devi, the woman revolutionary, who confirms through her words and her actions that love is a much wider emotion and loves – her people, her comrades, and Ramananda – with a matured clarity. This articulation of love represents the way Dutt has started imagining the nature of love through an interaction between romance, empathy, freedom, and imagination that remains significant for modern Indian theatre's perspectives on the relationship between theatre and the theatre-going public.

Dutt writes in *Towards a Revolutionary Theatre* that this play-text and its production in front of 'electrifying mass audiences for three years' transformed his writing for the theatre, eventually paving the way for bringing the myth-history of warrior ascetics of colonial Bengal on to the stage (2009: 173). The huge mass audience also reflected Dutt's success with the form of *Jatra*, the folk form of Bengali theatre. The literal meaning of *Jatra* or *Yatra* is journey, which alludes to the mobile troops of artists who put up plays in far-flung villages across Bengal.² The form of *Jatra* particularly charmed Dutt with its accomplished performers and its transformative ability without losing its popularity. He wrote in 'Ghure Fire' that political theatre needs to learn from *Jatra* the skill to write plays that captivate the attention of such huge audiences, the expertise in constructing events and characters on stage that entertain as well as educate, and the training of people's artists (1988: 397). In *Sannyasir Tarabari* he created a complex but entertaining political theatre for the mass audience. It is worth quoting from Dutt's own assessment of this play-text:

> I had at last thrown off the tendency to categorize the characters as simple statements of unilateral tendencies, and was able, partially I admit, to create them as complexes of warring contradictions, diverse and opposing desires, and was even able to present the contradiction, between what they wanted to do and what they were actually doing. (2009: 172)

Dutt's reference to creating characters as 'warring contradictions' between what revolutionaries wanted to do and what they actually did allows us to connect history with imagination. For Sudipta Kaviraj in *The Unhappy Consciousness: Bankim Chandra Chattopadhyay and the Formation of Nationalist Discourse in India*, the narratives of history and fiction intersect with each other in a fundamental way once historiography becomes the principal concern as 'history instead of being distinguished by the trueness of the story, is now distinguished by the storyness of its truth' (1995: 107). This process, Kaviraj argues, constructs imaginary history where the past is reconstructed not only through what actually happened but also through what might have happened. Imaginary history recalls the emotions that might have been at play in deciding the course of an event, including what alternative outcomes might have been possible if emotions had moved in a different direction.

Freddie Rokem's formulation in *Peforming History: Theatrical Representations of the Past in Contemporary Theatre* (2000) that theatre, while aesthetically retelling a historical event, is not just a secondary elaboration but rather allows the past to reappear and that the performance becomes a witness to the event is a useful ally to think through the links between imaginary history and political theatre of Utpal Dutt. Drawing from Rokem, I would like to explore in this chapter Dutt's retelling of revolutionary movements at different historical junctures of colonial and postcolonial Bengal through two play-texts – *Teer* (*Arrow*, 1967) and *Sannyasir Tarabari* (*The Crusade*, 1972). The principal analytical perspective consists of the layered meanings of love as an emotional, political commitment. The deeply political act of witnessing, when represented through performing history, invokes a gamut of emotions. The emotions ranging from fear, hate, and anguish to shame and contempt to trust, compassion, hope, and love circumscribe the 'event' – the way it happened in the past and the ways in which it might have happened. Identification of the actors involved in the event (then) and the performers (now) animates the emotional force of the space between the historical reality and the historical retelling. What these emotions 'do' to the spectator, the actors, and the theatre-maker, I would like to argue, largely constitute the politics of emotion inherent in performing history. Sara Ahmed's treatise (2014) on the cultural politics of emotion opens the field to consider emotions as connections between movement and attachment that circulate among and between bodies giving them solidity through repetition, as a structure of hierarchies that distinguishes between elevated emotions and baser ones and, of course, as politics because, following Ahmed, it is possible to argue that 'emotions show us how power shapes the very surface of bodies as well as worlds' (2014: 10). The fixities and boundaries of emotions, as they begin to represent different social histories, are rarely static since 'emotion' comes from the Latin *emovere*, meaning 'to move, move out'. The more important question, thus, is not only to focus on how it 'feels' but also to think what that feeling 'does' to an individual, to a collective, to multiple overlapping collectives that form a society. Sociality of emotions is not simply something that an individual or collective has but rather the very structures of connections through which the selfhood of an individual or a collective is shaped.

Dutt argues in the essay 'Bidroher Natok' (2005) that people's theatre[3] needs to bring critical historical events of mass mobilisations on stage to inform the spectator about the roots of communism within India, dispel the propaganda that it is an imported ideology, and that without the sense of history of struggles, the contemporary fight would become merely incidental. He continues: 'Rebellion signifies not only a crescendo in political mobilization, but can also be an apposite theatrical weapon. Each event of rebellion has had a cyclonic impact on the chronological progress of history. That is why each one them has the potential to keep the audience spellbound' (2005: 94).

Dutt provides a list of such rebellions ranging from the Sannyasi-Fakir Rebellion, the great Rebellion of 1857, the Santal Rebellion, and the Indigo Rebellion against the exploitative colonial system to relentless youth mobilisations against the British in Bengal-Punjab-Maharashtra, huge industrial strikes, and the naval mutiny. All of these, in his opinion, should have been the theme of Indian political theatre because historicising the romance around political upheaval on stage can create a politicised mass. This chapter aims to understand how events of protest and rebellion reflect moments of passionate politics in the political theatre of Utpal Dutt. It is an attempt to rethink two play-texts from the perspectives of imaginary history and the politics of emotion. This is an attempt to understand how Dutt engaged with the political philosophy of Marxism on the one hand with a sense of urgency in his theatre and on the other hand through creating historical references for contemporary political situations. I have focused on the ways in which love and politics have intersected with each other in constructing the politics of emotion in Dutt's theatre.

Lovers and enemies: the political theatre of Utpal Dutt

'Is it possible to write a history of love?' asks Sudipta Kaviraj in the chapter 'Tagore and Transformations in the Ideals of Love', and this profound question situates my concerns about the political imagination of love within a historical context (2007: 161). If love can be defined as, following Alain Badiou's position in *In Praise of Love*, 'deep and genuine experience of the otherness' where even the morsel of self-interest is surrendered to the risk of getting hurt and becomes 'a unique trust placed in chance' (2009: 8), how does one account for emotional appeal of a political ideology? If, following Lauren Berlant as she argues in *Desire/Love*, 'love is always deemed as the outcome of fantasy' (2012: 6), whether the lens is psychoanalytical, ideological, or institutional, how does one trace affective investments in carrying out certain political acts? These questions are enticing to the extent, in the context of this chapter, where Badiou broaches the subject of love and politics, or, more specifically, how identifying the enemy distinguishes love from politics. Enemy, in politics, is what 'you won't tolerate taking decisions on anything that impacts on yourself', while in love the greatest enemy is selfishness. In politics 'we really have to engage with our enemies', while love, with its own contradictions and violence, produces painfully bitter internal dramas between identity and difference (Badiou 2009: 59). Badiou, in fact, underlines at one point that 'love is not necessarily anymore peaceful than revolutionary politics' (2009: 56). The task for anyone embarking on the project of writing a history of love in the time of revolution, then, turns into looking for the traces where the internal dramas of love become entwined with enemies in the realm of the political. Traces, undeniably, are circumscribed by the conjunction of time, space, and place.

Dutt's engagement with love also entailed critical reflections on Bengali middle-class sensibilities around *prem* – the most popular contemporary Bengali expression of love. During his brief stint with the Indian People's Theatre Association (henceforth referred as IPTA) in 1950–1951, he felt 'IPTA took me by hands to an emotionally expressive comradeship with the people. I was intoxicated with an enlightened awakening' (2005: 446). This sense of exhilaration consolidated with depth and clarity in his political imagination of love – from individual romantic love with its internal drama to love for communicating with the audience and to love for the people.

Sudipta Kaviraj, in his attempt to conceptualise a social history of love in late colonial Bengal, has shown that there was a diversity available in the lexicon of love – *adirasa, shringara, sakhya, vatsalya* in Sanskrit literature; the Islamic traditions of *ishq, muhabbat, ibadat,* or even *junoon* (frenzy or excess of love) – that had informed the eighteenth- and early-nineteenth-century Bengali literature, principally the tradition of poetry (2007: 163). Such diversity, however, got lost as authors and artists of the late nineteenth century zeroed on to *prem* as the most suitable conceptual framework for describing love and developed it as a definition of ethical romantic love instead of bodily beauty, eroticism, and sexuality. The focus on *prem* is symptomatic of the emergence of the *bhadralok* or gentlemen within Bengali society who carefully constructed a moral universe based on colonial modernity. Sumanta Banerjee's work on oral subcultures of women in 'Marginalization of Women's Popular Culture in Nineteenth Century Bengal' elaborates how women in 'disrespectful' professions of sex work and performing arts mocked *bhadralok* ideals of domesticity, femininity, and conjugality through their songs and performances (1989: 127–179). Such resistance brought to the fore on the one hand that *prem* was not an uncontested site for scripting the new narrative of love and on the other hand exposed the exclusionary politics of colonial modernity in establishing ethical romantic love.

Dutt, with his inimitable sense of irony and satire, grasped this sleight of hand within *bhadralok* culture. The 'warring contradictions' within characters that he described with reference to *Sannyasir Tarabari* found interesting dimensions in his women characters from the dispossessed social sections, who could articulate love for individuals and collectives without hesitation. In *Teer*, tribal women peasants profess love for revolution in clear terms that are not limited by their individual romantic involvements. In *Sannyasir Tarabari*, Devi belongs to a rural landowning family and is falsely accused of adultery. She finds the courage to express her love to Ramananda Giri when she loses all her social capital. She becomes her own person through her fight against the British. The emotion of love in these women characters becomes enmeshed in romance, desire, sacrifice, and finally a sense of freedom. The exterior and interior of political theatre became connected through this dual imagination of love for revolution and revolution in love. The huge mass audience, whom Dutt wanted to entertain and educate with historical retellings of rebellion, possibly began to participate in his political theatre through this double imagination of love and revolution – in the public as well as in the private domain.

Liz Tomlin's *Political Dramaturgies and Theatre Spectatorship: Provocations for Change* shows that for European theatre history in the post-Second World War era, the principal debate has been 'the degree to which the dramaturgy aims to elicit desired political responses from the spectator or prioritizes the spectator's autonomy to produce their own interpretation' (2019: 1). Tomlin's excellent exploration of the debates around the autonomous spectator, an idea that has increasingly gained ground with the establishment of post-structuralism, cautions us against an unfettered celebration of the autonomous spectator in the age of neoliberal capitalism that continuously invests in consumerism rather than an informed response to any art form (2019: 11–12). The critique of Rancière's *The Emancipated Spectator* (2009) – that the spectator in theatre must become a participant instead of being a passive voyeur, and the theatre-maker must involve the spectators instead of being a boring pedagogue – in Andy Lavender's 'Viewing and Acting (and Points in between): The Trouble with Spectating after Rancière' (2012) draws attention to the limits of the production of autonomy only as individuals within the political logic of market economy. Analysis of the affective response of the spectators towards theatre, as Reinelt reminds us in '"What I Came to Say": Raymond Williams, the Sociology of Culture and the Politics of (Performance) Scholarship' (2015), is perhaps better served through the idea of 'structures of feeling', of residual and emergent culture, where the notion of culture is less related to autonomy and more to 'common' as in common ownership of cultural practices and production. Reinelt refers to Raymond Williams's conceptualisation of 'structures of feeling', elaborated in *Marxism and Literature* (1977). From Williams's explanation of 'characteristic elements of impulse, restraint, and tone; specifically, affective elements of consciousness and relationships: not feelings against thought, but thought as feeling and feeling as thought', it becomes possible to understand the affective response of the spectator in terms of the internal relationship between affect, experience, and sociality (1977: 132). Reinelt's suggestion finds an unexpected, but not entirely unlikely, ally in the words of Bijan Bhattacharya – a committed actor and playwright to people's theatre. Bhattacharya said in an interview with Samik Bandyopadhyay: 'in my conception, communism is a strong wave of love ... a wave that encompasses every aspect of life and progresses towards the realization of life-force as a consciousness' (2017: 16). This idea of a strong wave of love is much greater than rational political choice and individual romance – reflecting a structure of feeling that speaks to the romance around political activism with an ideological conviction.

The immense popular success, however, also begs the question: is creating great spectacles essential for political theatre? Would it not reduce the audience to passive voyeurs? And, of course, the theatre intellectuals of Bengal have raised Brecht's name with reference to Dutt's creation of sumptuous spectacles in his political theatre. In an essay 'Rajnoitik Natak, Ekti Kalaha' (1998), Dutt, an ardent reader of Brecht who was a key figure in establishing the Brecht Society of India in 1964, responds rhetorically to his critics:

> Is Brecht's audience and our audience the same? Hasn't the difference in the systems of production in two different countries shaped the emotional and intellectual universe of the theatre audience in these two countries? The cultural residues shape the outlook of the audience, the myths, religions, oral cultures, land systems, land owners, intermediate beneficiaries, nature, landscape, neighbours, state, taxes, exploitations – all are factors. That is why the rational German audience is different from the Bengali audience immersed in the culture of *Jatra*. (1998: 227)

Dutt begins to delve into creating a sociality of emotions through responses to audience reactions. In performing histories, Dutt argues, the audience reaction was crucial to the representation and interpretation of characters on stage because the audience 'brought their actual life-experience to bear upon the stage' and their reactions from 'the standpoint of their own personal sufferings [have] the strength to alter the values enshrined in a performance' (2009: 19). Let me give an example where it becomes quite clear how Dutt imagined the reciprocity with his audience and how his political imagination of love included not only 'noble' emotions like honesty and empathy but also ambiguous emotions like shrewdness and guile. He especially refers to his performance as lawyer Liebowitz in *Manusher Adhikare* (based on the Scottsborough Trial, 1931) and gives a long description of the transformations in his interpretation of the character (2009: 19–20). The audience compelled him to reflect on the cunning and brutality of a lawyer who had to fight dirty to win against a racist system because his audience could not see an honest Messiah in a lawyer from their own experiences. 'The resultant Liebowitz, I make bold to say', remarks Dutt, 'was more human, more wholesome, more complete' (2009: 20). This is what I would like to call Dutt's articulation of the political imagination of love – it contained everyday experiences of the people who came to watch the play, and because of that it could construct a reciprocal structure of feeling.

I have relied largely on Eva Illouz's 'Love and Its Discontents: Irony, Reason, Romance' (2010) for this argument since she alerts us to the cultural practices and cultural politics around love in modern times. By linking historical transformations in the ideas of the rational individual, property relations, and the spread of capital with love, Illouz shows the shift in the frame of love from seduction to irony – the irony that is hewn from cultural norms of equality, consensuality, and reciprocity (2010: 29–30). Though Badiou rejects such a modernist frame of love, his repeated emphasis on an individual with the freedom of choice as the principal protagonist of love puts his discussion fairly and squarely within historically marked constructions of the modern individual vis-à-vis the collective. Dutt's representations of romantic love on stage through the ideals of equality and consensus and his reciprocal structure of feeling with his audience encompasses modern Indian political theatre's imagination of love. The equality and consensus on stage, however, are often depicted through clashes between, to borrow from Raymond Williams again, archaic and residual elements of male chauvinism and women's self-realisation as emancipated agents – often making women characters the 'emergent' aspects of a new modern sociality. In fact, irony in Dutt's theatre is often used as a theatrical weapon to expose the limits of colonial modernity, rather than the modernity of equality and reciprocity among his subaltern characters or his relationship with his audience. The following discussions on *Teer* and *Sannyasir Tarabari* will further unpack the issues around identifying the tribal and peasant groups who never hitherto came into the middle-class imagination in the context of equality and reciprocity in romantic love, love for revolution, and the romanticism around revolutionary violence.

Teer (Arrow): incomplete text of an unfinished revolution

In 1967 Kanu Sanyal[4] wrote the 'Report on the Peasant Movement in the Terai Region' in the wake of the police firing on hundreds of peasants who had gathered on 25 May 1967 in Prasadujote village, killing seven peasant women, two men, and two children, and the following peasant mobilisation in the Naxalbari police station area in northern West Bengal. Naxalbari, since then, became a reference point of the radical peasant movement in contemporary India. Sanyal's 'Report' continually refers to the heroic peasants of Terai.[5] Apart from mentioning rich, middle, and landless peasants, and particularly the leadership of the landless peasants, Sanyal, however, does not define the huge, amorphous category of landless peasants. It is in Utpal Dutt's play-text *Teer (Arrow)* that representative faces within this category appear – Shukra Tudu, Gabriel Santal, Gajua, Shanicharoa and Birsa Oraon, Gangee and Sanjho Orain (Oraon woman), Ranbahadur Thapa, Upasu, Jonaku, Debari, and Somari Rajbangshi. People who belong to different tribal and caste communities but are all landless agricultural labourers occasionally working as casual tea-garden labourers. The significance of *Teer* as a cultural document increases when we are informed that Dutt and a couple of his colleagues from the Little Theatre Group (henceforth referred to as LTG) toured the villages after the uprising and interviewed many activists.

The status of this play in Utpal Dutt's formidable oeuvre of original plays, however, has remained precarious ever since Dutt withdrew his support from the Naxalbari movement in 1970. Dutt writes with enough detail that he withdrew *Teer* because of his disillusionment with the revolutionary politics of the movement as it descended into frenzied political violence, unleashed in the name of armed struggle – resulting in unprecedented state violence. Dutt was arrested a week after *Teer* was produced, allegedly for propagating armed violence against the Indian nation state, and the ensuing political debate led to the disintegration of the LTG. The political debate centred around the Naxalite ideology of armed revolution and the democratic Left's insistence on functioning within the norms of parliamentary democracy. Dutt has written about misplacing valuable documents on funding and other organisational details during this ideological turmoil, which possibly led to missing documents regarding the history of the production of *Teer* (2005: 462). Dutt himself is rather reticent in spite of a brief reference to its successful debut in Calcutta at Minerva on 16 December 1967. A few photographs of the production survive, freeze-framing the horror of the police firing of 1967 that killed eleven people, including seven women, and give a glimpse of the scenography (2005: 338). There is, however, little available academic work on *Teer*. The precarity of the play intensifies as the published text of the play is incomplete.

Comparison of the published text with a facsimile of the manuscript of the play reveals that names of the leaders of the Naxalbari uprising, references to names of villages, and references to the historical past of peasant uprisings were omitted in the published text.[6] Asit Basu, one of the members of the LTG during the production of *Teer*, said that such omission was necessary for various reasons.[7] Protection of the group from state surveillance, making it relevant for the audience coming from different political positions, the practicalities of total runtime of the production, and finally, to create a reciprocal relationship with the characters on stage rather than those in real life through symbolism contributed in the final edited version. The structure of the play-text – divided into chapters instead of scenes – indicates a particular kind of visual imagination following cinematic visuality, Basu added. The chapter where the news of the police firing reaches metropolitan Calcutta and multiple reactions of the urban middle class and intelligentsia are represented through the opening and closing of several windows with representative characters shooting dialogues towards the audience was referred to by the group members as the 'television scene'. This specific visual imagination continued in the chapter on the peasants' attack on the rice depot of the exploitative landowner and the final battle scene.

This visual imagination builds on the episodic chapter-wise structure of the play. It was initially decided that the group would enact certain relevant episodes during public meetings or mass gatherings and disappear among the people before either the police or their political opposition could intervene.[8] This performance structure allows for considering the presence of strong women characters in each of the episodes, speaking about revolution and 'doing' revolutionary activities. Even though the archival visual frames of the play capture only the slain women and the bereaved survivor, the play-text is a testament to the robust presence of women as agents of revolutionary change and definitely not only as victims of retaliatory state violence. The characters of peasant-woman-guerrilla perform political violence, explain theoretical arguments, and are part of decision-making as much as men. In fact, women love both their revolutionary male comrades and the ideal of revolution, at times with more emotional intensity, which is a contrast to the largely gender-blind historiography of Naxalbari (Sinha Roy 2011). Their love for revolutionary ideology and complete commitment to revolutionary violence represent, depending on his primary ethnographic material, possibly some of the 'real' women revolutionaries. One of the important aspects of women characters in *Teer* is their vocal articulation of theories and strategies of revolution, which is, again, a contrast to their relegation into silence and passivity in much of Naxalite historiography. Speaking positions, Janet Lyon argues in 'Transforming Manifestoes: A Second Wave Problematic' (1991), emerge within a discourse through political struggles, and Dutt was opening up this space of political struggle in his play-text by changing the speaking codes of explaining revolutionary ideology and strategy on stage with women characters. Unlike the metropolitan Naxalite leadership, for whom the 'real' tribal-peasant-woman-guerrilla remained outside the history-making process of revolution, women on stage in the production of *Teer* bridged the gap between the 'real' and 'imagined' women of Naxalbari.

The dynamism between love for revolution and revolution for love emerges with interesting gendered ramifications. Debari Rajbangshi defies her father and the customary practice of paying bride-price to marry her beloved Jonaku at the beginning of the play; Gangee Orain explains the strategy of guerrilla warfare through the Oraon parable of elephant hunt when all other villagers fumble with a translated text of Mao-tse-Tung's treatise of guerrilla warfare; Sanjho Orain keeps the morale up for the guerrilla group during state repression, and they do all of these while laughing, speaking, and celebrating everyday life. Women's speaking positions open an exploration of patriarchal structures through the tension between love and violence, and Dutt does not shy away from implicating the ostensible 'hero' Jonaku. Large-scale emotional moments are created where the characters of Jonaku and Debari – the newly wed couple – reveal their social difference in terms of access to literacy, and unlettered Jonaku displays a crisis of masculinity when he violently reacts to Debari's request to learn. A similar kind of tension exists between the characters of Gangee and Shanicharoa, who are lovers but are from different ethnic backgrounds, which prevents them from becoming a revolutionary couple, and Shanicharoa resorts to alcohol. Emotion, consequently, is freed from the groove of idealised feminine passivity and turned into an exploration of gendered selves and sexed bodies. Dutt continues with his conviction to present revolutionary characters who are human because they are not perfect and explores how the feeling of love sharpens such humane qualities.

These explorations of heterosexual romantic love build on the modern cultural norms of equality and consent, underlining the crisis of masculinity in the figures of male revolutionaries and articulating agency in the characters of women revolutionaries. The question, however, remains whether love, bound as it may be with sexuality, desire, eroticism, pleasure, and romance, is something more than the summation of all of these terms; whether there is a different possibility of framing love in terms of ethics. Badiou has refused to consider the politics of love in the way Derrida explores the politics of friendship through ethics in *Politics of Friendship* (2006) because in politics, people engage with the 'other' whom they do not love but remain ethically committed, and love, for Badiou, is not entirely defined by ethics (2009: 57).[9] Reiterating Badiou's argument that love is often no less peaceful than revolutionary politics, however, also compels us to consider love's relationship with violence, especially revolutionary violence, and in that context the framing of ethics reaches beyond peace – approaching the ethical limits of love during violent conflict.

Sannyasir Tarabari (*The Crusade*): love and war in a historical frame

Five years after *Teer*, the peasantry of north Bengal again entered Dutt's realm of imagination in *Sannyasir Tarabari* as a *Jatra*, produced by *Loknatya Jatra* group on 24 September 1972.[10] The chronology of Dutt's theatre shows that Dutt went back to history when he confronted ideological crisis. Taking his lead, I would like to think that after his disillusionment with the Naxalite movement, he went back to the history to make sense of the forces that produced the crisis. *Sannyasir Tarabari* is, perhaps, his way of confronting the complexities of geopolitical history of that region and the sociality of emotions around peasant rebellion. It may be equally important to remember that the play is a rewriting of Bankim Chandra Chatterjee's two novels on the same historical event: *Anandamath* (1882) and *Debi Choudhurani* (1884). Tanika Sarkar's reading of these two novels in *Hindu Wife, Hindu Nation: Community, Religion and Cultural Nationalism* (2003) reveals tenets of Hindu revivalism, a characteristic feature of late colonial Bengal, within their proto-nationalist narratives. In Dutt's play, Chatterjee's novels become historical allegories of the contemporary peasant unrest of the 1970s as well as a critique of masculinist political violence that pervaded Bengal across the border in 1971 – *Muktijuddho* or the Bangladesh War of Liberation and the Naxalite movement. During *Muktijuddho*, militarised Bengali masculinity was confronting the brutal repression of the West Pakistan army, most notably through the mass rape of Bengali women, while the Naxalbari movement had entered its most violent phase in 1971 (Sinha Roy 2011; Mookherjee 2016). The state and revolutionary violence possibly compelled Dutt to explore the emotional crevices of cruelty, bloodshed, and perversion as the crisis of masculinity through the course he knew the best – performing history in combination with the present.

The realm of imagined history in Chatterjee's novels and Dutt's play, two retellings almost a century apart, expands the original eighteenth-century rebellion in terms of both nationalism and revolutionary romanticism. The dynamic relationship between love and violence, in both retellings, focuses on the ferocity of revolutionary violence that can dehumanise revolutionaries and the potential of love to transcend such futile violence. The principal difference, however, remains that the warrior ascetics turn from Hindu nationalists in Chatterjee's novels to syncretic revolutionaries in Dutt's play-text – signifying a definitive turn towards the political imagination of love in the time of secular modernity.

Sannyasir Tarabari is important because of both form and content. Dutt has argued at several points in his long career that in people's theatre, creating large-scale emotional moments is the key to engaging the audience. For him, the speed and innocence (*sarolyo ar gotimoyota*) of such moments are at the heart of *Jatra*. His own play-texts for *Jatra* productions, 'Jatra-theatre' as he puts it, are evidence of his growth as a people's artist, and the success of *Sannyasir Tarabari* taught him the form's impact on the masses. This form – larger than life with qualities of innocence and speed – allows him to perform history with a set of straightforward emotions without compromising subtler nuances of such direct emotions. Quoting his own words on *Sannyasir Tarabari* is worth its while:

> The conflicts within the revolutionaries, the delight in butchery that Ramananda Giri displays, the famine which dehumanizes the peasants, the people turning away from their own champions, the lonely revolutionaries being burnt out

of their forest-hidings, the change in Rennell from an opium-smoking, tired, cultured Englishman to a savage successor of Hastings, and the revolutionary's final death in chains, totally alienated from his own people, secretly poisoned and thus deprived of even the halo of martyrdom – all these were elements that built a dialectical view of the patriotic war. (2009: 172)

Dutt represents straightforward emotional tensions through Devi Chaudhurani's transformation from an able administrator of her absentee husband's estate and a caring mother to their only child to an accomplished revolutionary who leaves her beloved child behind contains the heart of this *Jatra*. By allowing this tension to escalate to tragedy, Dutt fulfils the typical expectations from the *Jatra*. The subtler textures of emotion emerge through the character of Rennell, a historical figure who is a conflicted colonist – loathing intensely what he does to the people he is supposed to govern and yet loves to get 'the job done'. The layered interaction between love and violence finds expression through the semi-historical character of Ramananda Giri, the revolutionary leader, who transforms from a compassionate revolutionary to a grotesque assassin.

As the tension between love and violence spirals into love for violence, it becomes, in Dutt's political imagination of love, symptomatic of the crisis of masculinity. Love for violence ends the possibilities of revolutionising love as an equal, reciprocal, consensual emotion. The ethical limits of love are stretched beyond peace – peace in the sense of absence of war – because love for violence continuously redraws the lines between compassion and ruthlessness by protecting friends and destroying enemies. It is Major Rennell who says that love is not a weakness, but he also contradicts the same assertion by deceiving Ramananda into drinking poison. Rennell secretly kills his prisoner, whom he clearly admires far more than his superior, Warren Hastings. Perhaps Rennell is more cynical than Ramananda Giri in the effective application of violence and more aware of the devastating affective implication of committing violence. The quick succession with which dignity, love, honour, and cruelty overlap each other in the triadic interaction among Ramananda, Devi, and Rennell calls attention to the volatile nature of the relationship between love and violence when it is framed by ethics.

In lieu of a conclusion

Performing history with layered meanings, love, and violence has to negotiate continuously with the thorny but unavoidable question of balance between popular success and reciprocity with the audience. Dutt's political theatre has been committed to intermingling because to be politically effective, theatre must be so popular that it must reach as many people as possible. He never wanted to do experimental theatre just for the sake of celebrating the precarity of experiment, where his audience would become alienated from the practice of theatre. Dutt believed that in a postcolonial country like India, the unlettered people can always be emotionally moved by theatre, and performing history on stage would become valuable in disseminating historical facts, as well as in igniting popular imagination about what history might have been.

Both *Teer* and *Sannyasir Tarabari* enjoyed popular success despite their different forms. *Teer* as proscenium theatre presented novel scenography that brought forth on stage a tribal village of northern Bengal, while the speed and innocence of *Sannyasir Tarabari*, with its powerful dialogue and songs, moved the mass audience of *Jatra*. *Teer* in 1967 was more about an immediate past event, where the protagonists were completely unknown to the theatre audience of metropolitan Calcutta, while *Sannyasir Tarabari* in 1972 was more about making distant history relevant for contemporary times, where familiar legends were recreated with semi-historical figures. Dutt's foray into retelling both contemporary history and the distant past laid out the complex matrix of the sociality of emotions concerning love for the people and romanticism around revolutionary violence while challenging Rokem's argument that performing history on stage recounts failures of revolutions. I would like to contend that performing these histories of rebellions invites the audience to rethink the questions of injustice and structural violence from the perspective of people's theatre and the theatre of rebellion, where intricacies of interactions between love and revolution can be rethought within the frame of historical accountability.

In present-day India, rife with the communal question between Hindus and Muslims, revisiting Dutt's political theatre as historical accountability needs to be aware of the intricate interweaving between religion, ethnicity, caste, and class in each retelling because history has become a contested ground of fact and truth. Dutt has argued in *Towards a Revolutionary Theatre* that 'revolutionary theatre must be violently aetheistic to its own practitioners' but cautioned against directly attacking the audience's religious beliefs (2009: 36). 'The people', Dutt continues, 'have no obligation to renounce religion before they begin to fight', but the practitioner must engage with religion through its history and must realise that the long struggle against religion may have 'no relevance to the immediate need for political struggle' (2009: 36). This measured approach, I would like to emphasise, involves clarity regarding historical accountability in terms of the ethical framing of Dutt's imagination of love – both the articulations of romance and freedom on stage and the interactive reciprocity with the audience as love and romance can forge links between different communities, religions, and castes, opening up the imagination of transgression without undermining the divides. Let me end with the final contention that this imagination of love in Dutt's political theatre is still an unfinished journey. The traces indicate that his writing and performing love in the time of revolution is a mobile grid of emotions within the space of political theatre, changing, as it were, with different framings of modernity, ethics, and violence.

Notes

1. *Jatra* refers to the Bengali folk form of theatre, arguably prevalent as oral literary culture from the sixteenth century. Before the written tradition in theatre consolidated in the nineteenth century, *Jatra* mainly consisted of songs and performances of lyrics strung together with a minimalist plot. From the latter half of the nineteenth century, for the next one hundred years *Jatra* became associated with melodrama based on mythological stories, performed in the open air with colorful costumes and make-up, and showcased a specific cultural sensibility of the rural masses.
2. Though traditionally *Jatra* relied on *Puranic* or mythological themes, it became radically transformed from the 1930s with the playwright-performer Mukundadas, who introduced nationalist themes and characters of freedom fighters in *Jatra*.
3. In India it became a tradition from the 1940s, with contributions from both the activists in the communist movement and anti-fascist artists.
4. Sanyal was a peasant leader from the village Hatighisha in the Naxalbari police station area in the Siliguri sub-division of Darjeeling district in West Bengal.
5. Foothills of the Himalayas are locally referred as *Terai*.
6. I could access the facsimile of the manuscript from his personal papers due to the generosity of Dutt's daughter, Professor Bishnupriya Dutt.
7. Telephone conversation with Asit Basu, 7 April 2021.
8. In my conversations with Professor Dutt this new idea of 'guerrilla'-style performance was discussed.
9. Defining the relationship between friendship and politics to a large extent has guided the discussion around the formation of the 'political' in the twentieth century. Derrida's foundational text on the politics of friendship explores Carl Schmitt's writings along with Montaigne, Kant, Nietzsche, and Blanchot to reflect on Aristotle's quote 'o, my friends, there is no friend' and explains that Schmitt's emphasis on the distinction between friends and enemies largely defines the space of politics itself. Derrida, through memory and mourning inherent in experiencing friendship, offers a new vision of friendship that would undergird the future of inclusive democracy.
10. After LTG broke up, Dutt formed a *Jatra* group 'Bibek Natyasamaj', which seems more like a transitory phase. In 1970 Bibek Natyasamaj gave way to People's Little Theatre, the group in which Dutt remained as a mainstay until his death in 1993. Dutt, however, wrote and actively participated in several *Jatra* plays, which were produced by professional *Jatra* companies from 1968 to 1988.

Bibliography

Ahmed, Sara. 2014. *The Cultural Politics of Emotion*. Edinburgh: Edinburgh University Press.
Badiou, Alain. 2009. *In Praise of Love*. London: Serpent's Tail.
Bandyopadhyay, Samik. 2017. 'Nabanna Prasange.' In *Nabanna*, by Bijan Bhattacharya, p. 16. Calcutta: Dey's.
Banerjee, Sumanta. 1989. 'Marginalization of Women's Popular Culture in Nineteenth Century Bengal.' In *Recasting Women: Essays in Colonial History*, edited by K. Sangari and S. Vaid, pp. 127–179. Delhi: Kali for Women.
Berlant, Lauren. 2012. *Desire/Love*. New York: Punctum Books.
Chatterjee, B. 1937 (1882). *Anandamath*. Calcutta: Bangiya Sahitya Parishat.
Chatterjee, B. 1944 (1884). *Debi Choudhurani*. Calcutta: Bangiya Sahitya Parishat.
Chatterjee, Indrani. 2013. *Forgotten Friends: Monks, Marriages, and Memories of Northeast India*. Delhi: Oxford University Press.
Derrida, J. 2006. *Politics of Friendship*. London: Verso.
Dutt, Utpal. 1997. *Natak Samagra*, Volume 5. Calcutta: Mitra O Ghosh.
Dutt, Utpal. 1998. 'Ghure Fire.' In *Utpal Dutter Godyo Sangraha*, Volume 1, edited by S. Bandyopadhyay, pp. 392–399. Calcutta: Dey's.
Dutt, Utpal. 1999. 'Rajnoitik Natak, Ekti Kalaha.' In *Utpal Dutter Godyo Sangraha*, Volume 1, edited by S. Bandyopadhyay, pp. 226–236. Calcutta: Dey's.
Dutt, Utpal. 2005. 'Bidroher Natak.' In *Utpal Dutt: Ek Samagrik Abalokan*, edited by N. Saha, pp. 90–94. Calcutta: Utpal Dutt Drama Festival Committee.
Dutt, Utpal. 2005. 'Little Thiyetar O Ami.' In *Utpal Dutt: Ek Samagrik Abalokan*, edited by N. Saha, pp. 439–463. Calcutta: Utpal Dutt Drama Festival Committee.
Dutt, Utpal. 2009. *Towards a Revolutionary Theatre*. Calcutta: Seagull.
Ghosh, S. K. (ed.). 1992. *The Historic Turning Point: A Liberation Anthology*, Volume 1. Calcutta: S. K. Ghosh.
Illouz, Eva. 2010. 'Love and Its Discontents: Irony, Reason, Romance.' *The Hedgehog Review* 12(1): 18–32.
Kaviraj, Sudipta. 1995. *The Unhappy Consciousness: Bankim Chandra Chattopadhyay and the Formation of Nationalist Discourse in India*. Delhi: Oxford University Press.
Kaviraj, Sudipta. 2007. 'Tagore and the Transformations in the Ideals of Love.' In *Love in South Asia: A Cultural History*, edited by F. Orsini, pp. 161–182. Delhi: Oxford University Press.
Lavender, Andy. 2012. 'Viewing and Acting (and Points in between): The Trouble with Spectating after Ranciere.' *Contemporary Theatre Review* 22(3): 307–326.
Lyon, Janet. 1991. 'Transforming Manifestoes: A Second Wave Problematic.' *The Yale Journal of Criticism* 5(1): 101–104.
Mookherjee, Nayanika. 2016. *The Spectral Wound: Sexual Violence, Public Memories and the Bangladesh War of 1971*. Delhi: Zubaan.
Pinch, William. 2006. *Warrior Ascetics and Indian Empires*. Cambridge: Cambridge University Press.
Rancière, Jacques. 2009. *The Emancipated Spectator*. London: Verso.
Reinelt, Janelle. 2015. '"What I Came to Say": Raymond Williams, the Sociology of Culture and the Politics of (Performance) Scholarship.' *Theatre Research International* 40(3): 235–249.
Rokem, Freddie. 2000. *Peforming History: Theatrical Representations of the Past in Contemporary Theatre*. Iowa City, IA: University of Iowa Press.

Sarkar, T. 2003. *Hindu Wife, Hindu Nation: Community, Religion and Cultural Nationalism.* Delhi: Permanent Black.
Sinha Roy, Mallarika. 2011. *Gender and Radical Politics in India: Magic Moments of Naxalbari (1967–1975).* London: Routledge.
Tomlin, Liz. 2019. *Political Drmaturgies and Theatre Spectatorship: Provocations for Change.* London: Bloomsbury.
Williams, Raymond. 1977. *Marxism and Literature.* Oxford: Oxford University Press.

Part III

Subjectivity

12

Revolutionary intimacies: Friendship, love, and theatre

Silvija Jestrovic

Set to explore friendship, love, and theatre as notions and practices closely related to the idea of communism, this chapter is a journey down the rabbit hole of elusive categories that escape certainty. Is it possible to think about categories of friendship, love, and theatre as having the potential to epitomise a form of micro-communism? And if so, what insight might be gained from this approach? I am looking here into the correlation between theory and biography, the latter being understood as a form and evidence of practice – a mode of revolutionary being/doing that could offer an entry point into exploring these categories as forms of micro-communism.

However, what is meant here by this term micro-communism? The term has seldom been used and mostly in relation to the political economy and governance[1] to describe ways in which the communal economy is organised in small-scale communities around common property and labour distribution. The notion of micro-communism here does not centre on governance but rather foregrounds a bottom-up approach in the direction of the individual to the communal/community. Alain Badiou writes: 'Three basic elements – political, historical, and subjective – are needed for the operation of the "Idea of Communism"' (2010: 1). Taking my cues from Badiou, I argue that the idea of micro-communism enables a closer look into the subjective within the categories of political and historical.

Micro-communism refers to two related aspects: first, a kind of daily life practice of relations, actions, negotiations, radical refusals, disappointments, acts of solidarity, betrayals, and intimacies. This micro-communism emerges as a way of being/doing with others within 'concrete time specific sequence in which a new thought and practice of collective emancipation arise, exist and eventually disappear' (Badiou 2010: 2). The mode of politics, however, in which this thought/practice unfolds always involves a historical dimension. Badiou brings up large-scale events – the French Revolution 1792–1794, the People's War of Liberation in China 1927–1949, and Bolshevism in Russia from 1902 to 1917 – as examples of emancipatory historical events that arise, exist, and eventually disappear. Nevertheless, I am also interested in the role of concrete time-space sequences that unfold on the level of everyday life: at times, within significant moments of collective emancipation (such as those identified by Badiou). And at other times, on a large scale, they appear as not significant enough or even not significant at all. Such events develop as daily practices, and while too insignificant to be part of large historical narratives, they still make their way into other forms of narratives, such as biographies. In this sense micro-communism could be understood as a kind of communism of the everyday.

The second aspect of this notion of micro-communism concerns the relationship between the public and the private, trying to go beyond the binary and perhaps negotiate the place of the personal within the communal. I am aware that zooming in on the personal in the context of the Left and the idea of communism means entering a contested ground – the aforementioned rabbit hole of elusive categories. The focus on the individual is seemingly misplaced in this context as it echoes the notion of bourgeois individualism that rests on the possession of private property and is positioned in an antagonistic relationship with the collective and the communal. With Marx and Lenin, the bourgeoisie as the class enemy is epitomised in possessive individualism, holding on to private property and a risk-free private sphere. Badiou stresses that his notion of the Subject 'cannot be reduced to an individual' (2010: 2), not even empirically. He offers a definition of the Subject in relation to the idea of truth as 'a material existence of a truth in the making in a given world' (Badiou 2010: 2). He writes:

> This is the moment when an individual declares that he or she can go beyond the bounds (of selfishness, competition, finitude …) set by individualism (or animality – they're one and the same thing). He or she can do so to the extent that, while remaining the individual that he or she is, he or she can also become an active part of a new Subject. (2010: 3)

This process that Badiou calls subjectification opens the possibility 'for an individual to understand that his or her participation in a singular political process (his or her entry into the body of truth) is also, in a certain way a *historical decision*' (2010: 3). This understanding is at the heart of the communist idea, which for Badiou 'exists only at the border between the individual and the political procedure' (2010: 3) as the individual projects him/herself into history. Yet Badiou's notion of subjectification does mention small, personal acts of activism as they contribute to the making of big historical moments: 'To give out a flyer in the marketplace was also to mount the stage of History' (2010: 5).

If we take this as an invitation to zoom in on that individual who – accompanied perhaps by some activists/friends – hands out leaflets in the marketplace, I see Badiou's notion of subjectification (even if risking a too-liberal reading of the concept) as an opening for a biography to take place in the narrative of political becoming. In other words, how can biography as a form enable a unique insight into this process of becoming a political subject? Biography allows us to explore the interlinking of political activism with personal passions, politicising the private sphere and giving activism – and even large-scale emancipatory moments – dimensions of intimacy. As Maurice Blanchot notes, the relationship between everyday life and the political is 'a question of opening the everyday onto history, or even of reducing its privileged sector: private life. This is what happens in moments of effervescence – those we call revolution – when existence is public through and through' (1987: 12). How do we open the questions of the everyday, including its privileged sector of private life, to history in those moments that entirely lack effervescence? How has the process of subjectification been shaped through the ordinariness and complexities of the everyday? This is not about focusing on the individual in isolation from the macro-history but rather about foregrounding the relational aspect as key in the process of one's subjectification. The attempt is to understand the subjectification process as unfolding in the close proximities and intimacies of small groups – to identify the emancipatory potential that takes place in a circle of friends, a team of collaborators, or a pair of lovers.

Biographical glimpses

To explore these questions, I will cast some brief glimpses into the life of the prodigious Eleanor Marx, a life that her biographer Rachel Holmes describes as 'varied and full of contradictions as the materialist dialectic in which she was, quite literally, conceived' (2015: xviii). The discipline of history has recently seen a revival of the so-called *biographical turn* that seeks to bring human actors back on stage.[2] While biography has had a bad reputation seen through the positivist lens as solely focused on the mere retrieval of facts, reducing the conceptual dimensions of analysis and interpretation to personal psychology, contemporary histography begins to understand it as a hybrid genre that does not exclude theoretical engagement but rather aids it. In this chapter I am taking the *biographical turn* as a methodological approach of borrowing from biographers and historians (here most notably from Holmes, whose writing brings detail and vividness to both pivotal and quotidian moments of Eleonore Marx's life). These biographical glimpses allow a closer, at times almost intimate, look into acts of friendship, love, and theatre as manifestations of micro-communism and often as catalysts in the process of subjectification. My use of biography, thus, is neither aimed at presenting new facts nor as the sole interpretative strategy of the existing material, but rather as a methodological tool – a means of theorising the idea of micro-communism.

First biographical glimpse

Eleanor Marx's subjectification[3] in part begins with friendship when as a teenager, she meets the freedom-loving and fiercely political Irish sisters Mary and Lizzy Burns. The sisters, who lived together in a free union with Engels, were dedicated players in the Irish Republican movement. Engels was the closest friend to Eleanor's father, Karl Marx, and the entire family, on whose intellectual and financial support they could always count. Like her own father, Engels and the Burns sisters had a crucial impact on Eleanor's political education and activism. Holmes's biography details how a fortnightly visit to Engels and the Burns sisters, where the Fenian uprising of 1867 and the accounts of its brutal suppression were passionately discussed, turned the thirteen-year-old Eleanor into a lifelong supporter of the Irish Republicans. A year later Colonel Thomas Kelly recuperated the movement and made Manchester its headquarters. However, soon he was arrested. During an attempt at his rescue, a policeman was killed. The English police arrested thirty Irishmen in connection to the incident, five of whom stood trial, and three were hanged in Manchester in one of the last public executions in England. In the political vernacular of the Irish movement, they became known as the Manchester Martyrs. Their death fuelled Fenian radicalism, resulting in several terrorist acts in London. Marx and Engels sympathised with the movement but were very strongly against violence. Young Eleanor, however, a dedicated reader of *The Irishman* newspaper and a loyal friend to the Burns sisters, begged to differ.

Second biographical glimpse

Fast forward twenty years, in 1886 we find her en route to the US, invited by the Socialist Labour Party to give a series of lectures. By then she is a seasoned activist. The primary objective of this lecture tour was to internationalise the socialist organisation of America and bring together the exiles of the 1848 Paris Commune and the ongoing Irish revolution. By this time she had made a clear and precise distinction between socialism and anarchism, more in line with her father's and Engels's views against terrorism, calling the audiences of her American agitation tour to 'throw three bombs amongst the masses: agitation, education, organisation' (Holmes 2015: 285).

Third biographical glimpse

A year later, and back in London in the thick of the Irish Home Rule that epitomised the economic strife and political unrest, Eleanor writes: 'Everywhere large meetings are being held and for the first time the English working class is supporting *Ireland*' (2015: 297). On Sunday, 13 November Eleanor and her lover Edward Aveling were marching at the front of the rally heading to Trafalgar Square. It was in response to the government ban on all the meetings at Trafalgar that the Metropolitan Federation of Radical Clubs, the Irish National League, and the Socialist League called for a protest to demand freedom of expression under the slogan 'To the Square'. The ongoing 'Kill the Bill' protests that started in 2021 in London and across the UK against the bill that proposes to introduce a range of anti-protest measures are not dissimilar from their precursor from almost 140 years ago. Like a dedicated Extinction Rebellion or Insulate Britain activist of today, Eleanor was at the frontline of the protest, among the demonstrators attempting to force themselves into the heavily barricaded Square comprising armed guards and four thousand policemen. When the fight broke out, the police were brutal, kicking the men and women that had fallen and forcing people under their horses' hooves. Hundreds were injured, arrested, charged, and later sentenced; three people died. The event became known as Bloody Sunday and is considered 'one of the most notorious attacks on civil liberties in British history' (Holmes 2015: 300). Eleanor was dismayed by the police brutality but perhaps even more distressed by the cowardice of her fellow protesters: 'only after I shouted myself hoarse calling on the men to stand and show fight, did a few Irishmen closed round. These attracted others, as you will see from the papers, we on Westminster bridge made a fair sight. But it was sickening to see the men run' (Holmes 2015: 299). Two policemen tried to catch her, but she escaped, showing up at the doorsteps of Engels's home 'her coat in tatters, her hat bashed and slashed by a blow' (Holmes 2015: 299). Edward Aveling, the man she was ready to die for (but that is another story), was nowhere in sight. He was among the first who ran away as fast as they could.

In these biographical glimpses into Eleanor Marx's life, practices of friendship, reaching all the way back to her teenage years, turn later in the process of political becoming and into expressions of solidarity. They emerge in forms of political thought and activism whereby friends eventually become comrades. Friendship, and even love, transpire as the key factors not only in shaping the process of subjectification but also in revealing some of the complexities of this process, where the personal and the collective become interlinked, often through contradictions between the individual's courage and cowardice, solidarity and betrayal, action and rhetoric.

Friends and comrades

In his work 'The Politics of Friendship', Derrida investigates definitions of friendship from Montaigne, Kant, and Nietzsche to Carl Schmitt, all shaped through binary opposition of friend–enemy. According to Schmitt, the friend–enemy binary underlies every political idea, while war is seen as the most extreme manifestation of this binary. Working through the binary, Derrida turns to Aristotle, who in *Nichomachen Ethics* holds that 'the highest expression of justice' is 'in the nature of friendship' (1993: 383). Deliberation and equality are at the heart of his understanding of friendship. A relational dimension, implicit in notions and practices of deliberation and equality and in friendship, viewed as the highest form of justice, is always turned from self to other. Derrida arrives at redefining the notion of friendship through a logical sequence that has the other at its centre, rather than the friend–enemy binary: 'there is no thought unless it is a thought of *the other* and the thought of the other as *a thought of* the *mortal*. Within that same logic, there is no thought, there is no thinking being, at least if thought has to be thought of the other, except in friendship' (1993: 362). Derrida adds: 'One would have to specify that justice has two dimensions, one not written and the other codified by law: thus friendship founded on utility – and this is the case for political friendship – can likewise be moral or legal' (1993: 383). Instead of the friend–enemy binary, Derrida proposes a friend–friend dynamic as a defining frame of friendship, which allows us to think of friendship as a form of micro-communism. The binding forces of shared politics and ethics are also intrinsically intertwined with a range of emotional registers and are no strangers to love and passion.

In her book *Comrade* Jodi Dean finds a similar dynamic to Derrida's political friendship in the term comrade 'as the mode of address, carrier of expectations, and figure of belonging in the communist and socialist traditions' (2019: 3). For her, comrade is 'the generic figure for the political relation between those on the same side of the political struggle' (2019: 3). Hence, comrade, rather than friend, is a form of political belonging that is always directed towards the other. While friend, albeit relational, is also individualistic, as in 'I am someone's friend', it would be less common, if not unusual, to say 'I am someone's comrade', but rather 'we are comrades'. Both categories are relational, but the latter does not operate, according to Dean, as a marker of individual identity and connection but as a way of collective belonging. In its relationality, friendship is self-reflexive, while comradeship is binding through action – requiring solidarity and courage – and oriented, as Dean claims, towards the egalitarian future of the society emancipated from the determinations of private property and capitalism. In the recuperation of the term comrade, she sees a new opportunity: 'Rather than remaining stuck in the ruins of communism, we can scavenge the ruins for the past hopes and old lessons and put these remnants to use as we organize and build' (2019: 25). She, however, insists on a distinction between comrade and friend for, it seems to me, two key reasons: first, to point out that the term friend still contains its opposite and, thus, echoes Schmitt's friend–enemy binary, but also, more broadly, as a non-political category shaped through the conditions of neoliberalism; second, friendship, even if political, is more individual than collective, while comradeship requires 'intense collectivity' (2019: 38) that party discipline necessitates. For Dean, there is no collective belonging without a collective body, and that body is the party, which requires both discipline and a significant level of defacement.

To illustrate this point, she uses Brecht's Leherstück *The Measures Taken*, which depicts, in her view, the antithetical relation between individual identity and the comrade. Four agitators are on trial in front of the Control Chorus for the murder of their Young Comrade, who – by repeatedly asserting his own judgement over that of the party – endangered the mission of agitating workers in a Chinese factory. Brecht shows the necessity for party discipline to which the individual's identity needs to submerge when all the agitators put on masks in a deliberate gesture of self-defacement. During the mission, however, the Young Comrade is unable to suspend his own views when confronted with the miserable conditions of the workers – and in an emotional outburst that the revolution cannot wait, he tears off his mask, exposing his identity and endangering the whole mission. Thereafter, the comrades have a dilemma: abort the mission and spare the Young Comrade, or kill him (as his identity has been exposed) and rescue the mission. They choose the latter. The Young Comrade, realising his mistake, and being courageous as a comrade should be, agrees with the decision. The Control Chorus – resembling a mixture of a jury, public forum, and citizen assembly – accepts that the right decision has been made.

Would friends have made a different decision? Could there be a compromise – mission delayed but still accomplished and the Young Comrade spared? The collective versus individual here is also positioned as the rational/strategic versus affective/improvisational approach to the mission. The latter that the Young Comrade embodied has been too easily dismissed as useless and downright dangerous, but we do know now how important affective registers can be in political mobilisation and that, in some instances, improvisational acts can save the day.

It is difficult not to view this didactic cantata of Brecht's differently from the author's intention and in opposition to Dean's insistence on comradeship as political belonging made effective only through party discipline and defacement. We have, of course, seen the danger of utopian ideas of belonging through defacement and party discipline degenerating into nightmares of totalitarianism. Can comrades be rescued from this danger through friendship? Can comrades belong to the collective body without the party as a centralised body? And to what extent can comradeship effectively work through dissensus? Friends can disagree and still maintain a bond, even a political bond. I propose to define political friendship as a more individualised and self-reflexive form of political belonging, while comradeship is a more collective and action-oriented form of political belonging. In practice, there is an opportunity for these categories to serve as modifiers of one another. Micro-communism, as it zooms in on biography and everyday life, necessitates friendship to save comradeship from dogmatism, from drastic measures lightly taken, and comradeship to rescue political friendship from self-absorption, which by reducing the struggle to 'a matter of the individual's feeling, attitude, or comfort level' (Dean 2019: 16) risks making the politics of the struggle opaque.

In the brief biographical glimpses into Eleanor Marx's journey of subjectification, we could see her emerging through both political friendship and comradeship – in her early political initiations through friendship, parental love, and even friendly disagreements with her father and Engels over Irish Republicanism. When she goes to the US on a political mission and talks about the Paris Commune and the Irish question, she is already very much a comrade, yet no doubt very individual in her voice, body, and gestures, as well as in her framing of the political argument. It is this subjectivity within the collective struggle, rather than defacement, that makes her speeches effective. When she takes part in 'To the Square', she is indeed part of a collective body. She could be any of the figures pushing through the police cordon – defacement is effective in those moments of collective mobilisation and comradeship in action. Thereafter, it is friendship again (personal and political) that brings her, angry and dishevelled, to the door of her friend Engels. All these episodes are interlaced with a personal and collective impulse of solidarity – that epitomises political friendship in action.

What's love got to do with it?

In 1884, the same year Engels's seminal book *The Origin of the Family, Private Property and the State* was published, Eleanor Marx was madly in love. She moved into a room on 55 Russell Street opposite the British Museum to live in a free union with Edward Aveling. A year earlier, in the reading room of the British Library, she locked eyes with this young, intelligent academic who shared her political views and her love for theatre. This is the same Aveling who ran away from the violence of Bloody Sunday – one of his many betrayals. The final betrayal will take place fifteen years later when he leaves her for another woman. Soon after, Eleanor will be dead. Suicide by poison is stated as the cause of death. Yet speculations that Aveling killed her (some metaphorically minded, others quite literal in that claim) have never stopped. For Victorian England, Eleanor's move to live with her lover was almost as radical as Engels's book, which she had also helped shape. In this treatise, Engels offers an unflinching critique of the monogamous Victorian family through a long historical view into its origins based on economic foundations and 'conditioned on class positions'. Hence, monogamous marriage is always 'a marriage of convenience' and at the root of 'brutality towards women' (1884). The proletarian marriage emerges as a real possibility with women becoming breadwinners so that no basis for male supremacy is left in the proletarian household – 'the proletarian family is, therefore, no longer monogamous in the strict sense, even if there is passionate love and firmest loyalty on both sides' (1884).

Two years later, Eleanor and Aveling's writing and activism, inspired by August Bebel's essay 'Women and Socialism' (1879), aimed to introduce socialist feminism to Britain, asserting that there is no emancipation without gender equality and that this should be made integral to the worker's movement. For Eleanor, her free union with Aveling was, on the one hand, a feminist gesture and the possibility of proletarian marriage (without marrying). On the other, it was a very Victorian affair – Eleanor did not have much choice to begin with as Aveling was already married although estranged from his wife. She wrote to her friends announcing their union:

> I am going to live with Edward Aveling as his wife … You know he is married, and that I cannot be his wife legally, but it will be a true marriage to me – just as much as if a dozen registrars have officiated … we shall set up housekeeping together, and if love, a perfect sympathy in taste and work and a striving for the same ends can make people happy, we shall be so … I shall quite understand if you think the position one that you cannot quite accept, and I shall think of you with no less affection if we do not any longer count you amongst our immediate friends. (Holmes 2015: 210–211)

Aveling, however, had no inkling or need to write any such letter to anyone. Neither did Engels, who lived in a very unorthodox, free-loving relationship, but he did understand that such radical leaps were more precarious for the women than the men of his time. As Holmes notes in the biography of Eleanor Marx, Engels was very aware that class and social contradictions for him as a socialist man would play out differently than for Eleanor as a socialist woman: 'Engels studied the historical sources with his usual scholarly rigor, but it was observing at close quarters the modern lives of Eleanor and her friends that inspired him to think about sex, socialism, free love and revolution in the early 1880s' (Holmes 2015: 214).

Love is the most complicated form of micro-communism. It has emerged in the context of revolution and politics in various forms – from the urgency to reformulate romantic love to the big, abstract love of the revolution. The question of love and revolution is closely linked to redefining the place of the private and intimate within the collective movement. It is a search for a new form of love that would follow or emerge from the new social and political structures of life. It should, thus, come as no surprise that Lenin addressed the 'women's question', most notable in his 'Letter to Inessa Armand' and in 'The Right to Divorce', abolishing subsequently the inferior position of women, permitting divorce and abortion, and allowing women full control over their property. He seemed less open to more radical approaches to love and sexuality, criticising Alexandra Kollontai for her famous proposal that in communist society, satisfaction of sexual desire should be as simple as drinking a glass of water: 'The glass of water theory has made our young people mad, quite mad ... I think this glass of water theory is completely un-Marxist, and moreover, anti-social' (quoted in Zetkin 1924).

The emancipatory moment of the Soviet Revolution took a conservative turn all too soon, and free love gave way to increased state control of everyday life. Mayakovsky's satirical play *The Bedbug* dramatises this U-turn: romantic love has been declared the relic of the bourgeois past, ridiculed and obsolete; in the revolutionary future, where mechanical hands vote to make all the decisions, the collective body is cleansed of the messiness of any amorous desire. In both real life and in the Soviet theatre of the late 1920s, the rigid regulatory apparatus of the state became antithetical to love.

Both Badiou's *In Praise of Love* and Srećko Horvat's *The Radicality of Love* ponder on love, revolution, and communism. They describe love as 'minimal-communism' (akin to our micro-communism), communism for two (Badiou 2012: 90). However, they also point out that love is as difficult as communism and can end up as tragically as some communist dreams have (Eleanor's love for Aveling is a case in point). For Badiou, love should never be confused with political passions, although love has often emerged in collective political contexts as love for the party, or the leader, or for the revolution itself. This indeed becomes a dangerous love as it can turn strategic and transitional means of political struggle (such as the party) into a fetish. While according to Badiou political love and passion need to be viewed critically, he sees in a world of 'free association and equality' an opportunity to 're-invent love' more easily than when 'surrounded by capitalist frenzy ... The meaning of the word "communism" doesn't immediately relate to love. Nonetheless, the word brings with it new possibilities for love' (2012: 73).

For Horvat, 'every act of solidarity contains love, it is a sort of love, but love can't be reduced to solidarity' (2016: 7). He gives a few examples of what he calls a '*sign* of love' (2016: 73). One such example is the feminist protest that started at Tehran University in 1979 when Khomeini ordered women to wear the chador and in the course of a few days grew into a protest of several thousand people. The echoes of this we recognise all too well in the current struggle for political freedom and against the veil in Irian that has been met with (sometimes deadly) violence towards the protesters. Horvat describes how in the 1979 protest, when the members of the 'Party of God' came to attack the protesting women 'in order to protect them, men – friends, lovers, brother – made a circle around them' (2016: 73). He distinguishes between the '*sign* of love' which is reactive – a solidarity response provoked by an event – and a deeper love, which comes from internalised commitment to the given cause:

> To love would mean to do it even when there is no event, no special occasion, or level of consciousness. That would be the true event: when love is not only provoked by extraordinary cracks in the world, but can be found in the seemingly boring daily activities, even repetitions, or – reinventions. (2016: 8)

Horvat foregrounds the quotidian dimension as necessary to sustain commitment not only to a particular cause but as a certain political ethics that requires a continuum on a small scale – of mundane everyday life – as much as on the large scale of Badiou's *Event*. Hence, when Eleanor marches on Bloody Sunday along with others to protect the democratic right to protest, when she stays risking police violence while others run away, this is a '*sign* of love'. Yet the love that requires one to 'go a step further' (2016: 8) is harder to identify within a particular event as it grows slowly through friendships (that, even if political, cannot be reduced to political bonds only), in conversations and quarrels (some serious, some forgotten the next day), in nursing each other's political disappointments and broken hearts. It is the biographical mode that often depicts these moments of the everyday within which the '*sign* of love' becomes love itself with all its complications and messiness (political, romantic, and other). Biographical glimpses give us insight into how – within the quotidian – cultural materialism theory, political activism, different kinds of love, and different genres of theatre (in Eleanor's case, and in Badiou's for that matter) become entangled.

But, what's love got to do with our ill-fated Young Comrade from *The Measures Taken*? When he tears off his mask in a gesture of solidarity with the exploited factory workers, this is indeed a '*sign* of love' and a tactical mistake. The concept of comrade and comradery in the play is duty-bound – there is no room for love rooted in political friendship or in any other form – the comrades here are co-workers and co-conspirators. They need not share any form of belonging other than to the party. The loyalty is not to one another but to the task and the larger revolutionary struggle of which they are a small part. The communism in the play is an ideological belonging, yet devoid of the communal quotidian. It is communism without a community. There is no room here for love to endure in the everyday, nor even for the solidaristic '*sign* of love'. If there is love at all, then it is a singular love for the revolution epitomised in the loyalty to the party and the fulfilment of the task.

Badiou is sceptical of political love, yet he believes that through the communist ethos and relationships, we will learn to love better. In Horvat's view, for revolution to succeed, it needs 'to deal with the "human factor" (to organise things, channel energies, etc)' (2016: 102), and this also includes affective registers, desires, and the question of love. 'Intimate lives' of those 'doing the revolution' are inseparable from the revolution itself (2016: 102). As complicated as this may be, forms of love are necessary for communism to become a community, for the abstract idea to turn into care for commons without means of violence to secure discipline and successful outcomes. Such love cannot be of a singular kind – neither for the revolution nor for one's lover. It must be a multifaceted, plural love not only to show its *sign* bravely when an *Event* (Badiou) occurs but also to grow in the dullness of the everyday. Love in various forms, and friendship as one of its manifestations, is essential in knowing how to be an individual subject of communal belonging who 'acts politically' (Kear in this collection), whether it be in the mundane repetitiveness of everyday existence or when 'extraordinary cracks in the world' (Horvat) happen. There is a need for an embodied political belonging – through encounters among individuals within the collective political body. This is where love begins and where some form of microcommunism might take place.

Theatre's communism

Art (unlike politics and religion) is, for Badiou, 'very closely linked to love, since the latter is basically the moment when an event breaks into existence' (2015: 78). Theatre, perhaps more than other arts, has a potential to be a form of 'minimal communism', where politics and love intersect. For Badiou, theatre is 'from its origins thinking in-the-body, embodied. ... The relationship of a thought to space and movement is complicated. It must be at once spontaneous and pre-mediated. This is also what happens in love' (2015: 85).[4] The communist philosopher speaks of theatre's capacity to embody thought from the first-hand experience of a dramatist and a performer. In a stage dialogue at the Avignon festival that will become the book *In the Praise of Theatre*,[5] Badiou responds to Nicolas Troung's opening question on where his love for theatre comes from. The philosopher recalls a theatre production he saw at age fourteen, which left a lasting impression on him and how he got to perform the title role in his high school rendition of the same, and later his discovery of Vilar and the People's National

Theatre, where he understood that 'theatre is more an art of possibility than of actualisations' (2015: 2).

Like Badiou, Eleanor Marx loved theatre and aspired to become a professional actress. Shakespeare was the most beloved dramatist of the Marx household, and her father learnt English memorising phrases from his plays. Eleanor, then in her early twenties, and her childhood friend Clara Collet gathered a circle of young British radicals, and in 1877 they formed an amateur theatre group – the Dogberries – named after the pompous constable Mr Dogberry from Shakespeare's *Much Ado about Nothing*. Their meetings, it transpired, were under surveillance by Scotland Yard. They organised play readings at Eleanor's house and outings to Henry Irving's premiers. 'The Marxs at 41 Maitland Park Road became London's most homely radical bohemian theatre salon between 1875 and 1883', writes Holmes (2015: 126). Marx enjoyed the readings but never read a part; he and Engels were the first to join in the post-reading discussions and games. In whatever ways the participants contributed to the Dogberries' amateur dramatics, they were a community bound by radical politics, friendship, and theatre.

Even Eleanor's ill-fated love with Aveling included theatre as they contributed 'Dramatic Notes' (in the early 1890s) for Belford Bax's progressive cultural magazine *Time*.[6] She wrote with precision and wit on the varied repertoires of London theatres, from performances of Shakespeare's tragedies and comedies to pantomimes and French vaudevilles. While she certainly recognised socio-political themes in the plays and performances, she never directly equated theatre as a medium with potential for political activism. Her comments on the controversies over Ibsen's plays show a preference for the *Ghosts* and *The Doll's House* over the more overtly political and male protagonist-driven *The Enemy of the People*. She does make a direct comment on theatre and socio-political reality over the withdrawal of the 'offending burlesque of strikers' from the 'Joan of Arc' show – made especially insensitive to workers at the time of ongoing Scottish Railway Strikes. In her brief comment (co-written with Aveling), she points to the classist blind spots of theatre:

> Only actors, managers, and authors should clearly understand the exact meaning of the pit and gallery objection. Working men have no objection to good-humoured fun. They know the moment a thing is caricatured, that is evidence it is of serious importance. But they do not forget that the theatre, as at present constituted, is like the rest of our institutions, on the side of the classes, not of the masses. (1890)

This little note is a very clear critique of the theatrical apparatus and the responsibility of representation situated in the triangulation of form, content, and context. However, she does not go as far as to propose a deep analysis of the form and content dichotomy or to suggest that some aesthetic choices might be more progressive than others.

Marx preferred to write on political economy rather than on the theatre's potential for communism. Yet Marxism has been the ideological basis of political theatre of Brecht. He, too, criticised the bourgeoise theatrical apparatus while searching for new ways of theatre-making in popular forms and spectacles, in sports events, and in non-Western aesthetics. For Brecht, the socio-political dimension of theatre is predominantly in the method – less in what it represents and more in how it is represented. While he recognises that theatre can be a powerful medium of political activity, Brecht does not assume an innate potential for micro-communism in the operation of theatre as such.

However, in his book *Passionate Amateurs*, Nicolas Ridout explores theatre's potential for communism that is situated neither in the content nor in the aesthetics but has to do with the division of labour, perception of time, and the experience of work as non-work or play:

> The communist potential is to be found in theatre's occasional capacity to trouble some quite fundamental assumptions about both work and time – about the work of time and the time of work – that have come to shape social and cultural life at least since the consolidation of industrial capitalism in Europe from around the end of the eighteenth century. (2013: 6)

According to Ridout, this potential is inherent in the theatre's fundamental operational processes – even in ways in which members of a theatre company or institution live their working lives as theatre-makers. For Badiou, this inherent potentiality is not so much in the operation of theatre alone but rather in its capacity to make communities – both of theatre-makers and audiences. The inherent communal dimension of theatre is reinforced by its unfolding in the here and now of the theatrical event and is among the main reasons the state likes to keep an eye on theatrical events and theatre-makers. 'The theatre is a community and the aesthetic expression of fraternity', writes Badiou. 'That is why I argue that there is, in that sense, something communist in all theatre. By "communist" I understand that which makes the held-in-common prevail over selfishness, the collective achievement over private interests' (2012: 89–90). Eleanor Marx, in her love for theatre – where political activism, friendship, and amateur dramatics intersected – perhaps intuitively understood its communist possibility. However, it would be erroneous to view Brecht's search for a Leftist theatre aesthetic as antithetical to the ideas of theatre as a form of 'minimal communism', as they all, in different ways, formulate the art of communist possibilities – capable of, as Badiou claims, to 'restore completely' the 'intense power of the event. Only art restores the dimension of the senses to an encounter, an insurrection, or a riot' (2012: 78). Theatre, we might add, can depict both the intensity of the event and the drama in the dullness of the everyday – for example, the big brush strokes of the revolution and the mundane detail in micro-communism of the everyday.

Homely communism

Eleanor Marx died in the same year Bertolt Brecht was born – 1898. I wonder what she would have made of Brecht's didactic play *The Measures Taken* if she could have experienced it? Would this avant-garde play be a profound shock of the new to the Shakespeare-loving Dogberries? And what would Eleanor, her father, their friend Engels, and the Burns sisters think of the measures taken apropos the Young Comrade? Would they have a disagreement about the necessity of such measures like they had debated the means of struggle regarding the Irish question? And when the Young Comrade tears his mask down, what would Eleanor read in this gesture – betrayal of the revolutionary cause or would she have found in his bared face the eyes of a friend or even a lover?

We will never know. What we could claim with some certainty, though, is that Brecht would have become the subject of a lively debate at the Marxs' household, and his didactic play might have even received a staged reading from the Dogberries. A form of micro-communism took place at the Marxs in the late 1870s of which the Dogberries were one of the most prominent features, alongside various forms of political activism and radical hospitality. Every Sunday the house was open for friends and strangers. Eleanor was involved in curating these 'At Home' events, making sure that enough food was prepared for an indetermined number of guests. One of the visitors described the atmosphere:

> The strangers were numerous and shared the classic charm of great variety. There was one point of resemblance between them – for the most part they were impecunious. ... A goodly number have no doubt found their native land too hot to hold them – clever conspirators, to whom London was a chosen centre, political prisoners who had contrived to shake the shackles from their limbs, young adventurers whose creed was of 'if-there's-a-government-I'm-agen-it' order. (Holmes 2015: 128)

While the historical role of Eleanor's father, their friends, and Eleanor herself is commonly seen through their political thought and actions – in ways they have inspired historical *Events* (in Badiou's sense of the word) – these biographical glimpses also depict a special sort of Leftist being in the world and in the everyday. I propose to name it 'homely communism'. Not unlike utopian performatives (Dolan) of theatre, homely communism unfolds in fleeting moments of conviviality amid fallouts, betrayals, disappointments, injustice, exploitation, violence, heartache, and loss. The idea of homely communism uses hopeful thinking/doing as a strategy to imagine moments of small realised utopian performativity into an actual alternative. Like the art of theatre, and perhaps love – that 'communism for two' (never too far from bitter disappointment and even tragedy) – it needs some willing suspension of disbelief. Homely communism is a different concept of being at home(s) – where the door is wide open to friends and strangers, where the living room can easily turn into theatrical stage, or party headquarters, or into shelter for political refugees. Yet one quality of homely communism is that it is never fully homebound, for the door is always open so it can spread out to 'provoke extraordinary cracks in the world'. Like theatre, and perhaps love, homely communism is the realm of possibilities.

Notes

1 Political economist F. L. Pryor (1990) wrote about micro-communism in political economy of very small states with less than a million inhabitants.
2 See Renders *et al.* (2016).
3 While I am concerned here with political subjectification rooted in Badiou's thought of communism. For further consideration of the notion of subjectification within the context of moral philosophy, see Butler (2005).
4 See also Badiou (2013) and Puchner (2009).
5 Both *In Praise of Love* and *In Praise of Theatre* first took place as stage dialogues with Nicolas Truong at the Avignon Theatre festivals and masterminded, by the famous theatre director Antoine Vitez, 'Theatre of Ideas', who directed the Badiou play *The Red Scarf* at the Avignon.
6 Aveling used the pseudonym Alec Nelson.

References

Badiou, Alan. 2010. 'The Idea of Communism.' In *The Idea of Communism*, edited by C. Douzinas and S. Žižek, pp. 1–15. London: Verso.
Badiou, Alan. 2012. *In Praise of Love*, translated by P. Bush. London: Serpent's Tail.
Badiou, Alan. 2013. *Rhapsody for the Theatre*. London: Verso.
Badiou, Alan. 2015. *In Praise of Theatre*, translated by A. Bielski. Cambridge: Polity.
Bebel, August. 1910. *Women and Socialism*. New York: Socialist Literature Co.
Blanchot, Maurice. 1987. 'Everyday Speech.' *Yale French Studies: Everyday Life* 73: 12–20.
Butler, Judith. 2005. *Giving an Account of Oneself*. New York: Fordham University Press.

Dean, Jodie. 2019. *Comrade*. London: Verso.
Derrida, Jacques. 1993. 'Politics of Friendship.' *American Imago* 3(3): 353–391.
Engels, F. 1884. *The Origin of the Family, Private Property and the State*. www.marxists.org/archive/marx/works/1884/origin-family/index.htm. Accessed on 27 March 2023.
Holmes, Rachel. 2015. *Eleanor Marx*. London: Bloomsbury.
Horvat, Srećko. 2016. *The Radicality of Love*. Cambridge: Polity.
Lenin, V. I. 1976. 'Letter to Inessa Armand, January 24, 1915.' In *Lenin Collective Works*, pp. 182–185. Moscow: Progress Publishers.
Lenin, V. I. 1916, 1924. 'The Right to Divorce.' Marxist Internet Archive. www.marxists.org/archive/lenin/works/subject/women/abstract/16_08.htm. Accessed on 16 February 2024.
Marx, Eleanor, and Edward Aveling. 1890. *Dramatic Notes*. www.marxists.org/archive/eleanor-marx/1890/theatre.htm. Accessed on 27 March 2023.
Pryor, F. L. 1990. 'The Political Economy of Micro Communism.' *Communist Economies* 2(2): 223–249.
Puchner, Martin. 2009. 'The Theatre of Alain Badiou.' *Theatre Research International* 34(3): 256–266.
Renders, Hans, Binne de Haan, and Jonne Harmsma (eds). 2016. *The Biographical Turn: Lives in History*. London: Routledge.
Ridout, Nicholas. 2013. *Passionate Amateurs: Theatre, Communism and Love*. Ann Arbor, MI: University of Michigan Press.
Zetkin, Clara. 1924. *Reminiscence of Lenin*. www.marxists.org/archive/zetkin/1924/reminisence-of-Lenin.htm. Accessed on 21 March 2023.

13

The fraught act of speaking for/about the communist women

Urmimala Sarkar Munsi

Recent writings (Kumari and Kidwai 1998; Ray 1999; Sarkar 2008; Karat 2016; Loomba 2019) on women political/public figures and leaders of the communist movements have often reviewed the stories of the women leaders in a selective fashion and written critiques of the subservient/subjugated and often invisible state of their existence within the spectrum of the activities of the Communist Parties of India. Tanika Sarkar, one of the prominent historians on modern India, records her uneasiness about this recent trend of undermining communist women's agency and positions within the Communist Parties of India. She writes: 'women's actual, intentional political work as world-transformative and self-transformational activity' has been understood as a sphere in which women are largely manipulated or marginalised by men (Sarkar 2005: 541). Malhotra and Lambert-Hurley argue that 'women's voices and thus their self-representation may be convoluted, elusive, paradoxical, and metaphorical' (quoted in Sarkar 2005: 541), but they cannot be assumed to be insignificant or absent and have to be accepted as their own version or their way of telling their own story. They write:

> the challenges involved in recovering women's voice should not indicate a lack of voice. On the contrary, if the women had the temerity to negotiate with their own cultures in order to speak, so do we have a duty as scholars, to uncover and understand the cultural context in which their speech was created. (Malhotra and Lambert-Hurley 2015: 12)

The basic question that frames this chapter is whether it is possible to read the biographical and autobiographical accounts of the women in the communist movement in India without delegitimising their commitment and work beyond categories such as non-feminist or anti-feminist. Instead, I will argue for a reading of their works within collective programmes and as part of grassroot mobilisations. This will be apt for understanding the roles and contributions of women in the Left movements. As part of their ideological commitments, they never highlighted the individual self, and although they wrote autobiographical memoirs, they were primarily to understand the movement and the roles they carved out for themselves in a self-critical mode.

This chapter is based on four textual analyses of the (auto)biographical writings of Manikuntala Sen (2001, 2010), Hajrah Begum (1962), Vidya Munsi, and Reba Roychowdhury (1999) to investigate their agency through their work, principally focusing on the activities in the 1940s and 1950s in the context of their involvement and association with the women's movement in India of those times. These specific voices are chosen as

Figure 13.1a

Figure 13.1b

Figure 13.1c Covers of *Chalar Pathey* and *Ek Shathey*, two women's periodicals published by the women's organisations belonging to the Communist Party of India (CPI) and the Communist Party of India (Marxist) (CPI(M)) (© author)

representatives who are known names that have made a range of significant contributions both locally and nationally and yet have remained in the margins of mainstream communist memory. These narratives are treated here as important testimonies by women whose work and experiences have not been acknowledged specifically, as they have been repeatedly absorbed within the larger patriarchal narratives of communist history. This chapter looks at women's agency as 'polysemic' and sets out to 'uncover ways of locating and focusing on it' (Malhotra and Lambert-Hurley 2015: 13). The core understanding of agency in their work is read through the often matter-of-fact self-documentation of day-to-day activities within the communist movement and in following the party high command's orders. These women's choices to move away from families and work alongside male comrades, and at the same time also try to cull out a space for women's movement within the political environment largely shaped by patriarchy, need to be seen and identified specifically through their stories and not our interpretations – even if we, as the daughters of that generation of fiery women, feel like the privileged insiders to their stories. These narratives also tell us clearly that the thoughts expressed in these publicly available documents are sufficient to lend strength to these women's ideological positions. The chapter posits yet another parallel reading to the male-dominated discourse of the communist parties through these autobiographical observations. Carefully read, these narratives seem to provide a way to understand what mattered to these communist women and how they dealt with the dominant ideas of the time by selective and subjective transgression both in the domestic and the political public spheres (see Figure 13.1).

Thinking about the methodology

My research tries to create a space of recognition for the subjects' (in this case the communist women's) lifelong work and labour as construed, or even imagined, by themselves. This is essential to write women's histories by acknowledging them in the driver's seat and not just as extensions of their male counterparts within the social systems they dreamt of changing.

In Raka Ray's opinion, studies on the women's movements in different cities in India, such as Bombay and Kolkata, show that:

> [W]omen's movements are neither homogeneous nor pure products of modernization and development, but rather are embedded in particular histories and geographies. Political fields, which are the dynamic outcomes of local and regional processes, have thus shaped the women's movements in Bombay and Calcutta and elsewhere in India in very different ways. Activists within these movements consciously work to understand and assess the possibilities offered

by the field within which their organizations are embedded, negotiating optimal results given existing conditions. At the same time, their identities are shaped by the fields within which they are acting collectively. (Ray 1999: 159)

According to Sarla Sharma,[1] one of the founder members of the National Federation of Indian Women (NFIW), the documentation of narratives of the collective effort by communist women's organisations such as NFIW at the grassroots level and also national and international fronts is 'merely an indication of the voices raised by organized women not only in serious rallies and speeches' (Munsi *et al.* 2009: 20). Sharma's views are strengthened by Tanika Sarkar's observation that the historical, autobiographical, and biographical writings on communist lives focus almost exclusively on 'party programmes and lines' without mentioning their own political experiences: 'Communist women have thus been doubly marginalized: in Communist and in feminist histories' (2005: 557). She continues to assert that because of this, biased writing that actually undermined women's agency 'in radical refashioning of communist domesticities, familial worlds, gender relations' (2005: 557) is not visible to people reading communist history. Sarkar's work lends strength to my assertion on women's claims to the idea of 'work' through their own writings, which seem to have been undermined in the way scholars have the liberty to represent them.

Ania Loomba, in her recent book *Revolutionary Desires: Women, Communism and Feminism in India* (2019), notes that the absence of written history about the communists in India is 'even more true of communist women's lives' between 1920 and 1960. According to her, writings on communist women only 'extoll their public achievements, with little consideration of their everyday lives, particularly their domestic or emotional lives, or the debates that might have arisen within the organizations as a result of women's participation' (2019: 3). While acknowledging that the 'communist and other radical women in India did produce many personal narratives – autobiographies, memoirs, fragmentary accounts' (2019: 3), her book highlights the silences about the parallel private lives of these public figures – the communist women – whom she sees as cautiously avoiding direct critique of the political party that they themselves chose to be a part of. Loomba sees this unwillingness to document a direct critique of the ideology located in the realms of public and private worlds structured within and by the patriarchal social system. She asks: 'How does one get to the other side of this type of silence?' (2019: 8) and writes in her conclusion: 'Today, the gaps and omissions in the attempts of these communist women to fashion an alternative world are only too evident – insufficient engagement with questions of caste and rank, for example – and they are widely, and often smugly, remarked upon by critics of the left in India' (2019: 305). Janaki Nair, in her review of Loomba's book, points out that she (2019: 28) 'declares the need for some methodological promiscuity' that is 'occasioned by the object of study itself: women who were in the public eye, and yet shrouded many aspects of private life in their narrations' (Nair 2019: 23) to justify selective and occasional references to the oral history archive in Loomba's writings.

The universalisation of communist women's experiences all over India and the selective negations of their own narratives create an uncomfortable ethnographic hierarchy even in powerful writings such as Loomba's. It also appears to be dismissive of how the women saw and wrote about themselves. If their writings have not yielded what Loomba calls 'revolutionary desires' and have not provided detailed descriptions of their private lives, there is no other way but to take these silences as a form of the prioritisation that these women were reflecting. While that can be seen as a deliberate or forced and submissive omission, as a feminist I see it as a choice that an ethnographer must accept. It becomes important to acknowledge that they had their logic for choosing to perform their gendered presences and their ideological positions in a specific manner in such writings.

This chapter begins with reading Loomba's reference to 'revolutionary desire' parallelly to the idea of the 'communist desire' used by Jodi Dean (2013: 5). In her writing, Dean discusses Wendy Brown's writing on the 'left melancholy' as a result of the 'unavowedly crushed ideal', the 'unaccountable loss' (Brown 1999: 19–27) and of the hopelessness thereafter. Brown's analysis of the fallouts of 'the fears and anxieties of a left in decline, a left that is backwards-looking, self-punishing, attached to its own failure and seemingly incapable of envisioning an emancipatory, egalitarian future' (1999: 19–27) are seen by Dean as an acceptance and a facilitating process for a possible reformulation of the Left ideology, through 're-conceiving communist desire' (2013: 5). In this parallel placement of the two ways of looking at desires by Loomba and Dean, the individual and collective desires are differentiated.

In the women's movement in India, this phase of melancholia has brought recrimination and lament that usually suggests that the communist women have been silenced by their own scripts about what their performance needed to be as an ideal communist. In revisiting the writings by/on the communist women, thus, the reading of their desires and commitments may need to be approached differently, and one of the ways is suggested by Dean when she iterates:

> Although our political problem differs in a fundamental way from that of communists at the beginning of the twentieth century – we have to organize individuals; they had to organize masses – Georg Lukács's insight into individualism as a barrier to the formation of collective will is crucial to the theorizing of communist desire as collective desire. (2013: 19)

She reiterates: 'Collectivity is the form of desire in two senses: our desire and our desire for us; or, communist desire is the collective desire for collective desiring' (2013: 31). My readings of the autobiographies and biographies yielded time and again this very ideation of collective desires mentioned by Dean, as a focused outcome born out of a framework of collective belongings and aspirations mentioned by the women whose voices and works in the grassroots I have chosen to foreground and many others who I could not include in this chapter.

The 'grassroots' work was usually with women (and men) who were often not members or sympathisers of the Communist Party. Mostly, this was a distinctly different world from the leadership positions. While the leadership positions meant 'public' acts of mobilisation through large rallies and meetings and strategising at a very visible and public level, choosing to be in grassroots mobilisation meant preparing the ground in a very different manner. Small meetings, often within low- and middle-income localities, party classes, small face-to-face membership campaigns, organisations of local health clinics for women and children, discussions on specific issues concerning women, that is, the right to make decisions regarding bearing children, domestic violence, unorganised labour, publicising women's rights, anti-dowry campaigns, literacy drives, local exhibitions of posters for a literacy drive, and publishing vernacular magazines for women were some of the regular activities to activate political microcosms. These organised and collective political actions created an identifiable working group as well as a resistive awareness.

In Dean's words, 'Precisely because such struggle is necessarily collective, it forges a common desire out of individuated ones, replacing individual weakness with collective strength' (2013: 22). Many women's writings talk proudly about their work in mobilising and enhancing awareness of the Communist Party, and its importance in creating resistance against local-level socio-political conditions and systemic oppressions.

This niche space for mobilisation also brought its specific requirements of being a private (that is, less public, less threatening, and less patriarchally controlled) domain, where hegemonic masculine and familial controls could be subverted or at least ignored for a little while. For such spaces to be used for grassroots mobilisation, the timing of the meetings also had to be liminal – existing or fitted into small slots, almost stealthily taken out by the attendees from the free time that they got between work and family responsibilities. Thus, these meetings were open to women coming in and going out according to their unchangeable everyday routine, respecting their spaces and times along with their needs to bring the youngest children with them. Afternoons often became the only available slot for women to 'sit and waste time' in non-essential political 'activities' that clearly were not seen as their rightful place, even by their Left-leaning families.

Voices, choices, scripts, and logic: women's documentations

Raka Ray's use of the term 'political culture' by which she refers 'to the acceptable and legitimate ways of doing politics in a given society, strongly influenced by but not reducible to the complex web of class, gender, race, religion, and other relations that order society' (1999: 8) gives us yet another way to make sense of the individual/collective, private/public spheres of involvement of the passionately political (even perhaps somewhat romantically so) and committed communist women, whose autobiographies and biographies demand a critical but incisive reading. According to Ray, 'The dominant discourse within a political culture defines what politics is, who legitimate actors are, and what can or cannot be put on the political agenda' (1999: 8–9). This definition strengthens the need for detailed studies of regional movements and the socio-political networks of grassroots mobilisation processes, where the links between these 'her' stories and the toolkits for their work are conceived through the often-repeated words: 'collective', 'grassroots', 'mobilisation', and 'movement'. These autobiographies create a script of these women's convictions, of thinking beyond the social frames of family, a spirit of activism and sacrifice, and maybe to imagine a better world (not for self but for a larger community of women in particular and society in general). The script is played out through becoming involved in public/private activities for the mobilisation of women, in repeated imprisonments and even violent anti-state activities, in the choice of independent decision-making, in the willingness to learn a new vocabulary for the women beyond the socialised structures, in the sustained efforts to belong to an overly dominating patriarchal structure of the central body of the party.

The patriarchy that has plagued the political structures and created hindrances to women's participation has to be challenged through historiographic and archival references at the same time. That makes autobiographical and biographical presences of women even more essential. The communist women that I am speaking of registered themselves as agents of their own decisions, and their narratives foreground their 'choice' to join the communist movement, placing them in the time and particular social spaces they came from. These choices must get placed within the social milieu that framed them before and after they started their 'work'.

The research entailed extensive as well as in-depth and critical reading of the autobiographical, biographical, and political writings of and about Aruna Asaf Ali, Hajrah Begum, Renu Chakraborty, Vimla Dang, Kanak Mukherjee, Vidya Munsi, Sudha Roy, Reba Roychowdhury, Manikuntala Sen, Sarla Sharma, and also the oral history archival records of Stree Shakti Sanghatana.[2] For the limited scope of this chapter, I have chosen Munsi, Sen, Begum, and Roychowdhury's documentation of their work/life and choice/path as my primary source of information. Trying to desist from making assumptions about their lived realities, this chapter seeks to read the choices and ideological drive in these women and the 'labour' invested in commitment and ideology. What started as methodological meanderings to link several 'her' stories to configure a 'collective' also pushed me to look at these readings through a feminist lens. With the growing familiarity with some of the common factors in their worldviews, there emerges a performative (often confrontational and headstrong) rendition of not only 'being' communist but also 'doing' communism as a collective through words and work. The choice of placing the political over the personal in these women's cases was actually also a part of building new collectives and solidarities.

Prioritising the women's question from within the Communist Party: Vidya Munsi nee Kanuga[3] (1919–2014)

Vidya Munsi, a founder member of the NFIW, said in her interview to feminist scholar Samita Sen:

> My induction into the women's movement was through communism. I am a communist first and it is communism which led me to examine the women's issue and to realise its importance.

> I feel that I have to raise the women question within the party. When I shifted to 'Samity' (Paschim Banga Mahila Samity) work, many friends within the party deplored my decision. They said that I was a good journalist and should continue in that work. But would they then do Samiti work? Of course not. Women in the party, have a special responsibility, I believe, to give priority to the women's question I cannot accept that women's issues can wait for anything. It has to be a running battle with all other battles and *it was my decision* [emphasis mine] to concentrate on this particular battle.

She continued:

> I do not believe Feminism to be 'false' position. I believe that patriarchy has to be fought separately from class. Patriarchy may have originated as the first means of extracting surplus, but it has survived capitalism and seems even capable of surviving socialism. Thus it has to be fought separately from class struggle. (Sen 1997: 161–162)

Munsi, later, also said in her recorded interview,[4] 'I had to work at the grassroot level with women. I could not be the "elite" – I had to learn and unlearn at the same time.'

Munsi had gone to England to study medicine and had joined the Communist Party in 1942. The Communist Party of India (CPI) was still illegal in India. She told Sen that the Federation of Indian Students Societies of Europe (FEDIND) was affiliated to the All India Students' Federation

(AISF). There were regular political classes that both member and non-member students attended. Munsi's involvement with the women's movement came much later. She recalled that on 8 March 1945, she was invited to speak at a meeting on the occasion of International Women's Day. 'I remember Dange[5] helped me prepare my notes. That was the time when I really put my mind to the "woman question"' (Sen 1997: 151).

During November and December 1945, as the Secretary of FEDIND, Munsi attended the conferences of the World Federation of Democratic Youth (WFDY) in London and the Women's International Democratic Federation (WIDF) in Paris. In both the conferences, she represented the All India Students Federation (AIDF). In her role as the representative of the Girl Students' Association of the AISF, she met Ela Reid, one of the founding members of the Mahila Atma Raksha Samiti (MARS), who had travelled from India. This was followed by her trip back to India to set up a preparatory committee for the South East Asia Youth Conference. She elaborated:

> Women were very active in youth movement and they were given positions of great responsibility. There was no discrimination. It was a time of great struggle. Men and women had to pull together. As a result the women had begun to assert themselves and rework their relations with and their positions within the family. ... There has been a slide back in last fifty years. I no longer see women being given responsibilities and given visibility in positions at organisational level. I no longer see that creative energy that is perhaps unique to a time of great movements. This, I believe is the general patter in the women's movement ... When we went to the World Youth festival of Prague (1947), we saw lots of women. In the South East Asia Preparatory committee almost half the members were women. (Sen 1997: 152)

In the NFIW Bulletin (2009), Munsi wrote about the way Indian representatives explained the conditions and organised movements of women at the IDF Congress in December 1945:

> What did we Indian delegates say in our report to the WIDF Congress? We spoke of effects of two centuries of British colonial rule and its dismal record of impoverishment, illiteracy, incredibly high rates of infant and maternal mortality. ... They shuddered to hear Ela Reid describe the Bengal famine, which had taken the toll of over a million lives in 1943. We told them of the part the Indian women had played in the struggle for Independence. (2009: 4)

In the same essay Munsi described the everlasting inspiration from her meeting with Dolores Ibárruri (popularly known as La Pasionaria), a prominant leader of the anti-fascist struggle of the Spanish people and, at that time, general secretary of the Spanish Communist Party in exile. She wrote: 'Though I could not understand a word of Spanish, such was Pasionaria's power of oratory that I would clutch the arms of my chair and listen breathlessly to the end' (2009: 7). Munsi remained committed to the CPI throughout her life. Her course of work till the year 2001 – when she became largely homebound after a paralytic stroke – seems to have stemmed from the pledge that all attendees of the WIDF Congress of December 1945 took:

> We solemnly swear to struggle tirelessly for the final wiping out of fascism in all its forms, forever, and for the establishment of true democracy all throughout the whole world. We solemnly swear to struggle without respite to assure a lasting peace in the world, the only guarantee for the happiness of our homes and the full flowering of our children. Long live the WIDF! (2009: 8)

While helping Munsi edit her autobiographical book *In Retrospect: War-Time Memories and Thoughts on Women's Movement* (2006), I understood how much of her political life had remained unknown to me – her only offspring. A trained and professional journalist, she took documentation very seriously and put together her memories of the war years spent in England and at the headquarters of the World Federation of Democratic Youth, visits to different countries as representative of the women's movement, and some important debates and events on women's problems in India. Her family life would make an important book by itself, but none of that was significant enough for Munsi to include in her writings.

'The dangerous woman' committed to women's welfare: Manikuntala Sen (1910–1987)[6]

In her autobiography Manikuntala Sen (West Bengal State Legislative Assembly member from 1952 to 1962 for the undivided Communist Party) wrote an account of her work at the grassroots level. At the end of the autobiography is a section of police records on her compiled by Shikha Sengupta (Sen 2010: 323–326).[7] The police records (henceforth referred to as PR, translated by me) are important to understand the scope of such grassroots work mobilised by the CPI, the role of leaders such as Sen, and the responses from the authorities:

> PR – 05-04-1939: Women from Barishal B. M. College and Sadar Girls' School have created a Women Volunteers' Group. All of these girls are Communists.
>
> PR – 21-08-1941: Subject: Manikuntala Sen – After graduating from B. M. Collage Barishal, she joined Metropolitan Institution as the Assistant Head Mistress of the school. She was sharing accommodation with the erstwhile women political prisoners from Mahila Rashtriya Sangha (MARS)[8] in Kolkata.

The records trace her involvement with the women's movements and the conference of the All India Womens' Federation in 1937:

> PR – 30-11-1943: Police intercepted a letter sent by Sen to Nikhil Chakraborty, 44 Bahubajar Street, Kolkata, where Sen has reported the medical emergency

caused by large scale spread of Malaria in areas within Medinipur (Sutahata, Nandigram, Mahishadal). She urged the Party leadership in Kolkata to urgently arrange to send a medical team to the region.

Shikha Sengupta observes that in the turbulent times[9] of the early years of the 1940s, Manikuntala Sen worked tirelessly at the grassroots level all over undivided Bengal to establish the MARS as a self-defence group for women:

> PR – 15–03–1944: Sen along with Sucharita Das (the then Head Mistress of Tamluk Girls School) has delivered a public address at the Regional Conference of the MARS in Tamluk, in Medinipur District of Bengal. She is identified as a 'dangerous' woman – who needs to be kept under surveillance.

Sikha Sengupta, in her own writings about the police records, notes that Sen was jailed multiple times in that period, on a variety of charges:

> PR – 10–05–1947: After being arrested Sen gave a statement emphasising that her mobilization work was related to building social awareness regarding upliftment and progress of the women. Sen is recorded to have stated that the work for women's welfare necessitated constant working together with ordinary women on issues of progress and development with many women's organizations whose works are well-known and are accepted as progressive and developmental.

> PR – 03–03–1949: The records note that the Intelligence Bureau of Calcutta Police has sent a radiogram to the Police Department in Kharagpur asking them to keep Sen under severe surveillance. Sen is recorded to have been arrested on 08–03–1949 as a result. She was on a hunger strike and carried on her mobilizing activity relentlessly within the prison till she was released on 08–04–1951. From 1948 – 1949, she had been consistently working to help and organize the women refugees as well as in helping to build unorganised women workers' resistance. After her release from Jail in 1949, she was given the responsibility to create an organization with the Women Refugees from East Bengal.

The grassroots Communist Party campaign and mobilisation, of course, was a simultaneous activity among the women she worked with and on an everyday basis. Regarding the identification of the need for the work that was necessary to organise the women, Sen[10] mentions the formation of the MARS. She wrote in her autobiography:

> We would form our organisation primarily with middle class and lower middle class working and peasant women. Sitting in Ela di's house, the objectives of the Samiti and a memorandum were drawn up. What would the Samiti be called? Renu said, 'The men are doing "people's protection". Our samiti would be for women's atma raksha or self-respect. (2001: 74)

Gargi Chakravartty translates Kanak Mukhopadhyay's autobiography *Nari Mukti Andolon O Aamra Eksathe* (1993) to provide the programmes identified for the MARS in the initial meeting:

An eight-fold programme was issued. This included: 1) a propaganda campaign, 2) creating public awareness against the Fifth Column, 3) building civil defence, 4) collecting funds, food, and cloth for famine-displaced people, 5) helping in the evacuation of ordinary inhabitants from military-occupied places and ensuring that they get work as compensation and for their rehabilitation, 6) demanding government-aided fair-price shops run by district cooperatives, 7) organising women's defence groups with training in the use of lathis, martial arts etc., 8) assisting the farmers to grow crops and other grains. (Chakravartty 2017: 180)

Sen's continued work to build organised networks among women for self-help and self-defence led to her becoming one of the founder members of the MARS, which remains one of the most significant moments marking women's organised participation in the political struggle in Bengal.

Quest for workers' and women's rights: Hajrah Begum[11] (1910–2003)

Hajrah Begum was drawn to communism while studying in Britain. In her extensive recorded interview to the Nehru Memorial Museum and Library (NMML), she asserted that she was a communist and a nationalist at the same time and that these two commitments rested comfortably with each other in her political life as a citizen of India. Her fight for railway workers' rights and as the founder and secretary of the Allahabad Railway Coolies Union may be mapped alongside her involvement and active engagement with important international conferences of the World Peace Council, Vienna (1952), the Women's International Democratic Federation, Copenhagen (1953), the World Congress of Mothers, the Afro-Asian Women's conference, Cairo (1961), among others. She also became the first secretary of the NFIW.

In her speech as the secretary of the NFIW at the WIDF Congress in Copenhagen in 1953,[12] Hajrah Begum said:

> Today we have 30 women members in the House of the People and the Council of States, as well as women members in almost all state assemblies.
>
> This however, does not mean that the women in India have won equality in the social, economic and political field. Laws have to be implemented and in the attempt to make the right a reality our women's organisations face tremendous difficulty.
>
> That women are becoming more conscious of their responsibilities to determine the future of their country was clearly demonstrated. (Munsi *et al.* 2009: 9)

Hajrah Begum drew international attention through this speech to the fact that in the post-independence election, in several areas more women than men went to the polls and showed a zeal and enthusiasm not witnessed before. She also said that the women teachers, industrial workers (in industries such as jute, leather, tea and coffee plantations, coal mines, glass, rice mills, textile, and many others) have begun to organise themselves to protest and sit on hunger strikes for their rights to better work conditions, equal pay, living wages, better health and child care, and, most importantly, their right to organise. She said that they

> [H]ave demonstrated their urgent desire to win for themselves a decent life. In the peasant areas of the South, in Bengal and Uttar Pradesh, thousands of women have united and organized the demand for food and land. They have faced brutal attacks from the feudal landlords and the police. Thousands were imprisoned and hundreds dies either in prison or as a result of bullets, but the women carried on undaunted. (Munsi *et al.* 2009: 12)

Hajrah Begum became a well-known labour leader to work extensively in the state of Uttar Pradesh to organise grassroots workers' protests. In her narratives recorded as a part of the Oral History Archives at the NMML, she has recorded her frustration with the Communist Party working structures and strategies regarding the urgent requirement for focused organisational work among women as well as men. As the leader in the CPI and AIWC, and also the editor of the AIWC journal *Roshni*,[13] she raised 'the question of organizing women on an all India basis' (Begum 1994).[14]

To sum up Hajrah Begum's commitment, it would be important to quote Elisabeth Armstrong from her book[15] on the history of the changing landscape of women's politics in India: 'Hajrah Begum was an open communist and author of Why Women Should Vote Communist, a CPI pamphlet published in 1962' (Armstrong 2013: 35). Begum's pamphlet appeals for collective actions from women at the grassroots, who were already enclosed in individual domestic spaces. Like the other women in this chapter, she also identified the need to encourage collective subjectivities as essential, which can be achieved through the collective determination to perform the right to vote.

Honing performative tools for political mobilisation: Reba Roychowdhury[16] (1925–2007)

A little different from the rest of the communist women is the contribution and work of Reba Roychowdhury, known for her contribution as a member of the central Squad of the Indian People's Theatre Association (IPTA),[17] as the sister of Binoy Roy,[18] and an acclaimed actor of the Bengali cinema. In the introduction to Roychowdhury's autobiography, *Jeebaner Taney Shilper Taney* (1999), a well-known leader of the MARS and the Communist Party of India Marxist (CPIM), Kanak Mukhopadhyay,[19] writes that in this autobiography, Roychowdhury has brought together art and politics through her revolutionary understanding and writing capability. Against the backdrop of the Second World War, undivided Bengal experienced a tumultuous wave of resistance to fascist aggression, anti-imperialist protests, accentuating the freedom struggle, a devastating famine, mass mobilisations, organised resistance, and cultural expressions of dissent. It was the time of a new and historic moment of the people's revolution. The spontaneous commitment, the spirit of mass participation, and the celebration of life come through in Reba's reminiscences of her experiences of those times from 1941. Even during her illness, while writing this autobiography, Reba relived those spirited moments when she selflessly contributed her art and her activism to the cause as a true communist (Mukhopadhyay 1999: Introduction).

Roychowdhury was introduced to students' politics after starting her undergraduate studies at the Rangpur College in undivided Bengal. In spite of several warnings to her father by the principal, Roychowdhury continued with her commitment. Her memories are filled with real-life stories of extraordinary women from undivided Bengal who came together to build the MARS and its work base together. Describing the times, she writes:

> Hitler's force attacked Soviet Union. There started a people's war. We used to read the editions of People's War Weekly as soon as they arrived. I had become a member of MARS by then. The land owners, money lenders and hoarders had started playing their games. That was the beginning of the man-made famine in Bengal. The year was 1943 ... We started working to organize women from different communities, the scavengers, the upper caste, the erstwhile 'untouchable's – and proceeded with a large procession to collect relief from the Magistrate's Bungalow. All of us worked day and night with total dedication to provide food through a public distribution system that we opened in different localities, and also provided medicine from local pharmacies. We used to sing Haripada Kushari'e Song to mobilize the volunteers:

> 'Death is at our door; How would you survive if you still are not together; The golden Bengal is turning into a land of the dead; Lets us all come together'. (1999: 7; translation mine)

Roychowdhury learnt songs of protest and revolution that soon became an important part of all political gatherings, public meetings, and processions. She says: 'I also chose songs as my weapon from the struggle' (1999: 8). Roychowdhury's description gives us an idea of her initiation into the cultural squad and also her participation in a series of fundraising performances for the Bengal Famine. She left her home against her father's wish along with her brother, Binoy Roy, after she got her membership of the

Communist Party, and soon after went to Mumbai in 1944. She reminisces about the performances:

> Bengal famine was portrayed in *Anteem Abhilasha* (The last wish). The production was presented by the 'Voice of Bengal' Squad. This production was staged all over Gujarat and Maharashtra as the voice of those who were suffering in the Bengal Famine. We travelled for eighty to ninety miles on a Truck to go into to perform every day. Our dedication, practice, focus and commitment to our political ideology moved and charged people. (1999: 12; translation mine).

Roychowdhury's descriptions give us insights into the establishment of the Central Ballet Troupe and also the later contradictions that affected the cultural wing of the communist movement in India in the later years. She mentions:

> The three years (1948–1950), there were constant protests and confrontations between the newly formed government of Independent India and the members of the Communist Party on the streets and in factories, offices, banks, schools, and colleges. There were confrontations and strikes for demands around land rights. Thousands were in prison. The streets were covered with the blood of the martyrs. But still, we went on with meetings and protests right under the very nose of the police, sometimes without their knowledge and often openly in defiance. We were part of these struggles; we presented plays in support of strikes, in support of land rights for the farmers. (1999: 39)

According to Roychowdhury, she continued to act in protest and emancipatory plays. Even two days before her wedding,[20] the cultural wing of the Communist Party staged a play, *Shob Peyechhir Deshe* (*In the Land where We Have Everything*) in Hindustan Park (Kolkata). According to Roychowdhury, the police arrived and cordoned the auditorium in the middle of the play. The actors completed the play, mixed with the audience, and managed to slip away from the police. Roychowdhury comments: 'Such was the everyday of the communists' (1999: 39). Roychowdhury clearly sees such acts as inevitable political precarities as essential training for all communists across genders.

Individual commitment towards a collective movement

How does one read the individual stories told/written by all of these women about joining the Communist Party in different regions of India, from different economic, social, political, as well as ideological spaces? Are these women's decisions to dedicate their lives to communism, then, not agentive decisions? Would such influences be read differently in cases of male members of the communist movement? Voices such as those featured in this chapter demand agency, as they speak of a collective organisation building through their individual narratives of work. Renu Chakravartty sums up the involvement of the communist women at the grassroots and leadership levels by saying:

> The form employed by communist women were also varied. In the early days it was difficult to approach women except by going from house to house. Convening of a meeting meant hard house-to-house squad work, for several days, followed by reminders a couple of days before, and on the day of the meeting, calling them from house to house to take them to the meeting. ... [But] in almost all meeting, in order to hold the attention of the women and to attract them, dramas, songs and dances were staged, often written and directed by the organisers themselves. (1980: 226)

As a daughter of two communists, Vidya and Sunil Munsi, I have grown up hearing the term 'grassroots', used as a specific identifier of the particular kind of commitment the Party wanted out of their members. Munsi would often assert what she wrote in her book (2006): 'It was the communist-led democratic mass organisations of women who demonstrated before our entire women's movement how effectively constructive work among women could be organised if it was done in the spirit of self reliance and mutual help and not as charity' (2006: 240).

Conclusion

The women leaders 'mobilising' such spaces were conscious that the 'performative' public mobilisation would be differently energised and enabled from these spaces. They chose to respond to the needs specific to these smaller spaces by making them deliberately non-performative in character to make them speak softly and meaningfully and yet non-threateningly to the participants who saw any performative public character of larger meetings as something that could invite the attention and ire of the family. As the specific requirement of their political constituency, they chose less performance-reliant ways of mobilisation, and therefore had less of a presence in the political register. Such non-presences have not been documented and are often trivialised as non-political acts as they are not public acts.

Performance remains an interesting, if challenging, word in this context. On the one hand, it assumes a falseness – of the subject appearing to be what she is not, or what she is role-playing and pretending to be. Here the deliberate non-performative stance while working at the grassroots level needs to be read as an informed choice to clearly establish a non-threatening and everyday level of communication, which for them was a political tool for working among and with women at that grassroots level. In a feminist reading situated in critically reflective time and space, the biographies and autobiographies are statements of views and choice, not just a way of marking presence. They are performance manuals of women who were also creating a script of the work that they felt required urgent documentation.

Notes

1 The Communist Party of India split into two separate political factions in 1964 due to major differences in political views. While the original name, that is, Communist Party of India (CPI), remained unchanged for one of the factions, the other faction became known as the Communist Party of India (Marxist). See Sarla Sharma's chapter in Munsi *et al.* (2009).
2 Stree Shakti Sangathana conducted a series of oral history interviews that have been put together in the book. Please see for more details Sangathana (1989).
3 See Munsi's book *In Retrospect* (2006) for more details.
4 Recorded audio interviews of Vidya Munsi (Kanuga) on her relationship with the communist women's movement. Kolkata, 14 June 2008.
5 Shripad Amrit Dange was a founding member of the CPI. He is known as one of the leaders and a stalwart of the Indian trade union movement. See www.marxists.org/archive/dange/comrade-sadange-english.pdf.
6 See Sen's autobiography for more details.
7 See Shikha Sengupta's detailed compilation of Manikuntala Sen's Police Records from 1936 to 1954 in the compiled volume *Janajagaraney Narijagaraney* edited by Samik Bandhyopadhyay. Published on her birth centenary year, 2010, this volume contains Manikuntala Sen's autobiography as well as other unpublished writings, along with writings by her comrades from Mahila Atma Raksha Samiti (MARS) and other researchers. Sen was known for her disillusionment with party decisions, and she distanced herself from active politics after the split in the CPI. Her writings contain many critiques and clear dissent side by side with her detailed recounting of the work, responsibility, and the commitment she dedicated herself in from the mid-1930s till the beginning of the 1960s.
8 MARS was first established in 1928, as one of the forerunners of political organisations largely by and for women for creating political consciousness and a sense of inclusion within women in Bengal.
9 Please see Gargi Chakravartty's chapter 'Emergence of Mahila Atma Raksha Samiti in the Forties – Calcutta Chapter' (2015) for details on the beginning of the Second World War and the man-made famine of 1942–1943 and the crisis in policies within the communist movement in Calcutta (Kolkata). While the Communist Party itself was harshly criticised for its war-related policies, the organisation of volunteering work by the students' and women's wings of the Communist Party have been lauded for the relief and distribution of medical help as well as food organised on a multi-party platform to serve the interest of a city severely in crisis.

10 Please see Manikuntala Sen's memoires *In Search of Freedom* (2001). The book helps construct her world within the Communist Party while simultaneously searching for a sense of 'freedom' both for India and for its women citizens.
11 Hajrah Begum, born in a progressive Muslim family, was drawn to communism while in England at the same time as the group of students she interacted with in London — Sajjad Zaheer, Z. A. Ahmed, and K. M. Ashraf. She returned to India and began working with the All India Progressive Writers Association (AIPWA) and the All India Women's conference (AIWC). The late 1920s and thereafter witnessed the emergence of a viable Left alternative within the Indian Nationalist Movement.
12 See the NFIW publication (2009) for details.
13 The journal *Roshni* was first published as a quarterly in English in 1938. All printed copies are available at the MCM Library at the Central Office of AIWC in New Delhi. More information is available at www.aiwc.org.in/pdf/History.pdf.
14 For more details, please access Hajrah Begum Ahmed's interview: Oral History Project, 19 September 1994, Nehru Memorial Museum and Library Archives, New Delhi, India.
15 See Armstrong (2013) for more details.
16 See Reba Roychowdhury's autobiography *Jeebaner Taney Shilper Taney* (1999) for details.
17 See Malhotra and Lambert-Hurley (2015) for more details.
18 Binoy Roy was one of the well-known songwriters/theatre directors from the Bengal cultural Squad and became one of the office bearers of the Indian People's Theatre Association (IPTA). See details in Sumangala Damodaran's book *The Radical Impulse* (2017).
19 See Kanak Mukhopadhyay's own autobiography *Nari Mukti Andolon o Amra* (1993) for details on the women's movements in Bengal.
20 Roychowdhury married Sajal Roychowdhury in 1949. See details in her autobiography (1999).

Bibliography

Armstrong, Elisabeth. 2013. *Gender and Neoliberalism: The All India Democratic Women's Federation and Globalization Politics*. Delhi: Tulika Books.
Asaf Ali, Aruna. 2010. *Words of Freedom: Ideas of a Nation*. Delhi: Penguin.
Begum, Hajrah. 1962. *Why Women Should Vote the Communist*. Delhi: C. P. Publication.
Brown, Wendy. 1999. 'Resisting Left Melancholy.' *Boundary 2* 26(3): 19–27.
Chakravartty, Gargi. 2015. 'Emergence of Mahila Atma Raksha Samiti in the Forties: Calcutta Chapter.' In *Calcutta: The Stormy decades*, edited by T. Sarkar and S. Bandyopadhyay, pp. 177–203. London and New York: Routledge.
Chakravartty, Renu. 1980. *Communists in Indian Women's Movement: 1940–1950*. Delhi: People's Publishng House.
Damodaran, Sumangala. 2017. *The Radical Impulse*. Delhi: Tulika Books.

Dang, Vimla. 2007. *Fragments of an Autobiography*. Delhi: Asha Jyoti Booksellers & Publishers.

Dean, Jodi. 2013. 'Communist Desire.' In *The Ends of History: Questioning the Stakes of Historical Reason*, edited by A. Swiffen and J. Nichols, pp. 5–22. New York and Oxon: Routledge.

Karat, Brinda. 2016. 'Our Politics Is Still Regressive vis a vis Women Representation.' In *The Hans India*, 9 January. www.thehansindia.com/posts/index/Andhra-Pradesh/2016-01-08/Our-politics-is-still-regressive-vis-a-vis-women-representation-Brinda-Karat/198958. Accessed on 23 February 2019.

Kumari, Abhilasha, and Sabina Kidwai. 1998. *Crossing the Sacred Line: Women's Search for Political*. Delhi: Orient Blackswan.

Loomba, Ania. 2019. *Revolutionary Desires: Women, Communism, and Feminism in India*. New York: Routledge.

Malhotra, Anshu, and Siobhan Lambert-Hurley. 2015. 'Introduction: Gender Performance and Autobiography in South Asia.' In *Speaking of the Self: Gender, Performance and Autobiography in South Asia*, edited by A. Malhotra and S. Lambert-Hurley, pp. 1–30. Delhi: Zubaan.

Mukhopadhyay, Kanak. 1999. 'Bhoomika (Introduction).' In *Jeebaner Taney Shilper Taney: The Autobiography of Reba Roychowdhury*, by Reba Roychowdhury. Kolkata: Thema.

Mukhopadhyay, Kanak. 1993. *Narimukti Andolan-O-Amra*. Kolkata: National Book Agency.

Munsi, Vidya. 2006. *In Retrospect: War Time Memories and Thoughts on Women's Movement*. Kolkata: Manisha Granthalaya.

Munsi, Vidya, Hajrah Begum, and Sarla Sharma. 2009. *International Women's Movement: Early Years of Women's International Democratic Federation and National Federation of Indian Women*. Delhi: NFIW Publication.

Nair, Janaki. 2019. 'Histories of Love and Revolution.' *Economic and Political Weekly* 54(23): 21–24.

Ray, Raka. 1999. *Fields of Protest: Women's Movements in India*. Minneapolis, MN, and London: University of Minnesota Press.

Roychordhury, Reba. 1999. *Jeebaner Taney Shilper Taney: The Autobiography of Reba Roychowdhury*. Kolkata: Thema.

Sanghatana, Stree Shakti. 1989. '*We Were Making History…*': *Life Stories of Women in the Telengana People's Struggle*. London: Zed Books.

Sarkar, Mahua. 2008. *Visible Histories Disappearing Women: Producing Muslim Womanhood in Late Colonial Bengal*. Durham, NC, and London: Duke University Press.

Sarkar, Tanika. 2005. 'Political Women: An Overview of Modern Indian Developments.' In *Women in India: Colonial and Post-Colonial Periods*, edited by Bharati Ray, pp. 541–563. New Delhi: Sage Publications.

Sen, Manikuntala. 2001. *In Search of Freedom: An Unfinished Journey*. Kolkata: Stree.

Sen, Manikuntala. 2010. *Janajagaraney Narijagaraney: Janma-shatabarshik Rachanasangraha*. Kolkata: Thema.

Sen, Samita. 1997. 'Interview (8 & 16 July, 1997): Vidya Munsi.' *Journal of Women's Studies* 2(1): 137–163.

Sengupta, Shikha. 2010. 'Poolisher Doliley Manikuntala Sen: 1936–54.' In *Narijagaraney: Janma-shatabarshik Rachanasangraha*, pp. 323–326. Kolkata: Thema.

14

One always fails to speak of the things one loves: Memories of border crossings

Shirin M. Rai

Fragments of a story

This story is my story as much as it is the story of my family. I crossed two borders, and that changed my life for ever – a geopolitical border of nation states and a border marked by race, ethnicity, and nationality. My parents crossed many borders – through the partition of the country they grew up in, of caste in marriage, and through their political travels. So, here I write about borders and crossings – borders that we carry on our backs, within ourselves, and borders that others draw and guard. Both create disturbances, mark new social spaces, memorialise old ones, draw lines seemingly to protect 'us' from assaults on territories and imaginations, and in doing so – through our being aware of these lines as well as through stretching them – make us what we are. Biography, as Silvija Jestrovic has noted, allows us to 'explore the interlinking of political activism with personal passions, politicising the private sphere and giving activism – and even large-scale emancipatory moments – dimensions of intimacy'; it also allows us insights into 'a kind of daily life practice of relations, actions, negotiations, radical refusals, disappointments, acts of solidarity, betrayals, intimacies' (2021: 3, 2). A family biography is also, of course, an autobiography which raises the issues of how to separate myself from my parents' lives enough to be able to stand back and ask questions, sift the archives, both personal and political, and dig through memories to write about me/them. These two intertwined biographies meet and expand within the evolving landscape of the Left in India. Indeed, the two are inextricably linked – Marxism and the practices of the communist movement deeply affected my parents' and my life. As we face a period of decline of the Left in India (and elsewhere), reflecting on the history of the Left in India through the biography of my family helps me to make sense of this decline.

The Communist Party of India (CPI), which led the Left movement until its split in 1964, was founded in 1925 and held its first congress in 1943. Because of the strict control of political strategy of Communist Parties across much of the world by the Soviet-supported Communist International (Comintern), it was both a support to the Indian communists as well as a constraint upon their intellectual and political horizons. For example, after the signing of the German–Russian Non-Aggression Pact in 1939, Communist Parties across the world, including the CPI, were asked to oppose the war effort against Nazi Germany in the name of opposing imperialism. This policy was reversed when Hitler invaded the Soviet Union in 1941. It was this constraint that my father chafed against as a Party member; it was also the reason that my mother decided not to join the Party. In 1947 B. T. Ranadive was elected party secretary and soon declared the end of the progressive role of the bourgeoisie as leading the independence struggle and that the Indian partition had 'accentuated the hatred between religious communities, contributed to the communalisation of the army, and helped to reinforce imperialism' (Reynolds 2020: 7; see also Rai and Prakash 2022). This ambivalent position of the CPI laid the foundations of its unstable position within the postcolonial, independent India – it remained dependent on the Comintern, then after splitting the CPI remained close to the Congress, generating fissures in the Left movement.

I do not write this history of my family, my own history, and the history of the Left movement in India from systematic research, sustained archival searches, or even from a comprehensive biography of my parents. It emerges from fragments of memory, of particular archives, and of India's political history – fragments that in their episodic nature raise more questions than provide answers. However, in the words of Chatterjee, the 'virtues of the fragmentary, the local, and the subjugated' can be mobilised to challenge the metanarratives of history (1993: xi). It is in this spirit that I have written this chapter.

Partition/crossings/modernity

In terms of the partition and its impact on my family, I found this story difficult to unravel as no one talked about these crossings very much – life looked forwards not backwards; those who looked back perished, or so it felt whenever I looked through the cracks that occasionally appeared in the smooth mirror of everyday lives of my parents. Of the uprooting of lives that were scarred deeply as they pushed and were swept away in the roiling of hate and fear, there were hardly any traces. 'We were very lucky' was the refrain; we were lucky to have had to leave our homes, our streets, our histories, our friends … we were lucky. Of course, we were lucky not to have been raped, beaten, castrated, cut, and burned; our limbs were intact even as our minds struggled to cope with the changes that were not of our making. We were fortunate where others had been less so; that surely was enough to be getting on with. It was important to build on this foundation of precarious awareness; we had nothing without this urgency to build – we had seen too much destruction, tearing apart, and leaving behind. Building was forgetting; forgetting was needed for building ... it was all fine; we were fine. 'That is that', as my mother was fond of saying. This of course chimed well with the political concern of 'nation-building' in their new home, India. The horrors of the partition had to be put behind them, a public awareness needed engendering that dwelt not on the past grievances but on a shining new future where India will be great again and play its part on the world stage – modern, secular, democratic. Nehru's speech at the moment of independence was taught in schools as foundational of Indian ambitions on the national and the world stage:

> Long years ago we made a tryst with destiny, and now the time comes when we shall redeem our pledge, not wholly or in full measure, but very substantially.
>
> At the stroke of the midnight hour, when the world sleeps, India will awake to life and freedom. A moment comes, which comes but rarely in history, when we step out from the old to the new, when an age ends, and when the soul of a nation, long suppressed, finds utterance. (1947)

For some reason, perhaps because the Red Fort was associated with the prime minister speaking on Independence Day (14 August at midnight) from its ramparts, I always imagine Nehru making this speech from that stage – standing small but erect high above the newly independent citizens of India, with the national flag unfurled and flying proud. In actual fact this speech was made in the Central Hall of what became the Parliament of India (see Rai and Spary 2019), with the Constituent Assembly members as his immediate audience. Millions, however, heard this speech on the radio. This was a speech that we read in school as part of our work on nationalist history, too; it has become iconic and was included in *The Guardian*'s great speeches of the twentieth century.[1]

In 1950 'the people of India' gave 'themselves' the Constitution that encapsulated the democratic nation state postcolonial aspirations. The rights to citizenship were granted to all, with an optimism that this new independent country could be a new India that could be built on the foundations of a deeply unequal and diverse society. 'A formal manifesto of legal rights, aspiration to socio-economic equality and secular civic life and group-differentiated citizenship' (Jayal 2013). And yet Nehru's India, as it was also called, was complex. During this early period of effervescent freedom, thousands were put in prison – including communists who refused to accept this bourgeois vision of independence, and the first Communist Party-led government in Kerela was undemocratically dismissed. Ambedkar, the chairman of the Constituent Assembly, resigned because he could not see reflected in the

Constitution the commitment to challenge and overthrow the hierarchy of caste prejudice. Those who challenged this narrative of progress were shut up through public disapprobation, through containment, and through incarceration. India was on the march forward, wherever this path to progress led us. There was no point looking behind at the bloody boundaries, across which lay broken bodies, deserted homes, and diminished lives; there lay the corrosiveness of history and paralysing anger of the weak.

I grew up in New Delhi with this narrative of forward-looking modernity – of nation-building through prescribed school textbooks on civics and history, through exhortations on the state-owned media – Doordarshan – watching Bollywood films that confirmed this story of India's march from freedom to development (*Mother India*, for instance), and through conversations around our dining table. The past was just that, a past, occasionally invoked, often humorously, when my parents spoke of their 'home' and pretended to quarrel over the merits of their home or adopted cities – Lahore and Multan – and cultures. I could only guess at this past through occasional comments, momentary recalls shared sometimes in the context of anniversaries, days of birth, death, and festivals. We did this; my father always said that; my mother insisted we went there; we played so – fragments of memory casually brought into view, which I lapped up and stored. I asked questions, too, and got honest answers: I did not like Multan, always wanted to get away from it … I escaped to Lahore as soon as I could and tried not to go back home to Lyallpur – answers to be picked at carefully later for clues to histories of families and of my parents.

It seemed to me that there was this world behind a curtain – an opaque yet definite world that I wanted to devour but could do so only in small morsels; I could not disturb the curtain, rip it away – it was too fragile, insubstantial, and important to those that took shelter in front of it. The proscenium arch, carefully constructed, served a purpose – to separate out the audience (me and my brother) from the actors (my parents) as they carefully narrated their stories through the complex process of forgetting, remembering, and reconstructing. Slowly, however, a picture began to emerge of a different life that linked so directly to mine. A picture of border crossings – borders of nations, of citizenships, of minds and hearts, into new beginnings. It felt good to connect with a world I had never seen, of people I had never met, of sounds and smells that I had never experienced.

The Left movement through an everyday lens

The first memory I have of this history of my family is about discovering that when my father said he 'was underground', he did not mean that literally – it was a political statement; he had been a member of the Communist Party of India, a 'whole-timer' who worked 'underground' for the Party. My mother was inspired by but remained on the periphery of the Party; she was not a member and yet donated 10 per cent of her salary as a college teacher to Party coffers – a tithe that she was happy to pay, even with many family responsibilities. My father had been enchanted by this beautiful woman who wanted to buy Party propaganda literature at a public stall; 'my friend said she would get me into trouble, and she did' – my father used to laugh out loud as he said this; my mother blushed and smiled a shy and most lovely smile. However, where was this all happening? Multan, Lyallpur, Lahore, Amritsar, Ludhiana, Chandigarh, Delhi – places and spaces that told stories of my family, leaving traces that I had to follow to and fro myself but never really with them. Their place was my home in Delhi.

A second memory that I have is when I got my ears pierced or rather our neighbour got my ears pierced in my mother's absence. I had been wanting this symbolic marker of growing up for months but was refused every time I raised it. So, when the peripatetic ear cleaner and piercer came to our neighbour's flat, I asked to be done too. Raj auntie (the neighbour) agreed without much ado as she always thought my mother needed guidance with the gendered rituals of everyday life. My mother was not happy, I was crying because it hurt, and I knew I had crossed a line I should not have. My mother told me then that my father would be cross and told me the story of her father who took his 'ear-pierced' daughters to the local swimming pool and pulled out the thread from their ears, which meant that it was only much later that my mother could wear earrings. 'My father didn't believe that girls should have their bodies pierced when boys didn't,' she said. Oh, I thought – how strange! Who was this man – my *nana* – who, in provincial Multan in the 1930s, flouted tradition and could think of equality between girls and boys; who did not like pierced ears on his daughters?

Political arguments, even rows, around the dining table were common – we talked, we ate, we argued, or, as my parents preferred, had discussions about politics. So robust were these discussions at times that old scabs of other wounds often came off, and I realised that these domestic disturbances had a long history of political engagements and personal entanglements and wondered about these. Of course, my politics aligned most easily with my father's – it was radical, certain, and clear. My mother's nuances, hesitations, and questions just irritated me/us. However, she was not one for turning – she stood her ground and with a grace that I envied. This was a 'modern' marriage – an equal partnership, but one which was embedded in gendered histories long established. Negotiating the terrain of intimacy, love, and friendship within this marriage was an everyday struggle and celebration.

I left home in 1985 to go to the UK to do my PhD. Me leaving home also made me want to tell my story – who was I? I was a stranger in a land which was familiar through books, plays, music, and even buildings and spaces, but utterly unfamiliar with the everyday meaning of place. I could have reinvented my past in response to questions about my hinterland; instead, I wanted to know more about my past so that I could understand myself to recount to my friends, my lover and husband, and later my children my life's story. Crossing borders has that effect – of leaving behind and seeking what is left behind. Children make it imperative, really, that I tell my story – how will they know their own history without that? Silences have to be overcome, histories revealed. I need to know so that they can know. I need the narrative of my past to tie me to my future, my children. I need to know and then tell my story, *meri kahani*. My parents died, as parents do, leaving behind incomplete histories, memories, and images. The pain of my loss, first of my father in 2004 and then my mother in 2009, was deep and manifested itself in small and big ways for years. One of these was a re-engagement with their histories and, through them, the histories of space, time, and violence of their everyday. Below I tell the fragmentary story of my mother – on the Left but not a Party member, committed feminist, scholar, and activist – to make sense of different borders that affected my life and help me make sense of my past, present, and future.

My mother's story

'One Always Fails to Speak of the Things One Loves' was the title of Roland Barthes's last essay (Lotringer 2011). The book he wrote before he died, *Camera Lucida*, was a response to the photograph of his mother – 'that has been' he wrote, and that is what the photograph tells us; in so doing it also alerts us to our death – what has been is not with us. And yet, I wonder. It has taken me nearly ten years to view the interview with my mother; every time I tried to see it before now, I was overwhelmed with my loss. So, opening it up again took all my courage, not just my technical ability! And how I have cursed myself for not doing an interview with my father, who was such a wonderful raconteur! Many of the stories that my mother narrated I had heard all my life – growing up, growing away, returning. It would have been the same with my father – repeated tales of love and friendship, of politics and of activism. And yet a long narrative also picks up on and explains some gaps, silences, moods, and atmospheres of the past and present. It connects the autobiography with biography – theirs and mine.

Riessman has noted 'long stories that appear, on the surface, to have little to do with the question' (2012: 167); they seem to go on and on!

However, upon reflection, Riessman thought that 'participants were resisting our efforts to fragment their lived experience into thematic (code-able) categories' and that, looking back, she was 'embarrassed and instructed' for not valuing this in the first place (2000: 169). My mother's interview did just that. When I look back at this interview from such a long distance – ten years, many moons – I note with similar embarrassment my attempts to nudge her into familiar channels of storytelling – speaking like the political historian that she was, explaining to me her thought process, making visible analytical worlds that I would learn from, offering explanations of historical moments that I know of but did not quite understand, such as the Partition of India. I wanted her in didactic mode, not telling long stories – digressing, rambling, repeating herself. And yet, half an hour into the interview, I was able to stand back and see all this, to step back and let her speak in a register that was hers alone, to stop nudging her but enjoy her voice as it wove her tale. This was not easy for her, I realised – she had been recently widowed (this was 2007 and my father, her soulmate, had died in 2004) and she was vulnerable; going over her life brought back memories that were intimate as well as political and intertwined with his life – life stories are never individual stories; they are always relational. As Plummer has argued, 'For narratives to flourish there must be a community to hear … for communities to hear, there must be stories which weave together their history, their identity, their politics' (1995: 87). I wondered who did she think she was speaking to when she laid out her life? There was me and my friend Anjali, the daughter of a close family friend, behind the camera. Would she have spoken differently if the camera was not there, if it was only a voice recording? How aware was she of being filmed, of being the actor, performing for an audience? Was there a community beyond us that she conjured up for herself as she spoke of leaving her home at the time of the Partition and reflected upon making the Partition the object of her research? Bamberg and McCabe point out: 'With narrative, people strive to configure space and time, deploy cohesive devices, reveal identity of actors and relatedness of actions across scenes. They create themes, plots, and drama. In so doing, narrators make sense of themselves, social situations, and history' (1998: iii; also see Riessman 2003).

Watching and listening to her interview, I see all these moves – in self-conscious and careful ways. There are times she invokes and others that she refuses to engage with; she reveals the identity of a middle-class Hindu family and then disrupts it with stories of political engagement; she tries to give me a sense of her life and reveals and conceals moments important to her. There are smiles, pensiveness, reverie, tiredness – all mixed up in conjuring up memories, which, at the end, exhaust and emotionally unravel her, but she holds on with the occasional wiping of the tears.

The Partition, like any event, was experienced differently by the people who were affected by it – Hindus and Muslims, and Sikhs. We know the stories of violence, of murder and rape, of scores being settled, and lives unsettled. In some ways the violence was intimate – neighbours killed neighbours, and as my mother's story tells, girls were particularly vulnerable to kidnapping and sexual violence. My *nana* had opted to stay on in Multan when the Partition was announced. I heard this story many times when I was growing up. He did not want to leave his home and his property in Multan. He did not believe that countries could be partitioned. My aunt – who had just become a doctor – did not hesitate; she signed to go to India. My uncle was already in Kanpur. The Partition – even before it happened – was dividing families. On 11 August 1947 my grandfather came home for lunch from the school where he was headmaster. Halfway through having his food, without saying a word to his wife and children, he got up and ran back to the Post Office. He pleaded with the postmaster and got his form of selection out of the postbox and changed his option – the family would move to India. It was only when he came back home that he told my *nani* (maternal grandmother) the reason for his hasty departure – on his way home, earlier from school, a teacher had stopped him and told him that some Muslim men were planning to kidnap his girls. The teacher who had told him this and advised him to leave to protect his daughters was also Muslim.

The family left on 12 August, with my grandfather insisting that he would be back to 'hand over his charge' to the next headmaster. They took nothing with them except some clothes – the jewellery was buried in the garden, as it was in a million homes. There are so many stories much worse than this – the train from Bahawalpur that had come in from India the day before had been stopped by Hindu and Sikh mobs, and whole carriages had been slaughtered. Going the other way, the very next day was traumatic for my mother's family – my younger *masi* (my mother's sister) cannot remember the journey at all; fear-induced amnesia remained with her as I spoke to the whole family about the Partition in 1997 – fifty years later. I distinctly remember my mother saying to me how puzzled she was when she and her family arrived across the border from Pakistan to India – 'everyone was celebrating – laughing with relief and shouting, not remembering that they had lost their homes and their communities, their neighbours and friends, and that they were facing an uncertain future'. I have never forgotten this because it did seem to encapsulate the duality of loss and gain, of relief, and nostalgia that haunted that generation. Undoing lives took different forms – those who suffered and those who suffered less. Veena Das (2006) and Urvashi Butalia (2017) interviewed women who did not speak of the horrors of the Partition and suffered long-term depression alone. They also tell stories of rejection by the community because of gendered norms of sexual purity in the context of violence and violation of women – rape and sexual assaults during the Partition. My mother's family experienced none of this. Instead, in Kahror Pucca, my doctor Masi worked in the camps resisting Rashtriya Swayamsevak Sangh (RSS) thugs who did not want her to tend to Muslim women. Suturing the wounds of the other was one way that Asha escaped the narrowness of family life and experienced the rewards of gratitude.

Veena Das, writing about a woman who had experienced the horrors of Partition, says that she is 'not asking how the events of the Partition were present to consciousness as past events but how they came to be incorporated into the temporal structure of relationships' (2011: 9). I would add to this how they are folded into everyday life. It was 1984 and the horror of the anti-Sikh violence in Delhi had left thousands burnt, scarred, and traumatised. Led by Veena Das, students (including me) were gathering testimonies of this violence and bringing as much succour as they could through this 'storytelling'. My mother wanted to join this group – she made it to the gate of our garden and stopped; she could not go further as the horrors of her own from the time of Partition came crowding in.

Figure 14.1 NFIW – the women's wing of the Communist Party of India (CPI) (© author)

My mother was from the generation that was part of the nationalist struggle and of the building of postcolonial India. Her generation grew up with the experience of everyday colonial oppression and saw the dawn of independence and the departing colonial rulers. And yet the undoing of the partition was already stitched into its making. My mother says in her interview that for her (and my father), communist politics of the 1940s took away the excitement of independence – *ye azaadi jhhoothi he* (this is a false independence) was the slogan of the CPI. This counter-narrative of independence can only be understood in the context of Left politics in India. For my mother excitement came from being in the Left movement, the students' movement (particularly for her the Youth Welfare Association), and the women's movement.

Left engagements and the women's movement

In her interview my mother speaks of how she got involved in, but never joined, the Communist Party. Indeed, this peripheral but long-term involvement in the Party, as it was always called, is an integral part of her subjectivity as well as her romance with my father. They met when she went to buy *People's Democracy* at the People's Bookshop where my father was helping out. The real independence was yet to come – that could only be a socialist revolution, an equal society where markers of religion, gender, class, and caste melted away in a new dawn. This was a time of nationalist and Left mobilisations, of great optimism in the face of violence of colonialism – they could see that their world was changing, but into what? The clashes between liberal and socialist as well as between secular and religious ideologies were central to the nationalist movement (see Bidwai 2015; Rai 2021). The independent nation state that emerged resolved many and presented other new challenges, and my parents' lives were enmeshed in both of these.

Independence saw freedom, but in 1948 my father was incarcerated for eighteen months on charges of bomb-making that were never proven, and if you knew my father could never have been proven; he did not even know how to change a light bulb! As I have written elsewhere (2021), my father spent his incarceration in YOL jail in the now Himachal Pradesh, and this period was formative and perhaps the start of his long goodbye to the Party. He was in solitary confinement because he was a political prisoner with a master's degree, so he was isolated from the ordinary prisoners, had an '*ard-alli*' or 'batman' (a pickpocket who used to entertain my father by picking his pocket to demonstrate his skills) to look after him, and any number of books he could read, once they had passed the prison authorities; I read his copy of Howard Fast's *My Glorious Brothers* sent to him in prison by his friend Roshan Khosla, which bore the stamp of the jail authorities. During this period the Party under the leadership of B. T. Ranadive gave a call for a hunger strike in prisons and confrontation with police and army. So, while in prison, he also participated in the hunger strike that was called to challenge state authority from within; the strike lasted for eighty days, during which my father, like many others in the movement, was force-fed. My father's anger at this 'left adventurism' of BTR, as Ranadive was called, was palpable whenever he spoke of the strike – 'it was madness – I stuck it out not because I believed it was the right thing to do but because I was not going to let any working class Party member tell me that I as a bourgeois member couldn't stick it out!' he would say. Perhaps this time in prison was also a time of reflection on his politics, his life, and the political direction of the CPI. Decades later, in the newspaper *The Guardian*, I read an article about Indian prisoners in the Andaman Islands (Scott-Clark and Levy 2001). There, too, the prisoners went on hunger strike and were fed forcibly, and many drowned in the milk fed to them by tube, which went into their lungs instead of their stomachs. I felt ill as I realised that this could have happened to my father as he, too, was force-fed in prison. The real physical sense of outrage as well as shock when I realised this was very real.

My parents married in 1959, nearly ten years after they first met. My father was still a 'whole-timer' but getting restive; my mother was doing her PhD on the Indian Partition at Sapru House, the Indian Council of World Affairs' Library. It was the premier collection of documents on international relations in India and was one of India's finest and most coveted research libraries, located in the heart of New Delhi on Barakhamba Road, on which also sat my own school – Modern School. She often went to work in the library at Sapru House, before picking up my brother and me from school, when we needed to stay on after the school day. At this time my mother was also teaching at Hindu College, Delhi University, and helping her family, who were living in the Railway quarters allotted to my *masi*, Asha, who was now a Railways doctor. The family was large, and the responsibility of supporting them was on the two sisters. The displacement of the family meant that my grandfather no longer worked, and so the two sisters met the needs of the two younger brothers' education and the life expenses of the whole family. My mother's sense of confidence in herself perhaps came from being able to take on this role; it also, of course, meant that it was clear that she did not want a family of her own until her responsibilities to her natal family were delivered. My father, however, was impatient to set up home with her, visiting her in New Delhi from Chandigarh, where he was studying for his own PhD, which he never finished. The negotiation of pressures – romantic, familial, and professional – have been considerable for my mother.

My mother was appointed as a Lecturer at Hindu College, University of Delhi, in 1960, the year that I was born. The College timeline for the 1960s reads as follows: Dr Raj Narayan Mathur, alumnus, becomes Principal. The first lady lecturer, Satya M. Rai, is appointed.[2] She was not just the first but, for a long time, the only woman in the Politics department at Hindu College, which presented challenges that were both social and political and which she negotiated with her usual grace and determination. It was, therefore, not surprising that she became a feminist before I did! During this period, my mother became involved with the National Federation of Indian Women (NFIW), the women's wing of the CPI, and eventually became a vice-president. NFIW was established in 1954 by several women, including Aruna Asaf Ali.[3] Asaf Ali remained important to NFIW, but Vimla Farooqui was prominent in the organisation in Delhi. While I remember going to Vimla auntie's house many times as a child, Asaf Ali was a more remote figure who I saw very occasionally when accompanying my mother. The other important figure in Delhi was Anusuiya Gyanchand, my friend Anjali's grandmother, who, together with her husband Gyan Chand, were socialist activists and were close family friends (see Loomba 2018). My mother was committed to this organisation and its work with women – against violence, for peace – and many decades later, when she and my father moved to the home they built in Vaishali (north Delhi) near their retirement, she continued to invite women activists to the neighbourhood 'women's association' that she set up. She defended this work against my father's critique – that the CPI was a revisionist organisation, which had no vision for socialism and had become an adjustment of the Congress because of its abjection vis-à-vis the Soviet Union – robustly; she felt that the organisation that she worked with made a real difference to the lives of poor women on the ground. However, when it came to the CPI officially supporting Indira Gandhi's Emergency powers and the NFIW agreeing to this, it was too much for my always-independent mother to swallow, and she resigned from her position.

The Emergency, declared in 1975, suspended the rights of citizens, and thousands of opposition activists were imprisoned, except for CPI cadre. My father was at this time active in the Indo-China Friendship Society, as well as travelling and giving lectures to young people affiliated with the CPI, Marxist-Leninist. I remember clearly coming back from school one day and finding my father in our bathroom – he was trying to flush down the toilet old copies of *Beijing*, the political magazine he used to receive from the Chinese Embassy. Then we received a letter from my grandfather saying that the police had visited him in Jalandhar (the town that his family had settled in after their journey across the border in 1947), asking for his current address; my grandfather was frightened for my father. Nothing happened until after the Emergency was lifted, when my father was stopped at the university by a person who told him that he had 'kept him under

Figure 14.2 Satya M. Rai with the Cuban Ambassador, Eloy Valdez, 1970s (© author)

surveillance' throughout that period. His earlier and continuing activism then cast a long shadow much later in my parents' life. So, undoing the Partition was part of the counter-politics of the Left movement – however much we quarrel with the form and the strategic failures of this.

Travelling – political and geographic – was an important part of my parents' lives. As I rifle through family albums, I see glimpses of these travels – Prague in the early 1950s, where my father lived and worked for the World Peace Council for a short while; Moscow and Helsinki where my mother went as a delegate of the NFIW; Yunnan, China, where both of them went as part of their work for the India-China Friendship Society; there are even photographs in North Korea, but none that I can find from Egypt. Their departures for these trips were marked by family and friends coming to wish them safe travels – travelling 'abroad' not being as common as it is today; it also meant my brother and I being left under the supervision of Amma (our nanny) with relatives and friends mobilised to keep an eye on us. Travel brought art, clothes, and music from far-flung parts only seen on maps by my brother and me into our home; it generated a deep feeling of needing to cross boundaries in me.

Learning Left

This thumbnail sketch of my family life among a community of Left activists and sympathisers was my bubble when growing up. Neither of my parents were members of political parties; both of them were deeply politically committed to socialism and active in politics of the everyday – teaching with political as well as intellectual commitment, activism in women's organisations, peace organisation, giving public lectures, organising demonstrations, participating in trade union strikes in the university. As I sit in my London flat and think back to the arc of their life, I see it connecting in many ways to my life now. Teaching 'otherwise' has remained a pleasure for me, and also my attempt at politically reshaping the curriculum and pedagogy to bring radical new ideas to my students, hoping to sow seeds of change in a depressingly neoliberal world. What is the purpose of teaching if not to introduce new ideas, challenge established ones, and to open up space for self-expression and self-doubt? My father used to say that education should respond to Marx's observation that dominant ideas of an age are the ideas of the dominant class – and he wanted to present to his students ideas that challenged the dominant ideas and did not reproduce them (Althusser 1971; Giroux 1985; Friere 2000). My mother's pedagogic style was less overtly political but totally committed – I should know, as she taught me a course on Indian nationalism! I can see myself trying to follow in the footsteps of both my parents – engaging students and challenging them.

Towards the end of their lives, both my parents spoke of their political disappointments. However, because of their critical approaches to socialism, the crumbling of the Soviet Union came not as a surprise but as confirmation that freedom and justice together must underpin any new visions of social transformation. My mother continued to be active in bringing women of their neighbourhood together to discuss issues of gender justice and social justice; my father retreated to his music and his garden and told me that he was sad that, for now, socialism as a system had crumbled but glad that it was not his responsibility any more to fight to revive it – that, he said, was for my generation. This was ironic as in his activist days, he often used to get angry at the way in which age was connected with growing out of idealism and growing into acceptance of 'reality' and cite Victor Serge – 'young people with souls of pensioners and mentality of a pawn broker'![4] Neither was regretful of the politics that had guided them in their public and everyday lives.

Situated imaginaries, embedded histories

'In this fragmented world, after grand ideological narratives of communism have crumbled, how does one recuperate a Leftist ethos to address contemporary inequalities of class, caste, gender, and race against the backdrop of the rising Right and mounting environmental crisis?' ask the editors of this volume. I am suggesting here that one way of recuperating a Leftist ethos is to narrate the politics of the Left through the everyday lens. Storytelling – biography of individuals, families, groups, communities, objects, time, and space, for example – sometimes has a beginning, middle, and end, but sometimes, an introduction to fragments of memory of the everyday allows for the reader's imagination to construct new stories that look back as well as forward, crossing temporal borders in unexpected ways. As Andrews says, 'Not only can we time travel, but do it all the time. We must. We constantly move backwards and forwards in our mind's eye, and it is this movement which is a key stimulus behind our development' (2014: 3). 'Stimulus to what?' one could also ask. We learn things from our pasts, but what things? Often, looking back can reproduce prejudice, deepen borders between communities, and generate narratives of continuity rather than change. As Stoetzeler and Yuval-Davis argue, 'it is crucial to theorize the imagination as situated, that is, as shaped and conditioned (although not determined) by social positioning' (2002: 315). And, of course, biography is intimately connected to (dis)location, as is memory and storytelling. I have often wondered how biographies take shape and are remade in different locations as we cross borders – geographic, social, and political – sometimes through partial memory work and at others with intent. However, the everyday is an important worksite of politics – in the home as well as outside it. Understanding the ways in which we remember and connect these two is important to know ourselves and our politics, and to develop alternative strategies of change. Van Dijk and Rietveld (2020: 1) argue that imagination must be seen 'not as de-contextualized achievement by an individual but as an opening up to larger-scale "affordances," i.e. the unfolding possibilities for action'. It is the potential of stories to help this opening up of larger politics that is important.

So, what is the political story of my family narrated here in fragments? What traces of Left politics can I notice through doing this? What do I understand and what can I pass on and to whom? I am aware that the narrative that I construct smooths over many cracks – gaps that I cannot fill, gaps that I do not want to fill, and gaps that I might be able to fill if I tried harder to excavate family archives and my own memory banks. I deal in fragments of memory casually brought into view, which I lapped up and stored or forgot and now worry about. I worry about stories not passed on and what they signify. And about stories passed on; what family narratives are privileged, and how do families reconstruct themselves over space or time? In today's political vacuum, we find neoliberalism and populism, and in India, Hindutva-led politics of hate, thriving and posing grave challenges for humanity; we urgently need a critique of capitalism that is not bound by narrow party discipline, which is able to think outside the box and connect the national with the international and be, at the same time, self-critical. There is an urgent need for global strategies for progressive change. Through the fragmented biography of one family, I wished to understand the contemporary relevance of these earlier debates about socialism as well as the imprint of these ideas on our everyday lives. As the Left finds itself confronting the rise of Right-wing populism and neoliberalism, we need to think through alternative models of political activism, of memory work and theory-building that develops new solidarities challenging the emerging boundaries of nationalism and identity politics.

And what does it do for me? In one of his letters to me (see Rai 2021), my father wrote:

> a Left intellectual's first 'commitment is to the struggle of his [sic] people for changing the present social order based on exploitation, inequality, hunger, illiteracy and disease … [the second is] to oppose imperialism, colonialism, neo-colonialism, and racialism everywhere … The Left intellectual is thus a champion of the people right at home and consistent anti-imperialist abroad.

I wonder if I can ever rise to this challenge; have I done enough? A family story of Left activism becomes my burden to carry even as every day I try and rise to it.

Notes

1 www.theguardian.com/theguardian/2007/may/01/greatspeeches
2 See https://hinducollege.ac.in/ab-history.aspx.
3 She was an active participant in the Indian independence movement and is widely remembered for hoisting the Indian national flag at the Gowalia Tank maidan, Bombay, during the Quit India Movement in 1942. She also became the first Mayor of Delhi in 1958. Aruna Asaf Ali was the President and an influential voice in women's activism at the national level even after leaving the Communist Party in 1956 in protest against Khruschev's attack on Stalin; she was more a socialist than a communist and close to the Nehru family, which she supported through the Emergency years of 1975–1977.
4 I have not been able to find this quote anywhere, so it could be that he misremembered the author.

Bibliography

Althusser, Louis. 1971. *Lenin and Philosophy and Other Essays*. New York: Monthly Review Press.
Andrews, Molly. 1991. *Lifetimes of Commitment*. Cambridge: Cambridge University Press.
Andrews, Molly. 2014. *Narrative Imagination and Everyday Life*. Cambridge: Cambridge University Press.
Bamberg, M. G. W., and A. McCabe. 1998. 'Editorial.' *Narrative Inquiry* 8(1): iii–v.
Barthes, Roland. 1993. *Camera Lucida: Reflexions on Photography*. London: Vintage Classics.
Bidwai, Praful. 2015. *The Phoenix Moment: Challenges Confronting the Indian Left*. New Delhi: HarperCollins.
Butalia, Urvashi. 2017. *The Other Side of Silence: Voices from the Partition of India*. New Delhi: Penguin.
Chatterjee, Partha. 1993. *The Nation and Its Fragments: Colonial and Postcolonial Histories*. Princeton, NJ: Princeton University Press.
Das, Veena. 2006. *Life and Words*. Los Angeles, CA: University of California Press.
Das, Veena. 2011. 'The Act of Witnessing: Violence, Poisonous Knowledge and Subjectivity.' *Cadernos Pagu* 37: 9–41.
Freire, Paulo. 2000. *Pedagogy of the Oppressed*, 30th anniversary edition. New York: Bloomsbury.
The Guardian. 2007. www.theguardian.com/theguardian/2007/may/01/greatspeeches. Accessed on 22 February 2024.
Giroux, Henry A. 1985. 'Toward a Critical Theory of Education: Beyond a Marxism with Guarantees – A Response to Daniel Liston.' *Educational Theory* 35(3). doi.org/10.1111/j.1741-5446.1985.00313.x.
Jayal, Niraja Gopal. 2013. *Citizenship and Its Discontents: An Indian History*. New Delhi: Harvard University Press.
Jestrovic, Silvija. 2021. *Performances of Authorial Presence and Absence: The Author Dies*. London: Palgrave Macmillan.

Loomba, Ania. 2018. *Revolutionary Desires: Women, Communism, and Feminism in India*. New Delhi: Palgrave.

Lotringer, Sylvère. 2011. 'Mourning, Fiction and Love: The Final Thoughts of a Great Writer.' Frieze, 1 January. www.frieze.com/article/barthes-after-barthes#:~:text=On%20the%20day%20of%20his,his%20illustrious%20predecessors%20had%20done. Accessed on 22 February 2024.

Nehru, Jawaharlal. 1947. *Tryst with Destiny*. www.cam.ac.uk/files/a-tryst-with-destiny/index.html. Accessed on 22 February 2024.

Plummer, Ken. 1995. *Telling Sexual Stories: Power, Change and Social Worlds*. New York: Routledge.

Rai, Shirin M. 2021. 'Introduction: Many Shades of Red: A Personal Reflection on the Life and Times of Lajpat Rai.' In *Indian Debates on the International Left: Selected Writings of Lajpat Rai*, edited by S. M. Rai and A. Prakash, pp. 1–42. New Delhi: Sage.

Rai, Shirin M., and A. Prakash. 2021. 'Indian Debates on the International Left.' https://spectrum.sagepub.in/book/indian-debates-on-the-international-left-shirin-m-rai-9789354792113/7?fbclid=IwAR1-1SAWt1KU08IYtgsGdu1w6t-EPsJckRfeLL4iIUElsf0M_dNuuEx5XmA. Accessed on 22 February 2024.

Rai, Shirin M., and Carole Spary. 2019. *Performing Representation: Women Members of the Indian Parliament*. New Delhi: Oxford University Press.

Reynolds, Nathalène. 2020. *Failure of the Revolutionary Path: Mid-Life Crisis or Terminal Decline?* Sustainable Development Policy Institute. www.jstor.com/stable/resrep24387.5. Accessed on 22 February 2024.

Riessman, Catherine Kohler. 2012. 'Analysis of Personal Narratives.' In *Inside Interviewing: New Lenses, New Concerns*, edited by J. Holstein and J. F. Gubrium, pp. 331–346. Washington, DC: Sage.

Scott-Clark, Cathy, and Levy Adrian. 2001. 'Survivors of Our Hell.' *The Guardian*, 23 June.

Stoetzler, Marcel, and Nira Yuval-Davis. 2002. 'Standpoint Theory, Situated Knowledge, and the Situated Imagination.' *Feminist Theory* 3(3): 315–333.

Van Dijk, Ludger, and Erik Rietveld. 2020. 'Situated Imagination Phenomenology and the Cognitive Sciences.' https://doi.org/10.1007/s11097-020-09701-2. Accessed on 22 February 2024.

15

Why I am still a socialist

Janelle Reinelt

There was a certain point in my political (and emotional) development when I embraced socialism explicitly and identified as a socialist from then on. Unfortunately, I do not remember exactly where or when that moment took place! Let us conjecture that I was about eighteen; the year was 1968. I am now seventy-six, and the year is 2024. In this chapter I would like to share with you why it is still meaningful to me to identify as a socialist. This will mostly be a story about the meaning of socialism within the US context as well as a political memoire. More recently, I find that daily global and local (macro and micro) events and a decade of living and working in the UK (2006–2016) have shored up my commitment to socialism in my elder life and times.

During the 2020 presidential election in the US, I recognised a phenomenon that catapulted me back to several other moments of national history in my lifetime. This well-known tactic is called 'red-baiting', dating from the late nineteenth century and used extensively in the American 'Red Scares' of the first half of the twentieth century. It was basically guilt by association – accusing someone of being an anarchist (1870s), or communist, socialist, or fellow traveller (1920s, 1930s, and 1950s).[1] This time it took the form of a Trump campaign strategy claiming that various Democrats running for Congress were socialists and, therefore, radically deranged Leftists who would wreck the country if elected. As ridiculous as that sounds, especially to some non-American onlookers, it was surprisingly effective in keeping Democrats from being elected to the Senate and the House in a number of races, especially in the South and the Midwest. Joe Biden was also said to be 'socialist' although he explicitly denied it; in the end the fear-mongers were not able to keep him from sustaining a victory and becoming president in spite of the 6 January insurrection and other attempts in the courts to discredit the election results.

This aspect of the 2020 election recalled another moment when 'socialism' had an overwhelmingly negative valence in the US: the run-up to and events of the revolutions of 1989 that put an end to 'really existing socialism' in a number of Eastern European countries and, foremost, the USSR. The socialist experiment had failed, so it was thought; it was, as Francis Fukuyama said, the 'end of history' (1992). Almost overnight, the lexicon of socialism (socialist, Marxist, communist, and Leftist terms and discourse) disappeared from much intellectual and artistic chatter in the US. It was embarrassing in some academic quarters to be quoted or caught out using the language of the demolished ideologies. I remember my naivety in thinking that 'we' must keep the language of socialism alive at all costs in our scholarly work and in the theatre, believing that employing, reiterating, and resounding the word and its associated vocabulary could thereby retain socialism in common usage so that after a suitable period of time it could be redefined and refashioned for a new age. That proved much harder to make operative than I could have imagined – for some decades!

I have happened, by chance, to be born into the generation now known as 'baby boomers'. As a consequence, my personal fate has collided with some sizeable national and international milestones. I came of age in the late 1960s, a time when socialism seemed possible in the US; it was then that I first identified myself among its adherents. Marx and Brecht were my master-teachers, making for me a life/profession match based on politics and aesthetics. By the mid-1980s, no longer a student, I was teaching a feminist theatre workshop and classes on contemporary British and French theatre. I eschewed American realism in my research and teaching, becoming impatient with the bourgeois family drama that was the American paradigm, embracing instead British epic playwrights of my generation (Caryl Churchill, Howard Brenton, David Edgar, John McGrath, Trevor Griffith, and more), beginning to publish as a feminist-socialist theatre scholar.[2] Coming through Second Wave Feminism, the Reagan/Thatcher years, and the Fall of the Wall were personal as well as historic events. Since then, environmental degradation and the global refugee crises, as well as the domestic turbulence of the Trump years with their racist, anti-abortion, and transgender policies, closed border, and Make America Great Again (MAGA) economics, have given us baby boomers plenty to reconsider and decry. It is sometimes hard not to despair as we see work we thought had been accomplished coming undone, such as the 2022 Supreme Court decision contravening Roe v Wade (1973), protecting womens' right to abortion for these many fifty years, or the thirty-four election reform laws passed in nineteen states in 2021 that make it more difficult, not less, for people to vote – particularly people of colour, especially Black Americans (Brennan Center 2021). I also suspect that I had an inflated idea of the power of intellectual work in a country such as the US that is doggedly anti-intellectual in public culture, under the guise of being anti-elitest.

In 2020, baby boomers were on the cusp of turning over our domination of this era to the younger generations who helped elect Joe Biden and supported

Bernie Sanders and who do not necessarily find socialism a dirty word, perhaps because they know so little of its history but perhaps also because that history, if known, connects directly with their present lives in which daily issues of equality, environment, and social justice mobilise them mightily. 2020 was, of course, also the year of COVID and other testaments to boomer vulnerabilities. We are vulnerable because we are on our way to being aged and infirm, but politically we are also confronted with our failures to change our world in ways that secure the common good. So many hopes and dreams, so many disappointments. How did we get to a juncture where far-Right populism seems to be a significant world force alongside certain autocracies that would have been called fascism in an earlier time and which even now can bring on fierce controversy if alluded to publicly? As I drafted this chapter, the UK Home Secretary, the ultra-conservative Suella Braverman, was condemning a BBC journalist's tweeted comments characterising the language of her legislation to stop migrants from crossing the Channel on small boats as similar to language used in Germany in the 1930s. For this, conservative MPs were calling for journalist Gary Lineker to be dismissed. Subsequently, he was taken off the air by the BBC but reinstated a week later after his colleagues and other sports writers refused to do their own shows out of solidarity and protest, causing disruption to coverage of that week's matches (Lineker is a highly paid freelance sports broadcaster who hosts BBC's flagship football show *Match of the Day*).[3] This is just one example from the daily life and times of the present in one country I happen to consider my second home.

In the introduction to this volume, Silvija Jestrovic and Bishnupriya Dutt write about the importance of finding ways to recuperate and re-energise the political ideas and dimensions of the Left in the context of everyday life, something that speaks directly to my baby-boomer predicament: searching for a way forward, for a new Left strategy of inclusion and solidarity, for a way to take some of the goals and methods of our Left legacy forward to the future. It seems to me that recapturing faith in socialist values and cultivating faith in possible new modes of daily life, activism, and art are the only ways to find a meaningful life-exit strategy for baby boomers like me.

The historical backdrop to socialism in America

The history of socialism in the US is different from that of our European allies and the rest of the Americas. The stigma associated with socialism in my country is arguably more virulent than in many other Western democracies. Why should that be so?

If we take a simple definition of socialism, according to Dictionary.com, as 'a theory or system of social organization that advocates the ownership and control of the means of production and distribution, capital, land, etc., by the community as a whole, usually through a centralized government', socialism in the US can be traced all the way back to the American revolutionary period in the figure of Thomas Paine, author of *Common Sense* ([1776], 2014) and *The Age of Reason* ([1794], 2014). He was involved in both the American and the French Revolutions, and his ideas about a guaranteed annual income, pensions for the elderly, universal public education, and pre- and post-natal care can be seen as precursors to later programmes such as the New Deal and Social Security. Sometimes claimed by the Right – remarkably, Ronald Reagan liked to quote Paine – he is more often embraced by the Left. In his short history of American socialism, John Nichols begins with Walt Whitman and Thomas Paine, claiming that Paine's *Rights of Man* ([1791], 2014) and *Agrarian Justice* ([1797)], 2014) 'both contained content that provided, if not quite a Socialist Party platform, then surely the rough outlines for a social-democratic response to inequality' (2015: 37). Paine opposed slavery as well.

However, if there were socialist ideas embedded in the first years of the nation, they were not called socialist at the time. Socialism as a nomenclature comes into the US through immigrants who established utopian communities in the early nineteenth century, particularly in Midwest states such as Wisconsin and Indiana, where Robert Owen set up his New Harmony experiment in the 1820s. The Socialist Labor Party was established in 1876, and in 1901 the Socialist Party of America elected local officials and ran national campaigns. Eugene Debs, a railway union organiser, and leader of important strikes, was elected to the Indiana state Senate and House and ran for president as a socialist five times, garnering 6 per cent of the vote in 1912. In these early years socialism was legitimate if a minority party. However, in what has been called the first 'Red Scare', the demonising of socialism began. This came about because of the opposition of the Socialist Labor Party, Debs, and other Left leaders to the First World War. In 1917 Congress passed the Espionage Act, making it a crime to speak out against the war or oppose the draft. Thousands of socialists, including Debs, were subsequently arrested. At the same time, the 1917 Russian Revolution caused fear that a workers' revolt might happen in the US. Suspected socialists and other radicals were rounded up and jailed; immigration from Italy and Eastern Europe was curtailed. The charge that socialism was 'unpatriotic' has followed it ever since.

The second Red Scare emerged shortly later, in the 1930s, in the midst of the Depression, which labelled F. D. Roosevelt a socialist for his New Deal policies that brought about our first social welfare programmes, such as Social Security. After the Second World War, Cold War politics that had developed between the USSR and the US brought on a third wave of Red

Scare. 'Communism' was indistinguishable from 'socialism' for Senator Joseph McCarthy, and a cluster of terms that included socialism, Marxism, communism, and the Left could bring charges against any possible associate, causing them to lose a job or even be prosecuted for sedition. However, the Communist Control Act of 1954, which outlawed the Communist Party of America and made it a crime to belong, was later found unconstitutional by a lower court in Arizona. The Supreme Court has declined to take up the matter at any time since, and it is not enforced today. Still, the 1950s decade when people were fired, careers ruined, and blacklists drawn up remains a powerful memory in the public imagination and makes socialism suspect for a large number of ordinary voters.

While the Republican Party has continued to capitalise on anti-socialist tendencies in its campaign attacks on those who profess socialism, the success of Bernie Sanders in managing a serious national bid for president and for holding his Vermont Senate seat for sixteen years while daring to admit to being a democratic socialist is striking. More recent socialist elected officials such as Representatives Alexandria Ocasio-Cortez and Rashida Tlaib have been roundly accused of being traitors, but only a few are even democratic socialists (Epstein and Qiu 2019). A research report on the results of the 2020 election found that 'The "Dem potpourri" of attacks meant to brand Democrats as "radical" was effective – especially where there wasn't enough positive bio early and where campaigns failed to respond to the lies' ('Post-Election Analysis', quoted in Burns 2021). Red-baiting is still a popular sport in American politics.

Living on *Main Street* in Hollister, California

My parents were Roosevelt Democrats. Both of their families lost dairy farms during the Great Depression. I was always told my Grandfather Bettencourt died 'of a broken heart' because of losing his farm when the bank foreclosed shortly after he had borrowed money to expand. My Grandfather Gobby died when my father was ten, and his twelve brothers and sisters and their mother struggled to work their farm successfully, only to lose it anyway. My parents viewed Franklin Roosevelt as the country's saviour, someone who 'looked out for the little guy' instead of big business and whose social welfare programmes of the New Deal helped the country get back on its feet. However, my parents were also Catholics, and my father was a veteran of the Second World War: they were strongly anti-communist on ideological grounds and would never have considered voting socialist. I was born in 1947 when the McCarthy era was already underway, but my memories of it come some years later when I overheard my father tell my mother in a low voice that so-and-so might be a communist. To their credit, my parents knew that McCarthy and the hearings of the House on Un-American Activities Committee (appointed in 1938) were wrong; they did not think people should be outed and fired or imprisoned. Nonetheless, their ambivalence was clear to me – they thought being a socialist or a communist or a 'fellow traveller' was not good, not a good thing to be. I was too small (probably six or seven) to have an opinion as yet.

When I got a little older, I began to understand better: I heard about the Hollywood Ten blacklist and some of the stories about theatre people who were questioned by the Committee on Un-American Activities. I was very clear that you should never 'tell' on your friends so instinctively I felt the injustice of the Committee's wanting people to name names of friends or associates who might be suspected communists. (The number of theatre people and other artists who were persecuted, prosecuted, or banned during this period is disproportionately high.)[4]

I began to be aware of my small rural Californian town's character as I got older: I knew that the businesses were run by Protestants and the farms and ranches by Catholics, mostly Italians. I knew there was an Italian mass each Sunday and an Italian priest assigned to our parish, but that the large population of farm workers and other Mexican residents had no Spanish priest or weekly mass. I knew that there was one Black family in the whole of Hollister and that they lived on the edge of the town, and that the Jewish family (I guess there was only one of those too) owned the men's department store, and people referred to them as 'the Jews'. The mayor and town council were largely Protestant and owned the major retail businesses from car dealerships to clothing stores (except, of course, for the Jewish men's store). I also saw how everyone knew everyone else, and nobody's business was private. My Portuguese and Swiss parents moved to Hollister when I was three; ten years later I heard my mother saying that even if you lived there for a decade, you were still considered newcomers. I felt the small and petty climate of this town deeply and knew it was unfair to others besides me and my mother, much more unfortunate. I was pretty unhappy but at least began to develop a sense of social justice. I remember reading Sinclair Lewis's 1920 novel *Main Street* (2018), a novel about small-minded people in the small-town Midwest and telling my English teacher that Lewis must have been writing about Hollister because it described our own hypocrisy and prejudice exactly! (At sixteen, I was a tad self-righteous and pompous, I know, but my experiences were a good training ground for future socialist politics.)

The 1960s were my teenage years: I turned thirteen the year President Kennedy was elected, and I was sixteen when he was assassinated. The Vietnam War was debated in my high school history and civics classes, and I went on my first political demonstration against the war in 1967. I was eighteen and nineteen when the term 'hippie' was coined, and I lived in the epicentre of the Love Generation, close to San Francisco. Intellectually, I was leaving my small-town existence for the world of the university, reading Marx, Freud, and John-Paul Sartre. I saw my college production of *Marat Sade* three times, and I talked about it endlessly into the night with other students while we listened to Jefferson Airplane or sang along with Janis Joplin. I learnt about Woody Gutherie and his son Arlo's folk music written about labour protests, depression experiences, and other socialist themes (Woody wrote *This Land Is Your Land* in 1940; Arlo wrote *Alice's Restaurant* in 1967). In Golden Gate Park I saw the San Francisco Mime Troupe perform for the first time – I remember an environmental scene: there was an actress with a huge balloon-like costume painted as a globe with the oceans and continents; she was coughing and choking because of the bad air, the result of corporate pollution. They were just a local theatre to me, but of course they became one of the most researched and revered of the US socialist theatre companies from that period, along with Teatro Campesino which, closely linked to the Farm Workers' Movement and the protests in the lettuce fields and during the grape harvests, settled in San Juan Batista, about five miles from where I grew up and home to the California Mission where I married Herb Reinelt in 1968.[5] The theatre was such a vital part of civic life and politics in those years that I never questioned if it was powerful or irrelevant to real power. And it might have been preaching to the converted, but, honestly, there were a lot of us converted in those years. The feeling that my generation might really change the world was an empowering experience. I think it gave activists fuel to struggle, to fight another day, and to not give up. As Brecht insisted, we need a long anger to avoid the Great Capitulation.

    I have had many opportunities to see how different ideas about socialism have appeared in theatres around the world. From my early experiences with the International Brecht Society in the 1980s and early 1990s to the ten years (1995–2006) I spent as part of the University of Helsinki's annual doctoral summer school, where students from many countries worked together to understand how their countries' theatres and polities interconnected, I gained a new understanding of and appreciation for how making theatre is making politics. My decision to concentrate on the UK in my research gave me access to a country with a rich socialist history and tradition, introduced me to thinkers such as Raymond Williams, Stuart Hall, and Paul Gilroy, and helped me expand my vision of socialism as a lifelong practice of hope (to gloss Raymond Williams). As a result of my work on playwrights and directors in the UK, I was able to develop deep and treasured friendships with some of my British theatre heroes, especially Howard Brenton, David Edgar, and William Gaskill. (Bill's death in 2018 and Jane Brenton's in 2021 were very sad personal losses.) David was Jerry's best man at our backyard wedding in 2003. Jerry Hewitt and I have also collaborated on a book about David Edgar's political theatre (2011). The long-term partnership with Jawaharlal Nehru University, of which this book is the most recent evidence, began in 2008 when Bishnupriya Dutt, with whom I shared feminism as well as socialism, suggested to me that we might collaborate across our schools/departments. Indian histories of socialism and radical theatre practices added new knowledge and appreciation to my international grasp of committed theatre across the globe. Back in 2003, when I was still living and working in the US (I accepted a position at the University of Warwick in 2006), I realised, mainly as a result of my long involvement with the International Federation for Theatre Research, that the most pressing political issue for our field was a true internationalisation of theatre studies and a more inclusive and wide-reaching embrace of scholarship and practice across the globe. This aspect of our field has broadened and strengthened over time, and I am glad to have had some small part in making it so.

Life in the complex present or baby boomers' micro-plane

Living in California once again in retirement, I am trying to grapple with the political polarisation that characterises this national moment. Trump is out of office, but he is not gone; nor is the knowledge that his support base is large and a good-sized portion of the US populace still does not see the 2020 election as legitimate. It is going to take a long anger to sustain a national turn away from the Trump agenda in coming years, if not from the man himself. I am hopeful we will have what we need from the young people who have organised around climate change, the Black Lives Matter movement and protests, the Me Too movement and its follow-up, from ordinary people who have struggled through COVID, lost loved ones, perhaps survived grave illness. The original economic agenda of President Biden was close to the New Deal in terms of its size and impact. His infrastructure plans proposed two trillion USD for roads and bridges but also for education and internet provision, and cleaner energy sources.[6] This plan triggered an important national debate around what counts as infrastructure, and to me, this is a truly socialist idea: that education, clean water, and internet capacity are aspects of the infrastructure of society, as surely as roads and bridges.

In the first two decades of the twentieth century, when socialism had its initial electoral successes in the US, its appeal was most visible locally and at state levels. 353 cities and towns elected socialist candidates, including 130 mayors. Over a thousand socialists were elected overall, including two members of Congress and a number of state legislators (Ross n.d.). This is history I do not think most citizens, especially young ones, know. The governance of our neighbourhoods and cities is often the worksite where people struggle for equality, opportunity, fairness, and possibility. The battle takes place at close quarters, on the ground. Today's school boards that try to ban books or prevent the teaching of Critical Race Theory in schools are a charged site of struggle in need of articulate and knowledgeable parents and teachers who can push back against this attempt to censor legitimate scholarly theory and history. Small-town struggles for transgender rights often involve conflicts over inclusive toilets (shades of separate toilets for 'coloureds'). In larger cities, too, micro-politics are very specific to place and context. Gun violence in Chicago cost the first Black woman mayor her re-election in March 2023 because people in Chicago were frightened by the uptick of violence and therefore, while she was progressive (a word preferred now to 'Left' because it seems less radical), she was accused of being 'soft on crime' because she favoured police reform.[7] Along with local school boards, city councils, and voter registration efforts, the theatre can also create a site for struggle when it addresses its audiences and their specific contexts and lives. It can open up imaginative possibilities or highlight connections between communities across space and time. I am talking about the arts as part of the fabric and texture of the political micro-plane of everyday life, comparable to town hall meetings or civic projects, but utilising the tools of the aesthetic realm.

I missed my colleagues and friends in the UK very much during COVID, and as I age, it is clear I will not be able to keep them close spatially as travel becomes more difficult both for me and for the environment to bear. Once again, I find in theatre and socialism both a promise and a comfort. The comfort comes whenever I see a wonderful performance that enriches my theatrical archive or when a protest, piece of legislation, or judicial finding upholds a socialist principle; the promise comes when a theatre piece illuminates the values of equality, interconnectedness, and social justice that remain the socialist ideal. As long as we continue to imagine the world otherwise, critique the injustices, and portray the possibility of achieving change, there is hope for a socialist future, even in the face of dire predictions (climate change) and gross injustices (race, gender, disability, food shortages, massive human displacements, and wars).

In a recent book in our field, *Toward a Transindividual Self: A Study in Social Dramaturgy* (2022), Ana Vujanović and Bojana Cvejić offer an ambitious and capacious effort to theorise a new way to approach collectivity for political purposes through the lens of performance. Convinced that the current neoliberal conjuncture has only heightened a form of capitalist individualism that blocks notions of the social, the authors aim to show that a transindividual formation of the self can bring about different courses of action and a more socially driven imagination. 'The theory of transindividuation', they argue, 'shows that there is no real and unavoidable clash between the individual and the collective in the onto-historical sense' (2022: 262).

The authors present a complex argument leading to hope – hope in the ability of the Left to regenerate itself in a form appropriate to a future beyond the neoliberal straight jacket of the present; hope also in a theoretical break in the deadlock over individualism and communitarianism that has fuelled so many academic debates in performance and other humanistic disciplines. Transindividuation, they assure us, shows how 'we form ourselves on the basis of interdependence, sharing, commonality, as well as indispensability of the individual as the agent of creativity/knowledge, freedom, and change, who "possibilizes" their own conditions of formation' (2022: 261).

In March 2023, armed with these new theories, I had an unexpected and delightful boost to my faith in both theatre and socialism. I had finally managed a short eight-day trip to the UK to see beloved colleagues and friends. On the last day of my visit, Bishnupriya Dutt arrived from Delhi for two weeks at Warwick, and we were able to spend the day together and attend the theatre that evening. She selected the show: it was a musical called *Sylvia* at the Old Vic, and I did not know anything about it beforehand. It turned out that the 'Sylvia' was Sylvia Pankhurst, the socialist suffragette who broke with her mother and sister over her commitment to enfranchising working-class women as well as the middle class. Her mother Emmeline, the head of the twentieth-century suffragette movement (First Wave feminism), secured the vote for privileged women but not for all women. Sylvia was an independent thinker who embraced socialism and worked especially with East End London women to gain their voice. The musical is a celebration of her determination, and yet it also rehearses with great alacrity the historical splits in feminism around issues of class.

However, the production choices of director and author Kate Prince and the music by Josh Cohen and DJ Walde catapult a historical pageant drama into something far more innovative and pertinent: the cast is largely made up of Black British actors, and the music is a combination of hip-hop, soul, blues, and funk with citations to Motown, Madonna, and Aretha among others. The effect is not at all realistic: we are not asked to see the historical characters as Black, exactly; it is more like we are asked to embrace storytelling, which explicitly links today's issues of race, civil rights, Black Lives Matter, Me Too, and economic inequality to the historical past. This easily could have been a tedious forcing of interconnectedness, but the virtuosity and skill of almost all members of the cast, especially Sharon Rose as Sylvia and Beverly Knight as Emmeline, made this a surprising, delightful, slightly surreal experience for spectators while still beating out the historical suffragette facts. *The Guardian*'s Arifa Akbhar wrote: 'the sheer chutzpah of its vision is phenomenal' (2023). For Bishnupriya and me, the show was an intellectual and emotional pleasure from beginning to end, and viewing it together was an additional thrill. Best of all, when we looked around, the full house was very diverse and young compared to an average Old Vic audience, so the show appeared to be attracting a variety of spectators. In the end everyone jumped up and roared and cheered for the cast and the performance. I had not been in such an energised audience for a very long time. It felt like a wave of enthusiasm and assent. And in that moment, I knew, once again, why I am still a socialist.

Notes

1. There is an extensive literature dealing with the various Red Scares. Here are some sources that have been valuable to me: Murray (1955); Fariello (1995); Cornell (2016); Goldstein (2016).
2. My first two publications reflecting this professional identity were in 1985, followed by my book on British Epic theatre in 1994.
3. For a concise article about the 'row', see Abdul (2023).
4. For a full account of HUAC and Hollywood, see Doherty (2018). For an account from an important theatre critic, translator or Brecht, and playwright, see Bentley (2002).
5. For an excellent resource on the Mime Troupe, see Mason (2005); for an account of Teatro Campesino, see Broyles-González (1994).
6. After compromises, the legislation passed with one trillion dollars, about half of the original proposal. Education slipped out of the deal, although internet provision was funded (White House 2021).
7. Lori Lightfoot was the first Black woman and first openly gay woman to serve as mayor. 63 per cent of Chicagoans said in a poll that they did not feel safe in a city where gun violence reached an all-time high in 2021 (3,500 shootings), although it dropped in 2022. Ironically, in the run-off election, the progressive candidate Brandon Johnson won over the law-and-order candidate Paul Vallas (Korecki 2023).

Bibliography

Abdul, Geneva. 2023. 'Gary Lineker: It Was Factually Accurate to Call Refugee Policy Cruel.' *The Guardian*, 6 April. www.theguardian.com/football/2023/apr/06/gary-lineker-it-was-factually-accurate-to-call-refugee-policy-cruel. Accessed on 13 April 2023.

Akbar, Arifa. 2023. 'Sylvia review: Storming Show Sets Suffragettes to Soul, Funk and Hip-hop.' *The Guardian*, 15 February. www.theguardian.com/stage/2023/feb/15/sylvia-pankhurst-review-old-vic-london. Accessed on 20 April 2023.

Bentley, Eric (ed.). 2002. *Thirty Years of Treason: Excerpts from Hearings before the House Committee on Un-American Activities 1938–1968*. New York: Thunder's Mouth Press.

Brennan Center for Justice. 'Voting Laws Round-Up: December 2021.' www.brennancenter.org/our-work/research-reports/voting-laws-roundup-december-2021. Accessed on 13 April 2023.

Broyles-González, Yolanda. 1994. *El Teatro Campesino: Theater in the Chicano Movement*. Austin, TX: University of Texas.

Burns, Alexander. 2021. 'Democratic Report Raises 2022 Alarms on Messaging and Voter Outreach.' *New York Times*, 6 June. www.nytimes.com/2021/06/06/us/politics/democrats-2020-election.html. Accessed on 19 April 2023.

Cornell, Andrew. 2016. *Unruly Anarchism: U.S. Anarchism in the 20th Century*. Oakland, CA: University of California Press.

Dictionary.com. 'Socialism'. www.dictionary.com/browse/socialism. Accessed on 22 February 2024.

Doherty, Tom. 2018. *Show Trial: Hollywood, HUAC, and the Birth of the Blacklist*. New York: Columbia University Press.

Epstein, Reid J., and Linda Qiu. 2019. 'Fact-Checking Trump's Claims That Democrats Are Radical Socialists.' *New York Times*, 20 July. www.nytimes.com/2019/07/20/us/politics/trump-democrats-socialists.html. Accessed on 13 April 2023.

Fariello, Griffin (ed.). 1995. *Memories of the American Inquisition: An Oral History*. New York: Avon Books.

Fukuyama, Francis. 1992. *The End of History and the Last Man*. New York: Free Press.

Goldstein, Robert Justin (ed.). 2016. *Little 'Red Scares': Anti-Communism and Political Repression in the United States 1921–1946*. New York and London: Routledge.

Korecki, Natasha. 2023. 'Lori Lightfoot becomes the first Chicago mayor in 40 years to lose re-election.' *New York Times*, 28 February. www.nbcnews.com/politics/elections/lori-lightfoot-becomes-first-chicago-mayor-40-years-lose-re-election-rcna71997. Accessed on 20 April 2023.

Lewis, Sinclair. 2018. *Main Street*. Boston, MA: DigiReads Publishing.

Mason, Susan Vaneta. 2005. *The San Francisco Mime Troupe: A Reader*. Ann Arbor, MI: University of Michigan Press.

Murray, Robert K. 1955. *Red Scare: A Study in National Hysteria 1919–1920*. Minneapolis, MN: University of Minnesota Press.

Nichols, John. 2015. *The S Word: A Short History of an American Tradition … Socialism*, second edition. London: Verso.

Paine, Thomas. 2014. *Selected Writings of Thomas Paine*, edited by I. Shapiro and J. E. Calvert. New Haven, CT: Yale University Press.

Reinelt, Janelle. 1985. 'Bertolt Brecht and Howard Brenton: The Common Task.' *Pacific Coast Philology* 20(1–2): 46–52.

Reinelt, Janelle. 1985. 'Elaborating Brecht: Churchill's Domestic Drama.' *Communications* 14(2): 49–56.

Reinelt, Janelle. 1994. *After Brecht: British Epic Theatre*. Ann Arbor, MI: University of Michigan Press.

Reinelt, Janelle, and Gerald Hewitt. 2011. *The Political Theatre of David Edgar: Negotiation and Retrieval*. Cambridge: Cambridge University Press.

Ross, Jack. n.d. 'Socialist Party Elected Officials 1901–1960.' Mapping American Social Movements Project (University of Washington). https://depts.washington.edu/moves/SP_map-elected.shtml. Accessed on 20 April 2023.

Vujanović, Ana, and Bojana Cvejić. 2022. *Toward a Transindividual Self: A Study in Social Dramaturgy*. Oslo: Oslo National Academy of the Arts.

White House. 2021. 'Factsheet: The Bi-Partisan Infrastructure Deal.' www.whitehouse.gov/briefing-room/statements-releases/2021/11/06/fact-sheet-the-bipartisan-infrastructure-deal. Accessed on 20 April 2023.

Index

ableism 73, 83
Abraham, Chris 146, 155
activism 2, 5–7, 10–12, 38, 45, 74–75,
    81, 84–87, 220–223, 227, 244,
    251, 257, 262, 270, 277
    Left 4, 12–13
    Muslim 75
    online 50, 52
    performance 114, 124, 126
    political 3, 11–12, 81, 94, 206, 221,
        229, 231–233, 257, 272
    quiet 74, 81
    weekend 45, 50
Agamben, Giorgeo 60
agitprop 122, 135, 158
Ahmed, Sara 202
Ahsan, Hamja 12, 15, 73–82,
    84–87
Akhtar, Ayad 156
Amazon 2
Ambedkar, B. R. 23, 34, 259
anachronism 6
anarchist 87, 150, 275
Angar 180, 182–184, 186–189,
    192–194
Angelaki, Vicki 8
anti-capitalist 177
anti-communist 279
anti-immigrant 40
anti-protest 43
anti-socialist 279
Arendt, Hannah 60
Aristotle 224
Armed Forces Special Powers Act
    (AFSPA) 69
art, political 3

Aspergistan 73–74, 76–78, 86–87
assemblage 56, 168, 191
The Assembly 146, 149–150, 152–159
Aston, Elaine 124
Auschwitz 60
authoritarianism 6, 25, 32
autism 83–84
autobiography 11, 241, 243–244,
    247–248, 250, 254, 257, 262
avant-garde 233
avatar 42
Azad, Chandrashekhar 24
Azoulay, Ariella 99–100

baby boomers 276–277
Badiou, Alain 4, 14, 102, 113, 203,
    207, 210, 219–220, 228–233
Balkans 41
Banerjee, Sumanta 204
Barthes, Roland 79–80, 101, 262, 273
Battleship Potemkin 183, 189, 192
Baxi, Upendra 26
Begum, Hajrah 237, 244, 249–250
Benjamin, Walter 95–99, 101–103, 163
Berliner Ensemble 186
Bharatiya Janata Party (BJP) 23–24,
    27, 30
Bharucha, Rustom 6
Bhim Army 24
Biden, Joe 275–276, 282
biography 10–11, 15, 219–222,
    226–227, 243–244, 254,
    257–258, 262, 271–272
Black Lives Matter 93, 103, 107, 110,
    152, 158, 282, 284
Black Panthers 73

Bloody Sunday 223, 226, 229
Bolsonaro 2
Bonnett, Alastair 164–165
bourgeois 137, 141, 189, 267
    nationalist 139
bourgeoise 131, 138, 220, 232, 258
Braverman, Suella 277
Brecht, Bertolt 14, 93–97, 100–103, 131–132, 146, 157, 180–181, 186, 189, 206, 225, 232–233, 276, 281, 286
Brexit 2, 142
British Academy 2
British East India Company 199
British Medical Association 69
Brown, Wendy 74–75, 81, 135, 143, 163, 242, 255
Burns sisters 222, 233
Butler, Judith 25, 36, 72, 146–149, 152–154, 158–159, 164

Calvinism 138
Calvinist Reformation 138
capitalism 2–3, 114, 139, 163, 224, 232, 272
    market 163
    predatory 23
capitalist 3, 30, 32, 80, 86, 98, 114, 122, 124, 228
    development 138
    exploitation 140
Chakkajam 112, 115–118, 124
Chakrabarty, Dipesh 121–122
Charlesworth, Simon 112, 114
Chatterjee, Bankim Chandra 211
Chatterjee, Partha 6, 8, 123–124, 258
Chaudhuri, Una 170
Chernishevsky, Nikolay 10
The Cheviot 13, 129, 131–137, 139–140, 143
citizen 56, 75, 77, 86, 99, 118, 122–123, 132, 146, 157, 225, 249, 259, 268, 283
    middle-class 123
    modern 123
citizenship 56, 73, 75–76, 81, 84, 122, 125, 259–260
    Australian 76
    conditional 75
    social 125–126
Clinton, Hillary 40

Cold War 163, 278
    era 1, 3
collective
    action 46
    activist 80
    identity 46
    spectatorship 8
colonial
    aesthetics 13
    capitalist 99, 103–105, 110
    government 64–65, 67
    oppression 266
    power 64
    prison 64
    state 64, 67
colonialism 26, 104, 189, 194, 200, 266, 272
common culture 8
communism 1–2, 114, 219–220, 224, 228–230, 232, 241, 245, 271, 279
    homely 234
communist 245, 275–276, 280
    domesticities 241
    history 240–241
    Indian 258
    movement 15, 113, 236, 240, 252, 257
    women 15, 236, 240–242, 244, 250, 253
Communist International (Comintern) 258
Communist Party 247–248, 250, 252, 259, 266
Communist Party of America 279
Communist Party of India (CPI) 245–247, 250, 257–258, 261, 266–268
Communist Party of India Marxist, CPI(M) 115, 250
Communist Party of India (CPI), Marxist-Leninist 268
community
    political 9
Congress Party 258, 268
connective action 46
consensus 6, 12, 135, 207
Conservative government 142
Conservatives 39, 142
Constitution 12, 23, 26–28, 32–33
    Indian 12, 23–24, 26–28, 30–34

Constitutional Amendment Act (CAA) 9, 24
constitutionalism 26–27
corporeal state 57
COVID-19 24, 31, 160, 277, 282
    lockdown 78
    pandemic 2, 149
cultural
    aesthetics 9
    materialism 9, 229
culture
    political 244

Dalit 23–24
D'Arcy, Margaretta 60–61, 69
Dark Web 40
Dean, Jodi 4, 113–114, 126, 224–226, 242–243, 256
Deavere Smith, Anna 93, 103–110
De Certeau, Michel 48–49
Deleuze, Gilles 52
Delta Avenue Citizens Organization (DACO) 47–48
Derrida, Jacques 210, 214, 223–224
democracy 1, 25, 27, 34, 41, 52, 54, 84, 104, 113, 145, 156, 165, 171, 208, 277
    radical 159
    substantive 125
democratic socialist 279
democratisation 13, 52, 122, 124–125
Democrats 275
depoliticisation 8
dialectics 4–5, 14, 16, 101, 122
Didi-Huberman, Georges 93–96, 100–101, 103
Disgraced 156
disjunction 6, 95, 174
dissensus 3, 9, 12–13, 225
dissent 11, 42, 75, 120, 251
dissident 23, 57, 59–60, 69
    bodies 57
Dogberries 231, 233
Don't Drown Belgrade movement 44
dramaturgies
    Leftist 13, 15
dramaturgy 10–11, 13
Dundee Rep 129–130
Dutt, Utpal 1, 14–15, 96, 107, 180–195, 197, 199–214

Eastern Europe 1, 278
egalitarianism 34, 113, 122, 126
elite
    culture 8
Engels, Friedrich 3, 18, 222–223, 226–227, 231, 233, 235
Ernaux, Annie 1
ethnic chauvinism 3
Ewing, Winnifred 137

Facebook 39, 42, 46
Fahrenheit 11/9 145, 160
Farm Workers' Movement 281
far Right 41, 44
fascism 277
fellow traveller 275, 280
feminism 10, 32, 149, 282, 284
    First Wave 284
    Second Wave 276
    socialist 227
feudalism 139
First World War 3, 40, 278
Fisher, Tony 8–9
Floyd, George 46
Foucault, Michel 49–50, 56, 80, 104
free market 1
Freud, Sigmund 281

Gandhi 64
    Gandhian 12
Gandhi, Indira 268
Gaon Se Sehar Tak 112, 121
gestic 96
gestus 14, 94–96, 105, 108, 110
Gilroy, Paul 281
Glasgow Unity Theatre 132
globalisation 164, 167–168, 170, 177
Global South 1, 165
Goffman, Erving 56
A Good Night Out 131
Gopal Jayal, Niraja 125
governance 3, 7, 199, 219, 283
Gramsci, Antonio 6, 9
    Gramscian notion of popular tradition 131
Gray, Freddie 106–107, 109
Great Depression 278–279

Haksar, Anamika 13, 112, 118–121, 124, 126
Hall, Stuart 9, 73, 89, 141, 281

Haltung 101–103, 106, 108
Hamilton 93, 97–98
Harding, Warren G. 40
Hastings, Warren 199–200, 212
Hashmi, Moloyashree 13, 112, 117, 125–127
Hashmi, Safdar 115–116, 118
hegemonic
  common sense 6
  didacticism 9
  discourses 6
hermeneutics
  interdisciplinary 5
Hikikomori phenomenon 73, 76
Hindu
  revivalism 211
Hindustan Socialist Revolutionary Association (HSRA) 57, 59, 64–67
Hindutva 272
  project 23
historical materiality 148
historicisation 93–96, 101, 168
historiography 10, 98–99, 201, 209
  critical 10
Hitler 251, 258
Hollywood Ten 280
Holston, James 56
Hunger 62
hunger
  artist 57–58, 68
  fasts 12–13, 56, 64, 70
  protests 56–57, 63–64, 67–70
  strikes 58–59, 61–62, 64, 66–69
hyper-historian 136, 151–153
hyperperformativity 96
hyper-sites 115
hyperspace 12–13, 40–42

immigrant 145, 278
immigration 70, 146, 155, 278
imperialism 26, 99, 139, 258, 272
Indian Constitution 26, 259
Indian Medical Service (IMS) 67
Indian People's Theatre Association (IPTA) 183, 194, 204, 250
individualism 4, 45, 122, 220, 242, 284
  capitalist 283
insurgency 26, 71
insurgent 12, 26, 56
  body 57

citizenship 12–13, 57, 70
constitution 12, 26
constitutionalism 12, 28
possibilities 23
International Federation for Theatre Research (IFTR) 7–8, 282
Irish
  movement 222
  Republicanism 226
  Republicans 12, 57–60, 64, 66–67, 222
Iron Curtain 1
Islamophobe 155
Islamophobia 3, 6
isolationist 40

Jameson, Fredric 41, 54, 95, 97–98, 102
Jana Natya Manch (Janam) 8, 112, 115–117, 121, 126
Jatra 194, 199, 201, 206, 210–213
Jatra-theatre 211
Jawaharlal Nehru 259
Joseph, Jino 164, 166, 168, 172, 176

Kafka, Franz 57–58, 68
Kallol 180–181, 183, 186, 188–189, 191–195
Kaviraj, Sudipta 201, 203–204
Kelly J. Nestruck 155–158
Kerry, John 40
Kershaw, Baz 137
keyboard warriors 51

labour 7, 10, 13, 98, 113–116, 118–119, 121, 167, 182–183, 240, 245, 250
  child 169
  codes 115, 121
  cultures 126
  disputes 115
  distribution 219
  division 232
  immigrant 168, 173, 177
  migrant 168
  migration 167–168
  practices 123
  protection laws 120
  protests 281
  rates 168
  relation 164, 166, 168
  tribunals 115

labour *(continued)*
  unacknowledged 97
  unorganised 243
Labour Party 39, 137, 142
laissez-faire 114
Latour, Bruno 155
Left 1–6, 8, 10–11, 13–16, 27, 32, 38–39, 52, 73, 80, 86, 117, 126, 130, 133, 137, 140, 142, 146, 154, 157, 163–166, 177, 208, 220, 257, 262, 272, 277–279, 283–284
  activism 272
  activists 270
  aesthetics 4, 74
  agendas 12
  American 15
  cultural 189
  cultural politics 5
  cultural practices 10
  culture 16, 126
  discourses 5, 13
  dramaturgies 16
  dramaturgy 13
  echo-chambers 73–74
  Indian 195
  mobilisation 266
  movements 165, 236, 258, 270
  nostalgia 13
  politics 74, 112, 122, 181, 266
  populism 13, 88
  protests 13
  radical 13, 57, 143, 154
Left and Right binary 4
Leftist 4–5, 8, 174, 180, 183, 275–276
  agendas 2
  ethos 2, 10, 271
  histories 5, 16
  ideas 10
  ideology 78
  imaginations 9
  nostalgia 13
  performativity 10
  political resistance 3
  political subject 16
  politics 12, 14
  practices 12
  praxis 10
  protests 166
  radical 74
  state 13
  street theatre 8
  subjectivities 16
Left-wing
  agenda 126
  nation 143
  theatre 130, 132
  theatre companies 133
  theatre-makers 131
Lenin, Vladimir 1, 10, 220, 228
LGBT 12–13, 33
liberal
  state 6, 75
liberalisation 113, 117
Little Theatre 184
Little Theatre Group 191, 208
Littlewood, Amy 76
The Living Corpse 186
The Lower Depths 186

Mahabharata 23
Mahila Atma Raksha Samiti (MARS) 246, 248–251
Malayala Kalanilayalam Nadakavedhi 164
Manusmriti 23, 36
Marat Sade 281
Marschall, Anika 15
Marx, Eleanor 221–223, 226–229, 231–233
Marx, Karl 3, 220, 222, 232, 270, 276, 281
Marxism 232, 257, 279
Marxist 27, 113, 122, 180, 228, 276
  ideas 6
  imaginations 9
  literature 6
  scholars 5
  thinkers 39
mathi 164–170, 172, 175–177
Mathi (performance) 164–167, 169–171, 173–174, 176
Maxim Gorky Theatre 186
Mayakovsky Theatre 181, 187
Mayakovsky, Vladimir 181, 187, 228
Mbembe, Achille 104–105, 108–109
McGrath, John 14, 129–137, 139–142, 276
McQueen, Steve 62

melancholia 164
  Left 163–164
Me Too movement 282, 284
Mevani, Jignesh 23
micro-communism 11, 15, 219–221, 224, 226–228, 230, 232–233
migration 75
mimesis 94, 96, 100, 105
Minerva Theatre 182–183, 186–187, 189, 192, 195, 208
minimal communism 11, 230, 232
minimalism 14, 194
modernity 164–165
Modi, Narendra 2, 114
Moore, Michael 145
Mouffe, Chantal 6, 13, 145
Munsi, Vidya 237, 244–247
Murphy, Maeve 61

Nabanna 186, 194
Nairn, Tom 135, 137–140, 143
National Federation of Indian Women (NFIW) 241, 245–246, 249, 268, 270
nationalism 3, 14, 57, 81, 158, 165, 211, 272
  Indian 270
  nostalgic 88
  postcolonial 13
  revolutionary 139
  Scottish 130, 137, 139, 142
  socialist 137
Naxalbari 207–209
  movement 211
Naxalite
  ideology 208
  movement 210–211
Naz Foundation 32–33
necropolitics 105
necropower 105
neoliberal 3, 80, 122, 163, 225, 272
  capitalism 114, 130, 205
  culture 7
  governmentality 6
  state 4
neurodiversity 74, 76, 83–84
Non-Aligned Movement 3
noncitizen 75, 77
nostalgia 113, 138, 141, 163–165, 168, 173–174, 177, 264
  anti-colonial 165
  feudal 177
  Left 177
  radical 165
Notes from the Field 93, 103, 105–106, 108–109

Obraztsov, Sergei 190
Occupy movement 3, 12, 76
Ocean 181, 187
Okhlopkov, Nikolay 180–181, 187–189, 195
Old Vic Theatre 284–285
online campaign 52

Pankhurst, Sylvia 284
panopticon 49
Passionate Amateurs 232
Pathalgadi movement 12, 24, 28–32, 37
performance activism 145
performance art 85
performativity 11, 13–14, 25, 40, 147, 152–153, 234
  bodily 147
  linguistic 147
  political 149
polarisation 122, 146, 149, 154–155, 158–159, 282
political
  assembly 13
  chronotope 147
  efficacy 9, 166
  love 228, 230
  party light 39
  prisoner 59, 64, 76, 266
  Right 2, 39
polysemic 240
popular culture 8, 131, 138
populism 6, 8, 113, 123, 140, 155, 158–159, 272
Porte Parole 146, 149–152, 154–155, 157–158
postcolonial 213, 258, 266
  aspirations 259
  Bengal 202
  experimentations with space 13
  lens 13
  theory 165
  times 113
Prasad, Vijay 113

privatisation 1
proletariat 113
protest 13, 38, 42–47, 49–52, 60–64, 66–67, 69, 75, 112–113, 115, 148, 160, 169, 173–174, 223, 229, 250, 252, 277, 281–283
  anti-imperialist 251
  anti-protest 223
  anti-racism 46
  avatar 42
  campaigns 121
  collective 64
  dirty 60–62
  ephemeral 100
  event 203
  farmers 121
  feminist 228
  form 58–59
  Hong Kong 47
  intermittent 38, 43, 45, 47, 50–51
  Kill the Bill 223
  march 170
  mass 51, 145
  modalities 100
  movements 52
  Muslim-led 24
  narratives 57
  non-violent 64
  online 51
  political 50–52, 104
  procession 171, 174
  public 25
  sites 24, 114
  social 107
  songs 251
  strategies 12
  street 42, 76
  students 70
  traditional 38
  Umbrella 47
  walk 43, 48–50
  women's 60
  women-led 24
  by women prisoners 61
  workers 250
Pushkin Theatre 186

queer movement 32
Queer Pride 32

racism 3, 14, 73, 75, 93, 103, 105, 108–109
  systemic 158
radical
  dissensus 13
  imaginations 165
  movements 35
  political practices 12
  political thought 10
  politics 10, 12, 26–27, 231
  protest practices 12
radicalisation 75
radicalism 164–165
  Fenian 222
Rancière, Jacques 9, 205
Rao, Mayo 23
Rashtriya Swayamsevak Sangh (RSS) 265
Rau, Milo 74
Reagan, Ronald 40, 276, 278
realism 133, 173
  American 276
Realistic Theatre 188
red-baiting 275
Red Scare 278–279, 286
Republican Party 279
republicanism 57
resistance
  quiet 12–13
revolutionary love 15
Ridout, Nicolas 7, 177, 232
Right 2, 4, 12–13, 27, 42, 146, 157, 271, 278
  discourses 13
  far-Right populism 277
  radical 154
Right-wing 44
  agenda 126
  culture 121
  mobilisation 123
  populism 6, 113, 272
  state 6
Roe v Wade 276
Rokem, Freddie 136, 151–153, 201, 213
romanticism
  revolutionary 211
Romanticism 138
Roosevelt, F. D. 278–279

Index

Roy, Arundhati 2–3
Roychowdhury, Reba 237, 244, 250–252
Russian Revolution 278

Sacks, Oliver 28
Sanders, Bernie 277, 279
Sannyasir Tarabari 199, 201–202, 204, 207, 210–211, 213
Sartre, John-Paul 281
satyagraha 64
Schrödinger, Erwin 48–50
Scothorne, Rory 140, 142
Scottish
    identity 140
    society 140
    theatre companies 133
Scottish International 137, 139
Scottish National Party 136–137, 139, 142
Scottish Reformation 138
Scullion, Adrienne 132, 140
Second World War 251, 278–279
semiotics 148, 154
Sen, Manikuntala 244, 247
Sen, Sova 181–182, 186–187
Serbian Left 44
Serbian Left Movement 42
Serbian Progressive Party 41
Shaheen Bagh 24
Sharmila, Irom 68–69
shy radicalism 12–13, 15
Shy Radicals 73–82, 84–88
Silent Grace 61
slacktivism 45
Smith, Patti 11
social networks 39–40, 42, 44–45, 52
socialism 57, 163–164, 275–279, 281–282, 284
    American 278
socialist 15, 69, 275–276, 278–283, 285
    artist 15
    politics 280
    Realist 183, 189
    revolution, 64, 266
Socialist Labour Party 222, 278

Socialist Party of America 278
sovereignty 29, 32, 105
Soviet Revolution 228
Spanish Communist Party 246
spectacularisation 7
spectator citizen 9
Star Theatre 188
statecraft 73–74, 78
Stefanović, Borko 42
Stokoe, William C. 28
Stree Shakti Sanghatana 244
suffragette 67, 284
    facts 285
    movement 284
    prisoner 67
suffragists 12, 66
sustainability 4, 177

Taylor, Diana 25
Teatro Campesino 281
Teer 202, 204, 207–210, 213
terrorism 6, 171, 222
testimony 14–15, 59–60, 106–107, 109, 134, 152, 240, 265
Teyyam 175
Thatcher, Margaret 62–63, 276
theatre 11, 284
    amateur 166, 231
    Bengali 184, 192, 201
    British 8, 130, 276, 281
    of conjuncture 9
    documentary 13, 104, 145, 149–151, 154–155
    experimental 213
    feminist-socialist 276
    French 276
    ideological 9
    Leftist 10, 14, 180
    Leftist political 14
    Left political 166
    people's 189
    political 6–9, 93, 113–115, 132, 148, 157–158, 167, 175, 193, 201, 203, 205–207, 212–214, 232, 282
    Progressive Left 8
    proscenium 13, 194, 213
    radical 282
    radical bohemian 231

theatre (*continued*)
   revolutionary 115, 180, 184, 196, 213
   of the roots movement 174
   rural 166
   Scottish 132
   socialist 137
   Soviet 187, 228
   street 113, 125–126
   studies 282
   US socialist 281
   verbatim 105
theatricalisation 96, 98, 173, 177
theatricality 2, 11, 13, 96–97, 100, 102, 109, 150, 170, 172–173, 176–177
theory of transindividuation 284
Three Penny Opera 186
Tiner Talawar 189, 195
Titas Ekti Nodir Naam 187–188, 192, 195
Tomlin, Liz 8–9, 205
Tories 142
trade union 6, 112, 114–121, 124, 196, 270
transindividuation 284
Traverso, Enzo 163–164
Trump, Donald 2, 40, 145–146, 149, 152, 154–155, 157, 159, 275–276, 282, 286
Twitter 39, 42, 46

Verfremdung 99, 101
Vietnam War 280
visuality 94, 208
Vučić, Aleksandar 41–43

Washington, George 54, 97–98
Weiss, Peter 154
West 1, 27, 163, 207
Williams, Raymond 7–9, 52, 205, 207, 281
Women Against Imperialism 60
working class 13, 113, 116, 118, 122, 125–126, 132, 158, 177, 183–184, 223, 267
   Aberdonians 134
   audience 131–132
   consciousness 121–122
   cultural practices 121, 122
   culture 121, 123
   experience 131
   inhabitants 185
   life 122, 183
   migrant 167
   movement 122
   political traditions 140
   practices 122
   protests 122
   rights 120
   subjects 126
   theatre 131
   women 284
worksite 10–14, 272, 283

xenophobia 2, 158

Young Comrade 225, 229, 233
YouTube 39

zooesis 13, 170

EU authorised representative for GPSR:
Easy Access System Europe, Mustamäe tee 50,
10621 Tallinn, Estonia
gpsr.requests@easproject.com